SHEETS OF SCATTERED SAND

LIU INSTITUTE SERIES IN CHINESE CHRISTIANITIES
Series Editor: Alexander Chow, University of Edinburgh

Christianity is the fastest growing religion in both mainland China and a large, linguistically and culturally diverse Chinese diaspora, which encompasses more than a fifth of the world's population. Any consideration of the future of world Christianity must now take into account the role of Chinese Christians and their distinctly Chinese interpretation of the Christian faith. Despite the development and influence of this tradition, the academic world has been slow to invest in this timely subject. This series features titles that offer new perspectives on the vast and expanding field of Chinese Christianities in all its diverse forms, providing a forum for cross-disciplinary conversation. Books are welcome from a variety of disciplinary approaches, including but not limited to historical, theological, social scientific, and sinological perspectives. The University of Notre Dame's Liu Institute for Asia and Asian Studies is pleased to support sustained quality research on this rich and varied religious tradition that merits greater understanding.

SHEETS OF SCATTERED SAND

Cantonese Protestants and the Secular Dream of the Pacific Rim

JUSTIN K.H. TSE

University of Notre Dame Press

Notre Dame, Indiana

Copyright © 2024 by the University of Notre Dame
University of Notre Dame Press
Notre Dame, Indiana 46556
undpress.nd.edu

All Rights Reserved

Published in the United States of America

Library of Congress Control Number: 2024941352

ISBN: 978-0-268-20871-4 (Hardback)
ISBN: 978-0-268-20874-5 (WebPDF)
ISBN: 978-0-268-20873-8 (Epub3)

To Jenny

How beautiful you are, my darling!
Oh, how beautiful!

—Song of Songs 4:1

...外國人批評中國人,一面說沒有結合能力,既然如此,當然是散沙,是很自由的;又一面說中國人不懂自由。殊不知大家都有自由,便是一片散沙;要大家結合成一個堅固團體,便不能像一片散沙。所以外國人這樣批評我們的地方,就是陷於自相矛盾了。

—孫中山,三民主義

CONTENTS

	Preface: "Do You Love Chinese Christians?"	xi
	Acknowledgments	xxiii
CHAPTER 1	The Secular Dream of the Pacific Rim and Sheets of Scattered Sand	1
CHAPTER 2	Secular Compromise: Hong Kong Revivalism and Pacific Rim Migrations	27
CHAPTER 3	"Each Person Can Only Speak for Themselves": Same-Sex Marriage and Institutional Autonomy	61
CHAPTER 4	Against "Homeland Politics": Cantonese Protestant Organizations and the Varieties of Pacific Rim Civil Societies	101
CHAPTER 5	The Fading Shadow of Tiananmen: Chinese Christians and Electoral Democracy	139
	Epilogue: Ten Years	177
	Notes	187
	Bibliography	227
	Index	249

PREFACE

"Do You Love Chinese Christians?"

Simon, son of John, do you truly love me?
—John 21:16

Sheets of Scattered Sand is a radical revision of the doctoral dissertation that I wrote in 2013 in the Department of Geography at the University of British Columbia (UBC) in Vancouver.[1] I have waited long enough—ten years—to move through a range of feelings, from relief to apathy to rage to acceptance, about my graduate work. I did not experience those affects because I do not stand by what I originally filed with the university. I still do like it, and it continues to be available from UBC's institutional depository.

I did it because I was asked a question when I graduated—"Do you love Chinese Christians?"—by a Chinese Christian auntie and not in a good way. "You have written such an excellent thesis," my interlocutor continued, commenting that she had never read six hundred pages of prose so quickly. She had found that there was nothing inaccurate, as far as she could tell, about the work, and that was her problem with it. I had exposed the "secrets," as she put it, of how Cantonese-speaking Protestant Christians, which I abbreviate in both the dissertation and this book as "Cantonese Protestants," organize political networks. Did I love "Chinese Christians," as she called them? What were my motivations for writing the dissertation?

There was a backstory to the question. I graduated six months after I filed the dissertation in 2014. On the day I walked across the stage, an article for which I was interviewed came out in the *South China Morning Post*. It concerned the activities of some concerned parents, many of whom identified as Chinese Christian, at the Vancouver School Board, which was deliberating about adopting a policy for transgender students. The Chinese Christian parents opposed it. The journalist Ian Young, whose beat has since the early 2010s been to cover Hong Kong and Chinese participation in Vancouver's civil society, wanted to know why.

He asked whether there was something in "Christianity" or "Chinese culture" that could explain these concerned parents' opposition to transgender rights. I pointed out that it was not really about homophobia or transphobia but about what these "traditional family" activists themselves called "parental rights." I then said, "Chinese Christians have this vision for a rational orderly society. A particular reading of the Bible may inform this, a particular reading of the Chinese classics may inform this. But at the heart of it, it's about a rational orderly society, where parents are the primary educators for their children. What they are seeing instead with this kind of stuff [the board's proposals] is that this is irrational and disorderly. That's why there is such a strong pushback."[2] I also mentioned that I was about to graduate with a dissertation on this topic, and when the article came out, Young included a sidebar that detailed what I had written.

Not all doctoral dissertations get a newspaper article written about them, let alone two. In the previous year, another journalist, Douglas Todd of the *Vancouver Sun*, had also found out about my dissertation research. I had been in the middle of writing the very chapter on sexuality issues (the third one in this book) that Young interviewed me about the next year, and Todd had wanted to know all about it. Calling me a "scholarly dynamo" who published in both "academic and popular secular Asian journals," he observed that I was quite open about my faith. He found, for example, a previous thesis where I thanked "the Lord Jesus

Christ" for help on the work (God knows I needed it). He then wrote that I said—accurately—that among Vancouver's "100,000 Chinese Christians . . . the question of sexual orientation is a very fraught one."[3]

Todd derived his numbers by taking the over four hundred thousand residents of Metro Vancouver who listed themselves as Chinese (18 percent of the population) and using the 2001 census counts that showed that 24 percent of that number listed themselves Christian, 8 percent Catholic, 16 percent Protestant.[4] For an article on Vancouver's Chinese Christians that I wrote in 2011, a member of the Vancouver Chinese Evangelical Ministerial Fellowship and I counted through the 2007 directory and found that 74 percent of the churches used Cantonese as their primary language.[5] There were similar numbers in my other sites of study on the Pacific Rim with some variation. In the San Francisco Bay Area, over 560,000 people said that they were "Chinese" as of the 2010 census. Although Chinese Christian scholars report that only 6.3 percent of them go to church and 39 percent of that number are Cantonese, they take up a disproportionate amount of newspaper, radio, and television space through financial and psychological services.[6] Of the seven million people in Hong Kong, the latest Hong Kong Christian Council estimates in 2021 indicate that roughly 22 percent of the population have been consistently Christian, about 17 percent Protestant and 5 percent Catholic, though its previous status as a British colony ensured that schools, hospitals, and charities were usually nominally Christian and influential because of it.[7]

Todd's 2013 article did not get me into trouble, but Young's 2014 one nearly did. Some of the concerned parents who were protesting the Vancouver School Board alleged that I was outing their tactics and demanded that I have the dissertation removed from UBC's website. They were worried. Someone even called my parents and declared that it had been downloaded over six hundred times (the running count as of the final revisions of this book is 2,006). As things escalated, my father—a pastor associated with a church but who has since moved into full-time hospital chaplaincy—arranged for a sit-down with one of the most vocal aunties. It was at this meeting that she both complimented me on the thoroughness of the thesis and castigated me for exactly the same reason. *Did I love Chinese Christians?* she needed to know. What were my motivations for writing it?

I replied that of course I loved Chinese Christians. That is why I had spent six hundred pages trying to understand them. She retorted that if I had had any understanding of the situation, then I should have known that Chinese Christians have a hard enough time in politics without having to be written about in such detail. I replied that it seemed that queer communities, at least from my limited perspective as a straight man and therefore an outsider, also seem to have it hard in politics, as they often seemed to wrestle with how they wanted to be publicly represented versus how they could foster a sense of kinship among themselves. That seemed to calm her down. Her husband, visibly bored by our conversation, went out to buy pineapple buns to celebrate the end of our discussion.

And yet, over the last eight years, that question of whether I "love" Chinese Christians has since eaten at my mind. Love, as my colleague Ting Guo points out, is a tricky word. It is a political term that has been used since the reconceptualization of China from an empire to a nation-state, she has argued.[8] Its usage in Chinese politics has tended to refer to a feeling of affection not toward a person but toward a nation, a people, even a government. And so in asking that question, my interlocutor reminded me that my research was not only based in the San Francisco Bay Area and Vancouver. I had gone to Hong Kong too, a place where Guo also notes that the "politics of love," as she calls it, is at work. In 2012 when I did fieldwork there, the city was already known for being a place of protests, even before the celebrated 2014 Umbrella Movement, reprised in 2019 until the draconian measures laid down by the 2020 National Security Law seemed to put an end to it, had taken place. In 2010, the Hong Kong government had offered what seemed to be an olive branch to the pan-democratic parties. Promising to move the city toward democratic election of its leaders, the government rolled out an electoral reform package. Part of the deal was that candidates who ran for office would have to "love Hong Kong and love China." The democrats rejected it as a form of "democracy with Chinese characteristics"—not a hprotests with their demands for "genuine universal suffrage" that engulfed the city a few years after I finished my fieldwork there.

I want to offer this monograph as a gesture at a response to my interlocutor on the question of loving Chinese Christians, especially given how charged the question of love is. The historian Gary Okihiro points out that if the social sciences—which I profess to practice as a human geographer—are to be liberating to historically colonized communities, including the Cantonese Protestants I write about here, then someone like me must set out to study "the human condition."[9] But to reduce humanity to a science is a trap, and to get around it, Okihiro argues that what social scientists ought to do instead is to study what he calls the "social formation," the kaleidoscopic web of political, economic, social, legal, educational, and religious institutions that impinge on the everyday lives of ordinary persons. It is similar to the sociologist C. Wright Mills's classic call for his educated readers to develop a "sociological imagination," an account of how their private lives are constantly interpellated by public institutions.

This conception of the social formation is at the core of my radical revision. In the dissertation, I argued that Cantonese Protestants were acting in secular ways by privatizing their places of worship while leveraging an essentialized sense of their Chinese ethnicity to engage the civil societies in which they lived. It was a social scientific study of subjectivity, an attending to who Chinese Christians are and what they do. In this book, I want to attend to the social formation that contextualizes their activities. That social formation is what I am calling the *secular dream of the Pacific Rim*, the way that civil societies that are located in this region and yet remain necessarily autonomous from one another and work with private institutions that also prize their own autonomy share and manifest the dream of the "Pacific Rim" to integrate Asian and Anglo-American markets, states, and civil societies into a multicultural utopia do so in ways that reinforce concepts of the "secular" at various registers. As revisionist scholars of secularization have argued, what is meant here by the "secular" is not the absence of religion on the Pacific Rim but a set of theological assumptions that have a genealogy, mostly within Christian theology, that has been passed on through legacies of European colonization to the Asia-Pacific and the Americas.[10] I am interested in how Cantonese Protestants perceive and interact with such secularities in three Pacific Rim civil societies: Hong Kong, Vancouver, and San Francisco.[11]

In so doing, I hope that I have offered my fullest response to the question of whether I love them. I do not know every single one of them personally, and like Hannah Arendt who said that she could only love her friends, I am not fond of using the word "love" with reference to abstract collectives. But I like to think that their humanity is never in question.

The transpacific dimensions of this project have been in play since my original conception of it as a doctoral student at UBC in 2010. In fact, it started as a study of Hong Kong proper, and it was reconceived as transpacific when people with whom I spoke in Hong Kong told me I did not have the chops to study Christianity there.

The project that I presented to my graduate committee for my first-year spring review in 2010 was on how a life-size replica of Noah's ark came to be built on Ma Wan Island, one of the islands that is included in Hong Kong's formal territory. The organization behind it, the Media Evangelism (TME), had been organizing trips since 2004 to Mount Ararat in Turkey, where the historic ark allegedly landed millennia ago. That was shortly after the severe acute respiratory syndrome (SARS) epidemic in 2002, which, on top of claiming 299 lives in Hong Kong and 774 worldwide, had been the context for the heroic story of Dr. Joanna Tse Yuen-mun (no relation to me), who had given her life as a SARS doctor. She had also been a Protestant Christian of a Pentecostal persuasion, and during her broadcast funeral on TVB, a song had played titled "The Covenant under the Rainbow." It was a convenient hook for TME, which had been making films for public evangelism since 1999 and had been touring them across Cantonese Protestant communities all over the world, including to our churches in the Bay Area and Metro Vancouver. In fact, one of TME's major figures, Siu Kam-chi—the wife of the late Roy Chiao of Hong Kong cinematic fame—used to stay with our family during these tours. I still remember Mrs. Chiao holding us spellbound with her storytelling while undermining our hospitality by moving to the kitchen sink to do our dishes.

With SARS came the opportunity for a new evangelistic tack. TME made arrangements with both a Turkish archaeological team as well as Christian fundamentalists from the Creation Museum in the United States to go to Mount Ararat to search for the ark. Meanwhile, they got to work on building the ark. There was a consortium of Protestant

Christian organizations—the Chinese Young Men's Christian Association of Hong Kong, the Angel's Luk Education Foundation, St. James' Settlement, and the Boys' Brigade—each of which I planned to study as an entry point to Hong Kong Christianity's place in the city's political structure. The theory behind the project, perhaps best articulated by the global Christianities scholar Robbie Goh in his own study of the ark after hearing me present my research proposals in 2010, was that there might have been a theological way into understanding the governance of Hong Kong, perhaps even in the Christian conception of love.[12]

What especially caught my attention were all the celebrity figures attached, if not to the ark project itself, then at least to the strains of Christianity that supported it. The most prominent one was the developer behind the ark project, Sun Hung Kei Properties. Owned by the Kwok brothers—the third richest family in Hong Kong at the time—it was widely known that the chief executive officer, Thomas Kwok Ping-kwong, was an evangelical Protestant. So, too, the 2004 film that TME made on the story of Dr. Joanna Tse, *The Miracle Box*, starred TVB drama actress Ada Choi in the leading role. The highest paid celebrity in Hong Kong, the Cantopop star Sammi Cheng Sau-man, publicly converted to Christianity in 2007 after a bout of depression and was baptized at Kong Fok Evangelical Free Church by Rev. Daniel Ng Chung-man. In the wake of the 2014 Umbrella Movement, Ng became notorious as a defender of the Hong Kong political system against the protesters, most famously in his refusal to let nearby demonstrators use his church's restrooms. Yet at the time, he was primarily known as a Bay Area pastor who had been a solidarity figure with the Tiananmen Beijing Spring in 1989 before returning to Hong Kong to fill a megachurch pulpit. In more scandalous news, the leaking of pictures from the actor Edison Chen's personal computer of Hong Kong celebrities in sexually compromising positions with him resulted in his making a transpacific move to Vancouver, where his mother reportedly was going to the same church where I worked at the time. The revivalist Jaeson Ma then said on his blog, "Through a series of divine circumstances in February God brought me to Edison, I shared the Gospel and God's personal prophetic word to him and Edison gave his life to Christ," a conversion that later became news on the Hong Kong tabloid scene.[13] Chen later got back into business with a T-shirt line that said, "Only

God can judge me." When that happened, I joked that I would wear it to my dissertation defense.

With this project in mind, I made my way to Hong Kong for the first time in my life in 2010. The trip was generously funded by UBC as part of an exchange university course on transnational cities and global flows with the National University of Singapore. It was on this trip that I learned that the project I had proposed on Noah's ark had some problems that did not lend itself to doctoral study. On April 25, 2010—just two months before I had arrived in Hong Kong—the TME team that went to Mount Ararat had held a press conference announcing that they had been 99.9 percent sure that they had found the historical ark there.[14] This had led to widespread embarrassment among Protestant intellectuals in Hong Kong, who questioned the findings and called the whole thing a celebrity sham.[15] Those I talked to about the project discouraged me from doing it. One, a pastor, even said that some at his church worked at TME but found their employment embarrassing and would not be forthcoming as research participants. Others gently helped me to understand that what I was interested in was terribly one-sided, perhaps the kind of news that one receives about Hong Kong in Cantonese-speaking Protestant congregations in North America but not representative of mainline Protestant denominations in Hong Kong and their friendly ecumenical relations with the Roman Catholic Church. At least four seminary professors from different institutions and across the theological spectrum gave me impromptu primers in their offices and over lunch. They described to me how Protestant civil society activism in light of the 1997 handover tended to revolve around democracy, even the social conservatives at the Truth-Light Society who have been decrying the Sexual Orientation Discrimination Ordinance's attempts to create an equal playing field for sexual minorities in Hong Kong since the mid-2000s.

While talking to me, these interlocutors also made subtle hints about some prominent ministers and academics who had left Hong Kong for places like Vancouver and the Bay Area to wait out the transfer of sovereignty. Those people, they said, had relinquished their right to comment on Hong Kong issues. Perhaps, they suggested, it was why my views of Hong Kong were so skewed. It was a veiled critique of my positionality, something they were much too polite to say up front. Subtly, they were insinuating that I was one of those people they were judging. I like to think that I had enough subtlety to get the message.

I am glad for my Hong Kong interlocutors' advice. Noah's ark on Ma Wan Island shut down in January 2012, and TME moved away from their theological interpretations of Hong Kong as a city into projects that centered on a nationalistic Chinese interpretation of Christianity on the Silk Road. If I had gone with my original idea, I might have had to change topics midway through fieldwork anyway.

The argument I make in this book is that Cantonese Protestants rarely described themselves as a united bloc. They were, poetically and by their own description, a "sheet of scattered sand"—ideologically fragmented, politically disunited, and institutionally disconnected across each of the sites I studied as well as within them. It was, to be sure, not a term that they used every time they described themselves, but that is more to the point. They were so scattered that they did not need poetry every time they said they were.

When I came across this phrase in my fieldwork in 2011 and 2012, it made sense to me as someone who had grown up in these communities. In 2004, my parents and sister moved with me to Vancouver from the Bay Area. As we pulled into our new home in Richmond, we noticed a sign on the lawn. "Vote for Alice Wong," it said, indicating that she was part of the newly formed Conservative Party of Canada. We were confused by how it might have ended up there. Was it, say, part of the previous owners' politics? Clarity emerged the next day when our neighbors, members of my father's new congregation, came by to tell us that Alice Wong was a parishioner too. They had put it there because, as they said, a pastor ought to support his parishioners.

Such a statement was difficult for our purportedly apolitical family to comprehend, though in all fairness, 2004 was an eventful year for Chinese Christians in the Bay Area too. In January of that year, the then-mayor of San Francisco, Gavin Newsom, ordered his city clerk to revise the marriage licenses to be gender neutral. Over the next two months, about four thousand same-sex couples got married in the city until the California Supreme Court shut it all down in March, ruling that Newsom had acted outside of his procedural abilities to change state law as a city mayor. Still, on April 26, an event that was later revealed to have been organized by a Chinese Christian activist, Hak-Shing William Tam, with the revivalist preacher Rev. Thomas Wang headlining it, brought about seven thousand Chinese Christians wearing matching red T-shirts that read, "1 man + 1 woman = 1 marriage" to Sunset, San Francisco's 49 percent Asian American inner suburb.

I still remember this day, though I lived in a suburb near Silicon Valley called Fremont. I was going to another evangelical church, one that billed itself as multicultural, just to get away from my father's church. No announcement about the event was made, but at the coffee-and-doughnut hour following the service, the parking lot was unusually busy. There was even a bus that had pulled up. This church had a Cantonese congregation that met on the premises, and I knew the pastor. Seeing him amid the commotion, I asked him what was going on, and he said that they were going to the protest in San Francisco. It was strange because I had not heard my parents speak about it, but when I drove back to my father's church, I was met with the same commotion in their parking lot. The whole church was going except for my family. My mother told me at home that day that she had in fact received a notice about the protest from a group calling themselves the Bay Area Chinese Ministerial Prayer Fellowship, though she was not sure who they were. She was also surprised that I would be interested in it and gave the flyer to me. It was the first item in the archives that form, in part, the basis for this book.

But why my family did not go was interesting. It was because my father had strong convictions that the space of the church should not be used for secular purposes. In fact, in his own interview with the *Vancouver Sun* about Chinese Christians back in 2006, that is what he thought he told them too. What had occasioned the call to my dad was that 2006 was an election year, and the Liberal Party candidate, the Tiananmen activist Raymond Chan, had complained to the press about the Conservatives' nominee, Darrell Reid, the former president of Focus on the Family Canada. "Some of my friends called me last Sunday," Chan had told *Vancouver Sun* writer Doug Ward, "saying they are little uneasy about seeing church elders handing out Darrel Reid flyers." He went on, accusing Chinese Christian pastors of telling their people to support Reid and thereby "mixing church and politics." As the article that was later published in the *Vancouver Sun* explained, the irony was that Chan himself was an "evangelical Christian" and "attends the Chinese Mennonite Church in Vancouver." "I've been a Christian all these years and when I go to church, I pray," Chan expressed, attempting to position those he accused in the wrong.

Technically, the accusation had nothing to do with my dad or his church. The problem, of course, was that it really actually did, and that was because of the public perception of that particular church as a Conservative Party stronghold, mostly because Alice Wong, whose lawn sign had been planted at our house when we moved there, went there on Sundays. My dad was not sure that he wanted to get sucked into the turmoil, but of course he was. It did not matter that that community was not actually an "Alice Wong church," at least not in the sense of her having any political monopoly or even leadership role within it. It was indeed her place of worship, though she did not hold any position within it and did not use the premises to campaign. In fact, it might have been less stressful for Dad if only she could have monopolized power within it because at least the lines of power might have been clearer. But the outspoken Conservative Party members had to coexist with Liberal holdouts in the congregation, not to mention others who felt that all this political rancor was secularizing the church. By the end of 2005, all that factionalism had given my dad a heart attack. The board and he agreed that, for health reasons, he did not need to come back to work in January.

It is one of those small ironies, then, that the journalist from the *Vancouver Sun* seemed to have thought that he had found the man who could represent Alice Wong's church in an article where Raymond Chan was complaining about Darrel Reid's Chinese Christian supporters "mixing church and politics." My dad was in the office that January day in 2006 because he was packing it up. In came the call, and my father sensed the opportunity to set the record straight for himself. Prefacing his remarks by emphasizing that the church does not tell people how to vote, he said of Reid, "We support him because he supports the traditional family system and he is thinking the way we stand from our Bible teachings.... We can not tell people what to do but from our standpoint we see which candidate would go along with our Bible teaching and what we think is right for our society."[16]

Despite the smoking gun words "we support him because," Dad came home with an air of victory that night. In the way he told the story, he had outsmarted the journalist, though I personally do not think he got off as clean as he thinks he did. But from his perspective, the *Vancouver*

Sun was trying to place the church in terms of secular party affiliation, that it was Alice Wong's church and therefore somehow a Conservative fortress. He believed that he had told the newspaper that the church was completely apolitical. He had not taken a partisan position, he said, and he had even saved the church from publicly associating with a political party one way or another. In his view, his words had positioned the church's actions solely within the private realm of theological reasoning, that all they were doing was acting according to the teachings of the Bible, not aligning with either the Liberals or the Conservatives.

What I have reflected on over the course of this project was the dissonance that my dad also had with the people who were purportedly under his pastoral care. In saying what he said to the *Vancouver Sun*—and indeed, in not attending the Traditional Family Day in San Francisco—it revealed that he had a position on how the church should relate to secular politics, and it did not match that of some of the most outspoken church members. I say this because readers perhaps should understand that my family has been part of the contentions that compose the scattered divisions in this book. But I do not think it compromises the research. It is rather the point that many of the Cantonese Protestants to whom I spoke in the Bay Area, Metro Vancouver, and Hong Kong wanted to convey. The first thing you have to know about Cantonese Protestants is that we really are a sheet of scattered sand.

ACKNOWLEDGMENTS

We write this to make our
joy complete.
—1 John 1:4

When I think of the persons to whom I must give thanks for being part of the process of writing this book, I realize that it will read as a record of all the communities that have given me intellectual life over the last ten years at least.

I begin with the many academic communities I have called home during my struggle with this text. This book started out as a doctoral dissertation in the Department of Geography at UBC under the supervision of David Ley. Ley is an urban geographer who came to specialize in the Pacific Rim because of his interest in gentrification and housing bubbles in Metro Vancouver, and it is from him, and the texts he made me read and the people to whom he introduced me, that I first came to understand that the Pacific Rim could be a framework for my theological inquiries. Henry Yu, an Asian American historian, was also on my committee and taught me everything I know about transpacific Asian American studies, including Gary Okihiro's dictum, "Asians did not go to America; America went to Asia." Another com-mittee member was the late Claire Dwyer, who as an established senior scholar in feminist geography at University College London visited UBC when I was early in my program and took me on ethnographic excursions with her in Richmond, British Columbia, where

I was living. She had gotten the idea from Dan Hiebert, another geographer in the department who was one of my examiners. In fact, I first encountered the concept of globalization as a first-year undergraduate student at UBC from Dan's lectures on migration geographers David, Henry, Claire, and Dan deserve so much credit for my intellectual formation, especially for showing me that a theological reading of the secular concerns that animated their scholarship was possible. In a beautiful email that Dan wrote me after my defense, he said that my work on theology in the secular academy felt a bit like how he had been influenced by the music he was listening to in college to get into migration studies. Some will call us anti-intellectual, he said, but it is from such poetry that scholarship begins. I also hope this book honors Claire's memory. I miss her very much.

Early on in my graduate work, I also became a regular attendee at the Asian Pacific American and Religion Research Initiative (APARRI). My encounter with APARRI was serendipitous; some might call it providential. I was visiting my childhood church, Chinese for Christ Church of Hayward, in the summer of 2009, where I met Asian American Christian historian Timothy Tseng, who encouraged me to attend the conference at Claremont School of Theology that year. It was at APARRI that I met some of my most important interlocutors who heard and gently encouraged the formation of my own engagements with Asian American religious studies. My conversation partners at APARRI, as well as at the Asian North American Religions, Cultures, and Society (ANARCS) group at the American Academy of Religion (AAR), include Russell Jeung, Carolyn Chen, Jerry Park, Sharon Suh, Jane Iwamura, Grace Kao, Khyati Joshi, Himanee Gupta, Tammy Ho, Chris Chua, Neil Gotanda, Rita Nakashima Brock, David Yoo, Janelle Wong, Sylvia Chan-Malik, Gale Yee, Melissa Borja, Jaisy Joseph, Mike Karim, Christopher The, Helen Jin Kim, Brett Esaki, Daniel Lee, David Chao, Ann Tran, Bianca Mabute-Louie, Chanhee Heo, Hope Chang, Shirley Lung, Joyce Chang, Karis Ryu, Annie Li, and SueJeanne Koh. Because of APARRI, Rudy Busto served on my committee, taught me important lessons about the politics of race in religious studies, and put the University of California, Santa Barbara's religious studies department on my geographer's radar as a powerhouse to which I should attend. It was also at ANARCS that Grace Kao pushed me to think philosophically while working through this material, so much so that we established an annual coffee appointment at the AAR. Carolyn recently told me that they consider me an "APARRI baby." I am honored by the designation and recognize myself in it.

Since leaving UBC in 2014, I have traversed several academic communities, where the arguments and narratives of this book have been workshopped among colleagues and students. At the American Association of Geographers, the Geographies of Religion and Belief Systems Specialty Group provided a home base for me to branch out to other academic societies, and I found conversation partners across those communities to whom I remain grateful, especially Anna Secor, Banu Gökariksel, Betsy Olson, Murat Es, Justin Wilford, Vincent Artman, and Ed Davis. James Wellman supervised my postdoctoral fellowship from 2014 to 2015 at the University of Washington's Comparative Religion Program, and it was there that I met important interlocutors who took the theological dimensions of this work very seriously, including Artur Rosman, Mx We King, James Felak, Mike Williams, Mika Ahuvia, Philip Tite, Joel Walker, and Tony Lucero. I am also indebted to the generosity of Katharyne Mitchell and Matt Sparke, both intellectually and materially, and found in conversation with them that I was indeed interested in fusing the study of the Pacific Rim with questions of political theology. Students in my courses on American religion and transpacific Christianities also became fellow travelers; some of those who helped me refine the telling of these stories include Eugenia Geisel, Meg Hirai, Cody Lynn, Julie Bellefeuille, Mariam Mathew, and Taylor Steger. Being in Seattle also made it possible to have conversations with colleagues at Seattle Pacific University (SPU), where Billy Vo, Bo Lim, Brian Bantum, David Leong, and Jennifer McKinney had countless coffees and meals with me as I worked out the significance of this work for theologies of race. It is because of those meetings that I was also able to teach with Soong-Chan Rah, both of us guest lecturers for a two-day course at SPU, where I came to see the importance of this work for informing Asian American pastoral ministry. I also found accompaniment with two men I am proud to call brothers, Sam Rocha and Sam Tsang. Rocha demanded philosophical rigor from me despite my ethnographic proclivities. Tsang insisted that I stay grounded within the intellectual currents of Chinese Christianity. Anna Scott also challenged me to rethink my masculine categories as I attempted not only to be serious about feminist practice but also to attend to how Chinese nationalism works itself out in the Pacific Rim.

In 2016, the Asian American Studies Program at Northwestern University, especially Ji-Yeon Yuh, took a chance on me as a visiting assistant professor. At the time, I was lecturing at Simon Fraser University, where I workshopped this book with twenty of some of the brightest students I have ever taught in a fourth-year course on cultural geography. Minelle Mahtani, a cultural geographer who had a radio show on Roundhouse Radio 98.3 FM, brought me onto the program in what she called the "grounded theologies" segment and often had me talk about what was going on in the course in relation to my work, which was more or less me struggling with this book. It was because of that show, I am told, that my new colleagues at Northwestern identified me as a public intellectual and had me teach courses on Asian American history and social movements, Chinese America and Chinatowns, and religion and conservatism. Teaching at Northwestern was transformative because of the seriousness with which colleagues and students took my arguments, along with their commitment to engage our scholarship with Asian American communities. I am deeply indebted to Ji-Yeon Yuh, Nitasha Sharma, Shalini Shankar, Cheryl and Greg Jue, Patricia Nguyen, Michelle Huang, Y Thien Nguyen, Wonhee Anne Joh, and Carlos Balinas for helping me understand at an existential level what it means to do research from within a community. Students also demanded that I stick to my ethical principles and stay intellectually consistent; I am especially grateful for the formative conversations that I had with Diana Fu, Irina Huang, Will Paik, Will Kang, Mok Zining, Ellen Zhou, Ying Dai, Celestine He, Lizzy Jang, Katherine Lo, Chloe Wong, Michael Postiglione, Jevons Liu, Abbey Zhu, Grace Park, Hyohee Kim, and Emily Ahn. Grace Yu, James Kang, and Stephan Dornauer were important presences in my years there too, demanding consistency and rigor from me in our conversations and shared practice about the transpacific, intersectionality, and theology. It was also because of this program that I was able to meet Gary Okihiro and to tell him that his work in *Third World Studies* is unexpectedly theological. I am grateful to him for adopting me as one of his students.

As I write this book, I have found intellectual homes in several communities with which I have regular conversation about how the book speaks to contemporary scholarship and public intellectual concerns. The first is my home institution at Singapore Management University's (SMU) College of Integrative Studies since 2019. I am deeply grateful to the leadership of our dean, Elvin Lim, in creating opportunities for intellectual integration across an unexpected and sometimes dizzying array of disciplines, and for our president, Lily Kong, for pioneering a way forward for us to position ourselves on the cutting edge of integrative thinking in the Asia-Pacific. With my colleagues here, I have found both hilarity and tenacity. They have torn into my arguments with love and sharpened my thinking. I want to especially thank Giovanni Ko, Orlando Woods, Aidan Wong, Darlene Espena, Fiona Williamson, Winston Chow, Wen-Qing Ngoei, Maartje de Visser, Nona Pepito, Daniel Seah, Jonathan Chase, Sayd Randle, Teng-Kuan Ng, Emily Soon, Joshua Luczak, Andrew Koh, Christine Henderson, and Chandran Kukathas.

I also found myself maintaining transpacific intellectual communities, both with my long-standing participation in APARRI and ANARCS but also branching out to new units too. One unit I have come to understand as responsible for all good things in my career, including having my monograph published with the Liu Institute Series on Chinese Christianities at the University of Notre Dame Press, is the Chinese Christianities Unit (CCU) at the AAR, of which I am now currently cochair with Stephanie Wong. It was the foresight of Alexander Chow, now our series editor, that allowed us a space to question the categories of "Chineseness" and "Christianities" in intellectually and ideologically diverse ways such that a book like this could be written. I am grateful to so many of my generous interlocutors at the CCU, who are friends both old and new, including Jonathan Seitz, Jonathan Tan, Fenggang Yang, Calida Chu, Francis Yip, Chloe Starr, Eric Hung, Easten Law, and Christie Chow. Another group I have been part of has been a monthly discussion on transpacific political theology organized by Kwok Pui-lan and Lester Ruiz, and it is at this group that I have also workshopped this manuscript and come away with fresh insight from Grace Kao, Jonathan Tran, Ki Joo Choi, Peng Yin, Francis Yip, Nami Kim, Sharon Bong, Yo and Yuko Fukushima,

Izak Lattu, Septemmy Lakawa, Michael Campos, John Boopalan, and Mary Yuen, among others.

Amid the ravages of the pandemic, I also came to understand that although this book is a monograph—it is solo authored, by me, and painstakingly so—it really cannot be written alone. Writing, it turns out, can only happen in the midst of friendship. In 2020, my friendships with Mok Zining in Singapore, Ellen Zhou in Chicago, and Xenia Chan in Toronto began to deepen to the point where we are unable to conceive of the intellectual work we do without each other. This manuscript has been workshopped through the weekly call I have had with Ellen, the monthly "paneer club" meeting I have with Zining, and the endless messages that Xenia and I share while living across an ocean and then some. Xenia also organized a series of meetings between me and some Cantonese Protestants in Toronto, including a two-part podcast episode on Canadian Asian Missional Podcast with Jon Nip, Shu-Ling Lee, and Bernard Tam, where we talked about the sheet of scattered sand. Through these engagements I met Christie Chan, with whom conversation about this work in our communities is always full of joy. I also want to remember here two friends from Toronto who have left us too soon. Helen Mo told me before she died that she was going to try to do what I did in Vancouver in Toronto. I had also just met Tim Tang, with whom before his passing I had been hoping to collaborate on furthering some of these insights in Toronto. I hope that these revisions are worthy of their memory.

Ellen, Zining, Xenia, and I began conceiving of ourselves as a re-search collective, and I started to organize the students who work closely with me as teaching and research assistants as a "lab" of sorts too, especially Teri Tan, Germaine Yeo, Prarthana Chandani, Dan Yi Jia, Madeline Yu, Chai JiaQi, Saw Min Nyo, Shanice Lam, Sophia Soon, Liu Enqi, Shania Yong, Renee Ong, Eileen Chang, and Ashley Sim. I am especially delighted to have become a thesis supervisor to one of these longtime "lab" participants, Renee Tan, who, along with her own collective consisting of Tay Shi Ying, Ray Yang, and Rachel Tham, has constantly pressed me to find joy in the work. It is here also that I began to become serious about applying for grant funding, and I cannot imagine having done this manuscript and the projects that are spinning off from it without Halyna Herasym at University College

Dublin and Ting Guo at the Chinese University of Hong Kong. I am also indebted to Matthew Lai Tsz-him, currently at Drew University, for helping me stay current with Hong Kong research. I am also deeply grateful to Sarah To as a fellow traveler, as we share humorous stories about this strange world of academia in which we both, in our different ways, get to work.

Reflecting on my own Christian journey in the time that I have spent writing and reworking this book, I find that I have traversed many churches and Christian communities and have sought to make intellectual communities of them too. I suppose my antics tested the patience of some, but as I reflect with gratefulness on the conversations I have had with persons in these communities who have talked with me, I realize that the supposed anti-intellectual bent of contemporary Christianity can be refuted, at least in small pockets of conversation. When I began the research for this book, I was attending St. John's Richmond, where Rev. Sean Love, Dan Hsu, David Jones, Robert and Kerensa Edwards, the late Howard and Esther McIlveen, Carl Hildebrand, Yucheng Zhuo, Erik Peters, and Lise Johnston especially made space for me over coffee, curry, and conversation to discuss this work. At Faith Community Christian Church, Rev. Ted Ng, Rev. Diana Gee, and Becca Hawkins showed me that intellectual inquiry could be woven into the fabric of Christian worship and folded into intimate conversation. When we moved to Seattle, we found welcome at Blessed Sacrament Church and the Catholic Newman Center at the University of Washington, especially from Frs. Łukasz Misko, OP, and Marcin Symański, OP, and an open invitation to offer talks based on my research to their congregations (some of my offerings were better than others). When I returned to Vancouver, Fr. Richard Soo, SJ, took my writing and thought so seriously, especially when I was stuck, that I asked him for spiritual direction and was soon received at Richmond Eastern Catholic Church into the Greek-Catholic Church of Kyiv. I have found conversation with Chris and Joyee Chiu and Richard Wu, among many others, especially to consistently sustain the work I must do after our parish hall banter. This pattern continued in Chicago, where my writing struggles and theoretical tangles were welcomed with open arms by Summer and Julian Hayda as we, with the support of Fr. Myron Panchuk of blessed memory, formed what used to be called the Kyivan Psychoanalysis Study Group, and then later St. Mary of Egypt Social Justice Fellowship. Thanks to Julian, I also got to work out some of this material on a show on public radio WBEZ 91.5 FM called *Worldview* and became friends with Jerome McDonnell and Steve Bynum in the process. In Singapore, I have also found myself engrossed in ecumenical conversation about the importance of secular friendship and free-flowing conversation with Fra. John-Paul Tan, OFM, Gerald Kong, and Nicole Ann Law.

This research would also have been impossible without the kind generosity of the people who housed and fed me while I was doing it. Some were family; others have become kin. In Vancouver, the Hos took me in for reduced rent, tolerated my earliest attempts at adult living, and regularly brought soup downstairs to aid my writing. In the Bay Area, the Andersons, the Aus, and the Huas offered space for my strange academic habits and friendship to keep me grounded. I am also deeply grateful to the Holy Cross Center in Berkeley, especially Fr. Harry Cronin, CSC, of blessed memory and Fr. Bruce Cecil, CSC, for letting me house-sit. Russell Jeung also let me borrow a car to get around. In Hong Kong, my aunt and uncle, whom I did not meet until I was an adult, offered me a room, Wi-Fi, and accessible Cantonese food and in so doing taught me that kin is more than affection—it is material.

Indeed, the only way that I could have conducted the research is through the generosity of those who are interviewed in the book, both as individual respondents and as focus group participants. It would be inappropriate to reveal too many names, except the ones who are quoted by name in the book, but suffice it to say that I was stunned by how willing people were to talk, to participate, and to contribute follow-up resources for me to consider in my study. My heart is full, and I can only hope that I have not only been fair and charitable but, more important, a worthy listener to their contributions.

Parts of this work have also been reworked with permission from already published material, including "Liberal Protestant Chinatown: Social Gospel Geographies in Chinese San Francisco," *Chinese America: History and Perspectives* (2015): 29–46; "Under the Umbrella: Grounded Christian Theologies and Democratic Working Alliances in Hong Kong," *Review of Religion and Chinese Society* 2, no. 1

(2015): 109–42; "A Tale of Three Bishops: Ideologies of Chineseness and Global Cities in Vancouver's Anglican Realignment," *Ching Feng: A Journal on Christianity and Chinese Religion and Culture* 15, no. 1–2 (2016): 103–30; "One Family, Many Systems? Ecumenical Alliances and the Defense of the Domestic in Post-handover Hong Kong," in *Gathered in My Name: Ecumenism in the World Church*, ed. William T. Cavanaugh (Eugene, OR: Cascade, 2020), 105–24; "'Fraught' Chineseness: 'Chinese Christians' in the *Vancouver Sun*," in *Ecclesial Diversity in Chinese Christianity*, ed. Alexander Chow and Easten Law (New York: Palgrave, 2021), 183–207; and "The Privacy of Hak-Shing William Tam: Imagining Asian Families in Proposition 8 in California," *Journal of Asian American Studies* 26, no. 1 (2023): 63–85. Biblical verses are from the English translation of my childhood, the New International Version.

I come, at last, to family. My parents, Philip and Gladys, and my sister, Joanna, saw the early stages of this research and, unexpectedly, encouraged and enabled it. My in-laws, Stanley and Janet, as well as my sister-in-law, Julia—and lest I be remiss, Bobby the dog—also supported the work without reservation, even and especially when it became difficult. There are also those I have come to consider kin who have seen this book take shape from the beginning and have shared in my joys and terrors about it. Chris and Annie Fong have been there from the original conception of the project and have always sought to ground me in the practical delights of home organization and housework, lest my head forget where my body is. Even before them, Edy, Michelle, and Agnes Wong heard about the research and rolled their eyes at how "boring" it was, as only kin can do. I especially relished the time that, as this manuscript took shape as a monograph, Agnes spent time at our apartment baking up a storm and involving me in kitchen work to keep me joyful.

It was also because of this project that I met my wife, Jenny. What I did not tell anyone at the time was that just before setting off for Hong Kong in 2010—at the very start of the project's original formulation—I had also just gone on a series of dates with her. Things were just getting good, so good that when my aunt and uncle discovered in Hong Kong that I did not have Wi-Fi at the place I was staying, they took me in. "You talk to your girlfriend till midnight, 1:00 a.m., no problem," they kept saying. Reader, she married me. When I came back from Hong Kong, we planned a wedding and got married before the dissertation was finished. Even Alice Wong, the Conservative politician our church friends told us to vote for back in 2004, came to the wedding. She gave us a wine stopper. I have used it many times while writing this book.

It is to Jenny that I dedicate this book. How can I not? We were in our early twenties when we began this book, and now we have traversed borders, states, oceans, and continents because of it. What Jenny has taught me is that where we are together, that is home. There is a quietness to it, even a kind of secrecy and privacy of which I am quite sure the Cantonese Protestants in this book would approve. It is too sacred to talk too much about, except to say that I realized in the late stages of revising this manuscript, what was more powerful than the adrenaline was the calm that I could sink into as we embarked on our weekend explorations, ate well, and slept better.

Here, we arrive at holy ground. I suppose the *Vancouver Sun* journalist Douglas Todd, who has read through all my theses as a student, will be wondering if I will, in a book like this, "thank the Lord Jesus Christ" again. There is some poetry to this question, especially because when I first received the preliminary agreement in 2019 to publish the book with the University of Notre Dame Press, I was heading to Montreal, where I promptly visited St. Joseph's Oratory and prayed for the healing intercession of St. André Bessette over the writing process. I now write these words, and submit this manuscript for production, on the anniversary of my baptism twenty-eight years ago. It was a different time and a very different church from the one I am in now, but it was immersion into the Body of Christ by water and the Trinitarian formula that makes it so impossible to know a life outside of the Christianities I have traversed. There is a song sung in Mandarin that every Cantonese Protestant knows that perhaps best describes my prayer for this book. The words ask that whatever we say and sing might be transfigured into worship and doxology. For all the flaws and faults for which I must take ownership in this book, I plead for divine mercy and hope that, at least for some readers, the prose will become a song and the sheets of scattered sand open up cracks of light and joy.

The Feast of St. Sophia and Her Daughters
Faith, Hope, and Love, 2023

CHAPTER ONE

The Secular Dream of the Pacific Rim and Sheets of Scattered Sand

To God's elect, strangers in the world, scattered throughout . . . Asia.
—1 Peter 1:1

Sheets of Scattered Sand situates Cantonese Protestants in the period 1989–2012 as part of the larger fantasy that I am calling the "dream of the Pacific Rim." Its main scholarly contribution is to offer, through the prism of Cantonese Protestant communities (which are usually described by some participating in them as a "sheet of scattered sand"), the beginnings of a theological reinterpretation of the Pacific Rim as a powerful imaginary that powers civil societies that have vied for their place as political, economic, and cultural hubs connecting Asia and the Americas. This offering also situates Hong Kong as one of the enduring flashpoints in what Shu-mei Shih calls the "Sinophone Pacific," the scattering of communities that tend to have fraught and tenuous relationships with Chinese nationalisms across the Pacific Rim while usually also being disorganized in their own right. In this way, I use "Pacific Rim" to signal a set of imaginaries that idealize multicultural civil societies and a vague sense of democratic participation in places like Hong Kong, San

Francisco, and Vancouver. There is, I must stress, no single institutional entity that represents the Pacific Rim as a whole. It is better conceived, I suggest, as ideological content that circulates through civil societies and private institutions that claim to operate autonomously from one another.

Although my case studies may give the impression that the Pacific Rim simply refers to the geography of the Asia-Pacific and the Americas, a critical reappraisal of the term in what Janet Hoskins and Viet Nguyen call "transpacific studies" positions it much more as an aspirational imagination. It is, as I will show, an ideological engine that motivates civil societies to frame themselves in the terms of multicultural diversity, economic viability, and geopolitical peacemaking, all by bringing the Asia-Pacific and the Americas together. That this vision might feel overly ambitious is the point. It is better described as a "dream" because it has always been an ideology in development and thus, in Freudian terms, a wish fulfillment fantasy. Some might argue that this dream, in the 2010s when geopolitical discussions were dominated by talk of far-right nationalist movements, antiestablishment rhetoric, and antiglobalist skepticism from various shades of the ideological spectrum, has passed its sell-by date. But as I show, the activities of Cantonese Protestants in those civil societies up to the present time of the much-celebrated Hong Kong protests since 2014, disorganized as they also usually were, suggests otherwise. Besides, dreams never expire. They are only ever repurposed and repackaged.

Cantonese Protestants, I am saying, find themselves as a set of Sinophone communities in societies powered by such imaginations. The three sites that I engage in this book—the San Francisco Bay Area, Metro Vancouver, and Hong Kong—are all Pacific Rim civil societies, not only in the sense of being geographically on the Rim but also in terms of their societies, their governing institutions, and the various private entities with which they interact sharing in a broad sense in the Pacific Rim's aspirational imaginary. I am not above admitting that there was some convenience in choosing these sites. I grew up in the Bay Area, went to university in Vancouver, and have had my dreams haunted by Hong Kong despite never having lived there. But it should also be noted that from the 1980s to the early 2010s, the Bay Area, Vancouver, and Hong Kong also served as three nodes in one of the most prominent stories that was told about how the Asia-Pacific and the Americas were being brought together. That story at one level involved Cantonese Protestants in the sense that they were among what the anthropologist Aihwa Ong calls the "transnational Chinese subjects" of the time, whose movements took place in the shadow of political developments in Hong Kong revolving around the time of its handover in 1997 from British colonial rule to the sovereignty of the People's Republic of China (PRC). Transpacific migration from Hong Kong during those years gave rise to figures that Ong describes as "the multiple-passport holder; the multicultural manager with 'flexible capital'; the 'astronaut,' shuttling across borders on business; 'parachute kids,' who can be dropped off in another country by parents on the trans-Pacific business commute; and so on."[1]

Focusing my scholarly gaze on Pacific Rim imaginaries, in turn, also means that I do not need the Cantonese Protestants I studied to be organized at all, much less offer a coherent account of their theological engagements with the world outside their churches. It also does not mean that all of the Cantonese Protestants I spoke to fled Hong Kong over 1997, stayed there as a matter of principle, or even staked out a claim about the whole affair. Some migrated in the 1960s and 1970s, others went back and forth between Hong Kong and North America, and still others have been in these civil societies for generations. In this sense, I am not attempting a theological critique of Cantonese Protestantism or even trying to theorize what a Cantonese Protestant subject could possibly be. Instead, I am critiquing the Pacific Rim as a secular apparatus that Cantonese Protestants, diverse and disorganized as they themselves are, engage as they interact with the civil societies where they live.

Although my consideration of events tapers off in the early 2010s, this retelling of a familiar transpacific story remains relevant as the prequel to the 2014 Umbrella Movement protests, ostensibly for democracy, for which Hong Kong has been celebrated in recent popular consciousness. It is beyond the scope of this book to cover the events surrounding the Umbrella Movement and its development into the Anti-Extradition Law Amendment Bill (Anti-ELAB) demonstrations in 2019, as well as the attempt to silence them with the National Security Law of 2020. That further timeline is for a second book to work through in due course. But what recent events also demonstrate is that despite predictions that Hong Kong and its global migrations would simply be absorbed into the PRC's orbit, it remains a place where the aspirations for an integrated Pacific Rim, with all the problems that come with such an imagination, are battled out. With the 1997 handover as a pivot point to examine these transpacific Hong Kong migrations, I offer in this introduction a framework of how Cantonese Protestants, sometimes inadvertently, reveal the power of the secular dream of the Pacific Rim in the civil societies they engage.

HONG KONG "FLEXIBLE CITIZENSHIP": AN ENDURING STORY ON THE SINOPHONE PACIFIC

In 1997, the cultural theorist Ackbar Abbas characterized the culture of Hong Kong as marked by a "politics of disappearance." For a global city that had never known—at least in its modern form—an existence without British colonialism, the handover of sovereignty in 1997 from the United Kingdom (UK) to the PRC precipitated a postcolonial problem. If Hong Kong had never existed without a sense of coloniality, then what could be said about Hong Kong culture after colonialism, except that it might simply disappear? In that handover moment, Abbas noted that the "immanence of disappearance precipitated an intense and unprecedented interest in Hong Kong culture."[2]

Since the Umbrella Movement protests of 2014, it is as if the culture that was supposed to have disappeared in 1997 remains stubbornly present in the 2010s and has even further crystallized. Likewise, some might say that the concept of the Pacific Rim, with its optimistic aspirations about geopolitical peace through market modalities, is itself outdated. But it is precisely in the present moment that Asian American scholars Christine Mok and Aimee Bahng have called for attentiveness to what they call "transpacific futurities." For Mok and Bahng, terms like the "Asian Century" and the images of a "New Asia" juxtapose dazzling urban spectacles, the creation of labor precarity for rural and coastal workers, and the continuing attempts to extract resources from the region. They are therefore suggestive of how the capitalist fantasy of the Pacific Rim continues to operate *and* how those who have lived within its coordinates are continuing to challenge it.[3] As the PRC's capitalist endeavors are implicated within these activities, it might be simply said that it too is an emerging power in shaping the region and in activating

The Secular Dream of the Pacific Rim   5

unexpected alternatives to its hegemony. In other words, both the Hong Kong story and the optimism of the Pacific Rim are not disappearing despite rumors that their sell-by date has already passed. The 1997 story continues into the tale of the protests now. The optimistic aspirations of the Pacific Rim, mired perhaps by the PRC's crackdown on protesters in Tiananmen Square in 1989, have developed into the talk of an Asian Century.

The migration of Cantonese Protestants that I discuss in this book lies at the intersection of these two stories in their earlier form, in the period after Tiananmen surrounding the 1997 handover. At that time, migration from Hong Kong, including those of Protestant Christians, became a Pacific Rim story, as they moved to metropolitan areas such as Auckland, Sydney, Melbourne, Los Angeles, San Francisco, Seattle, and Vancouver. When the transition turned out to be initially smooth—it was not until the aftermath of the 2014 Umbrella Movement that a more aggressive nationalist effort to integrate Hong Kong into the mainland began to be understood—scholarly and journalistic discourse turned to the possibilities of return migration to Hong Kong, with the possibility that Hong Kong's place on the Rim was beginning to wane in the shadow of Chinese capitalism.

The San Francisco Bay Area and Metro Vancouver have tended to dominate this out-migration narrative from Hong Kong as sites of investigation into what are called the "transnational" movements of such Hong Kong migrants. Scholars like Aihwa Ong and Donald Nonini noted that a number of wealthy families tended to split their family members across various cities on the Pacific Rim while claiming an essentialized "Chinese" culture to explain how they would also keep their wealth within a global familial "empire."[4] Working mostly with California examples while based in Berkeley in the Bay Area, Ong suggested that this capitalist strategy was a spinoff of a larger process that the Marxist geographer David Harvey describes as "flexible accumulation," the attempt to use leaner institutional units such as the family to accumulate capital at a global scale.[5]

The story was then picked up by geographers in Metro Vancouver, to use the Canadian shorthand for the unwieldy official designation of the region as the Greater Vancouver Regional District. These scholars examined the way that transpacific shuttling affected the everyday lives and emotional geographies of transnational Chinese families. Whereas Kris Olds and Katharyne Mitchell maintained Ong's line that the split family arrangement used "Chineseness" as well as Hong Kong neoliberal normativities to explain their ruthless property purchases in Metro Vancouver,[6] Johanna Waters, Sin Yih Teo, and David Ley probed the emotional impacts of such strategies.[7] Several important findings augmenting Ong's critique of "Chineseness" emerged. First, the Vancouver geographers were able to show that physical distance often compromised the emotional closeness of the family, often leading to marital strain and tensions at home; memorably, Ley quotes a respondent who tells him, "Don't tell me I have a big house. The house is a house of tears."[8] They also demonstrated that what lay at the heart of such strategizing was not only financial capital but also a capitalization of "quality of life" as Hong Kong and Vancouver provided for different needs around the life course.[9] Hong Kong might provide employment, for example, but Vancouver was a place for schooling, homeownership, and retirement. In so doing, they showed that "education," which might seem like a capital expenditure, is actually a form of "cultural capital" that can be deployed to raise one's social status and marketability along the Pacific Rim.[10]

This transpacific Hong Kong story was in turn part of an even larger imaginary, the Pacific Rim vision that powered the political, economic, and social institutions of metropolitan areas like Hong Kong, the Bay Area, and Metro Vancouver. Here, the tale pivots from the migrant subjects to the ideological constitution of the societies to which they migrated. Jini Kim Watson notes that the very language that produced the 1980s capitalist success stories of the "Japan and the four Asian tigers" of Singapore, Korea, Taiwan, and Hong Kong was a work of creative fiction and imaginary dreaming in which the powers in those societies participated.[11] The historian Bruce Cumings facetiously characterizes these narratives as "Rimspeak," the easy usage of the words "Pacific Rim" to denote a geographic region that should feel natural but is actually an ideological production.[12] The late Arif Dirlik even calls it a "euphemism for the powers that dominate the region," with the tall tale that the "ring of fire" that circles Oceania, Southeast and East Asia, and the west coast of the Americas can somehow be imagined as a region of integrated markets, geopolitical peace, and multicultural societies. Such imaginative aspirations, these critics agreed, in turn obfuscated which political entities, including those outside the geography of the Rim (such as the UK), actually dominated the region.[13]

And yet, these very critics of the "Pacific Rim" also point out that the term should not be easily discarded, not even, I would say, in the present moment. Problematic as it may be at a material level, the Pacific Rim as an "invented concept" remains useful as a matter of "discourse" that signals dominant modes of geopolitical thinking from the late 1970s onward. Indeed, as Dirlik puts it, it is best used as a term of reference to "relationships (economic, social, political, military, and cultural) that are concretely historical" instead of as a fact of "physical geography" and should include "global forces that transcend the Pacific, as well as relationships of hegemony and exploitation that are internal to the region." In so doing, "the idea of the Pacific is intended as much to express the aspirations of the people who inhabit the region as it is to contain intraregional contradictions and the relationship of the Pacific to other regions of the world." It is a discourse "that is problematized by the very relationships that legitimize it" and appropriated by the people who find themselves living within the coordinates of its fantasies.[14]

At a discursive level, recent scholarly work on the Pacific Rim as a kind of problematic discourse has tended to examine its militaristic manifestations in the nation-states in the region. It is, in other words, a fantasy with consequences for those who find themselves living within its coordinates. In most of these studies, the United States is often cast as the imperial power that has dominated the Pacific since World War II.[15] One thread of scholarship focuses on the American efforts to restructure decolonized countries after World War II, contain communism during the Cold War, and mobilize capitalist success stories in places like Japan and the so-called four Asian tigers against the various ideological turns in the PRC. These strategic impositions have in turn led to the traumatization of communities that have had to go along with the militarization of their homelands and the economic experiments that do not always work out for their benefit.[16] In another strain that resembles the depictions of Hong Kong migrants in the societies Ong and Ley describe, scholars critique American ideologues who tried to rehabilitate America's image in Asia by touting its embrace of Asian Americans—and by extension, migrants from Asia—as a "model minority." Another image of the Asia-Pacific emerges from this scholarly line, an orientalist success story where the supposed integrity of the Asian nuclear family and a belief in the education system chalked up to Confucian, Buddhist, Taoist, and other garden-variety Asian philosophical values would make way for personal prosperity.[17] Finally, some critique American empire for ecological destruction in the Pacific Rim. One of the major case studies is the treatment of the Pacific Ocean as a dumping ground that has produced what is being called the Great Pacific Garbage Patch. But more important, some have criticized the Pacific Rim as instantiating a "settler colonial" mentality that seeks to erase Indigenous modes of ecology. The activist strain in this scholarship opposes settler colonialism in an effort to discover more sustainable ways of making human society within planetary ecosystems.[18]

Taken together, these various critiques of the Pacific Rim constitute what Janet Hoskins and Viet Nguyen propose to be called "transpacific studies," an examination of American empire as it manifests from its treatment of Asian migrants in the Americas to its extensions of power through and across the Pacific.[19] But what powers these material manifestations of the Pacific Rim is much too incomplete and aspirational to be described as a vision. My preference is to call it a dream. There is, after all, a series of free associations: the region-wide market containment of communism, an imagined reversal of orientalism via model minority mythologies, an anxiety about ecological sustainability in the terms of economic growth. As scholars like Anne Anlin Cheng, David Eng, David Kyuman Kim, and Jinah Kim have each suggested, there is also a melancholia to these unfulfilled desires, say, for societies that are actually multicultural, transpacific social fields that actually manifest geopolitical peace, and racial formations that actually lead to personal actualization.[20] But what they (psycho)analyze in each of these cases is not really a transpacific "subject."[21] Instead, they are interrogating from the perspective of subjects in the region the structures of Pacific Rim civil societies for the desires that circulate through their laws, policies, formal activities, cultural production, and informal practices.

With the Pacific Rim articulated more as a dream than as a regional geography, its work as a fantasy engine that powers civil society imaginations can be analyzed through everyday lives in specific transpacific networks, where the waves of the unconscious break on the shores of underdetermined reality. It is here that what Shu-mei Shih calls the "concept of the Sinophone" becomes relevant.[22] Shih's project is to lay bare what she sees as the real stakes in the studies that emerged in the 1990s and 2000s on Chinese transnationalism, the "Chinese diaspora," and the imaginary of "cultural China" and its detractors in relation to the study of the Pacific Rim. As she sees it, there are two problems. First, transpacific studies enact a thorough critique of American empire, but it tends to ignore the rise of another hegemon in the region, the PRC with its Chinese Communist Party (CCP) attempting to claim the mantle of uniting Chinese peoples around the world under the culturalist banner of "Chineseness." A second problem then arises: terms that invoke Chineseness give the impression that there is a unitary sense of peoplehood among those who might be labeled Chinese, when there is not.

That the word "Chineseness" signals a neoimperialist project is problematic is without question, and in this sense, Shih's intervention is actually a continuation of those very studies of Chinese transnationalism since the 1990s that took the Hong Kong handover as a central point of reflection.[23] The term "Sinophone studies" is Shih's attempt to develop these various critiques into a field where the private idiosyncrasies and political disorganization of a number of Sinophone communities, including Cantonese Protestants, might be examined. In this way, her project is also continuous with the Asian American scholar Ling-chi Wang's advocacy for Chinese American communities to become politically self-determining, instead of being locked into what he called the "dual domination" of American pressure to assimilate and the demands of loyalty toward a Chinese nation-state across the Pacific. It is also to insist on understanding the breadth of the Sinophone as encompassing a scattering of languages across communities and networks that are called Sinitic, including all kinds of forms of Cantonese, Hokkien, Wu, Tibetan, Uyghur, and so on, their local variations, their accented relationships to Mandarin, and their linguistic contexts in societies that may be Anglophone. In this way also, the story that I tell positions Cantonese Protestants not in relation to other Sinophone communities but in relation to the social formation. If there is a foil that might clarify what is particular about these communities, it is in fact, I submit, what I am calling the dream of the Pacific Rim, which is a set of aspirations and free associations seldom articulated by Cantonese Protestants themselves and more often by governing structures and media outlets outside of their communities, usually Anglophone, typically white. In this way, the Sinophone meets the Anglophone in the dream of the Pacific Rim.

SHEETS OF SCATTERED SAND: CANTONESE PROTESTANT DISUNITY IN PACIFIC RIM CIVIL SOCIETIES

Sheets of Scattered Sand is the opening move in a scholarly research agenda that revolves around the theological critique of what I call the secular dream of the Pacific Rim. It might sound laughable to Cantonese Protestants that they are the protagonists in my first study, as their own organizational leaders and participants tend to describe themselves as scattered. But let me offer three stories from my research that illustrate this scattering, and then I will unpack why it is in fact the point of the larger Pacific Rim story I am tracing here.

Sinophone Scatterings: Fremont, October 11, 2011

In 2011, I was conducting a focus group in my hometown, Fremont, when one participant took it as a matter of obligation to criticize the Sinophone framing of my project. "Cantonese is a narrow subset of Chinese," he said, implying that it would have been better for me to call them "Chinese Christians." He then clarified his objections. Apparently, I was only interested in southern Chinese people whom he claimed were "richer" than their northern counterparts. Wealthy people, he said, were predisposed to being less interested in politics. Besides, he continued, they tended to be the ones who came to America first. Also, they grew up in Hong Kong, where "the colonizers will not allow you to oppose politics." He concluded by saying that, actually, Cantonese people do participate in politics, but they will not get "very deep and passionate."

I smiled. What did I know after all? I was being schooled here by a well-meaning critic because I am what my "uncles and aunties," adults in the communities in which I grew up, call in Cantonese a *jook sing*, a "hollow bamboo," who is said only to look Chinese but be culturally empty inside and prefer to speak English, raised by Hong Kong parents who migrated to North America in the 1980s.[24] It was not the only time it happened and not the only way either. At the end of my fieldwork in Hong Kong in 2012 the next year, I was having an informal dinner with a group I had met at a church when one of the elder statesmen of the group, hearing about my project, said that my work was doomed to insignificance. If I had really wanted to be groundbreaking, he said, then I would have tried to study Buddhists in China. But all I had done in his eyes was to study myself. He pounded the table and declared, "We Hong Kong people are not like those ABCs," using the colloquial shorthand for American-born Chinese, which was another way to refer to a *jook sing*, with the added assumption here that all that ABCs are concerned about is their own identities. "But I *am* an ABC," I replied. I also knew that I had made it. *Jook sing* me was, by the end of my fieldwork, mistaken for a Hong Kong person, fluent in Cantonese.

Still—and here I return to the focus group in Fremont in 2011—the criticism about the scope of my project made me feel less insecure than I thought I would be. I had already interviewed church leaders in San Francisco's Chinatown, some of whose families came in the nineteenth and early twentieth centuries from the Toisan area in Guangdong Province. Guangdong, which used to be called Canton, is where many variants of Cantonese are spoken; the Asian American historian Henry Yu even centers the Toisan migrants who built the early Chinatowns in his account of the "Cantonese Pacific."[25] The people I talked to had participated in the social justice movements in the 1960s that became known as the Asian American movement, which fought for the material empowerment of communities that had been economically and politically marginalized in white supremacist America.[26] I had also conducted interviews and focus groups in Metro Vancouver earlier that year. There, they described to me the difficulties of having mainland Chinese migrants, Mandarin speaking and from farther up north (to use the terms of my critic), come to their "Chinese churches" because the people in those churches were ill-equipped as Cantonese speakers to serve them.[27] So much, then, for Cantonese people being mostly rich and for the project being restrictive in terms of southerners and northerners on the Sinophone axis. As for passionate involvement in politics, I was also about to go to Hong Kong the next year in 2012 to speak with activists who were embroiled in antiestablishment democracy movements even before the 2014 Umbrella Movement protests.

After hearing out my critic, another participant spoke how she had first begun to think about politics during 6/4 (shorthand for the June 4, 1989, crackdown by the Chinese authorities on the Beijing Spring protesters) and had recently begun to be troubled by the emergence of homosexuality and abortion as the issues of "moral battle" of the day. An older man in the group cut in to say that he had not supported the solidarity movements for the protesters, that he found the gatherings to be "*caai waa waa*" (Cantonese slang for a noisy gathering), but that he had gone because he wanted to be there for his friend, who eventually gave up on supporting the movement. The woman who brought it up said that she had seen the events unfold on television, and she was actually unclear about what was happening at the time, but "this is in my memory," she emphasized, "it's my belonging, what I remember." Still another participant said that she was in Hong Kong at the time and that she remembered that no one had any motivation to go to work at the time. She had told her daughter that they were going to go for a walk to Victoria Park, where the demonstration that became known as the Million Man March was beginning. It was a grief, she said that her colleagues said, that was "worse than your own father dying."

Then it was another older participant's turn to speak. She said she was already living in the Bay Area at the time, and she had never been to a prayer meeting outside of her own church—and this is where the Protestant Christian dimension is important, as discussions were inevitably drawn back to churches as one of the basic units of community. But as she was grieving the crackdowns, she went to a gathering that was organized by a network of Cantonese-speaking churches. In her words:

> My feeling is that it's like Chinese people actually have a new awareness because Chinese people often like to say, "Chinese people are a sheet of scattered sand." But in that moment, as I recall it, it's not so; I saw that Chinese people are not a sheet of scattered sand. When there are these events that come up, those people will come together for the same issue, the same goal, to weep and to be in prayer. That's my biggest feeling at the time.

That romantic feeling of Chinese unity, however, would have to be restricted to 1989, as her views were not shared by everyone in the group.

Soon, another participant said that his friend brought up another interesting point of view. He said that the students at the time had affected the political operations of the government, which meant that a crackdown was necessary unless they really wanted to entertain the possibility of radical change. Then he commented on how political machinations had changed since Tiananmen. The top-down crackdown, he suggested, was a bygone way of doing politics. He cited the United States as an example in recent years, especially during the War on Terror in which he accused politicians of opening up theaters of war in Afghanistan and Iraq and needing to cut their budget for social security, which would affect retiring people like himself.[28] He concluded in Cantonese, "Politics now is very smart. They will not say, 'I am the boss.' They will say, 'You are the boss. I am your servant.'" Then to add emphasis, he switched to English. "You are the master. I am your servant," he said. Then he returned to Cantonese to say, "So you will vote, and then I will do the work. But once they have done the work, now you are their servant."

Participants in the group shifted uncomfortably as he spoke about these political games, though some later also spoke about how "politics," which included protests, was indeed a dirty game to play.[29] There was little ideological unity within the group, not even about what seemed to be the formative event of the Tiananmen Beijing Spring for Cantonese Protestants. But there was also a sense that disunity coalesced around the feeling that there was something to be avoided about politics. It was a realm that was supposed to lie outside their everyday concerns, an unknown space that was to be engaged at their own risk.

"We Did Not Push Him Out": Burnaby, January 16, 2012

The dynamics of this Fremont group represented a common one in my field research in 2011 and 2012. In February 2012, I was conducting another focus group, this time in the Vancouver suburb of Burnaby. It so happened that a municipal election was getting heated in that city, with contention being generated by a newly formed grassroots school board slate called Burnaby Parents' Voice. Ostensibly founded by a group of concerned parents across the political spectrum and ethnic communities to assert parental agency over their children's education, its main platform was opposition to the school board having implemented the

Sexual Orientation and Gender Identity policy to develop curriculum and programming to "address educational policies, practices, and procedures that perpetuate homophobia, transphobia, and heteronormativity."[30]

One of the more prominent members of the slate was a Cantonese Protestant named Charter Lau. Until his advancement to political candidacy, he had been the vice chair of the Christian Social Concern Fellowship (CSCF), which was a collective of Cantonese Protestants that gathered to discuss the relationship between their practice of faith and secular political topics and to generate Sunday school curriculum based on their conversations for local Cantonese churches. Lau's ties to the group generated some unwanted publicity during the school board campaign. English-language news accounts emerged on November 17, 2011, that CSCF's website had all sorts of controversial material. First, there was an anti-pornography video that had been allegedly produced by the group depicting nude children as part of a campaign to underscore the horrors of sex trafficking; in advance of the news breaking on *Burnaby Now*, it was removed. But second, what was still up on the website were comments by the then-chair of CSCF, Rev. Wayne Lo, about Christians having to step up a prayer campaign to counteract Muslim influence in Canada.[31] Both items dogged Lau's campaign, undermining his credibility as a moral crusader on the one hand and as a political figure able to work in a multicultural, secular coalition like the Burnaby Parents' Voice slate.

However, Lau did not think that *he* was the problem. Rather, he blamed those who had read his published materials for misreading him. "There's a pending legal action against whoever attempts to disgrace me by false accusation," he commented to CTV News about these two problems. "OK, so I really can't comment about the action we are taking now."[32] Lau, in other words, did not see his ties to CSCF as a liability. Instead, he saw the group as being falsely represented in an unfriendly media arena—precisely the dirty politics that my Fremont focus group participants were referencing—which was why he was threatening legal action.

Presumably, then, the proper context for reading CSCF's Chinese-language website would have been within Cantonese Protestant networks in Vancouver. I therefore asked the Burnaby focus group, which was composed of Cantonese Protestants, whether he was their candidate of choice. The response I got was laughter. "We didn't push him out," a middle-aged woman I now anonymize as Mrs. Mak remarked in Cantonese, with "push" referring to whether Lau emerged from the popular will of Cantonese Protestants in Burnaby. To say that they did not push him out was tantamount to saying that Charter Lau—and for that matter, CSCF—did not represent Chinese Christians. Of course, Lau and CSCF may have framed themselves as representing Chinese Christian views, but that framing was problematic because representation requires the people being represented to recognize themselves in that group. Lau was not someone who bore the mantle of the community, she was saying. He was an outspoken person who happened to be a Cantonese Protestant seeking to engage Canadian civil society. Her husband agreed with her: "Yes, he came out on his own. We have no means as a community to push him out." There were, in other words, no institutional mechanisms that Cantonese Protestant churches or other organizations could use to bolster Lau's campaign. Lamenting the disorganization, this last participant then sat back and sighed. "Truly, Chinese people are a sheet of scattered sand."[33]

"Killing and Burning": Hong Kong, April 1, 2012

A pattern I had begun to see at that point was emerging around what might be seen as the rhetoric of Cantonese Protestant communities as "scattered sand." That set of words, I suggest, was less important than what they described, which was that Cantonese Protestant communities and organizations tended to be perceived by Cantonese Protestants themselves as disorganized to the point that any claim that someone who was part of those networks represented them—or worse, "Chinese Christians," if not the "Chinese community" itself—would be laughable, even doomed to be the community's next political failure.

This dynamic also emerged in a tense exchange at one of my focus groups in Hong Kong in 2012. Toward the end of the conversation, one of the participants began criticizing a Catholic priest, Fr. Franco Mella, who had moved to Hong Kong from Italy in the 1970s. Mella had come to be known by the locals as Kam Chai, a play on his translated last name into Cantonese. That he had his own nickname and public persona suggested that he had come to be seen as a local Hong Kong personality.

Indeed, he played the part well. He speaks fluent Cantonese and has become a ubiquitous presence at democracy protests with his guitar, singing Cantonese folk songs he usually wrote himself with lyrics that advocated for human rights and social justice for marginalized groups in Hong Kong.

The participant in the focus group, however, was not taken in by the romance of Mella's popular persona. Without being altogether clear about which of Mella's protests he was referring to, he opposed what he called Mella's "killing and burning" (Cantonese, *saat jan fong fo*) based on his own Protestant Christian biblical principles. Not having heard that arson was among Mella's activities, I asked him for some clarification.[34] "I would ask him," he said, "because he organized this event, then how would he respond that someone might kill and burn? Would this be in accordance with the Bible's principles? Because he loudly proclaims that this is a thing that Christians should do. So he's killing and burning, then is he doing what a Christian should be doing?" As the participant, with the help of other group members, clarified what he meant by "killing and burning" (though another one whispered that he had "no idea" what was being discussed), it became clear that the protest he was referring to was a pivotal one in Hong Kong's history after its 1997 handover to Chinese sovereignty.

Another participant then said that there was a protest with a group of "right of abode activists," though no one was clear that the events they were referring to had happened some twelve years before. The "right of abode" references long-standing problems in immigration law since the 1997 handover of Hong Kong to the PRC. The mini-constitution of Hong Kong, the Basic Law, states in Article 24 that anyone who has lived in Hong Kong for seven years has the "right of abode" there, a kind of permanent residency. But the practice of the Hong Kong government since 1999 was to exclude certain groups from this right, including children born to Hong Kong parents while living on the mainland as well as domestic workers from the Philippines and Indonesia. Mella was on the forefront of fighting for the right of abode as a matter of fairness for these disadvantaged groups under the law. If there was a protest for the right of abode, then Mella was definitely there.[35]

The original respondent continued that "at that event, someone threw a bottle of gas, and it caught on fire and killed someone." He was talking about a mainland Chinese activist named Shi Junlong, who had been occupying the Immigration Building demanding the right of abode in Hong Kong. When immigration officials refused, he and other activists reacted swiftly on August 2, 2000. They doused the room with gasoline and lit it on fire, injuring fifty government staff workers and killing two people, one immigration official and one protester. The focus group participant then pivoted back to Mella as the one responsible for this "killing and burning." Mella, he reasoned, was also an activist who promoted right-of-abode activism based on Christian principles. "Now it's that team of people," he said. "Kam Chai might have warned him, but the thing got out of control, but out of control is his responsibility too. It's like if this was a corporate firm, and Kam Chai is the boss, and if your team is out of control, then isn't it your fault?"

It turns out, in other words, that it was not exactly that Mella had been "killing and burning."[36] Just as the Burnaby group felt that Charter Lau could not represent them because of his own self-proclaimed leadership, this participant was arguing that Mella was one of the Christian faces of right-to-abode activism, yet he was unable to control the movement he had started, framed in the mind of the focus group participant as an ideally organized corporate entity in and of itself. Even though he did not use the words "sheet of scattered sand," he was also gesturing toward the inevitability of political action being messy and that leadership in politics included an impossible sense of liability too because a movement *is* an institution already.

There was also a deeper significance to the 2000 Immigration Building fire incident in terms of Hong Kong's civil society history. The participant in the focus group was giving voice to a common sentiment among the respondents that protests should be "rational" as opposed to "radical." In fact, this dichotomy can be found in the news reporting about the 2000 incident. A protester who was at the Immigration Building that day had told the *Hong Kong Daily News* that there had been two factions in the demonstration, one "radical" and the other "conservative," with the former willing to use violent tactics while the latter preferred reasonable communicative action.[37] My research participants were voicing an alignment for the "conservative"—or as they put it, "rational"—faction, in the sense that a competent leader should organize a civil dialogue that would lead to gradual steps toward justice. A movement, in other words, was perceived as corporate and, ipso facto, institutional; for some reason, movements were also never organized, although my respondents wished that they would become rational someday.

Interestingly, that wish for rationality, and what my respondents might have foreseen as its eventual denouement into radical action, began to play out the very next year, after my fieldwork was finished. In January 2013, the constitutional law professor (and practicing Protestant Christian) Benny Tai Yiu-Ting and his colleagues, the Baptist minister Chu Yiu-ming and the sociologist Chan Kin-man, began to organize a movement called Occupy Central with Love and Peace (OCLP). Using precisely the language of "rational" in opposition to the word "radical," they proposed to enter into a yearlong set of deliberations about democratic reform in Hong Kong that would culminate in a nonbinding referendum to overhaul the system. OCLP would, in other words, be precisely the kind of organized corporate effort to ensure rational discussion among its participants. After an orderly process that included the institutional mechanisms of deliberating and voting, the recommendations that emerged from the institutionalized movement would be taken to the government. At that point, if the authorities then refused to acknowledge, then they would turn to the more "radical" option of a street occupation in the business district known as Central that would threaten to shut the city's financial operations down for at least a day. When Tai was asked on television by journalist Michael Chugani and legislative councilor Priscilla Leung what would happen if someone decided to use those civil disobedience events for violence, he answered that he would demarcate who was and was not part of OCLP and say that the troublemakers were external to his initiatives.[38]

As my focus group participant could very well have predicted even in 2012, the movement got out of hand. When OCLP did not end up organizing the civil disobedience measures it had promised to initiate after the rational discussions did not bear fruit with the authorities—Tai went on *Bloomberg* to say that the movement did not have enough participants and that they would instead organize a "symbolic banquet" instead of an all-out occupation of the Central District[39]—student groups organized a school boycott in September 2014 that led to a series of democracy teach-ins and the occupation of an area adjacent to government buildings that had become popularly known a few years before as

The Secular Dream of the Pacific Rim 19

Civic Square. Police fired tear gas, against which protesters defended themselves using umbrellas, and a seventy-nine-day street occupation known as the Umbrella Movement came into being. Protests, my focus group participants were saying in 2012, do become unpredictable and uncontrollable. They end up being, if you will, a sheet of scattered sand that is more "radical" than "rational," even if one wishes to organize them corporately and institutionally. This reality, like the constant potential for community infighting that the focus group members spoke about in Fremont or the inability of self-appointed leaders to represent communities, as discussed in Burnaby, also led to some handwringing in Hong Kong, where respondents wished for what they called civil rationality precisely because they perceived the opposite to be happening on the streets.

SCATTERED ON A SHEET: CANTONESE PROTESTANTS AND THE SECULAR DREAM OF THE PACIFIC RIM

Taken together, the foregoing anecdotes suggest that the term "sheet of scattered sand" circulated among Cantonese Protestants as part of a discourse about community infighting, organizational dysfunction, and ideological disunity. Perhaps most fully illustrating this pattern of partial knowledges and nonrepresentational insistence, my participants did not tell *jook sing* me that they borrowed this term from perhaps the most renowned of all Cantonese Protestant community leaders, Sun Yat-sen. I had to find that out myself when I spoke about it at an academic conference. At a panel on Chinese religions, I spoke about how my interview participants would use this term, the "sheet of scattered sand," to describe their political engagements. A white man shouted from the back row, "That's Sun Yat-sen!"[40]

To be clear, it was not quite Sun Yat-sen. In fact, the term might as well have been more of a colloquialism than a quote. When my respondents used the term "sheet of scattered sand" (一盤散沙, *jatpunsaansaa*), they referred to themselves in Cantonese as a *pun* (盤), more a pot than a sheet. Sun's formulation, though, was originally a *pin* (片), an actual thin sheet. I justify my retention of Sun's "sheet" by being agnostic as to its depth. My respondents also used the term "sheet of scattered sand" slightly differently from Sun's conception of it in his lectures on *The Three Principles of the People*. For Sun, the term "sheet of scattered sand," rendered "loose sand" in the official English translation, was a term of criticism against his nation-building project, often directed at him by those he called foreign observers.[41] Normative loyalties belonged, as Sun lamented, "to family and clan and not to the nation," which means that the "scattered sand" referred to the way that each family and clan was out to serve its own purposes instead of what might be considered the fictional entity of the "Chinese people."[42] My research participants, however, were saying that the disorganization lay within their own communities, that crafting political networks and engaging in public action was difficult because of dysfunction within their own churches, seminaries, missionary agencies, publishing houses, and so on, if not also their very families at home. If it was Sun's critics who called the people of his new nation a "sheet of scattered sand," then the Cantonese Protestants I spoke with had thoroughly internalized the description, invented a new term altogether, and grounded themselves in an internal critique of their own political paralysis.

As I considered the radical negativity of the "sheets of scattered sand" in my ethnographic data, I also began to see that there was a point to this emphasis on disorganization. As a colleague reminded me when I was in the frustrated throes of revising this manuscript from dissertation to monograph—how, after all, does one say anything meaningful about a sheet of scattered sand?—there are two elements to the metaphor. For my research participants, the focus tended to be overtly on the incoherent scattering of grains that took the form of institutional splits, political disorganization, and uncontrollable action. But implicitly, there is also a sheet, where the sands are scattered matters; therefore, moving the focus from the scattering to the sheet itself might illuminate unexpected ways that the project hung together.

The argument of *Sheets of Scattered Sand* is that for Cantonese Protestants in these three civil societies—the San Francisco Bay Area, Metro Vancouver, and Hong Kong—to describe as "secular" that "sheet" on which they are scattered as sand also reveals something about the way that these three metropolises are ideologically and materially linked through what I am calling the secular dream of the Pacific Rim. Comparing the activities of Cantonese Protestants in these three metropolitan areas allows me to retrace this Pacific Rim mythology with an eye toward what my research participants reveal about its secularity.

TRIANGULATED METHODOLOGY: INTERVIEWS, FOCUS GROUPS, AND ARCHIVES

I undertook this research from 2011 to 2012. The research question I started with was, *What are the conceptions of civil society and concrete political networks and practices that constitute the engagements of Cantonese Protestants with the Pacific Rim civil societies of Metro Vancouver, the San Francisco Bay Area, and Hong Kong?* What I meant by "civil society" as I began the research—which is more or less still what I think now—was the constellation of local public institutions in the metropolitan areas where Cantonese Protestants lived in which they participated in the democratic work of deliberating how they wanted to be governed and what the nature of the society they lived in should be. I conducted this inquiry in three phases: semistructured interviews with Cantonese Protestant leaders, focus groups within Cantonese Protestant communities, and archival work on Cantonese Protestant engagements with Pacific Rim civil societies from 1989 to 2012.

In the first phase, I identified 142 interviewees—50 in Metro Vancouver, 47 in the San Francisco Bay Area, and 45 in Hong Kong—who could speak knowledgeably, either from positions of leadership in Cantonese Protestant churches and other organizations or from working closely with Cantonese Protestants in their engagements with civil society, about how Cantonese Protestants had engaged their local civil societies, what theological imaginaries they brought with them into such engagements, what ideological impacts they understood themselves to have made, what networks they formed to achieve such impact, and what reflections on Pacific Rim civil societies they might articulate through their activities. These interviews were semistructured, conducted in a mix of Cantonese and English, transcribed, and analyzed for narrative themes—that is, the stories that were being told about secular civil societies on the Pacific Rim and the relationship of Cantonese Protestant communities and networks with such secularities. I obtained full, informed, and voluntary consent from my contacts, most of whom allowed me to use their names for the study. Given the passage of time since my initial interviews, I have endeavored to anonymize many of them anyway, unless I am speaking about activities and statements that are already a matter of public record (including in the dissertation), in which cases I work as much from my assembled archives as from the interview transcripts. Initially, I worked with contacts whom I personally knew through family connections due to my own position within these communities, though the process of snowballing led to respondents I did not know and whose ideologies were unfamiliar to me.

Because I was conducting a study of Sinophone communities in Pacific Rim civil societies, the interviews made up only the initial phase of the study, which also deals with ideological disunity within Cantonese Protestant communities and networks as well as the way the dream of the Pacific Rim works its way through civil society. A frequent refrain I heard within the interviews referred to the "sheet of scattered sand," but the thirteen focus groups I conducted—five in Vancouver, five in the Bay Area, and three in Hong Kong—confirmed it. Because the purpose of the focus groups was to triangulate the interview data, the respondents were not randomized. Instead, I identified churches that I anonymized and asked members to self-select whether they wanted to be in the group; all their names have also been anonymized. I also requested that they not be church leaders, as those tended to be part of the first sample. Again, the focus groups were transcribed and analyzed according to the same themes that the interviews were.

The third phase of the study was then to check the interview and focus group data with documentation of Cantonese Protestant activities in Pacific Rim civil societies. At one level, this process involved trying to find newspaper reporting, advertising, radio and television spots, live recordings, and so on of the Cantonese Protestant engagements of which my interview and focus group participants spoke. But it also required me to understand what laws and policies they were trying to engage, so this process also necessitated scouring city hall minutes, legal proceedings, judicial decisions, the precise wordings of laws and statutes, and other formal records of the various engagements that my fieldwork subjects mentioned. In this way, I was often able to compare what Cantonese Protestants spoke about with how their activities were popularly portrayed, in addition to what formal apparatuses they were trying to engage.

Let me offer a final note on why I chose to focus on "civil society" that is more local than, say, a national context. My method is to tease out from the stories themselves—the interviews, the fieldwork, the documents that I track down—what the social formation of the Pacific Rim looks like. To provide a national context for each of the sites would suggest that one particular kind of social formation—the nation—determines what kinds of responses I am getting from the respondents, who are simply calling their experience of the world outside the church, which they are attempting to engage and negotiate, "secular." In so doing, they face multiple levels of secular politics, ranging from the press at multiple levels (there are the *New York Times*, the CBC, the *Globe and Mail*, and the *South China Morning Post*, but there are also the *Vancouver Sun*, *San Jose Mercury News*, and *Apple Daily*) to politicians at multiple levels (city, state/province/special administrative region, national/federal) and the legal system at multiple levels (some cases to which I refer include the federal American case *Perry v. Schwarzenegger*, the provincial British Columbian decision *Chong v. Lee*, and the experiment in "one country, two systems" in a case like Hong Kong's *Ng Ka Ling v. Director of Immigration*). What I try to do instead of overdetermining the places Cantonese Protestants live is to say that the dream itself is articulated in the structures with which Cantonese Protestants must contend and collaborate with—and which they themselves articulate in their activities. Those sites are the Bay Area, Metro Vancouver, and Hong Kong.

CANTONESE PROTESTANTS AND PACIFIC RIM SECULARITIES: AN AGENDA

Cantonese Protestants operate as scattered sand in the secular sheets of Pacific Rim civil society arenas. The next step is to consider what these Pacific Rim secularities might be and what Cantonese Protestants reveal about it. In the following chapters, I proceed in four movements.

The first movement, which takes place in the following chapter, is to clarify the theological coordinates of what I call the secular dream of the Pacific Rim and what the scattering of Cantonese Protestants through these societies reveals about it. I do so by working through a transpacific Cantonese Protestant community narrative around the word "church," which is anchored in Hong Kong, to understand what they considered to be the "secular." What I show is that they rooted themselves in the story of a revival movement that originated in the 1950s in Hong Kong that theorized the colonial state and its Protestant denominational bureaucracies through the terms of the secular and that was then exported to cities like San Francisco and Vancouver. These revivalist Cantonese Protestants understood the space of the church, with its practices of prayer, Bible study, and evangelism, to be threatened by secular apparatuses that were more interested in public and private fundraising and collaboration with political power. In so doing, I work through the period before 1989 in which these Cantonese Protestants founded new communities in San Francisco and Vancouver while participating in a nascent democracy movement in Hong Kong, all with this concept of the secular in mind.

The second movement then examines a crisis in this Cantonese Protestant secular imaginary, one that arguably produced the sheet of scattered sand. Having settled in Pacific Rim civil societies that are run according to narratives of liberal diversity, Cantonese Protestants have found themselves on a collision course with these metropolises when it comes to their conceptions of privacy and autonomy. Same-sex marriage and transgender rights dominated this conversation. But with the secular as outside the concerns of the church, what I demonstrate in this chapter is that Cantonese Protestants approached these concerns by insisting on the radical autonomy of all of their institutions. The sheet of scattered sand, I show, is rather the point.

In the third movement, these domestic units become scaled out institutionally. Cantonese Protestants may have insisted on a kind of institutional networking framed through radical organizational autonomy, but at the same time, they had to be legible to the civil societies they were trying to engage. What I show, then, is that Cantonese Protestants at this very time were also at work in reformulating their church congregations in secular terms. Here, the three comparative sites become important. Hong Kong, Metro Vancouver, and the San Francisco Bay Area each manifest different flavors of Pacific Rim secularity with various emphases. In this way, churches in the Bay Area restructured themselves according to what they saw as market "best practice" norms, while those in Vancouver reworked themselves as social services hubs and those in

Hong Kong as intellectual think tanks, sometimes with a whiff of collaboration with the post-handover government and at other times completely at odds with it. Those societies, in other words, were different from each other, though they were all located on the Pacific Rim, which means that it is difficult to speak of Cantonese Protestants as forming a coherent transpacific bloc either.

The fourth movement resolves the contradiction of domestic confrontation and institutional cooperation by theorizing a key word in Pacific Rim secularities: democracy. It does so by situating Cantonese Protestants within the political parties they worked with between 1989 and 2012. Because of their ideological inclinations, they often found themselves working with politically conservative parties in North America, though news of their strength as a voting bloc was, I show, overdetermined. Moreover, the overarching rubric for political participation was to showcase their own democratic voices, a point that is particularly salient in Hong Kong as they faced the threat of the security bill that came into view in 2003 and became effective in 2020. In other words, the space of political participation is no longer Cantonese Protestant communities but the very apparatuses of Pacific Rim secularities themselves, in political parties, action groups, and intellectual think tanks. In this way, this final step of placing Cantonese Protestants within the secular arenas of Pacific Rim societies—in their political parties—underscores how "democracy" became a central ideological term under discussion in secular Pacific Rim arenas. But that word itself did not provide coherence. It was, I ultimately show, the sheet on which the sands scattered.

In the epilogue, I gesture toward what relevance this story, which retraces the Hong Kong migration story from 1989 to 2012 through the San Francisco Bay Area and Metro Vancouver, continues to have in a time marked by the turn in the region to Chinese nationalism. There is a certain weariness with which Cantonese Protestants in the times that I spoke to them talked about the sheet of scattered sand. In gesturing to a future project to which this book might lead, I suggest that there is a way that this tale of Sinophone scattering on the Pacific Rim becomes even more pulled apart by the emergence of the PRC as a more pronounced secular global empire, that even though this monograph ends in 2012, what happens afterward is but a set of variations on the theme of the sheet of scattered sand.

CHAPTER TWO

Secular Compromise

Hong Kong Revivalism and Pacific Rim Migrations

What harmony is there between Christ and Belial?
What does a believer have in common with an
unbeliever?

—2 Corinthians 6:15

INTRODUCTION:
THE "SECULAR" IN CANTONESE PROTESTANTISM

Since the 1970s, Cantonese Protestant theologies have presumed, I hope to show in this chapter, a separation between the church and a world they presume to be secular. To scholars in Chinese Christianities, this division will sound entirely unsurprising. Lian Xi and Christie Chow have traced the emergence of this distinction among Chinese Christian revivalists during the Republican Era in the early twentieth century.[1] Tim Tseng has observed its "transpacific transpositions" to American urban centers such as New York and San Francisco after the Chinese Communist Revolution.[2] The field has already spoken, as it were, and not only in China but all over what has come to be known as the Pacific Rim.

But there is a story to how Chinese Protestant revivalism spread across Pacific Rim civil societies. In terms of the Pacific Rim's dream coordinates, most of the Cantonese Protestants I spoke to could narrate themselves in the secular terms of students moving to North America for school, highly skilled workers who settled in the Bay Area, semi-retirees who sought a slower pace of life in Vancouver, and entrepreneurs who kept a foot in Hong Kong for business opportunities. But the Cantonese Protestant church communities that they established offer a concurrent transpacific narrative. In this story, what spread throughout the Pacific Rim from the 1950s to the 1970s was the theological account of the church regarding the "secular" as a presence that compromises the purity of Cantonese Protestant church congregations to practice their faith without being dependent on political institutions outside the church. The prevalence of this theology among Cantonese Protestants in Pacific Rim civil societies, I intend moreover to demonstrate, was hard won. Strict separation from the secular was not the norm when they arrived on the scene, and their arrival resulted in political contests in which their theological vision became dominant from the 1970s onward.

I first set the stage with the Chinese revivalists in Republican China moving to Hong Kong and initiating a revivalist "student movement" that led to young Cantonese Protestants framing mainline Protestant denominational bureaucracies in Hong Kong as secular and breaking from them in the 1950s. I move to these students' subsequent collisions in the 1960s and 1970s with the Asian American movement in San Francisco and Chinese Canadian community politics in Vancouver, both of which they regarded as blocs of theologically compromised Chinese Christian church communities. The final part of this chapter focuses on developments in Hong Kong since the late 1970s in which this strict separation of the church and the world enabled the emergence of a theology of civil society from among Cantonese Protestant communities, which has arguably been carried over into the present in the democracy movements that have animated transpacific interest in the Hong Kong protests.

DENOMINATIONAL SECULARITIES: THE "STUDENT MOVEMENT" AND HONG KONG PROTESTANTISM

When I was conducting fieldwork in Hong Kong, a story that my participants narrated to me concerned what some called the St. Paul's Seven. As a composite of their hagiographic tale goes, seven classmates were suspended by St. Paul's School in the early 1960s because they began an evangelical Bible study and proselytized fellow students. While St. Paul's itself was an Anglican school, my participants suggested that the denominational establishment wanted complete control of theological activities at the school instead of recognizing the power of the Holy Spirit in their midst. The story of the suspension, at least from the perspective of my interviewees, is therefore the tale of a church institution that had become so compromised by its secular power that it could not recognize the movements of God.

I recount the story of the St. Paul's Seven because it invites reflection on a new understanding of the church's relation to the secular that was emerging in 1950s and early 1960s Hong Kong. One research participant who told me this story was the longtime general secretary of the Hong Kong evangelical organization Breakthrough Youth Ministries, Philemon Choi. He said that he had actually met one of the St. Paul's Seven and that he in fact had been led to Christian faith through this young revivalist's influence.[3] In fact, the St. Paul's Seven were part of a much larger movement that had an interschool evangelistic rally organized by the Inter-School Christian Fellowship (ISCF). ISCF in turn was the secondary school node of a networked set of institutions such as the Fellowship of Evangelical Studies (FES) and the Hong Kong University Christian Association.

Taken together, these fellowships composed what was described to me as a "student movement." One of the movement leaders from that time invited me to lunch and described a revival that "broke out," she said, in 1951 at a Baptist youth camp on the island of Cheung Chau. The new Hong Kong revivalism, she continued, emphasized pietistic practices that differentiated Christian life from a kind of secular worldliness as a matter of "purity." What that meant, she said, was that she "would not even pass in front of a cinema," though she had "no qualm about

TV." This seeming contradiction in practice, she added, had to do with the students' normative belief in what in some evangelical quarters is known as the "Rapture," a sudden event in which practicing Christians would suddenly disappear from the earth in preparation for God's judgment of the earth at the end of the world. A cinema, the students speculated, was a house of vice, an impure space. If they were in such a place, perhaps they would not be "raptured." A television set, by contrast, can be anywhere.

The Cheung Chau revivals generated, my respondent said, a set of gatherings calling themselves Gospel churches. They were spin-off congregations from the Baptist Convention, which she said had attempted to suppress the student movement just like the St. Paul's Seven had been suspended by an Anglican school. The reason for the repression, she added, was that the denominations were "suspicious of young people and spread rumors that they were communists."[4] What the students threatened, she suggested, was the temporal power of denominational institutions, which in turn were said to be compromising the faith. Indeed, a popular term that emerged from the time about the charities that these institutional apparatuses offered to refugees in Hong Kong fleeing the war-torn mainland was "rice Christians," people who claimed to have converted to Christianity but only for the material benefits it conferred on them. From the perspective of the students, the revivals seemed to threaten the denominations' material power by calling them on their spiritual bluff. For the revivalists, the denominations were in fact secular institutions, even though they were Protestant Christian in name.

The students saw themselves as distinct from the Protestant denominational apparatuses. But the politics of purity led to divisions among the students themselves. Indeed, having called the denominations out for secular compromise, they found that sometimes they were calling each other out for the same thing. One strand of the student movement developed into the joint youth fellowships that had led to Philemon Choi's conversion and networked it with the global network of university gatherings that came to be known as Intervarsity Christian Fellowship (IVCF). These groups retained the term "Baptist," my respondent emphasized, because the point of being Baptist was that they gathered in independent congregations; it was more of a theological indicator than a link to a denominational apparatus.⁵ But staying Baptist also made enemies of other students. A more radical vein of the student movement can be found, for example, in the activities of another Cheung Chau revival participant, David Ng Chu Kwong, who founded Peace Evangelical Fellowship as a public break from the more institutionally minded students. In a ministry that he later developed into a grassroots mission to New Territories squatters whose huts were subject to fire hazards, even clerical ordination was considered a compromise with the establishment, though Ng was later ordained himself to facilitate his migration to Canada as a member of the clergy.⁶

The student movement was in turn part of a larger informal network of revivalists that had rooted itself in Hong Kong. When I asked Philemon Choi how the student movement began, he named several revivalist preachers who had gotten their start in ministry on university campuses on the Chinese mainland in the 1930s and 1940s prior to the Chinese Communist Revolution in the late 1940s. They included figures like David Adeney and Rev. Philip Teng, as well as the founders of the Chinese for Christ network in California that I grew up with: Calvin Chao, Moses Yu, and Stephen Chiu. These men were themselves part of international student ministry networks too. Teng, for example, had attended student revival conferences in Chinese universities and had converted under the influences of American and Canadian missionaries like the China Inland Mission's Adeney and Dr. Stephen Knights, the founder of the Canadian branch of IVCF's university campus ministries.⁷

The Hong Kong revivals were thus part of a larger story of Chinese Christian revival movements, which in turn could be placed within some networks of global student revivalism, such as IVCF. At the same time, the move from the mainland to Hong Kong shifted the context of practice. Although a number of these revivalists sought to collaborate with the Republican Chinese regime in the early twentieth century, their move through Hong Kong in the 1940s and 1950s and their subsequent movements across the Pacific highlight a concept of the church that is hostile to the secular.⁸ Part of it has to do with the conditions of their migration from the mainland: most of them were fleeing the new hegemony of the Chinese Communist Party (CCP). Indeed, my own life story is caught up in these movements. My childhood pastor in the Bay Area, Stephen Chiu, was among the revivalists that Choi mentioned. Chiu recounts in his memoir how CCP agents incarcerated him and subjected him to harsh interrogation techniques. He writes of how he fled to Hong Kong by boat.[9]

From a newfound base in Hong Kong, some of these revivalists moved across the Pacific Ocean and founded church networks like Chinese for Christ and Home of Christ in the Bay Area, as well as the Chinese congregations of the Christian and Missionary Alliance association in Canada. Others, such as Philip Teng, stayed in Hong Kong and established influential churches, such as North Point Alliance Church. The founder of the Chinese Christian Mission, Rev. Thomas Wang (whom I also interviewed for this project), writes in an autobiographical account that he was converted in the 1950s by the preaching of the revivalist John Sung. He was also influenced by another minister in the same strain, Wang Mingdao. Both of them advocated for a strict separation of the church from secular compromise with the CCP.[10]

And yet, the routes through which these revivalists moved through Hong Kong and around the nascent Pacific Rim were not necessarily Chinese Christian. Certainly, a number of student movement participants migrated from Hong Kong to North America in the 1960s and brought their revivalist theologies with them. But here is where their theology needs to be put into secular perspective. They did not move for theological reasons, and they moved as part of a migration wave that was not exclusive to the revivalists. Their movements are in fact much more legible within the framework of a new geographical formation that was emerging at that very historical moment: the Pacific Rim and what the historian Madeline Hsu interprets as its casting of Chinese students and professionals as a "model minority" that could contribute to American and Canadian economies while presenting a viable ideological alternative to Chinese communism.[11] Moving away from Hong Kong opened educational and economic opportunity for a younger generation at the time. When they arrived in North America, they joined existing churches and started new ones, while also taking the opportunity to evangelize Cantonese speakers who had moved in the same migration wave.[12] It is the growth and eventual dominance of these revivalist congregations and networks, I show next, that led to dramatic clashes with Chinatown churches in San Francisco and Vancouver.

ASIAN AMERICAN SECULARITIES: "IMMIGRANT" REVIVALISTS CONFRONT SOCIAL JUSTICE MOVEMENTS

First Chinese Baptist Church (FCBC) on Waverley Place in San Francisco's Chinatown is the site where the members of the writer Amy Tan's Joy Luck Club met in the 1950s.[13] But when its longtime pastor, Rev. James Chuck, remembers the church in the 1970s, he remembers that the church split.

According to the *Bay Area Chinese Churches Report* that Chuck helped to edit, sixty members left FCBC in 1978 intending to plant another church "specifically to reach new immigrants."[14] What was different about the culture of these new immigrants, interestingly enough, was their theology. In my fieldwork, I spoke with Mr. Ho, who told me he had been part of the exodus. He told me that he had left FCBC for theological reasons. He said that he "found out that the church's faith content is *maamaa* [so-so]" and that when "the church broke," his family was able to switch churches.[15] Chuck also knew that theology was the problem. In a paper he presented to the regular pastors' gathering in San Francisco, the Chinese Christian Union, in 1970—eight years before the split—Chuck observed that there had been tremendous numerical growth among Chinese American evangelicals who were active in university campus ministries and congregational planting initiatives. He was worried about them and not because they were urban Hong Kong people coming to historically Toisan Chinatown. His anxiety revolved around their conception of the church in what he called "private" terms. If faith is "intensely personal," Chuck declared, "it is never private." He continued, "The Christian lives a 'separated' existence only in the sense that his life is different from, or distinguishable from that of the world; but the Christian never lives apart from the world."[16]

The implication was that churches like FCBC did not conceive of the church as "private" and "separated" and that newcomers from Hong Kong had thought precisely that. There is a story to how churches like FCBC in San Francisco's Chinatown did theology in a nonseparatist way. In fact, they had been developing engagements with secular society since the 1930s. In 1933, the Tahoe Christian Conference brought young people from a number of Chinatown churches to Zephyr Point, a

Presbyterian campground in the Sierra Nevada mountains. Some of the discussion there might have been characterized as secular, such as the identity "problems of American Chinese youth" that were "accentuated" by the material alienation of the Great Depression. But the conversations were also explicitly theological, especially when they mulled over what they noted as a "prevailing skepticism" among Chinese American youth to a divided American Protestant milieu, split as it was in the early twentieth century between "modernists" who sought to make the faith relevant to modern society and the "fundamentalists" who insisted on the scientific veracity of the Bible.[17] After World War II, the Tahoe conferences developed a postwar Chinese American theological agenda by joining with the Silver Bay Youth Conference and the Chinese Students' Christian Association. Together, they pushed for a postwar Chinese American generation to integrate Christian theology in their social activism, particularly in the "endeavor to integrate the minorities, more particularly the Chinese in America, into the larger American society and work toward a Christian world."[18]

These discussions came to a head in the 1950s. A very negative report about the Chinatown churches authored by Horace Cayton and Anne Lively for the National Council of Churches spurred the churches to come together as the National Conference of Chinese American Churches (CONFAB), the first meeting of which Chuck hosted at FCBC.[19] Addressing the Cayton and Lively report's claims that the Chinatown churches tended to be governed by American missionary boards with little interest in Chinese American community development, CONFAB's final report—which was compiled by one of the organizers of the Tahoe conference, Oakland Chinese Methodist Church's Rev. Edwar Lee—argued that Chinese American churches had to engage "racial tensions" in society at large and "the inter-group tensions within the groups." CONFAB also rejected the notion of "considering our own congregation as an entirely independent church" on the theological grounds that "we are saved not for isolation, but for fellowship." It met every three years, working to develop a bilingual hymnal to be sung in both Cantonese and English, to recruit young Chinese American ministers, to review clergy salaries, to provide theological training, and to aid in Chinese American refugee resettlement.[20] It also took federal funding from the federal initiative called the War on Poverty to start community organizations. Alan Wong recalls that the secular organization Self-Help for the Elderly was inspired by initiatives when "the National Council of Churches started senior centers at churches."[21] James Chuck recalls that when the Chinese Hospital in Chinatown was founded, "it was actually the church people that were on the boards and committees, and the early directors were church people."[22]

Taken together, CONFAB's initiatives positioned the churches to participate in what became known as the Asian American movement.[23] By most accounts, the high point of the movement revolved around college campus strikes in 1968 led by a multiracial coalition called the Third World Liberation Front (TWLF) to establish colleges of "ethnic studies" at San Francisco State College (SFSC) and the University of California, Berkeley.[24] They succeeded in 1969, with a department established at Berkeley and a self-governing College of Ethnic Studies at SFSC. The purpose of the TWLF had been to transform universities into community-based educational centers where the dynamics of oppression in marginalized communities in America could be studied in an international framework that linked racism in the United States with neocolonialism in what was then called the third world, and some people who were involved with CONFAB were also involved with the TWLF. Take, for example, the YMCA's Alan Wong, who was in charge of the Intercollegiate Chinese Students Association (ICSA). The ICSA became involved with the TWLF when Wong was transferred to work with students and was arrested with members of the Black Student Union who were rallying for the college. For Wong, participation in the strikes was a direct outgrowth of his church work; he said to me in an interview that he was inspired by Jesus's words in Matthew 25: "When you saw that I was hungry, you fed me."[25] In turn, Asian American studies in the sense of this radical movement transcended the Tahoe conference's original focus on Chinese American identity in American society. It linked the marginalization of Chinese, Japanese, and Filipino communities in the United States (the term has grown to be more capacious since the 1960s) to the postcolonial struggles of developing nation-states in Asia.

Some Asian American graduates of SFSC's College of Ethnic Studies, in turn, went to work for the churches. Rev. Harry Chuck, the executive director of the Presbyterian Church's Donaldina Cameron House from 1977 to 2001, cochaired the Chinatown Coalition for Better Housing.

With the help of some of the first Asian American students of SFSC's College of Ethnic Studies, Harry Chuck organized congregation members and local business owners to build a seniors' home at his church, the 175-unit Mei Lun Yuen Project at Cameron House. The origins of the project came from a fresh graduate in Asian American studies, a Cameron House staff worker named Gordon Chin. In 1972, Chin wrote a report that showed that the situation for senior access to affordable housing in Chinatown was dire. Over two thousand new units of senior housing would need to be built, and two thousand more renovated, in order to rectify the problem. Chin's report formed the basis of Chinatown's affordable housing agenda, which was presented to the San Francisco Planning Department.[26] However, the patch of land that Cameron House wanted to develop was a site that affluent Nob Hill residents adjacent to Chinatown wanted for redevelopment into a parking lot. New strategies from the strikes orchestrated by students in ethnic studies were thus deployed for Chinatown community organizing. With a coalition of Chinatown organizations, the Presbyterian Church in Chinatown rallied three hundred senior citizens, most of them members of the congregation, for a public hearing at Commodore Stockton School on January 13, 1977, and persuaded the city government to acquiesce to their demands.[27]

Across the San Francisco Bay, some Chinatown congregations in Oakland also saw themselves as part of the Asian American movement. Oakland Chinese Presbyterian Church's Rev. Frank Mar founded a series of nonprofit organizations in Oakland that remain in operation today. Advancing the cause of "Christian service," Mar was instrumental in starting many community organizations in Oakland's Chinatown that used the church's name as an official sponsor. Oakland Chinese Presbyterian Church became one of the formal sponsors of the Chinatown senior affordable housing project, Doh On Yuen, in 1969. An Elderly Nutrition Program followed in 1973, which in turn led to the formation of the Chinese Convalescent Hospital Committee and the Chinese American Health Organization to develop facilities to provide health care for senior citizens. Mar also cooperated with students from Berkeley's Asian American studies program to form the East Bay Chinese Youth Council at the Presbyterian Church's social hall. This group then formed the East Bay Asians for Community Action in 1970, out of which Asian Health Services and the Asian Law Caucus were formed in 1972.[28] The Asian

Community Mental Health Services was also a Presbyterian initiative, beginning with the efforts of social workers, supported by the community, and first headed in 1974 by San Francisco Presbyterian minister Rev. Dennis Loo. Mar was also involved in the Chinatown Project Area Committee to renew Chinatown's built environment in 1973, the Chinese History Research Project from 1975 to 1982, the Oakland Public Library's Asian branch in 1981, and the Oakland Asian Cultural Center in 1996.[29]

This Asian American movement reconfiguration of Chinatown churches in the Bay Area was the setting into which some student movement revivalists from Hong Kong, as well as China, arrived. In time, they came to outnumber the Chinatown congregations. Of the Bay Area Chinese churches that were founded between 1950 and 1972, sixteen were considered "theologically conservative" while nine, by contrast to the Chinatown churches, cited no denominational affiliation.[30] By mid-1996, there were 158 Chinese churches in the entire Bay Area, many of them suburban, with revivalist roots and without affiliation to mainline denominations to which the Chinatown churches were attached. By contrast, only 33 churches with 150 delegates nationwide were asociated with CONFAB in 1998, which in turn met its institutional demise in 2000.[31]

These new revivalist "church plants," as they were called, often traced their origins to small, family-style Bible studies. In San Jose—the southernmost tip of the Bay Area that became known as the Silicon Valley because of its concentration of information technology companies—revivalists grew their numbers among Cantonese-speaking migrants who came there to pursue secular careers. Rev. Abraham Poon moved to the South Bay from Calgary to plant a Christian and Missionary Alliance church. He began with thirty people, most of whom were college students, and as their numbers increased, they were slowly able in 1983 to afford rental space in Campbell and then build their own building by 1987.[32] This story of congregational growth and suburban church property purchase was typical. In 1962, New Life Church, Nazarene, constructed a worship center in 1966 on a 2.7 acre site.[33] Lord's Grace Christian Church began recruiting from Stanford University students and faculty in 1973 and met in Palo Alto's Masonic temple until they purchased property in 1989.[34] Chinese Baptist Church of San Jose began in 1975 as a family prayer meeting in the fellowship hall of the First

Baptist Church of Campbell in January 1976 and stayed there until they had means for a building of their own. Chinese Bible Baptist Church in Los Altos was planted in 1980, again mostly with a congregation from Hong Kong,[35] as was South Bay Chinese Baptist Church in Milpitas by twelve Christians who later moved to San Jose.[36]

The congregations were independent from each other; what linked the new Hong Kong revivalist immigrants together were missionary agencies. At first, the CONFAB churches did not seem to see the immigrant revivalists as an existential threat, as much as they might have worried that the encounter with their theologies would be problematic. One of the theological outgrowths of the movement was the Pacific Asian Center for Theologies and Strategies (PACTS) at the Pacific School of Religion in Berkeley. In 1976, PACTS published an anthology of Asian American theologies. In Mar's essay for the volume, he proposed that CONFAB collaborate with the immigrant revivalists. He listed eight missionary agencies that might be worth working with. Seven had revivalist origins: the Chinese Christian Mission in Michigan (with Rev. Thomas Wang), Ambassadors for Christ in Washington, DC (with Moses Chow), the Evangelize China Fellowship in Los Angeles, Chinese for Christ in Los Angeles, the Ling Liang World-Wide Evangelistic Mission in Los Angeles, the Chinese Christian Literature Society in Kowloon (presumably the forerunner to Breakthrough Publications), and the China Graduate School of Theology in Hong Kong. The only organization with actual links to the Asian American movement was Cameron House.[37]

One of the most prominent organizations in Mar's list was the Chinese Christian Mission (CCM), which eventually moved to the Bay Area north of San Francisco. CCM began in Rev. Thomas Wang's garage in Detroit in 1961 as a small congregation and merged with the Chinese Bible Church of Detroit in 1964. Its original English-language periodical was titled *Chinese Christians Today*, though later *Chinese Christian Mission* became a Chinese-language magazine supplemented by the English *Challenger*.[38] Wang also embarked on cross-country mission trips throughout the 1960s, gathering young students who became key staff workers at CCM. Rev. Wally Yew was one of those missionaries who later became the general secretary of CCM. He told me in an interview that CCM had moved to the Bay Area in 1972 to be nearer to another agency on Mar's list: Far East Broadcasting, a radio project that broadcast biblical teaching into the People's Republic of China. However, because land was "less expensive, more economical" in Petaluma, CCM purchased property there, thirty-nine miles north of its target site.[39] It then established a presence in San Francisco's Chinatown in 1979 with a book center that later became a Gospel Center that offers English-language and American citizenship classes.

The church splits of the 1970s, such as the one at FCBC, demonstrated that these immigrant revivalists also changed the theological culture of the CONFAB churches. Another church in San Francisco's Chinatown that encountered the new immigrants was Cumberland Chinese Presbyterian Church. While its pastor in the 1950s, Rev. Samuel King Gam, had been a core member of CONFAB, Rev. Ernest Chan's arrival from Hong Kong in 1965 signaled that a new game was in town. His first move was to consolidate power in staff pastors, as the church grew to about eight hundred members across Cantonese, Mandarin, and English congregations.[40] His pastors later became revivalist leaders throughout San Francisco. Cumberland's student minister, Rev. Chanson Lau, began Cornerstone Church with students and young families in 1975 in the Sunset District.[41] In 1987, Cumberland's Cantonese associate pastor, Rev. Wing So, led 140 people to merge with the Richmond District's Chinese Evangelical Free Church to form the San Francisco Evangelical Free Church in a residential area near Chinatown,[42] which in turn planted Hope Evangelical Free Church in the Sunset District in 1999.[43] In addition, Ernest Chan's assistant, Kenneth Yeung, later founded the Chinese herbal medicine and health food company Prince of Peace Enterprises.

Where CONFAB and the Asian American movement had engaged the political and economic structures of American society with a coalition, Cumberland's approach to social engagement was largely in-house. In 1979, Yeung—Chan's assistant at the time—encouraged Cumberland church members to sponsor large Vietnamese and Cambodian refugee families in the Bay Area. Yeung proposed that congregation members team up to sponsor large families, "like your family plus B and C couples, I mean, families, three of us sponsor this family of ten persons so they don't need to be separated into different states, different cities." When they arrived in San Francisco, Yeung mobilized church members to resettle the new immigrants: "So we get church people to help: find jobs, find housing, find school for the kids, take these people around, so they know how to be independent and live in the city and so it was a very good testimony."[44] Yeung's strategy also guaranteed that the separation of the church from secular institutions remained intact. Sponsorship and resettlement were individual acts of Cumberland membership; no state funding was involved.

Across the San Francisco Bay, immigrant revivalist churches advocated for an even stricter differentiation of church spaces from secular society. Part of the reason was because there were already English-speaking Chinese "fundamentalist" churches. Instead of having to re-orient those congregations like they did at FCBC and Cumberland, they simply had to establish Cantonese worship services at them. In Oakland, the Chinese Independent Baptist Church (CIBC) had been established after the 1906 earthquake in San Francisco and became independent from its San Francisco mother church in 1967 when a new building was constructed.[45] Even though many of its members could speak Cantonese, CIBC felt that speaking English could grow the church's numbers. Its position was also that the theologies of the Presbyterian and Methodist churches across the street, both affiliated with CONFAB, were overly secular. One of CIBC's former members, Asian American theologian Russell Yee, took me on a tour of Oakland's Chinatown in 2011. Clarifying that he no longer held the fundamentalist views he did when he was younger, he described the situation of CIBC on one side of the street and the CONFAB churches on the other as the spatialization of the "fundamentalist-modernist divide in Oakland Chinatown," a situation in which "we were the evangelizing, tract-passing, have-evangelistic-basketball-games kind of youth group" and the Presbyterians across the street "were going to have dances and not pass out tracts." When pressed about whether the churches ever interacted because of their close proximity to one another, Yee replied that the interaction was "zero, absolutely zero, just sinfully zero," for he, like many in the church, had internalized a narrative that evangelicals were growing inversely to the mainline's decline because of "God's favor."[46]

A Chinese church that saw itself in the same fundamentalist network as CIBC was the Chinese Bible Church. Its founder was Pastor Sen Wong. Although Wong himself was Cantonese speaking, he sought to proselytize English speakers. According to the church's current senior pastor, Steve Quen, Wong acquired a job at the local post office and started a Vacation Bible School, a summer evangelistic program for children, in 1956. As his children's ministry grew, Wong's search for new property led to the Chinese Bible Church renting a "large house" on East Twenty-Ninth Street. Slowly, he continued, "we converted to a church, then we rented the apartments one by one next door, eventually rented the whole apartment complex, twenty-something, thirty-something rooms, for our Sunday school as well as our school that we started in 1979." Like CIBC, the Chinese Bible Church described itself as "fundamentalist." "We were that brand of fundamentalism," Quen said, "where if you didn't believe exactly what we believed, if you were not for me, you were against me." This entailed strict codes in terms of Bible translation (they preferred the King James Version), dress code, and worship music. Quen pressed his point by stating that in the early days, even Southern Baptists were too liberal for them. Instead, they networked among like-minded American congregations, and sometimes even CIBC was "too liberal," although they held summer camps together.[47]

When the immigrant revivalists arrived, CIBC and the Chinese Bible Church were drawn into the orbit of Cantonese Protestantism in the Bay Area. CIBC later planted a CIBC Fremont in the 1990s farther south in the Bay Area. Pastor Sen Wong began a network of Chinese Bible Churches throughout California, including the Chinese Bible Mission in San Francisco, Chinese Grace Churches in Sacramento and Stockton, and the Fellowship Bible Church on the Bay Area peninsula. The Chinese Bible Church moved out of Oakland in the 1980s, renting property from San Leandro public schools to start the Cantonese-speaking Chinese Christian Schools while renaming itself Bay Area Chinese Bible Church. They also established Cantonese ministries because newer Chinese American students were also arriving. Indeed, Dr. Alvin Louie, a pastor who trained at the Chinese Bible Church before becoming CIBC's senior pastor in 1989, pressed this point in a piece published by CCM. "While ministering at the Oakland Chinese Bible Church as visiting director," he writes, "an influx of Cantonese young people began coming to our church and later, joining our visitation teams. . . . It was then I saw the need to speak Cantonese. Nobody told me this time. . . . I wanted to!"[48] Louie's passion for

Cantonese student ministries led him to take language courses from the University of California, Berkeley.

The new hegemony was now set. By the early 1980s, the story of CONFAB's involvement in the Asian American movement had been all but displaced by a narrative that cast them as agents of secular compromise. In their place was the growth of new revivalist churches throughout the Bay Area, with church splits in San Francisco's Chinatown, the English-language fundamentalist churches in Oakland drawn into a Cantonese-language orbit, and new congregations being established in the Silicon Valley. Most of these congregations saw themselves as independent of each other, but they were drawn together into a revivalist network by missionary organizations like CCM. It was also not the case that they were uninterested in engagement with secular society. It was just that these engagements needed to happen without the compromise of secular funding with putative strings attached, as they saw in the activist work of CONFAB and the Asian American movement, with the denominational churches in San Francisco in the place of the Hong Kong denominations.

COMMUNITY SECULARITIES:
CHINATOWN ORGANIZERS MEET HONG KONG REVIVALISTS

In Vancouver, the conflicts within Chinatown churches over the arrival of the new Hong Kong revivalists boiled over into a British Columbia Supreme Court lawsuit, *Chong v. Lee,* in 1981. Ostensibly, the *Chong* case concerned an internal "doctrinal dispute" in a historic Chinatown church, the Christ Church of China.[49] The petitioners who filed the suit represented "a small minority of the congregation, mostly elderly people."[50] They alleged that a new pastor from Hong Kong, Rev. Gentle Lee, had recently changed the mode of baptism from sprinkling to full immersion. These changes generated two legal problems. First, the petitioners argued that the changes altered the way in which persons could become legal members of the church. They alleged that because the mode of baptism had been changed, all previous members who were sprinkled at baptism were illegitimate.[51] This issue, the court noted, was further complicated by the list of membership for the church having been "in disarray" since

1975; according to the church's own rules, the judge observed, the current pastor would not have been a legitimate member.[52] Second, the theological change meant that the building had to be physically altered to accommodate a large baptismal font at the front of the sanctuary. Although the judge understood that the court system should generally not interfere with theological doctrines "except in so far as may be necessary for the determination of the legal rights of the parties concerned," the court heard the case because it was about legal property ownership in light of internal doctrinal disputes. "A majority of the congregation cannot divert the property to uses inconsistent with such defined religious doctrines against the opposition of a minority of the congregation," the decision read, "however small such minority may be."[53]

Chong suggests that, just like in the Bay Area, there were Chinatown churches in Vancouver that existed before the arrival of new Hong Kong immigrants. Indeed, they shared many of the similar problems of Canadian missionaries trying to maintain power over Chinese congregations, though there was no Cayton and Lively report to galvanize them into a networked collaboration like CONFAB and no Asian American movement that radicalized them. Instead, one response in the early twentieth century, long before the arrival of the Hong Kong revivalists, was to form a new, independent church. Members of the Chinese Presbyterian Church and the Chinese Methodist Church left their denominations to establish an independent congregation in Chinatown in 1913, the Christ Church of China of later *Chong* fame.[54] Initially meeting at the Chinese Benevolent Association with about one hundred attendees, the church represented, according to its pastor from the 1980s Rev. Stephen Lee (who was Gentle Lee's son), "an indigenized, independent and self-supporting church with no denominational or missionary affiliation" and included services for "worshipping God, proclaiming the Gospel, educating the illiterate, cultivating the virtues, helping the poor and being loyal to the Chinese nation."[55]

The founding of the Christ Church of China reflected broader developments among Chinatown churches at the turn of the twentieth century, including those with denominational affiliations. In 1896, Rev. Chan Yu Tan and his brother, Rev. Chan Sing Kai, arrived in British Columbia after organizing the first Wesleyan school in Hong Kong and established the Chinese Methodist Church in Vancouver.[56] Presbyterian and Anglican missionaries with some knowledge of Cantonese started missions with schools that developed into congregations still currently in existence, such as the Vancouver Chinese Presbyterian Church and the Anglican Church of the Good Shepherd.[57] It was in this church landscape that the Christ Church of China formalized Chinese power over a congregation of their own. The only difference between them and the denominational churches was that they were not beholden to missionary boards outside of the congregation.

Like their counterparts in the Bay Area, the generation of Chinese Canadians after World War II became leaders in Chinatown congregations. They soon found that they needed to defend their property against Vancouver's slum redevelopment project in the 1960s in which the city government proposed severe demolition projects in Chinatown to clear putatively dilapidated buildings to build a freeway through the city. Although the municipal authorities had promised not to touch the churches, the Christ Church of China was somehow slated for demolition in the second iteration of the development plans. As one alderperson put it, "The church has no architectural value . . . and it is holding up 300 units of public housing."[58]

Negotiating with the city required some legal creativity on the part of church members. Due to the threat of expropriation, the members of the church, represented by its committee's chair, a lawyer named Harry Fan, challenged the eviction on precisely the grounds that churches were not supposed to have been on the demolition list. Vancouver's city solicitor then replied that Fan's letter protesting the expropriation was "without validity" and that his proposal of an "exchange of properties" was "quite unrealistic" in September.[59] But negotiations between the city government and the church lawyers continued. They reached an agreement in December. Vancouver's city council passed a motion to compensate the church $21,000 in exchange for a public parcel of land on East Pender Street and Gore Avenue that would be sold to them for $40,000. There, the Christ Church of China constructed their new building, along with a senior's home called China Villa. The freeway never came through town.

The freeway debacle coincided with the arrival of the Hong Kong revivalists. One prominent revivalist was Rev. Augustus Chao, a Christian and Missionary Alliance pastor whose Canadian career began in the Canadian prairies before he moved to Vancouver. In 1960, he had moved from Hong Kong to Saskatchewan to plant Regina Chinese Alliance Church, the first Cantonese-speaking Christian and Missionary Alliance congregation in Canada. His ministry in Regina had gotten him involved with a group of students in Winnipeg, who called themselves the Winnipeggers, who had formed the Chinese Christian Fellowship on the University of Manitoba campus and later planted the Winnipeg Chinese Alliance Church.[60] Chao helped them organize the first Chinese Christian Winter Conference in 1961, which invited CCM's Rev. Thomas Wang as its inaugural speaker.

Chao moved to Vancouver in 1966. Chao's autobiography recalls a letter that a friend from his Bible college days, Joe Ottom, had reportedly sent him. "Here, very big fish in Vancouver," Ottom's letter had read, "lots of Cantonese." Chao then writes, "Regina was a small town and had only 500 Cantonese, but there were maybe 10,000 in Vancouver, so he urged me very much to come."[61] Ottom needed the help. He had established a Cantonese ministry at an Anglo-Canadian church, Tenth Avenue Alliance Church. When Chao arrived, he conducted the Chinese ministry at Tenth as well as a Cantonese afternoon service at Chinatown's Salvation Army hall; they also handed out evangelistic tracts in Chinatown. When the services grew to two hundred people in 1969, they bought property on Knight Street into which they moved with three hundred congregants in 1972.[62] This new building then became a base for other church plants in Victoria, Richmond, Burnaby, Chicago, and South America.

Although Chao never ministered at the Christ Church of China, his arrival in Vancouver arguably precipitated the events of *Chong*. Stephen Lee's account places revival speakers at the church as early as 1966.[63] In 1970, the congregation called another evangelical minister from Hong Kong, David Poon. Having served a Christian and Missionary Alliance church in the Aberdeen district in Hong Kong, Poon was subsequently ordained by Augustus Chao in Vancouver in 1971. Under Poon's leadership, the church outgrew its original thirty to forty attendees to about four hundred members by 1974. Unlike the old Chinatown guard, they were mostly new immigrants from Hong Kong who practiced revivalist theologies.

Almost repeating the slum clearance controversy, the building became yet again a site of contestation, but this time, it was between parties within the congregation itself. The church committee, which mostly consisted of the revivalists, received notices from groups calling themselves the Board of the Christ Church of China and the Trustee of China Villa. It turned out that these alternative boards were composed of the old Chinatown members and had "devised a scheme to sell the church building for a dollar to a new organization controlled by them."[64] On May 4, worshippers found the buildings locked by hired security guards, forcing the over two hundred members at the time (it later grew to four hundred) to hold church services in the parking lot and in the basement, an event covered on the front page of the *Vancouver Sun*.[65] The battle for the property's ownership lasted for two years and was settled in 1976 by the Supreme Court of British Columbia in favor of Poon's congregation, not the Chinatown members.

By the time that Rev. Gentle Lee was hired in 1978, contestations within the church over modes of baptism in relation to both membership and the building had become commonplace. That year, Poon had left the church over misunderstandings with a pastoral search committee.[66] Before Gentle Lee was hired, a special general meeting on October 22, 1978, passed a motion to change the mode of baptism altogether to immersion, with sprinkling "only in exceptional cases (such as those physically unfit for immersion) with special permission from the committee." It would also permit applications for church membership by those who had been either sprinkled or immersed, as they believed that "salvation came not through baptism by either immersion or sprinkling, but through the redeeming grace of the Blood of our Lord Jesus Christ, while men's justification came by faith alone."[67] Sensing this to be divine confirmation to participate in what he thought would be a revivalist movement in Canada, Rev. Gentle Lee was hired on November 28 from Hong Kong and arrived for work on October 1, 1979.[68] In March 1980, the general meeting resolved to build a new building on the Pender and Gore site with four hundred to five hundred seats, along with a large baptismal pool in the front and an adjacent park that would serve as a parking lot. They also appointed new deacons that did not include old Chinatown members.

These changes in the church's building and leadership structures led to the filing of *Chong v. Lee*, the court case in which older Chinatown members accused Gentle Lee of changing the modes of baptism. Anonymous letters from Chinatown members began to appear; at least one interviewee also remembered picketers outside the church.[69] Gentle Lee also recalls in his autobiography that a Chinese Canadian Protestant newspaper sided with the petitioners, filing accusations against him and, in his words, "publishing articles that falsely accused the pastor of fighting with his congregation in the courts, damaging many people's faith."[70] He writes that many of the church leaders were young students who held prayer vigils in the church.[71] In 1981, the petitioners' case was struck down, for the court held that as a nondenominational, unaffiliated church that could vote on its own internal practices, the claim that a fundamental church baptism tradition had been altered could not be made. In an appeal, the petitioners then alleged that the congregation had also changed infant baptism to believers' baptism. In *Re Christ Church of China*, 15 E.T.R. 272 (B.C.S.C.) (1983), the Supreme Court of British Columbia ruled decisively against the Chinatown petitioners and for the new Cantonese evangelicals, arguing that the church had not changed its theology and that the petitioners had no actual rights to the properties.[72]

Although these cases concerned one Chinatown congregation, the results were felt across Cantonese Protestantism in Vancouver. As one interviewee put it, "There was a lot of divisiveness, and the pastors came to here, and the elders went to there, and they went to many different churches. . . . [After moving to Calgary for a time] I came back here, and because all the people had left, and they became church leaders elsewhere."[73] Gentle Lee himself left for Toronto in the late 1980s, which led to the promotion of the pastor for the English-speaking second generation, Rev. Edwin Kong, to the Cantonese-speaking senior pastor post.

It was through these events that new evangelicals from Hong Kong altered the imagination of Cantonese Protestant congregational space in Vancouver. When I asked Edwin Kong about what drove what he described as his social service work at CCM Canada, he told me that it was a sense of guilt. He said that during his pastoral tenure from 1983 to 1999, he seldom engaged the Chinatown community:

> My failure as a pastor, many times when I recall at that time, I drove my car and pressed a button, the gate opened. I drive into my parking lot, the gate shut. I pushed another button, open the church door,

I use a key to go into my room, and then I *zyunsam ji keitou cyundou waisi* [devoted myself to prayer and the ministry of the word],[74] the traditional teaching. I preached my butt off. I taught the people. I did everything that a pastor should do. And yes, I did a good job, I always say, this is not pride, but I am pleased that I have done my years as a pastor. But I came to a point that I said, "So what?" The church is in Chinatown, but we are so cut off from Chinatown. The only thing that I know about Chinatown is the barbecue duck and the barbecue pork.

Kong then told me that he forced himself to reevaluate his theology. He discovered that he needed "to put away evangelism first. Do I really care about them? And if I said I care about them, then why? I have to soul-search myself. In the past, I care about you because I want you to sit in my church." Kong applied for the Christ Church of China to have a booth at the Chinatown night market in the 1990s that both distributed tracts and provided free medical services. But as Kong laments, "it wasn't very successful. After a couple of years, the excitement is gone. People like the excitement to start, the continuity, and then when you don't see the so-called result, fades, and I learned from this."[75]

Although the *Chong* case concerned only the Christ Church of China in a strict sense, it is instructive more generally about the emergence of Cantonese Protestantism in Metro Vancouver because of the drastic transformation of the space of the church from a community center to one, as Kong puts it, with a gate and locks. The theology that motivated this shift was revivalist, aimed at converting Cantonese speakers and growing the congregation's numbers. But the result was twofold. The first was that the church became detached from the Chinatown community. In addition, the fallout from the cases facilitated the spread of revivalism across new Cantonese churches, such as Vancouver Chinese Alliance Church and its many church planting projects, across Metro Vancouver. As Kong suggests, there was a shift in the 1990s during his tenure at CCM Canada in which he, out of a sense of guilt for the social effects of the theological separation of the church from the secular community, attempted to bridge that gap. The need for such bridging indicates that the revivalists' strict separation had also become hegemonic in Vancouver.

COLONIAL SECULARITIES:
THE HONG KONG MAINLINE ESTABLISHMENT MEETS
EVANGELICAL REVIVALISTS

The question, then, is whether such separatism actually separated the Cantonese Protestants in this transpacific Hong Kong revivalist network from the secular civil societies of the Pacific Rim. On reflection, the answer may in fact be tricky. In the Bay Area, Cantonese Protestant revivalists reconfigured both mainline denominational churches *and* fundamentalist congregations in Chinatowns and established new ones of their own to draw in new Hong Kong migrants. In Vancouver, these same efforts led to a series of lawsuits at a Chinatown church that, on the one hand, scattered its members to new congregations and, on the other hand, established precedents in Canadian law about whether internal doctrinal disputes could be brought to secular court, while inducing guilt among some church leaders about the detachment of churches from the neighborhoods in which they gathered. What this dynamic suggests is that there are unexpected possibilities for secular engagement in revivalist theology. The church is supposed to remain separate from the world to avoid secular compromise. However, there is also a way where this separation makes possible new forms of engagement with secular society. It is that possibility that manifested as the revivalists made their way in the 1970s back to Hong Kong.

When I asked some interviewees in Hong Kong who had grown up in the revivalist tradition about their interactions with secular civil society, they told me about what they called the Golden Jubilee incident in 1978.[76] The yearlong ordeal revolved around a Catholic girls' school in Ho Ma Tin, when teachers discovered that the accounting books kept by the headmistress of the Precious Blood Golden Jubilee Secondary School, Sister Beatrice Leung Kit Fun, contained irregularities.[77] When this was reported to the newly established Independent Commission Against Corruption, Leung resigned, stood trial, and pleaded guilty to charges of misappropriation of funds.

But that was only the beginning. The press had reported that the whistleblowers were leftists, and the school retaliated accordingly. Teacher contracts were revised, adjusting their terms of employment and lowering their salaries. Students took to the school playground to demand full disclosure of the school's financial situation. In response, the newly appointed Catholic bishop of Hong Kong, John Baptist Cardinal Wu, appointed another headmistress, who promptly set policies that forbade students from gathering for meetings, ostensibly because they might be planning revolutionary activities. Soon, a meeting of four students was discovered. They were suspended. Teachers protested. They were fired.

These events caught the attention of Szeto Wah, a pro-democratic activist who had himself been a headmaster at a primary school in Kwun Tong before he became politically active during a strike in 1971 against the government teachers' department, which had threatened to cut teachers' salaries. With Szeto at the helm, some four hundred students, along with their teachers, staged demonstrations and vigils at the Hong Kong Catholic cathedral compound throughout May 1978, demanding the dismissal of the new headmistress and the reinstatement of the suspended students.[78] As tensions escalated, the colonial government's Education Department, with the support of Cardinal Wu, did the opposite. They fired all the teachers and closed the school.

Closing the school escalated the crisis. Civil society groups, some of them religious, joined the movement. Fr. Franco Mella recalled that the event propelled Szeto Wah to prominence as a democratic activist and gathered some ten thousand people at Victoria Park to protest in support of the occupation; it was the largest gathering there since the 1967 riots. The diocese's own Justice and Peace Commission condemned the school's closure, which precipitated its own temporary suspension of operations by Cardinal Wu.[79] So too, it brought a Protestant group, Breakthrough Youth Ministries, to prominence in Hong Kong civil society. Two interviewees who were working for Breakthrough at the time told me that they had gone to the sit-ins carrying a Breakthrough Publications banner.[80] The Methodist minister Rev. Lo Lung Kwong remembers that one of Breakthrough's founders, Josephine So Yan Pui, called "the position of the Christian" in the Golden Jubilee incident "the great challenge facing the church in Hong Kong," as it would determine the position of the church in relation to human rights. In a tribute to So's legacy, Lo wrote that she was "not only a good counselor, a good sister, but more like a prophet of the era, of *the* era. With insightful care and compassion proceeding from your heart, facing the weight of an evil dominion of darkness in a suffocating world, you were brave enough to issue a prophetic voice."[81] The situation itself was finally resolved when the government opened a new secular school, Ng Yuk Secondary School, to which the majority of Golden Jubilee students and teachers went.[82]

The irony was that Breakthrough's social engagement, as well as the activist networks it established with denominational ministers like Lo Lung Kwong, emerged from the very revivalist movement that had become known for its separatism in the Bay Area and Metro Vancouver. The Breakthrough Youth Movement was launched in 1973 with the help of the Fellowship of Evangelical Students and its connections with IVCF. The timing coincided with the emergence of Chinese Protestants in the developments of the global reshaping of evangelicalism at the Lausanne Conference on World Evangelization in 1974. Of the 2,300 delegates from around the world, some 70 Chinese delegates attended. They decided to form a "Chinese Lausanne" for themselves and called it the Chinese Coordination Center for World Evangelization (CCCOWE), aiming to reach out to Chinese communities all over the world in order to mobilize them for missionary purposes.[83]

With the establishment of CCCOWE, some of the revivalist characters in this transpacific tale took on new prominence as the organization established a new home base in Hong Kong. Coming from the Bay Area, Thomas Wang left his post at CCM and served as CCCOWE's general secretary from 1976 to 1986. His successor in the 1980s and 1990s was Chan Hay Him, one of the founders of FES in Hong Kong. As part of its global missionary strategy, CCCOWE influenced Cantonese Protestant students from the revivalist tradition to return to Hong Kong for two reasons. First, they wanted to evangelize mainland China, gathering the scattered communities, as it were, for the nation. Second, they wanted to make their impact in Hong Kong's civil society. Both ends came together in the formation of the China Graduate School of Theology in 1974. Echoing the founding of Fuller Theological Seminary in Southern California with demanding academic standards that required "every faculty member to be an accepted and recognized scholar in his own field," Chan had an evangelical vision for academic work that could be used to conduct future missionary endeavors in China.[84] Chan contributed his connections to fundraise and to acquire Hong Kong land to build a seminary, while others recruited faculty members from around the world.[85]

The return of the revivalists to Hong Kong also led to the founding of Breakthrough. Josephine So Yan Pui was one of the returnees. So was a journalist who had studied in the United States and worked in Taiwan and Singapore before arriving in Hong Kong. So and Chan Hay Him collaborated to gather fresh university graduates to form an organization to shape youth media discourse. This new institution, Breakthrough Youth Ministries, drew inspiration from an iconic letter that Josephine So penned in 1972 titled "What Can I Do for This City?" She wrote of how Hong Kong's young people were, in her view, being negatively transformed by corrupt urban conditions:

> The city is growing too fast. There are too many changes. The only thing that has not changed is the sky. . . . Apart from this, even the ocean has changed (many bays have been filled as reclaimed land). The colors of the mountains have changed (many once green peaks have been razed to the ground). But the greatest change is in our society, our young people!

"We dare not trust our fellow human beings any more," she added. She lamented the stories she heard of how Hong Kong people had to live behind bolted gates for fear of being robbed and murdered. On the news, she had read about a mother and a child who were on an early morning stroll in the North District's reservoir area. She had also heard about how high school students were being pressured to join gangs. "Brute force," So continued, "the diminished value of life, the distortion of humanity has reached the limit." She emphasized that young people were both the perpetrators and the victims of this violence: "What disturbs me most is that the majority of crimes are committed by youths under twenty-one. These are our own young people! (Whose responsibility is that?)" She laid the blame on the church people who "attend regular meetings week after week, our members are all law-abiding middle class people." She concluded her letter, "'Oh God, what can I do for this city?'—all I have is a frail body, and my pen. I have never felt so utterly depressed about the sins and crimes of this world, I have never felt so drastically inadequate."[86]

The publication that Breakthrough Youth Ministries issued, *Breakthrough Magazine*, recast the revivalist separatism into an opportunity to reshape Hong Kong's public discourse.[87] Because of these aims, some church leaders accused Breakthrough of being a secular organization. One of the original editors of *Breakthrough Magazine* recalled in an interview that while members of Breakthrough must sign a statement of faith with evangelical theological propositions, the primary critique of Breakthrough was, "You should have a more clear voice, a stronger position, a more clear view; they say that you cannot avoid to have your editorial voice, which is true, but people don't see it as a Christian view." She also remembered that the activities that Breakthrough hosted were also controversial. The magazine featured a column called the "Heart Understanding Mailbox" (*mingsam seonsoeng*), named for its author, Ruth Chan Wai Ming, a counselor trained in English literature and psychology from the United States. The editor recalled, "The churches say and the pastors say, 'We counsel, no need for Christian counseling,'" implying that Breakthrough's emerging counseling department that Chan ran was threatening the church establishment. So too, the magazine was castigated for discussing sex. "We have to respond to the principal," the editor continued. "I remember we respond to the school principal who criticized that we have sex discussed in the magazine, it's polluting the minds of the students. So we have to explain, that we say that if we don't do that, the consequences are like that."[88] I also had a chance to interview Ruth Chan herself. She told me that because of these criticisms from the established church, "Breakthrough was influential to society more than to the church because many mainline churches were still holding back. They kept on asking how many people we led to Christ."[89] However, as both interviewees emphasized, Breakthrough's audience was not the church. They were trying to engage secular civil society itself. They saw it as a success, then, when Breakthrough's founders became frequent guests on radio shows. Schools, they also noted, stocked *Breakthrough Magazine*, which gave the periodical an extensive student readership.

By participating in the Golden Jubilee incident, Breakthrough signaled its intention to be a leading Protestant voice in reshaping Hong Kong's civil society. An official statement from Breakthrough Publications was issued on June 16, 1978, after the government closed the school. Jointly signed by eight Protestant organizations—though the matter concerned the Roman Catholic Church—the statement argued that the crux of the Golden Jubilee incident was "the worth of human beings and their dignity." It then issued a "positive proposal" to "put their focus on the Golden Jubilee students themselves."[90] The proposal focused on developing a rational public sphere and a civil conversation between all parties, a point elaborated in a follow-up article in the same issue by So herself. In "A Statement on Our Statement," So castigated public opinion for framing the students as leftist "troublemakers." She said that the public needed to form an objective opinion, based on biblical principles drawn from an evangelical hermeneutic, that humans are made in the image of God, which means that "everyone, regardless of rich or poor, big or small, is important and valuable in God's eye" and that "the term 'human rights' promoted by democracy is based on this."

So went further, moving from civil society to social structures themselves. The Education Department, she wrote, had violated the human rights of the students and the teachers by closing the school. Education is supposed to be a participatory endeavor, she emphasized, and "any political means taken to deal with educational issues is against the principle of education." She had words for the Roman Catholic Church too. The original catalyst of the events was Sister Beatrice Leung, she said. Leung had been dismissed on embezzlement charges. So wrote that if indeed the Catholic Church—and by extension, any other Christian church, Protestant or Catholic—"has attempted to cover the facts," that would make the "despicable crime of embezzlement" even "more despicable."[91] Indeed, therein lay the real secular compromise, to cover up dark deeds in the name of institutional stability.

The Golden Jubilee incident reconfigured the place of revivalist theology in Hong Kong, including its relationship with denominational institutions. As before, the revivalists commented on the conflicts of interest when state and church were entangled. But instead of advocating separatism, the organizational energy that coalesced around Breakthrough attempted to influence secular civil society itself. Revivalist separatism did not mean that the church could not engage in secular social issues. It meant instead that the church should simply remain disentangled enough from institutional interests that it could offer objective commentary on the capacity for social and political institutions to act in just ways.

What that also implied was that the hostility to denominational bureaucracies was no longer necessary. Indeed, Breakthrough formed a new alliance at this point with the Hong Kong Christian Council (HKCC), the local branch of the World Christian Council that served as a hub for interdenominational interaction. Following the Golden Jubilee incident, some HKCC clergy were inspired to continue its social critique and the fight for justice and human rights that it had initiated. As the sociologist Tinming Ko also recounts, the HKCC held a consultation in the early 1980s on the "Mission of the Church in Hong Kong for the 1980s." The initiatives that the final report suggested focused on missions to those in poverty, the church's participation in public policymaking, mainland China concerns, student ministries, and social values.[92] The implementation of some of these action items suggested that Protestant participation in the Golden Jubilee incident had indeed catalyzed a new social awareness.

Some of these HKCC pastors were ministering to congregations in Chai Wan, a working-class neighborhood on the easternmost side of Hong Kong Island. In 1974, Rev. Chu Yiu Ming became pastor at Chai Wan Baptist Church. In 1978, Rev. Lo Lung Kwong was appointed pastor of Chai Wan Methodist Church. Chu told me that a Chai Wan assignment meant that he had to get involved in his own people's concerns:

> You ask why do we Christians basically get involved like this? It's because in the Bible, it's very much emphasized that the church is for the people, and our local church here is with the local people. This is a very important point. If not, whether or not our church is in Chai Wan, it's meaningless. My church is in Chai Wan to be for the Chai Wan people and to be with them. Only then can this Gospel, this Bible's teaching, the strength of the Gospel be developed.[93]

Their first act of protest was to oppose a bus fare hike in 1982. Lo remembers the frustrating daily commute from Yau Ma Tei in Kowloon, where he lived, to the easternmost part of Hong Kong Island. Lo recalled that he first had to make a stop at Shau Kei Wan because that was where one bus line ended. The rest of the "Eastern Corridor" between Shau Kei Wan and Chai Wan relied on another route. When the bus fare increased, he took it personally:

> At that time, I was very angry. I was reflecting on the tram: why should the poor people have to pay more in terms of time, in terms of money? Right? And we had to change cars too. And then, in less

than a year of taking that car, the bus fare increased. So I was like, "How dare they! If they increase it again, I will oppose it." Then one year, another increase.

Just like in the Golden Jubilee incident, Lo's reflections considered "poor people" from the perspective of human rights. In place of the students and teachers, the residents of Chai Wan were being dealt a bad hand from colonial authorities and business corporations.

"Grassroots people," as Lo called them, needed to be considered as part of Hong Kong's civil society, and the place of the church in Lo's view was to empower them. In partnership with the China Graduate School of Theology, he launched the Grassroots Evangelist Educational Training, a program that accepted educationally disadvantaged workers directly into graduate seminary work in order to train them to minister to grassroots communities. These church communities in turn could be mobilized to engage social policy. In 1982, the HKCC mission conference theme was "Gospel for the Poor." Lo told me that his address to the gathering rallied the clergy around the bus fare issue:

> I raised my hand. I said, "We say, 'Gospel for the poor.'" But now, they increase the fare. The ones who will be the most impacted are the poor people. And so I said, "What position do we have?" And they were like, "Oh." The bishop was there, the president was there, and I was less than thirty years old at the time, 1980, thirty-two years ago. And they knew me, and they said, "Oh, OK, you proposed it, then you deal with it! And we will support you to deal with the bus fare increase." Well, anyway, I got my mandate.

Lo got to work. His new initiative brought into his network Hong Kong Christian Industrial Committee's Lau Chin Sek and the theologian Raymond Fung Wai Man, as well as the HKCC general secretary at the time, Rev. Kwok Nai Wang. They convened a press conference with Kwok as chair and Lo as the clergy spokesperson reading the press release. Lo recalls that this was "the first time that Hong Kong churches participated in a Hong Kong society-wide movement," which included both mainline and evangelical institutions as diverse as "the Alliance Bible Seminary's student association, the Baptist seminary's student association, our Chung

Chi College, Alliance Church, the Roman Catholic Church, the Labor Party, the leftists, Breakthrough (because of Josephine So)."

Revivalist theology had done its work in the most unlikely of places, then: in the denominational establishment itself. Undertaking such political activities, the HKCC effectively disentangled itself from the colonial government. "Scared those people to death because they saw the pastors come out as the spokespeople," Lo said to me, "holding public meetings in the church." A demonstration against electricity bill hikes soon followed. Lo also told me about this protest:

> Who regulates the public utilities? Even the public utilities are using a money profit-making operational principle. This is a service. This exposed many problems for people to discuss in forums. . . . We were a pressure group movement. A Catholic priest [Fr. Kwan Kin Tong] and I were central to this, opposing the bus fare increase, opposing the electric utilities fee increase, exposed these secret agreements between the bus companies and this government, this profit agreement, assuring them that they would have profit. And there was also the district issue, like the bus route plan.

When Protestant clergy acted for the construction of a hospital for the eastern district of Hong Kong Island, they also framed the issue as one of workers' rights premised on their democratic dignity.[94] Focusing on Chai Wan labor rights, Rev. Chu Yiu Ming told me that when factory workers in Chai Wan were injured, they would have had to travel to Queen Mary Hospital over ten kilometers to Wan Chai on the west side of the island. Yet again, clergy activism exposed parts of the colonial government's inaction as a problem of internal policy ineffectiveness, if not corruption. Chu recounted to me, "I discovered that the local community things can be done locally here, but this is a policy problem." A government report had in fact been filed in the 1950s arguing that an Eastern Hospital would be needed by 1972. However, the project had not yet been approved during the time of the clergy protest in the 1980s. Chu continued,

> And so we did some research and found that 1972 had already been the deadline for the government to build the hospital because residents were already moving east so that Wan Chai had fewer and

fewer people, but the medical services favored the western side of the island. And so, we and the residents, meaning the church with the residents—at that time, there were several churches with the residents lobbying for the hospital.[95]

The churches that rallied for the cause included both mainline and evangelical churches in Chai Wan, including the Baptist church, the Alliance church, the China Gospel Church, and the Wesleyan church. Lo also remembers that the hospital activism also leveraged the power of British parliamentarians who were in conversation with pastors about the "1997 issue" of handing Hong Kong back to Chinese sovereignty. "We even invited them to the groundbreaking," he said, "because the colonial government saw that the entire Eastern District's people signed their names."[96] Working off the exposure of church-state entanglement in the Golden Jubilee incident, the activism of Chai Wan clergy forced the state to consider the welfare of Chinese workers in Hong Kong.

The emergence of Cantonese Protestant activism in Hong Kong in the late 1970s and early 1980s clarifies the possibilities of revivalist theologies in relation to secular civil society. While the early student movement operated on a mythology that denounced the Hong Kong Protestant denominational establishment for secular compromise with the colonial state, the events of the Golden Jubilee incident paved the way for a new relationship. The story, I hope to have told, focuses on how student revivalists of the 1950s who argued for a strict separation of their churches from denominational bureaucracies and the colonial government could now rearticulate their theological agenda. Engaging the secular world was not the problem, at least in Hong Kong; being entangled with it was. What that meant was that the separatism that became prevalent among revivalists in the Bay Area and Vancouver was not the only possibility for where this kind of theology could take Cantonese Protestantism in Hong Kong. As organizations like Breakthrough show, an engagement with secular institutions and civil society could position Protestants as pointing out the political conflicts of interest that led to social injustice. This "prophetic" role also did not have to be separate from the denominational apparatuses that coalesced in the HKCC. Used wisely, Protestant institutions could also be used for prophetic purposes.

CONCLUSION:
HONG KONG REVIVALISM AND THE EMERGENCE OF
PACIFIC RIM SECULARITIES

The stage is now set. The story that I now tell follows from the specificities of this tale of the secular according to Chinese Christian revivalism as it passed through Hong Kong to the rest of the Pacific Rim. That their separation between their churches and a world they regarded as secular seems normative does not mean that it always was. When their revival movements emerged in the 1950s in Hong Kong, what was normal was for denominational bureaucracies to run the Protestant show as the charity arm of the colonial state. When they got to the Bay Area, the Chinatown churches had been in discussions since the 1930s about how to acquire secular funding for their racially marginalized communities and had just joined the radical Asian American movement in the 1960s to work for those aims. When they arrived in Vancouver, the Christ Church of China had been at the forefront of fighting for Chinatown not to be demolished to make way for an urban freeway.

Chinese Christianities, Alexander Chow reminds his readers, have never held to one ideology, not on the mainland and not in Sinophone communities around the world.[97] This ideological inconsistency suggests that there is also not one single view of the secular among Chinese Christians. That the revivalist strain among Cantonese Protestants became a dominant paradigm means that it had to be worked for, fought for, prevailed on. Churches split. There were lawsuits. New congregations had to be established. Communities had to be reoriented.

In so doing, what the Hong Kong revivalists unknowingly also contributed to is the long-standing theological debate on what the secular is. In what turns out to be a more complex theorizing of the secular than previously imagined, the Hong Kong revivalists figured the secular as a matter of moral compromise. Their initial activities were radical, calling for a complete break from denominational apparatuses only to realize that sometimes institutions are necessary and that they themselves might be called secular for participating in institutional building. Establishing churches, engaging in lawsuits (or rather, being engaged in one), and influencing the development of civil society all required a more nuanced account of the secular too, one that acknowledged that engagement with the world was necessary. What was objectionable, it turned out, was the compromise born of political entanglement. Separation, in other words, did not need to mean nonengagement. It simply had to include availability to point out injustices and how to rectify them institutionally.

The secular in this account refers, then, to the world, its institutions, and its ideologies outside of the church. Incidentally, those worlds in the 1960s and 1970s also facilitated the movement of Cantonese Protestants and their communities throughout the Pacific region. They were changing, reanimated by the imaginaries and dreams of the Pacific Rim as they began to take shape in the 1970s and 1980s. In the following chapters, the story turns to how Cantonese Protestants dealt with the secularities of the Pacific Rim in the heyday of its hegemonic power in the 1990s and the 2000s, with its focus on reaching the frontiers of multicultural equality within the limits of a market logic while praising the virtues of democracy without much defining it. In so doing, it also becomes a tale of how Cantonese Protestants became scattered on the sheet of the secular dream of the Pacific Rim, calling each other secular just like the revivalists established that they could when they first broke from the denominational apparatuses of Hong Kong while recognizing the necessity of working with civil society and state institutions outside of their churches.

CHAPTER THREE

"Each Person Can Only Speak for Themselves"

Same-Sex Marriage and Institutional Autonomy

> *But avoid foolish controversies and genealogies and arguments and quarrels about the law.*
>
> —Titus 3:9

INTRODUCTION: CANTONESE PROTESTANTISM AND PACIFIC RIM "PROGRESS"

A narrative of progress powers the dream of the Pacific Rim. Bringing together the Asia-Pacific and the Americas, the story goes that an era of multicultural peace would be established as migrants from places like Hong Kong replicated their entrepreneurial and technological success in Australia, New Zealand, Canada, and the United States. It was a plausible tale, though geographers, especially in Vancouver, have been at the forefront of pointing out the problems that these schemes produced:

rising house prices, business failures, new forms of anti-Asian racism that viewed Asian migrants as economic competition.[1]

In the 1990s and 2000s, Cantonese Protestants revealed yet another side to this disappointment in the Pacific Rim dream: the debate over same-sex marriage. One of the flashpoints in that drama centered on San Francisco, where its mayor had turned its marriage licenses gender neutral in the first four months of 2004. As the civil conversation about what came to be called "marriage equality" raged into the aftermath of the 2008 ballot initiative Proposition 8's call to ban the use of the word "marriage" to describe same-sex unions, Cantonese Protestants made their presence felt as concerned parents speaking up in public in ways that several commentators overblew as an initial entry in politics.[2] When similar developments unfolded in Canada, these traditional family values, as they were called, were framed in the press as the "homeland politics" of a conservative place of origin.[3] I remember finding that claim particularly laughable as I began my fieldwork and will explore my incredulity about it in chapter 4. Hong Kong, after all, was known for its cosmopolitanism, not to mention its long-standing openness with queer-presenting celebrity figures like Anita Mui and Leslie Cheung, the latter of whom plays the lover whose counterpart is played by Tony Leung in Wong Kar Wai's *Happy Together*.

This Cantonese Protestant confrontation with the secular dream of the Pacific Rim is, having had its commentary in the press at the time it was unfolding, overdue for a scholarly reinterpretation. Building off the revivalist separation of the church from the secular world in the previous chapter, I intend to shed some theological light on Cantonese Protestant activism in the 1990s and 2000s against same-sex marriage. But what I do not mean to do is to interpret their attitudes about sexuality as based on a certain reading of the Bible. Instead, I want to understand how they reconsidered the relationship between their communities and a world they considered secular, especially as it was being reshaped by a Pacific Rim imagination that held that the final fight for equality, after having overcome racial disparities through immigration schemes favoring skilled migrants, would be over the terrain of sexuality, marriage, and gender identity.[4]

In so doing, I hope to show that the most salient place to look for this theology is in how Cantonese Protestants considered their relationship with the "secular" as they struggled with how to deal with the politics of marriage equality. The story that unfolds is one of division. Cantonese Protestants scattered over how to relate to the secular, but that secularity was itself shaped by the Pacific Rim. In the Bay Area, Cantonese Protestants did their best to emphasize their autonomy from the socially conservative institutions that were mobilizing them for Proposition 8. In Metro Vancouver, their organizations often splintered over how to address what they considered, in the words of one focus group participant, "ridiculous" advancement of human rights without being drawn into a kind of religious pluralism.[5] In Hong Kong, they answered the accusation of being called an antidemocratic "religious right" by insisting that they were autonomous organizations advancing a rational and pluralistic democratic discursive sphere in the face of what they saw as a putatively irrational "sex-culture" revolution.

One memorable interviewee in Vancouver vigorously agreed with this framework of scattering. By the time I had gotten to him, I had already conducted over a hundred interviews total across all three sites and was in the middle of planning my own wedding—a straight one. I began the interview by telling him that I would be asking him to speak from his vantage point about the activities of Cantonese Protestants. I then hastened to add, "What I've noticed is that each person can only speak for themselves." "Exactly," he responded with a laugh, "*waa, lek zai*," he called me in Cantonese, which roughly translates to "smart guy."[6] I responded that I would simply allow him to speak for himself. I hope that I have done every person in this chapter the same courtesy.

THE DEFENSE OF HAK-SHING WILLIAM TAM: SCATTERING THE TRADITIONAL FAMILY COALITION

On January 21, 2010, the plaintiffs in the district court case *Perry et al. v. Schwarzenegger*, 704 F.Supp.2d 921 (N.D. Cal., 2010), called Dr. Hak-Shing William Tam, a chemical engineer turned chair of what he named the Traditional Family Coalition (TFC), as a hostile witness.

The context was Proposition 8. In 2008, five citizens of California had, with the signatures of 807,615 registered voters, acted as "proponents" to put on the ballot an initiative to amend the state constitution with what came to be known as the "fourteen words" of Proposition 8: "Only marriage between a man and a woman is valid or recognized in California."[7] It passed with 52.3 percent of the votes. In response, one gay and one lesbian couple, organized by an organization fronted by the Hollywood star Rob Reiner called Americans for Equal Rights, sued the California government over the measure's constitutionality.[8] The governor, who was Arnold Schwarzenegger, declined to defend the case, as did his attorney general, Jerry Brown. In their place came the proponents themselves, who were associated with a group that called itself ProtectMarriage.com, as defendant-intervenors. "Bill" Tam, as he called himself, was one of them.

Leading the *Perry* prosecution were two lawyers, Theodore Olson and David Boies, who had faced off in another high-profile case, *Gore v. Bush*, 531 U.S. 98 (2000). Once opponents—Olson had represented George W. Bush against Boies for Al Gore as they wrangled over whose the presidency was after the federal election in 2000—they were now brought together as a kind of bipartisan show. Their objective was to show that the fight for Proposition 8 could not withstand what in legal terms is called strict scrutiny, which has as its litmus test whether the state had a legitimate public interest in discriminating against a whole class of people—in this case, same-sex couples. One strategy to show that it did not was to show that the proponents were motivated by private "animus."[9] Perhaps, for example, they personally hated gay and lesbian persons. Maybe they were motivated by religious beliefs. Either reason would be a private one, inappropriate for application in a secular society and therefore failing strict scrutiny.

Tam was their hostile witness, the proof in their pudding. His responses under cross-examination by David Boies yielded a bonanza. The smoking gun in Tam's deposition before the trial opened was a private email that Tam had written to Chinese churches. Tam had stated that if Proposition 8 were to fail in California, then the states were likely one by one to "fall into Satan's hand."[10] There was more. In another memorable exchange, Boies asked Tam about where he could substantiate the claim on his website, 1man1woman.net, that "homosexuals are twelve times more likely to be pedophiles." He could not.[11] Asked later about how he knew that same-sex marriage would lead to polygamy and incest, he replied, "It's in the Internet."[12] In still another place, he said, "I think it's very important for our next generation to understand the historical meaning of marriage. It is very important that our children won't grow up to fantasize or think about, Should I marry Jane or John when I grow up?"[13] He continued at another point by way of clarifying the motivation of his concerns: "So children will fantasize about marrying either a man or a woman. And to us parents—you may say that I'm a paranoid Chinese parent—we get very, very upset about that."[14] When Boies was done, Tam already knew the ridicule was only just beginning. His concluding words on the stand were, "I felt like a naughty boy being put in front of a classroom and being mocked at."[15]

Tam said more about that day in his interview with me. "He grilled me for four hours," Tam told me, "but I fought him, I fought him, I fought him real. . . . At the end, I even teased him. I was saying indirectly: you are bullying me. Because you know, he's a top lawyer, it's the first time I was in a court. And [laughs] he was so surprised."[16] There was, in other words, a fight, which meant that there was supposed to have been a method to the madness, and it redirected me to reconsider the trial transcript and the various other documents associated with it. Tam had tried to put as much distance between himself, the organizations that had fought for Proposition 8, and the Chinese Christian churches and institutions of which he was a part, though he had, as the decision later pointed out, "signed a Statement of Unity with Protect Marriage . . . in which he agreed not to put forward 'independent strategies for public messaging.'"[17] In what he presented, he had been operating in sole capacity as the convenor of the TFC. Yes, he was also the secretary in a parallel organization called the America Return to God Prayer Movement (ARTGPM), but talking at length about his role in it would mean giving ground on the possibility that his views were religiously motivated. The group was simply made up of "different Chinese pastors," Tam said, and "there are presidents, vice-presidents, and other more important persons." Boies called him on his obfuscation. Tam retorted, "What's the power of the secretary in your company?" "Considerable," Boies replied.[18] Tam had also attempted to distance himself from ProtectMarriage.com. He kept saying that he had not been part of its "core group." Asked how many times he had "contact" with their leaders, he said he had phone calls "maybe four times" with the chair and even fewer with its public engagement office: "Very rare. Maybe one or two times."[19]

The question is whether Tam's strategy of obfuscation was spinning a fictional reality about the various organizations of which he had been a part. What I learned from conducting more fieldwork and interviews—including with Tam, who generously bought me not only a Quizno's sandwich but also a broccoli cheese soup—is that the missing puzzle piece from the public record is that TFC operated mostly by informally networking among Cantonese Protestants, and in that world, Tam's comments made perfect sense. Tam expressed frustration with the Cantonese Protestants he was trying to mobilize. In his book *Church, Stand Up as Salt and Light!*, he opined that many churches were doing a "wonderful job being the 'light' of the world sharing the saving grace of the gospel and the righteousness of God," but "not many are doing the 'salt' part, which is to slow down the moral decay," an urgent task because the "endless conflict between good and evil has deteriorated the society to a point where the standard of human decency has been degraded to that of animals."[20] In fact, there was seldom any unity among churches, he observed, especially in countering what he felt to be a very urgent situation. They also tended to be frustrated with each other, mostly because they disagreed over whether his kind of activism involved churches in too much of a secular cause. In this way, organizational atomization, which divided along the theological axis of secularity, was the way they narrated their institutional landscape. It made sense that that would also become Tam's defense strategy. It was the truth, the whole truth, and nothing but the truth.

Tam's approach was to engage the world head-on. Whatever other Cantonese Protestants thought of him, Tam of course felt that what he was doing was not caving in to the secular. By 2010, he had been working as a family values activist for quite some time, some fourteen years. He was also not shy about his record, neither with me nor in his TFC newsletters (nor in his filing to withdraw as a defendant-intervenor in the *Perry* case). The formative event, he said, had taken place in 1990 in San Francisco. There was a concerned parent initiative in 1990 to oppose Project 10, a proposal to launch LGBTQ+ counseling centers in the San Francisco Unified School District's public schools.[21] Tam went to the public hearing with three other concerned citizens (none of them Chinese, he recalled). They were also flanked by a media campaign in the Chinese newspapers and the English-language *Channel 7 News*. Tam recalled that half an hour before the proceedings started, an AIDS advocacy group, ACT UP, had already filled the hall. In a TFC newsletter, he says that he remembers them shouting slurs against both Asian Americans ("Go back to China") and Christians ("God is Gay" and "Jesus Is Gay"), while holding signs that showed "two naked boys, one behind another, sucking his thumb." "At that moment," Tam recalled, "I realized that the gay activists are aiming at our young children. I saw the danger if we did not fight for our children."[22]

These events surrounding Project 10 led to the founding of the Chinese Family Alliance (CFA) in 1990. CFA published literature that discouraged the passage of domestic partnership legislation at the state level in the 1990s while supporting Proposition 22 in 2000, the implementation of a Defense of Marriage Act in California's family code.[23] As a member of CFA, Tam also recalled fighting to have a book banned from the San Francisco school district's social studies curriculum. "It talks about some African tribes," he said to me. "They sewed up the vagina of the girls until they get married, then the husband gets to open for sex. That was a lesbian teacher. They used that book to teach how bad men are."[24] This skirmish generated some of the language that Tam had used in *Perry* about being a "paranoid Chinese parent."[25] He said that "one of them [school board members] said, 'You Asian parents, you are so overprotective,' one of those ladies said." Tam responded that that was exactly what he was. "Look at the Asian students, Chinese students," he said that he said. "We have the least teen pregnancies. We have the least sexual transmitted diseases. We have the least tardiness. We have the least problems of any kind. But we are the best in our grades, and that's because we are overprotecting them."[26]

These skirmishes with the secular San Francisco government paved the way for the CFA's engagement with same-sex marriage in 2004, when San Francisco's newly elected mayor, Gavin Newsom, directed his city clerk, Nancy Alfaro, to issue gender-neutral marriage licenses in defiance of the California family code. In the ensuing weeks, 4,013 marriages were performed at San Francisco City Hall, including by Asian American officials such as Mabel Teng (then assessor recorder), Donna

Kotake (a marriage commissioner), and Richard Ow (another marriage commissioner).[27]

On April 25, 2004, the pastors responded with Traditional Family Day. Much of what they say points to a lack of clarity about who was actually their leader, if they had one at all. The CFA organized some two hundred pastors in the Bay Area Chinese Evangelical Ministerial Prayer Fellowship to oppose same-sex marriage. One of its spokespersons was Raymond Kwong, who convened the Bay Area Chinese Christians for Traditional Marriage. He spoke of a "silent majority" in an interview with the *Christian Post* and lamented the ineffectiveness of the church in speaking up faster. "I think the key is pastors and churches—not politicians," he said. "They must teach the congregation the correct worldview. We have been so effectively neutralized. Pastors think they can't do anything about it because same-sex marriage is a political issue."[28] Tam said something similar in his interview with me:

> I talked to a couple of friends and they said, "Wow, this is huge. We Christians have to do something." So I called up pastors. They said, "No." I said, "Hey, what should we do?" One pastor said, "I don't know. Call up Pastor Y." Call Pastor Y, and he said, "I don't know what to do; call Pastor W." [laughs] Call Pastor W? "I'm very busy! Call Pastor Z!"

Tam said that at last he spoke with Rev. Thomas Wang, the founder of Chinese Christian Mission (CCM) and Chinese Coordination Center for World Evangelization who had since become the international director of the global missionary initiative called the Lausanne Movement in the mid-1980s before founding the Great Commission Center International (GCCI), another missions-oriented institution, in 1989. Tam reported that Wang said, "Yeah, of course, I read about it, of course we have to do something about it, or else we should not call ourselves Christians."[29] In my interview with Wang at the GCCI offices, he recalled, "I was one of the, if not the, instigator for the open-air rally in Nineteenth Street, San Francisco.... The first time in history, the Chinese Christians came out publicly for some public purpose like that, never happened before." Chinese radio host David Pang quickly invited Tam and Wang onto his secular talk show on 1450 FM KTSD and Tri-Star Radio KVSF. Pang recalled, "We directly influenced it because we personally, I know Bill Tam on the one man, one woman activism on Nineteenth Avenue with Rev. Wang, we directly participated, we called people to come out."[30]

TFC claimed on their website that "about 7,000 Cantonese Protestants" from "174 churches" around the Bay Area showed up.[31] They wore red T-shirts that read "One Man, One Woman" in both English and Chinese and held up signs promoting traditional marriage. The *San Francisco Chronicle* reported that at Larsen Park, Wang clarified in a speech that "we're not here today to antagonize or to hate people." But "true love and true concern," Wang said, mandated that they speak up about how "any deviation" from the first marriage between Adam and Eve—"one man and one woman"—"will bring disastrous results."[32] The crowd then poured into the Sunset District's main throughway, Nineteenth Avenue between Quintara Street and Holloway Avenue, calling on drivers to honk if they were supportive to their cause.[33]

The 2004 rally led to two developments within Cantonese Protestant networks. The first was that Wang founded the ARTGPM, the organization of which Boies wanted Tam to say that he was the secretary with "considerable" power.[34] ARTGPM organized a hundred-thousand-person March on Washington in October 2004, essentially repeating in Washington, DC, what had happened in San Francisco. Wang also compiled a collection of English-language articles in the anthology *America, Return to God*, printing pieces written by white American pastors and Republican apologists like David Barton, James Dobson, Carl Henry, Erwin Lutzer, and Tim LaHaye. The main thrust of the collection was to decry what it saw as the encroaching secularity of America as a totalitarian plot by "master planners of the other side" to "achieve the downfall of America—by steadily weakening her spiritual roots and moral fibers" and to "re-shape and re-constitute America into an atheistic and pagan country."[35] Wang wrote that the mission of "Chinese Christians" was to bring America back to "her God-ordained beginning, her noble Christian past, her struggles, her lurking and scheming enemies, and her need for spiritual restoration by returning to the 'faith of her fathers'—faith in her Creator and Savior Jesus Christ."[36] Five hundred thousand copies of this first edition, they wrote in the anthology, were sent to politicians, universities, professionals, and churches selected from a United States Postal Service directory.[37]

The second development was literally adjacent to ARTGPM, which operated out of GCCI's offices in Sunnyvale. With Wang's blessing, Tam founded TFC and housed it next to the GCCI office. It is here that the various organizations that Tam claimed to be autonomous from each other can be placed in proximate, yet distinct, relationship with one another. TFC may have been next door to GCCI, but they were separate institutions. So too, the umbrella organization that Boies wanted to lump Tam in with was called ProtectMarriage.com, but that argument for association could also have been construed as problematic in Tam's world. For one, TFC was not the same as ProtectMarriage.com, and ProtectMarriage.com was intentionally autonomous from other organizations with which it affiliated itself. Technically, it was the advocacy arm of the California Family Council (CFC) and its umbrella institution, the Family Research Council, but that is an autonomous entity that keeps the popular psychology organization Focus on the Family from being directly involved in political activity.[38]

Of course, in practice, things were a bit messier. Just as Wang had blessed TFC to be next door to his offices, the CFC had in fact, according to Tam, approached TFC as early as 2005 to collect signatures for the 2006 elections. "The top men came to me and asked me to join," he said, "saying that to protect marriage, we have to have the constitution stating this statement that marriage only recognize one man and one woman. So he said they would like minority groups to get into this also, and asked if I would like to join in this crusade."[39] Unsuccessful the first time, they tried again in 2007 and successfully placed Proposition 8 on the November 2008 election ballot. As the evidence in the *Perry* case showed, Tam indeed helmed the campaign's Asian Pacific Islander initiative, collecting some twenty thousand Asian American signatures, which was 2.48 percent of the required number of votes to get a citizen-propelled initiative on the ballot.[40] After Proposition 8 made it onto the ballot, Protect Marriage.com tapped Tam to participate in several broadcast debates about it, including two on the radio, one televised on New American Media, one on Cantonese-language KTSF *Channel 26 News*, and some that were reported in Chinese newspapers *Sing Tao* and *Ming Pao*.[41]

TFC also organized three Asian American "Yes on 8" rallies between July and November 2008, mostly in the Bay Area (there was one rally in Los Angeles). These rallies were large-scale events. On October

12, ARTGPM and TFC held a rally on San Francisco Chinatown's Portsmouth Square where attendees wore red T-shirts that read "1 man + 1 woman," while holding "Yes on 8" placards, chanting "Yes on 8," singing hymns like "Amazing Grace" and "How Great Thou Art," and giving speeches about the psychological importance of traditional families in Cantonese and Mandarin.[42] A second rally took place in Silicon Valley at Cupertino's Memorial Park on October 19. Held in English, Mandarin, and Korean, this rally presumed a more diverse crowd, though many Cantonese Protestants attended. One conservative website estimated that 3,500 people showed up; 1man1woman.net stated that "more than 4000 vowed to protect 1 man 1 woman marriage," and on TFC's website, the number, given here in Chinese, is "more than 5,000."[43] They sang Christian hymns and heard English-language speeches from Family Research Council and ProtectMarriage.com figures as well as Mandarin- and Korean-language addresses from Silicon Valley pastors. Then they proceeded down Stevens Creek Parkway calling for passing drivers to honk in support.[44]

And yet in all this—and this is the part that is relevant to the *Perry* defense strategy—Tam did not see himself as an agent of ProtectMarriage.com. If there was a group he was trying to represent, it was Asian Americans and Chinese Christians in the Bay Area, even though some Asian American activists saw him as homophobic and not every "Chinese Christian" wanted to participate in what they considered secular politics. In one media appearance that was later revealed at trial to have been unsanctioned by ProtectMarriage.com, Tam acknowledged to the *San Jose Mercury News* that there were multiple views of both "Christian" and "Asian American." Tam explained that the "No on 8" campaigners "have very cleverly portrayed homosexuals as a kind of minority" and gay marriage "as a civil rights issue." He was therefore aware that it would be difficult to "convince Asian-Americans that gay marriage will encourage more children to experiment with the gay lifestyle and that the lifestyle comes with all kinds of disease."[45] In fact, there was a counterrally that took place at the Portsmouth Square rally. Organized by Asian American groups such as Asian Pacific Islander Equality, the Network for Religion and Justice, Pine United Methodist Church, and Buena Vista United Methodist Church, the protest of the protest chanted "Equality for all," "No on 8," and "God loves everyone!"[46]

In fact, Tam's attempt to unite "Chinese Christians," as he called them, led to even more fracture. It was difficult, for example, to convince every Chinese Christian pastor in the Bay Area to fight for Proposition 8. Even when they did come on side, there were different motivations. The historic Chinese Christian Union (CCU) was internally divided about Proposition 8. At face value, Tam had them. The then-chair of the CCU, Salvation Army's Major Thomas Mui, had thrown his weight behind the October 12 rally at San Francisco Chinatown's Portsmouth Square. But Mui did not speak for everyone in the fellowship. I spoke to one disaffected clergy member whose church was located across the street from the demonstration. He said he was "very uncomfortable because it was a unilateral decision, and so I came back and talked to my council, and we decided not to show our support in any way."[47] Mui's supporters also had mixed motivations. An Episcopal priest, Rev. Franco Kwan, told me that he was in fact ambivalent about his stance on "homosexuality" because of the lack of clarity in the biblical passages supporting and opposing it and that in fact his bishop was often at the Gay Pride parades. However, he also felt that his parishioners were "harassed by members of other churches" for having "a homosexual bishop and homosexual priests," which left their faith in question. Kwan actually became the CCU chair after Mui, almost right after the rally. "I still support Proposition 8," he said, "because even though I am in the middle, I tend to the right because in the traditional morality, I think like this. This is my position. I always tell my bishop this."[48]

Similar drama played out in the Silicon Valley. In the wake of Tam's trial testimony in *Perry*, Gerry Shih of the *New York Times* went down to the largest Chinese American megachurch in the Bay Area, River of Life Christian Church (ROLCC), to see what he could find about the communities that Tam purportedly represented. The story he picked up on the "little noticed but burgeoning world of evangelical Chinese Christianity in the Bay Area," as he put it, was complex. There was some recognition of Tam as "the voice of a set of beliefs that resonates with them," even as having "galvanized evangelical Asians—drawn from a population of first-generation immigrants that have generally stayed aloof from politics—into a nascent but cohesive and potentially powerful political force." The problem was that ROLCC was not actually part of the movement, and the senior pastor, Liu Tong, told me that he had told Shih as much. Tam was "a figure," he is quoted as saying, but

Liu's "community traditionally shuns visible political activity." Their focus, Liu had said, was to "rekindle the fire, the hunger and they want more of God."[49] When the story appeared in the *New York Times*, Liu told me that he saw to his dismay that the article was accompanied by a picture of a prayer meeting that insinuated that the church was part of Tam's movement. He stressed in his interview with me that his church not being involved "was a very courageous move, let me tell you because all the Chinese churches are criticizing us." Liu's people had been "really not happy" with the story and had written a letter to the paper to complain.[50] But when I followed up the interview asking for a copy of the letter, I got no response. When I asked Tam whether he thought the article was fair, he said it was.[51]

Among my respondents, there was even a debate about whether *any* of the churches in the Bay Area were involved. At one large, prominent Silicon Valley church, two pastors who were on staff at the time gave vastly contradictory answers about the church's involvement. One said that his pastoral presence at the rallies implied that the church as an institution supported the measure. "In my thinking," he said, "if I am the pastor of a church, then even if it is individual, I am at the same time representing the church to go." In fact, he added that it would be in his institutional interest to be there. The results of Proposition 8 would, for example, affect the way that he taught premarital counseling courses and determined the church's rental policy for weddings.[52] By contrast, another staff member at the same church suggested that the church would take a "conservative" position by not participating in a formal way. "Still, it is not from the leadership level," he insisted to me. "I would even think during this time . . . that the leadership would not try to do anything too confrontational, up in the front line, even they feel that something ought to be done, they will do it at a more personal level." A "safe" and "more conservative" strategy was to frame Proposition 8 as a "biblical teaching" and hint at a private position at which each individual church member should independently arrive. In this way, he admitted of the red T-shirts worn by the protesters, "actually it's kind of created or designed by people in the church, but it's not really like a church event."[53]

At another Silicon Valley church, a focus group discussion suggested to me that even within the churches, Cantonese Protestants saw themselves as acting as individuals, not as institutions. Jeff, a midthirties male participant in my Silicon Valley focus group, told me to think of the power of the pastor in the case of Proposition 8 "in a simpler way." "When the pastor calls on people to serve," he said, "how many people really will go and respond? Like this is a simple response, taking on our consensus: if once the pastor says something and everyone is so united to do it, God's kingdom would flourish so much more!" The group laughed as he finished. Mrs. Ng then piped up. She had gone on the buses to the protests, and her pastor had taken a stand for Proposition 8. But she had first heard about the issues on television, not at church. "If your reflective ability is strong enough," she said, "tell you the truth, even if the church had not organized a whole bus to tell us to go, I would think about going along with some of my church fellowship members because I don't even know the place." The rest of the group then chimed in. "And even if you don't know the place," they said, "we'll give you a ride there."[54]

If there *was* a place that Cantonese Protestants were being mobilized, then it might have been Chinese-language radio. On the day following the 2008 elections, financial adviser and Christian organization leader Lam Sau Wing found the passage of Proposition 8 a cause for "celebration." Lam said, "We want to thank the listeners who heard our program and went out to vote Yes on Proposition 8 and those who advertised and campaigned for it."[55] Lam was not the only Cantonese Protestant on secular radio. David Pang suggested that he had been dismissed from his post on the radio after 2008 ostensibly because of budget cuts but most likely also because he had promoted Proposition 8 on his secular show.[56] Bill Tam also had a show, which likewise was on the secular Cantonese channel. It was called *Conscience for a Minute and a Half*, and it aired during rush hour. "So with that," he said to me, "I'm trying to reshape how people think. It doesn't matter they are Christian or non-Christian—as long as they are . . . listening to the radio, I put it at the rush hour when they get out of work, turn on the radio, and then there's me talking about certain things," like parenting and politics.[57]

But even then, there was some division over what my respondents thought about the show hosts. Radio, after all, was considered a secular space. Mr. Lee at one of my focus groups in Fremont said, "There is a very influential Cantonese radio host on AM 1450, Yeung Kwong. He opposes Obama. He puts his show online. His opposition to Obama makes a lot of sense. We doubt he is a Christian." Mr. Wong agreed with him: "The way he talks, he doesn't look like a Christian. He uses very coarse language."[58] But a woman at another Fremont focus group had more positive things to say. "You have to listen to him; there's no choice, because at 2:15 p.m., there's only Cantonese news," she said. "He speaks Cantonese on the radio. The tone isn't very good, though, because it's vulgar and provocative."[59] In other words, Yeung Kwong was not considered a Christian because his vulgarities did not match the affect of the church that my participants were used to. But for regular radio listeners, he was numbered among Christian radio hosts like Lam Sau Wing, David Pang, and Bill Tam because they all promoted similar ideologies. They were against Obama and for Proposition 8. What this suggested, Pang emphasized, was that the audience was in fact a secular one. When he invited Tam and Wang onto his show to talk about same-sex marriage, they were appealing to a broad Cantonese audience, not the church.[60]

In this way, Tam's defense strategy in *Perry* was more plausible than it might have seemed. In fact, it may have been more honest about what the TFC was than what he had said during the Proposition 8 campaign. As an activist, Tam had had to make the impossible case that most Chinese Christians, if not most Asian Americans, agreed with his views on the family. The result had been that ministerial fellowships, church leadership, and congregation members became divided, not so much on his views on sexuality but on whether their churches were institutionally involved in the activities around Proposition 8. But as a hostile witness, it was as if Tam could finally come clean. He may have been acting in coalition with ProtectMarriage.com, but it was literally coalitional. He too was an individual, and while he attempted to speak for Chinese Christians and intervene in Asian American politics, he was ultimately frustrated. Although the sheet of San Francisco's same-sex marriage drama may have afforded Cantonese Protestants more coherence than their organizational abilities deserved, they were scattered on it.

"RIDICULOUS":
REPRESENTATIONAL PROBLEMS AND HUMAN RIGHTS EXPANSION IN VANCOUVER

As I began my fieldwork in April 2011, I received an email that was circulating among Cantonese Protestants in Vancouver. It was about a new sexual orientation bill that had been introduced by the openly gay Burnaby-Douglas member of parliament (MP) Bill Siksay. Known as Bill C-389, it proposed to amend the Canadian Charter of Rights and Freedoms to ensure equality for bisexual and transgender persons. The email stated in both English and Chinese, "If you are concerned not only about economic, tax, health care and other social services but also about where different political parties stand on moral issues; then please read on for your reference." It then dubbed C-389 the "Bathroom Bill," alleging that it "would potentially allow men who say they are women to use women's washrooms and vice versa, increasing public safety risk in public facilities."[61] The proverbial Washroom Bill—adjusting here for the Canadian colloquial use of "washroom," as the Chinese is "bathroom facilities bill" (廁所浴室法案, *cisojuksatfaaton*)—became the talk of Cantonese evangelicals throughout my Vancouver fieldwork and the subject of pastor-led prayer meetings and peer-to-peer conversation as they opposed what they saw as its ludicrousness.

At a focus group in Richmond, I asked participants what they thought of Bill C-389. Mrs. Tam responded, "Ridiculous." I expected, then, that this group's members would have been readily mobilized for action against it by some of the more prominent Cantonese Protestant family values organizations, like the Canadian Alliance for Social Justice and Family Values Association (CASJAFVA) and the Christian Social Concern Fellowship (CSCF). They told me that they receive emails from these groups, just like the correspondence that I had been receiving. But they also said that they were taken aback when members from these mobilizing organizations attempted to coerce other church attendees to join their organizations, as well as the Conservative Party more generally. Mrs. Chin recalled that "once upon a time, there were some people in the church who told us to participate." During the social hour after the church service, a member of some of these lobby groups, a Mrs. Wong, "called on us to join the Conservative Party." While some joined, Mrs. Chin refused. So did the church's pastors. But there was still pressure. She said that "then those fellowship leaders ask whether Mrs. Wong found you, did she find you?"[62]

These responses set out a familiar story. When it came to same-sex marriage and transgender rights, my Vancouver respondents would talk about how the expansion of the category of human rights seemed ludicrous to them. The question, though, was whether and how they wanted to respond. Certainly, some joined political parties like the Conservative Party of Canada and started organizations like CASJAFVA and CSCF in an effort to counter these trends. But others, like those in the Richmond focus group, felt that these groups sometimes went too far. Mobilizing Cantonese Protestants in churches, for example, came off as inappropriate. There was also the problem of whether the Conservative Party, CASJAFVA, and CSCF could adequately represent "Chinese Christians" writ large. That was because they often skirted with the secular, and more often than not, such accusations precipitated these institutions dividing within themselves too.

What was intriguing, I also learned as I spoke with some pastors (contrasting the focus group's claims that pastors would never get involved in politics), was that the real story about pastoral participation on questions of sexual ethics was a little bit more complicated. It turned out that in the early 1990s—about twenty years before this focus group—it was a few pastors themselves who had opened the interface between the churches and politicians. Embarrassment might have motivated them. In 1991, some of them had supported the candidacy of a Tiananmen Square redress activist, Raymond Chan, to become Richmond's MP for the Liberal Party. Then in 1994, Parliament put forward Bill C-41, a hate crime bill that would amend Canada's criminal code to impose harsher penalties on crimes motivated by animus for a victim's sexual orientation.

Now they were concerned. One of them remembers a roundtable discussion they had with Chan with seven clergy present, most of them trained at Regent College, a graduate school of Christian studies (as it describes itself) on the University of British Columbia campus. They pressed Chan on how it would be determined that a crime had been motivated by homophobia, as that basis felt subjective to them. To increase punitive measures on such a basis, they also wrote in the Chinese newspaper *Ming Pao*, was to subject Canadian civil society to a social experiment.[63] "We are not saying that those who have homosexual behavior are criminals," another pastor from this group explained to me in an interview. "We are not saying that—this is their personal life. But we say that there are many, many hidden costs, social costs, there, that we warn the people that once the traditional view of marriage and family is changed, the Canadian society will collapse. I would say—we did use the word 'collapse.'"[64]

The pastors told me that the talks ended in failure. In fact, they recalled that other members of the ministerial fellowship often rebuffed their efforts as irrelevant to their revivalist agenda. Chan, for his part, voted in favor of C-41. He acknowledged in his contribution to the parliamentary discussion on the bill that he had "worked hard to correct the spread of misinformation by explaining to religious communities Bill C-41 will not prevent churches and religious instructors from talking about their beliefs regarding the morality of homosexuality." Chan also said that he had explained to the pastors that it was not true that "by not defining the term sexual orientation, Bill C-41 will open legal loopholes that will legitimize the actions of paedophiles."[65] In so doing, Chan made clear the political stage on which he was playing his part, and it was not on the terrain of the church, which is where the pastors were and seemed to expect him to acknowledge at the very least.

In 1997, sexual ethics activism among Cantonese Protestants took a turn away from the clergy. Over a breakfast at McDonald's, I spoke about this shift with a writer for the Chinese Christian newspaper *Truth Monthly* who was very involved in sexuality issues.[66] She told me that the British Columbia Teachers' Federation (BCTF) were trying to implement Bills C-41 and C-33 into the school curricula. Specifically, she objected to the school district in the Vancouver suburb of Surrey introducing into their curriculum three books that portrayed same-sex relationships as normal. She said that she felt dissatisfied after writing to "principals, the BCTF, educational boards, school boards," so she launched a petition campaign. In so doing, she said she leveraged influential pastoral connections to the Vancouver Chinese Evangelical Ministerial Fellowship (VCEMF). She also published an editorial about the Surrey case in the April 1997 edition of *Truth Monthly*.

Within a month and a half, this writer had collected some two thousand signatures for her petition. She also mobilized Chinese Christians to join a rally organized by the Citizens' Research Institute on June 7 to decry the passage of the sexual orientation bill at Vancouver downtown's Robson Square, an event that was also joined by another activist, Bill Chu, and his group, Chinese Christians in Action. The event turned into mayhem. The demonstrators (according to the writer, "some people said that we had 1,500 people") were surrounded by about a hundred people, who reportedly shouted and threw sand at them, while, as Chu alleged in an August press conference, the police stood by and did nothing.[67] Chu told me that following this event, he also approached the VCEMF to ask for their renewed support. They rebuffed him. "Bill Chu, you worry too much!" he remembers the pastors telling him. "And so I said, 'You know, I couldn't do anything,' and you know what? Pretty soon it become law and then they throw up their hands and say, *Oh, they are oppressing the Christians!* [laughs] The same group!"[68]

The narrative, in other words, became that the pastors were mostly unsupportive, though the history suggests that the real story is more complicated. But it was a mentality arguably that informed the formation of CASJAFVA. Their convener was a lawyer named K-John Cheung. He told me that he had watched the Robson Square rally on television, and he lamented the chaos that was happening "here . . . in a democratic country in North America," as "we are looking at freedom of speech, freedom of religion, freedom of assembly, what happened to those?"[69] In response, Cheung convened CASJAFVA in October 1997. He framed it as a secular organization, though its membership was predominantly composed of Cantonese Protestants. They laid out their agenda in ninety bilingual web quarterlies that were published between their start date in the autumn of 1997 till they went defunct in the summer of 2012.

CASJAFVA was perhaps most popularly known for being a lobby against same-sex marriage. In 2003, they collected twelve thousand petitions against it and organized a downtown rally with ten thousand demonstrators. Yet more broadly, they said that their agenda would more accurately be described as "parental rights," which seemed to have a broad focus on protecting the rights of persons in private domains to govern their own spaces. Their special target of ire was the BCTF and its associated professional body, the British Columbia College of Teachers (BCCT). In 2002, a public high school teacher, Chris Kempling, had been fired for publishing articles criticizing gay rights movements. CASJAFVA organized a protest on Kempling's behalf, narrating Kempling's actions as having gone against the BCTF and the BCCT's ideology and had suffered the consequences.[70]

CASJAFVA's strategy, in other words, was to identify and protest institutions, such as the BCTF, that they felt infringed on the private rights of citizens and communities. Parents, CASJAFVA argued, should be in charge of the families they governed, not these external organizations. In 1998, they staged a protest on behalf of a Vietnamese Chinese migrant, Mrs. Leung, whose child was taken into foster care when she showed up to school with bruises on her arm because she had been playing with her two brothers and had fallen from a bed. In 2009, CASJAFVA also took on the case of the Baynes family, whose children were taken from them by child services after their daughter was hospitalized after an accident while playing with her brothers. Their parental rights, they said, had been unjustly infringed on by an overly zealous state.[71]

CASJAFVA's problem, though, was that they did not have the unequivocal support of Cantonese Protestants. In fact, they were seen as an organization that skirted the line of inappropriately using church spaces for secular activities. One pastor said to me, "Maybe for me, I think it's a bit radical to some extent. . . . I think they go to another extreme . . . like a pressure group people, like we feel they are a bit perceived as a radical, as a 'fundamentalist,' they attack people openly."[72] So too, a younger respondent recalled that a pastor at her church had stopped CASJAFVA from distributing their newsletter on church grounds. She also said that she "purposely" did not want to be associated with CASJAFVA because she remembered "seeing one newsletter that—it was making fun of gay people—and I was really upset because if gay people saw this, they would be so turned off by this and they would say more things about how Christians bash us, how Christians don't like us."[73] Worse, as some in a focus group in the suburb of Coquitlam told me, CASJAFVA's sense of theology was problematic for some. Mr. Chan noted that CASJAFVA had become "very broad," evidenced in a recent fundraising dinner where the auction featured Buddhist statues on sale. He said that as a Christian (a revivalist, to be specific), he could not "touch" the Buddhist statues, adding that while "their motivations are very good, but when you're open to all, you include all kinds of different kinds of things. If your goal is very focused, and you're open to all, then it's no good."[74]

Cantonese Protestant dissatisfaction with CASJAFVA coincided with the formation of the CSCF in 2005. CSCF's main concern was that Cantonese Protestants had become apathetic in the face of same-sex marriage, which was legalized that same year. One of CSCF's founders,

Rev. Wayne Lo, explained to me that it was after the failure of activism against the hate crime bills in the 1990s and same-sex marriage in the 2000s that CSCF was "endorsed and facilitated by the VCEMF to stand out, to let CSCF to stand out and to voice out on behalf of Christians."[75] In the aftermath of the legalization of same-sex marriage, CSCF sought to educate Chinese churches about other pressing social issues, more or less repeating CASJAFVA's concerns that the state was ideologically policing their private family and church spaces. But it was also different, one of its members clarified to me. CASJAFVA, she said, sought to mobilize "Christians"; CSCF went for the pastors—the leaders of the Christians, at least in theory—mostly by organizing guest Sunday school courses at participating churches.[76] And yet it was also independent of the VCEMF. Indeed, another member told me that CSCF was independent of other Cantonese Protestant institutions too, even though, as he put it, CCM was "instrumental" in its founding. "We deliberately do not want CCM to take it over," he said, "and so that it won't be owned by an organization. It's easier for people to partake of things."[77]

CSCF, in other words, professed its Christian commitments in contrast to CASJAFVA's secularity, but the issues they considered were also remarkably similar. Lo forwarded me a list of topics they addressed in their Sunday school curriculum:

> Separation of Church & State; Participating in Politics; BC School Education; Drugs & Gangs; Abortion & Sex Ethics; Social Involvement with compassion; Euthanasia & Assisted Suicide; Witnessing God in the Public [Religious Freedom]; Parental Rights in Canada; Marijuana and Gender Spectrum[78]

Same-sex marriage fit into this array of key words, CSCF's instructor on sexuality told me, because it spoke to a slippery slope the state was on in infringing on the private rights of communities. He emphasized that there had to be a "boundary line" between what was and was not marriage, or else "if you can remove the line from gender discrimination, then by the same argument, you can remove age discrimination, and you can remove number discrimination. It's the same argument, you can remove these things." Repeating the arguments that the Cantonese mainline pastors and CASJAFVA had previously made, he asserted that this would be a slippery slope to "pedophilia." "Then over ten years," he continued, "then I accept pedophilia: then we move the line again? Then what will the society become? Then why do you need marriage? Maybe you don't need marriage. This is the homosexual activists' community agenda, I think, to go into marriage to destroy marriage."[79]

CSCF encountered the same kind of intransigence from Cantonese Protestant communities that its predecessors also had faced, so much that the organizational core eventually disintegrated and made their regular meetings increasingly sporadic. One CSCF member related that they "encountered many difficulties" because "many churches told us that they would not take sides, or that these things, if they prayed about it, it's enough; God would exercise his sovereignty from his throne. . . . What they do not see is that the whole environment will influence each person, influence even our children."[80] CSCF members had many explanations for this resistance. Some blamed the strict secular-religious divide in revivalist theology. "That is the teaching—this is secular, this is worldly," one said. "*Fanbit waising* [separated as holy]. I don't know—separated holiness means that you're still in the world but not of the world, you're still the salt and light of the world . . . and they label people doing social gospel."[81] Yet another blamed a "retirement mentality" among migrants who constantly traveled between Hong Kong and Vancouver for leisure and were therefore "not rooted in either place."[82]

There was, of course, a small problem about these organizational complaints about Cantonese Protestant apathy. It turns out that most of my respondents who were not part of CASJAFVA or CSCF actually *did* care about these issues. Indeed, they cared a lot about how the media, in their view, misrepresented CASJAFVA's protests in 2002 and 2003. They told me that news reports misreported their numbers. One woman, anonymized here as Mandy, recalled that counterprotesters attempted to get into the family values demonstration and "tried to cause some trouble by lying down and pretend that he was hurt or injured." Emphasizing that the family values demonstrators greatly outnumbered the counterprotesters, Mandy recalled "very clearly afterwards" her disappointment in the news report, including in the Chinese media. They "actually blew up the number of participants on the other side," she said, "and that was so vivid, so clear because we were there, we knew how many we were, and we knew how many they were." She expressed special disappointment at the Chinese media "because we thought that the Chinese media may be a little bit more conservative, if not sympathetic to the church" and said that even her husband, "being very quiet, seldom took part in things like this, but he went that time, and that was one thing he mentioned again and again, about the blowing up of the participants on the other side."[83] Those in my focus group in Richmond also commented on the amount of time they had on screen as opposed to the counterprotesters. One person who described herself as politically apathetic told the group that she was present at those demonstrations and was just as frustrated. "How many thousands did we have?" she asked. "Ten thousand? How many thousands? In any case, they in fact filmed those few people."[84] In Coquitlam, Mr. Chan also spoke about his frustration with the media at the same protests to the wide acclamation of the group: "So you go to the protest and you watch the news, and it's two different things. On the news, you saw maybe a few people waving, but there, it was like thousands of people, all lined up."[85]

Numbers and representation were important, my respondents told me, because they saw themselves as voicing the views of the majority over against sexual minorities—and for good reason, they emphasized, because they were trying to keep their own families from falling apart. They explained this expansion of what they took to be minority rights as a kind of organized criminality, one that began by splitting the family apart so that young people would move out of the home and have to fend financially for themselves. One respondent said, "Once you take apart the family, how expensive will it be? The two of you live apart, and then you're poor. You get one job, just an ordinary job, it's $3,000, and you're already poor. Would you say that one family is to save money, or two?"[86] Another interviewee expressed that "the Western values are very individualistic: if you are young and you grow up, you must leave. But in the East, there are many who have family concepts. If you have a family, you have a support. If you are in the family and you don't go outside, then how will you become homeless?" He then spoke of human rights as a "knife" that had been used the wrong way. "I mean, if you're a bad person, you use a knife to kill people," he said. "A good person uses a knife to chop vegetables. . . . [Human rights are] neutral. . . . Human rights is all for criminals now, not ordinary people. Which ordinary person needs to use human rights? Only criminals use it!"[87]

What in fact divided them was whether it was appropriate for the church to talk about these problems. When I asked my focus groups whether their pastors informed their political choices, they responded vigorously, usually in the spirit of this memorable line from the Richmond focus group, "No, no, no!"[88] At the Burnaby focus group, Mrs. Yang said that within the church, individual members often "talk about values," explaining that her friends "always look at the different parties and politicians coming out, and like children, we ask, 'Hey, are they good or cunning?'" She then suggested that the church itself was not part of these discussions. "I don't think it's the church that says this," she said. "When you talk about the church's education, in the church, I think it's not so good because we are not very united about voting or teaching. I don't think it's the church that does this." Her thoughts generated a conversation among the group about how their church had in fact failed to address anything political; it was only that "the church reminds us to go vote" and that the church should maintain neutrality in order to keep peace within its potentially politically diverse congregation.[89]

These lines of conversation were similar in the other focus groups. In Richmond, the conversation began with a statement that the church "overall tries to maintain its neutrality, don't want to make the society concerned, but at a certain position, it might get too close," to which another respondent replied, "I have been here for more than a decade. The church never says that you must vote for the Conservative Party or any other party." Instead, they said that Cantonese evangelicals had to "choose based on their own values, whatever is fair." In terms of pastoral leadership, one participant remembered, "I once heard my pastor say, 'You read your Bible, then whatever position is close to the biblical principles, then you pick that one. If you don't know which party to choose, then I will not tell you here which party to choose, but if you read your Bible, you can observe the different positions.'"[90] Although one pastor told me that such a statement was indeed code for "We prefer the Conservatives for the moral and biblical values,"[91] the focus group members read these statements as demonstrations of pastoral neutrality at best and apathy at worst. In any case, despite the many political conversations that I as a researcher had with pastors, the laity often viewed their pastoral staff as outside the range of people with whom they discussed secular politics. There was a pastor with whom I spoke who refuted quite eloquently the sentiment that this pastoral distance was somehow problematic. "This is really not fair," he said, "because the Bible says that pastors should pray and do ministry. . . . So I feel that it's a partnership, from God's perspective, it's a partnership; you cannot lose one person, and you cannot say that one person can do it all."[92]

It is these comments that make sense of the tension between Cantonese Protestants in Vancouver lambasting what they took to be the expansion of human rights discourse while distancing themselves from any leader from within their midst who could represent them. In chapter 1, I told the story of CSCF's cochair Charter Lau, who was part of a slate of parental rights activists trying to get themselves on the Burnaby school board to overturn Policy 5.45, which introduced anti-homophobic and anti-heterosexist pedagogy into school practice. These efforts were also paralleled across Metro Vancouver, with similar activities held in Metro Vancouver with the Non-Partisan Association's Ken Denike and Sophia Woo and in Richmond with the Richmond Independent Team of Electors' slate of Kenny Chiu and Jonathan Ho for school board, all running on platforms of parents' rights and what they called "non-partisan" curricula.[93] While these candidacies were successful in Richmond and Vancouver, Burnaby Parents' Voice was defeated in Burnaby, its demise attributed to death threats launched at supporters of 5.45 and derogatory comments about Muslims put on CSCF's website by Wayne Lo that were tied to Charter Lau.[94]

The history of the same-sex marriage protests repeated itself in 2011. Just like in 2002 and 2003, there was a counterprotest that attempted to drown them out; similarly, pastors claimed that they had not encouraged their congregation members to attend. In Burnaby, one pastor said that he told his congregation that they would need to be "wise as serpents and innocent as doves," encouraging his congregation 'to start a protest, a peaceful protest' without saying "that homosexuality is wrong." Instead, following the "parental rights" ideology, he argued, "Like we can't oppose the measure, but we can say that parents should have a voice, you can't just teach our youth without notifying us."[95] Another Vancouver pastor readily admitted to me that the 5.45 activism was a matter of individuals from his congregation crossing city lines to protest. "So we tell them if you don't want to go protest," he said, "you can sign a petition. But this is very individual, very individual. . . . I will make an announcement to raise the awareness that we are collecting signatures. That's the most that we've ever done, it's this thing."[96]

For my Burnaby focus group participants, though, neither these pastoral actions nor the activities of Charter Lau qualified them to be Chinese Christian representatives. One respondent said, "In Burnaby, on Parents' Voice, we are very clear about our values. But he was unable to articulate our values clearly. In the mainstream, they think that we are a nuisance, but if you look at the Chinese polls, 80 percent should have gone to him. So why doesn't the mainstream buy us?" In other words, Mr. Yip resented the notion of having to acknowledge Lau as a leader, for he had failed (in Mr. Yip's view) in his efforts to represent an ethnic Chinese Canadian population in Burnaby (much less Cantonese Protestants) to a non-Chinese audience.

The consensus, then, was that although Lau had been outspoken about his opposition to Policy 5.45, being vocal was not the same as him being a representative. Representation, of course, was impossible. It was possible for everyone to agree that the problem was what they saw as a "ridiculous" expansion of the category of human rights, perhaps in Canadian discourse, but also in terms that fit with the dream of the Pacific Rim. But a common vision did not imply coordinated action. Mobilization ran into the difficulty of intransigent churches interested in political neutrality. Protests ran the risk of media misrepresentation. Organizational strategies could be shown to be secular. Those institutions blamed the churches. Church members blamed their pastors. Pastors blamed each other. In the words of the Burnaby focus group member I recounted in the first chapter as he sighed and commented on this institutional mayhem, "Truly, Chinese people are a sheet of scattered sand."[97]

"RELIGIOUS RIGHT"? MEDIA ETHICS, "SEX CULTURE," AND ORGANIZATIONAL AUTONOMY IN HONG KONG

When I arrived in Hong Kong for fieldwork in 2012, part of the talk of the town among Protestants there was about whether there was a "religious right." Of particular interest were two organizations, the Society for Truth and Light (STL) and the Hong Kong Sex Culture Society (HKSCS). Interestingly, their accusers were themselves Protestant Christians. In 2009,

Daniel Cheung, who had once worked at STL, published a book titled *Too Bright*; its Cantonese title 論盡明光社 (*leonzeon minggwongse*) is better translated "clumsy STL."

Its portrayal of STL, though, is anything but clumsy. Advertised as an insider's exposé of STL as an antidemocratic institution, Cheung alleged that STL had constructed an elaborate network in Hong Kong that undemocratically controlled the voting patterns of some politicians in the Legislative Council.[98] Cheung's book spawned a sequel anthology, *Religious Right*, in 2010, edited by Lingnan University cultural studies scholar Lau Wing Sang and Chung Chi Divinity School theologian Kung Lap Yan.[99] They wanted to show that the church's influence during the colonial period paralleled the rise of an American religious right in the 1970s. Those influences were trying to remain in power, they claimed, in the form of a conservative religious right networked by STL that was pushing their moral agenda onto Hong Kong's secular civil society.

In response, STL and HKSCS advanced a picture of themselves as a loose coalition that prized institutional autonomy. Their first tactic was to respond that Cheung was acting as an individual with an axe to grind. The founder of the HKSCS, the philosopher Kwan Kai Man, told me that Cheung was in fact his philosophy student, but "I think our relationship turned sour because he was really dissatisfied with the way we handled these issues, so he writes a lot of things before publishing the book in November."[100] STL's head, Choi Chi Sum, remembered meeting with Cheung in his office prior to the publication of *Too Bright*. He reduced Cheung's book to a personal dispute between himself and Cheung, for Cheung had asked during that meeting "that whatever statements we put out, could we send it to him and he will read it for us first before publishing." Choi said that he responded that *he* was the general secretary, not Cheung, and accountable only to his board. Choi thus reduced the entire affair to a power struggle with a distant individual: "I think he thinks that we don't listen to his suggestions, but I think he's mistaking his own role. . . . If he has good suggestions, he can give it to us, but there's no way I'm going to let him approve it."[101]

STL and HKSCS then published their own response to *Religious Right* with Alliance Seminary Press. They challenged the portrayal of their organizations as a religious right. They were not, they pointed out, as connected as the institutions of the American religious right to the partisan operations of some quarters of the state. Indeed, the lead editor of *Religious Right*, Kung Lap Yan, admitted to me in an interview that it was a fair critique.[102] On reflection, I would also have to agree, as it does not take into account that STL and HKSCS had a background in revivalism, not the denominational establishment of the colonial state. This response argued that their organizations and churches had very little collusion with the government. Instead, they "lobbied all of the parties" and often worked "against the government" in their activism against sexual liberalization.[103] Indeed, Choi mocked the account as overly imaginative. "It's like that organization goes out and talks," he said, "and that church talks, and that person talks, and then they put it together like one picture, like the 'religious right' really has this power, a lot of close relationships with through the phenomenal lens of STL. I really think that this has no correlation to reality." Arguing that "they really do not understand the situation of Hong Kong churches," he pressed the point with a rhetorical question: "Do you think an organization can influence a congregation's pastor to do something?" He then said that his board was multidenominational and independent of any external governance. He gave the example of a megachurch pastor, Rev. Patrick So, whom their opponents loved to associate him with, especially when one time So made homophobic remarks from the pulpit. "What real ability do we have to tell Rev. So to do anything? He's a huge church's congregational pastor. And on the flip side, Rev. So also does not have the capability of telling me what to do.'" Instead, Choi emphasized that STL had to be "politically neutral" to be effective. They had a number of issues on their docket, ranging from gambling to sexual orientation to media ethics. They had to lobby every party, he said, and not be tied down to one.[104]

Unlike my experience in the Bay Area and Vancouver, the representatives of neither STL nor HKSCS bought me lunch, though Kwan once invited me into his home for a four-hour interview, after which I told him that I was going to interview his opponents. He was delighted, and he encouraged me to get the story from all sides. But as I considered the objections to being called a "religious right," I came to understand that just like in my sites across the Pacific, their claim to organizational autonomy was reasonable on their own terms. By their own account, they had started their activities around the time of the 1997 handover of Hong Kong to the People's Republic of China. What they had been concerned about then were ethical issues in media journalism and sexual liberalization. Kwan was there from the start. He was a rationalist philosopher who was one of STL's original board members. He had his doctorate in philosophy of religion from Oxford and had returned to Hong Kong in 1993. He was also connected to the revivalists who started organizations like Breakthrough Youth Ministries in the 1970s and taught two courses for Fellowship of Evangelical Studies on pornography and human rights. These classes formed working groups within the organization, which generated concern that "these kinds of moral problems seem to get worse and worse" and that their ad hoc groups would not be sufficient to address public policy issues adequately.[105]

These groups developed into the board for a new organization in May 1997 that became STL. STL's mandate revolved around journalism ethics. They were concerned about both the veracity of media content and the presence of pornography in mainstream broadcasting. In particular, STL decried the ways in which Hong Kong journalists often exaggerated news stories and violated privacy rights. They called for a boycott of the tabloid newspaper *Apple Daily* in 1998 when they printed what was later discovered to be a staged photograph of a man, Chan Kin Hong, who claimed that his wife and children had committed suicide after he started visiting prostitutes.

STL's boycott of *Apple Daily*, Choi told me, propelled it to public prominence. He himself was hired shortly afterward but for another reason. At that time, the government proposed a revision of the Control of Obscene and Indecent Articles Ordinance so that it would no longer regulate pornographic and violent content in the media. Choi was already known as an outspoken journalist about media ethics, so STL hired him as its director so that they could more effectively protest the press. Choi also told me that he felt a sense of "close thinking" with STL's values, especially in its respect for privacy and its call for the media to use higher ethical standards to promote substantive journalism.[106]

By 2000, these issues in media ethics expanded to what they began to call "sex-culture" (性文化, *singmanfaa*). Kwan told me that he had been following a secular social debate about "sex-culture" beginning around 2000 during an "intrusion of prostitutes" into the working-class district of Sham Shui Po, which was protested by the residents there. The primary antagonist for them was Dr. Ng Man-lun, a psychiatrist at

Hong Kong University who was given the ignominious label "Dr. Sex." Kwan described him as an "arch–sexual liberal" who was "quite radical and does not think that incest or bestiality are a problem." Kwan said that "many people think that we are promoting a sort of irrational moral panic—that is a common allegation of the liberals against us," but he had a list of news items "beginning with 2000 and in those few years, there are lots of cases about some sexual crimes which are really horrifying." At his home, he showed me his extensive archives. He had accounts of "sexual crimes" throughout East Asia, with newspaper clippings from 2000 to 2004 drawn from Hong Kong, Taiwan, and China that described serial rapists, incest, indecent thoughts, father-and-son gang rapes, teachers playing games with sexual connotations, pimping, the usage of peeping video cameras, and young boys engaging in oral sex rape. These stories were "sex-culture," he was showing me, the normalization of sex crimes in mainstream culture. "I think this is horrifying," Kwan said repeatedly to me.[107]

Kwan's horror effected what might be seen as the first rift among Hong Kong Protestants, which would come back to haunt him and his colleagues when they were called the "religious right" in 2012. Kwan recounted his objections to the government's Equal Opportunity Commission's (EOC) Sexual Orientation Funding Scheme in 2000. He had said publicly that "the fund was not used to educate people not to discriminate homosexuals, but it seemed to positively encourage a homosexual lifestyle. And we think that has crossed the line; that is not the original purpose of the education fund to reduce discrimination." His comments did not only earn him a rebuke from the EOC's Anna Wu Hung-yuk; they also created a rift between him and the feminist theologian Rose Wu Lo Sai, who was then leading both the Hong Kong Christian Institute and the Hong Kong Women's Christian Council. Kwan told me that he had been initially supportive of Wu's work, as well as the efforts of what is popularly called in Sinophone worlds the *tongzhi* movement (Cantonese, *tungzi*), a term that technically means "comrade" but is also code for gay rights. However, he said, "when I look deeper and deeper, I think honestly, I can speak with integrity, I do not only base my opposition upon my Christian belief, but as a scholar, as a person in the modern society who is concerned about a real pluralistic society and respecting the rights of different people."[108] In an article he wrote on the EOC—which became the fourth chapter of his book *Human Rights and Homosexuality* (2000)—Kwan considered that the ambiguous definition of "sexual orientation" could include acceptance of the very sexual crimes constitutive of the East Asian sexual revolution and could lead to widespread disease as well as reverse discrimination for heterosexual families.[109]

And so, there was a second division, albeit a more amicable one. To address sex-culture more pointedly, Kwan Kai Man convened HKSCS in 2001 as a separate institutional entity from STL. They began by organizing four study groups that first met in STL's offices. They tackled questions of what the "homosexual movement" was in relation to biblical sexual ethics, the problem of homosexuality, the issue of marriage, and the nature of family. There was, they claimed, a democratic dimension to what they were doing. One of their project directors told me that he had joined HKSCS in 2003 because eight sexual minority activists interrupted a Sunday mass in August 2003 at the Catholic Diocese's St. Joseph's Cathedral in Central and kissed in the middle of the church to protest the Vatican's opposition to same-sex unions. Although this project director was Protestant, he felt that this protest demonstrated the *tongzhi* movement's disregard for the rights of their opponents.[110] He then compared gay rights legislation to the anti-sedition constitutional clause Article 23, an interesting choice because Kwan's old friend Wu had been instrumental in organizing the Civil Human Rights Front (CHRF), a coalition that existed precisely to protest Article 23's possible infringements on freedoms of speech and religion. HKSCS said that antidiscrimination ordinations for sexual minorities were also "stripping away the freedoms of those who oppose homosexuality, their social freedoms and their freedoms to assembly."[111]

In 2004, these clashes escalated over the Sexual Orientation Discrimination Ordinance (SODO). In December 2004, the deputy secretary for home affairs, Stephen Fisher, announced a public consultation to investigate public opinion about homosexuality, indicating that the Panel for Home Affairs would propose SODO as a law if not more than 70–80 percent of Hong Kong people opposed it. The mainline Protestant denominations such as the Anglican Church, the Methodist Church, and the Christ Church of China broadly supported it despite their internal ambivalence about homosexuality.[112] But Kwan saw it all as quite nefarious. As he told me, Fisher had shown his cards. "But that is just wrong," he said. "From an interview, Stephen Fisher has pretty much said that 'the presumption is to go ahead, unless there is massive opposition.' Now we feel quite shocked and we feel quite pessimistic."[113] So too, Kwan's HKSCS director also recalled "feeling very shocked," comparing Fisher's actions again to Article 23. "I mean," he said, "Hong Kong doesn't have a constitution where it says that you have to legislate this kind of law, even if it's not like Article 23, it's similar, and it was not until the government could not withstand the protest of its citizens that it gave up."[114] At STL, Choi agreed about the possibilities for undemocratic actions to be conducted if SODO were to pass. He asserted that his organization "never told people to oppose homosexuals, and we have very sincere communication with the heads of homosexual groups; we will not think that, oh, they are homosexuals so that we do not talk to them or use an attitude of enmity." However, he opposed SODO on institutional grounds. "In the experience of many foreign countries," he said, "if we openly say that we do not support homosexuality or our organization—our organization will not hire homosexuals. But we do not think that this is discrimination; we think this is a question of our position because we also will not hire an open practitioner of Buddhism either."[115]

In response to Fisher's consultation, STL and HKSCS formed yet another organization, the Hong Kong Alliance for Family; "in fact," the HKSCS director noted, the alliance "was a Christian institution, and we were a member of it."[116] As Kwan recounted, HKSCS called on "church members and the citizens" to engage in a "one person, one letter" campaign because, as his project director put it bluntly, "the government wants to hear the public opinion."[117] This initiative generated fifty thousand individual letters opposing SODO. Second, they mobilized a petition campaign to oppose SODO, which was published in the major Chinese newspaper *Ming Pao* in April and was signed by 300 Christian organizations and 9,800 individuals. "Since 1989," the HKSCS director said, with reference to protests in solidarity with the Tiananmen Beijing Spring, "this was the largest newspaper announcement that was ever put out."[118] They also conducted their own surveys of public opinion. HKSCS hired Hong Kong University's Social Sciences Research Centre to conduct a survey independent from the government, which again found that the majority of Hong Kongers opposed SODO. Claiming to have "taken part in almost all of the major skirmishes and battles" on SODO while joining with STL to maximize this social impact, Kwan also wrote articles and advertisements for newspapers and spoke widely in churches, in social organizations, on the radio, and in high schools "to educate people about the possible impact of SODO."[119] For its part, the government shelved SODO in 2006.

These activities around SODO were important because they affected Hong Kong's post-handover democracy movement. During the anti-SODO campaign, HKSCS also offered an olive branch to Wu by organizing a conversation titled "Let's Not Talk Past Each Other but to Each Other" at Mong Kok Baptist Church on April 25. The proceedings and subsequent reflections were published in the *Christian Times*'s book *The Ends of the Rainbow*.[120] But in 2005, news broke in the press that there was a call for a boycott of the annual democratic protest on July 1—precisely the one that the solidarity movement Wu headed, CHRF, had helped to organize in 2003—because CHRF had arranged for a gay rights group to head the front of the protest.[121] Speaking for STL, Choi denied in his interview with me that he had called for the boycott. He said that he had been misunderstood by the press. He had told journalists, he said to me, that "if the *tungzi* group leads and waves a flag demanding SODO," he continued, "then I will oppose it because that will mean that the entire group supports SODO." Journalists, he said, misreported his hypothetical statement as prescriptive. The result was more or less an actual boycott; there were, he said, "much fewer people at the demonstration" that year, a claim corroborated by CHRF leaders to me too.[122]

SODO, STL and HKSCS representatives told me, may have brought these groups to public prominence, but what I had to remember, they emphasized, was that they were groups that advocated for media ethics, of which "sex-culture" was but a subset. In 2006, STL and HKSCS attacked a television documentary titled *Gay Lovers*, which aired on Radio Television Hong Kong (RTHK) in July 2006. In the film, a lesbian couple and gay activist, Joseph Cho Man Kit (who was popularly nicknamed Little Cho, or Siu Cho), expressed their aspirations to have a public policy that eliminated discrimination for them and enabled them to get married. STL and HKSCS reported *Gay Lovers* to Hong Kong's Broadcasting Authority. They said that the documentary had interviewed gay and lesbian couples about SODO and gay marriage without mentioning that there was an opposition, which (for them) demonstrated that the media was colluding with a gay rights movement and compromising its independence.[123] When the Broadcasting Authority sanctioned RTHK for not complying with its set media standards, Siu Cho appealed the entire matter for judicial review to the High Court in a widely publicized court case. The result was that the Broadcasting Authority's sanctions were reversed on the grounds that *tongzhi* activists had freedom of speech.

The *Gay Lovers* case earned STL and HKSCS their reputation as a united right-wing front. Kwan told me that when RTHK was first sanctioned, gay rights activists began to attribute every public contestation around sexuality and the media to STL, regardless of whether STL was actually involved in the activism or not. One example was when the Obscene and Indecent Articles Ordinance enforcement group confiscated a newsletter for a column allegedly containing pornographic material at the Chinese University of Hong Kong's Chung Chi College in 2007. "There is a rumor that the Society for Light and Truth—STL—who deliberately filed the complaint against the CU [Chinese University] magazine," Kwan said to me. "But that was a rumor. The people who did it complained were not related to us. If you ask me who it was, I forgot their names—so they were not related to us, but at the time, people seem to think that all the things are through the evil source of the STL. All the conservative actions." Kwan then told me an internet character called Oh My God sent the Bible to the same tribunal "because it contains stories about incest, say, Lot and his daughters. . . . They said, 'You should declare the Bible is an indecent article. According to the law of Hong Kong, you need to wrap it up in a plastic bag!'" They also gave STL and HKSCS a nickname: the "moral Taliban." In response, HKSCS held a seminar called "Who Is the Moral Taliban?" Kwan told me that, in fact, he was disappointed. "Well, of course, I think psychologically I felt depression," he said, "and of course, if the people debate with me reasonably, I think I am happy to do that, and I think that's not a problem for me because I am a philosopher; I am familiar with debates."[124] He had been, as he wrote at the time in the *Christian Times*, advocating for a liberal society where a multiplicity of positions could find overlapping consensus. In fact, he claimed, this name-calling by gay rights groups showed that they were the ones distorting the liberal democratic deliberative process.[125]

And then came the Domestic Violence Ordinance (DVO). In December 2007, the Hong Kong Legislative Council announced plans to revise the 1986 DVO to streamline the process for minors and the elderly to apply for injunctions against domestic abusers. However, as a Bills Committee was formed in May 2008, Legislative Council members from various political parties expressed that the bill should be gender neutral in coverage, expanding its scope to same-sex couples. While the Labour and Services Bureau countered that Hong Kong did not even recognize same-sex domestic partnerships (much less marriage), these members argued that same-sex couples should be entitled to equal protection under the law as stated by Basic Law's Article 25.

These policy conversations led the bureau to place same-sex couples in the amended version of the bill, which is when STL, HKSCS, and the Alliance for Family raised their objections.[126] Indeed, just like in SODO, the problem lay in the government's handling of the DVO. The HKSCS project director told me that he knew that there were "some new pro-family members" who had joined the Legislative Council "who told the government that they did not agree with this because we hear a lot of citizen voices telling us that they do not agree with these revisions, because they are wondering if our marriage system will continue to change." Yet at the public hearings, the "panel's chairman was very pro-gay," he said, saying that he would only accept the voices of organizations, not individual citizens. "This is so facetious!" he protested. "Which Legislative Council member would do such a thing? And this chairman, he's so-called pro-democracy! So we said, 'Hey, are you really pro-democracy or not?'" As a result, he recalled that over one hundred organizations applied to speak on their opposition to the inclusion of same-sex couples in the DVO, including many evangelical churches and Roman Catholics.[127]

But their strategy was not religious. Instead, STL and HKSCS adopted a purely secular strategy. As one initial hearing spilled into a second one because of the volume of applicants, STL and HKSCS made the simple demands that the words "family" and "marriage" be struck from the bill and that the bill be expanded to cover all domestic living arrangements, including roommates who could, for all they knew, be same-sex couples. "Eventually," STL's Choi told me, "they changed it to Family and Cohabitation Violence Ordinance, so we packed up. They said that it was both about families and cohabitation, not the marriage and arrangements equivalent to marriage, so we packed up. We accept the law."

The problem, though, was that not all Cantonese Protestants were on the same secular page. At a Sunday service in the week prior to the DVO public hearing, Rev. Patrick So, himself on the advisory board of HKSCS, called on his ten-thousand-strong congregation Yan Fook Evangelical Free Church to protest the DVO at Government House. He said that homosexuals that the church had tried to help were now rejecting Christ's substitutionary atonement and trying to lead Hong Kong society into an era of sexual "cohabitation" in which they would change sex into "just eating sandwiches."[128] As the HKSCS director recalled, this protest was itself a pivotal moment in evangelical activism, arguably demonstrating a level of public opinion to the Legislative Council that Hong Kong was not ready for same-sex couples' legal recognition, for "it made the Legislative Council members shocked because every day there are some people protesting there, and it's always the same people coming and going, but that day, all those people were those that they had never seen before. They did not protest very often."[129] So's words sparked outrage among *tongzhi* activists, who launched a protest at the church the week afterward on February 15, 2009, with the theme "Protecting Civil Rights from the Religious Right," chanting, "Patrick So, shut up! STL, eat bananas! Choi Chi Sum, shameless!"[130]

It was from this demonstration that the claim emerged that a nefarious "religious right," one that somehow linked Patrick So to STL and Choi Chi Sum, had arisen in Hong Kong. It was not an altogether unreasonable assumption. After all, when I was doing my fieldwork in 2012, STL's offices happened to be located in the building behind the church. But I also spoke with a pastor at Yan Fook, who recalled that the protest led to a structural clarification within the operations of the church. They learned, he said, that these issues needed to be "handled with care" and that "it should not be one person; it should be a whole team of people, and the agenda, we should have someone study it, and how to express it, maybe it's not every time that we need the senior pastor to express it. We can find a spokesperson to say it."[131] Kwan was more blunt in his assessment. He said that Rev. So had gone off script. "So after he came back," Kwan said, "he had to do a lot of explaining as well. And the way he wrote his speech—I had no way to know about that when he said that on the spot. So what could we do?" Kwan then acknowledged that "people lump us together and say, 'You are religious right,' because we do share some goals with Rev. So and in some work, that is correct." However, he stood by his claims to institutional autonomy. "But as I explained to you," he continued, "this is a loose coalition, and at every step, we need to explain if we should join, so we can only be responsible for what we actually do and what we actually believe in. We cannot be responsible for what others do and say."[132]

Defensive as these claims to autonomy might seem, they were supported by my focus groups at smaller churches in Tuen Mun, Sha Tin, North Point, and Mong Kok. There, I learned that the "religious right" and the Protestant supporters of gay rights who opposed them did not even register on the radar screens of most of my participants. In the Tuen Mun focus group where members were mostly middle class and in their early thirties, Mrs. Ng said that she had "never heard of these organizations" like STL and HKSCS. Mr. Chan (who had also not heard of them) said, "I will first inquire as to whether they have a biblical basis for their action, if they have a Bible verse, are these organizations centered on this? Then, based on the Bible, I will support them, but I will not be part of their movement." Other focus group members emphasized to me that this relative apathy was because their churches tended to be relatively apolitical, though they hypothetically disapproved of homosexual practices based on biblical teaching.[133]

At the Sha Tin focus groups, group members told me that they personally believed that homosexuality was wrong but that they had not actively participated in STL's campaigns. Mr. Lam only recalled hearing about STL when he was watching the news. He said that while he did not "conduct a very deep investigation," he simply reflected at home that while ordinary Hong Kong citizens might not think that it matters, Christians theoretically opposed what he understood to be the "legalization of homosexuality"[134] because of "the Bible, so we have a standard, and our standard does not fall." However, asked if they supported these activities, Mr. Lee said that he would "only secretly support it." "If we could circulate a petition in the church (we did not)," he said, "I would accept this action because it [homosexuality] conflicts with our faith. But we would not use our church's name."[135] Mirroring the Tuen Mun group, those in Sha Tin (as well as other very similar statements that I found in

North Point and Mong Kok) suggested that their support was only hypothetical, mostly because they had not really heard of these groups. Their ignorance of STL's work was indeed consonant with Choi's own assessment of his organization. "If you think we are that influential," he said, "you have overestimated the Society for Truth and Light."[136] They were not a religious right, he was implying. In many ways, the book that alleged that they were, Cheung's *Too Bright*, was more accurate than it knew. If anything, they told me that they were clumsy organizations.

CONCLUSION: ON NOT FOLLOWING THE MONEY

When I began my transpacific research on Cantonese Protestant opposition to same-sex marriage in 2011, I thought that I would find connections across Pacific Rim societies. The opposite turned out to be the case, at least in terms of how those involved narrated themselves. When I asked STL's Choi whether he had worked with North American organizations, he said that it was only through "mutual connections." "But if you ask about close day-to-day operations," he said, "we don't have that." Speaking, for example, on Proposition 8 in California, Choi said, "We heard about it, but we don't do anything about it, and they don't tell us what to do in Hong Kong, and we have no mission or donations from outside."[137] However, one pastor I spoke to was "friendly" with STL and sat on the board of Thomas Wang's GCCI Hong Kong office. But he emphasized to me that GCCI tended not to be active in Hong Kong but rather supportive of the American activities by printing their materials in Hong Kong.[138] So too, when Kwan told me that HKSCS had toured various family values associations like Focus on the Family and the Family Research Council and that he had shared "one lunch" with Vancouver's CSCF's Rev. Wayne Lo, he emphasized that these liaisons were strictly one-off visitations.[139] Although their materials subsequently copied from the CSCF's assertions that Vancouver's BCTF had fired Chris Kempling (one of the cases that CASJAFVA wrote about in their newsletters), these organizations suggested that they had heard about this through the free exchange of information available in public. Finally, when I finished interviewing Bill Tam in San Francisco, he asked me who else I was talking to. I reminded him that this was a transpacific study. He asked me to introduce him to his counterparts. I admit that I have dropped the ball on that request.

In the end, whether these transpacific links actually existed (and whether my respondents were trying to pull the wool over me by catering to a gullibility that was arguably reinforced by free food) became less ethnographically interesting to me than the practice of institutional autonomy that they insisted they were enacting. Certainly, other methodologies might have been able to discern whether there were material linkages among these organizations, say, by following the money. But these were not my methods. I was interested in how Cantonese Protestants in these churches and organizations narrated their own engagement with civil society, and the narration is one that insists on institutional autonomy. Whatever intentions might lie behind this narrative focus and whatever the story may have obscured, they also seemed to support the larger story of fragmentation among Cantonese Protestant communities, with a consistent tale that there was no one organization taking leadership on what seemed to be critical issues of concern to the people in them.

One way of narrating these divisions is through the theological narrative of revivalism. Nervousness about the secular provides a justification for institutional splintering, political inaction, and mutual blaming. But there is a way where the organizational *strategy* of autonomy seems to be a transformation from a narration purely based on theology. The story turns in the next chapter to what more Cantonese Protestants saw about their Pacific Rim civil societies that led them to articulate their churches and associated organizations in secular ways. In so doing, they reveal that the secular dream of the Pacific Rim is about more than progress along the lines of social and sexual equality. It turns out that interactions with local governing institutions are also very important in how they perceive civil society. It is to those transformations that we now turn.

CHAPTER FOUR

Against "Homeland Politics"

Cantonese Protestant Organizations and the Varieties of Pacific Rim Civil Societies

> *Love does no harm to its neighbor. Therefore love is the fulfillment of the law.*
>
> —Romans 13:10

INTRODUCTION: "HOMELAND POLITICS" AND THE VARIETIES OF SECULAR LEGIBILITY

In 2004, *Vancouver Sun* reporter Chad Skelton wrote about the "shifting immigrant vote" in Canada. He observed that the swing issues of abortion and same-sex marriage as well as the fact that new arrivals in Canada tended to be business owners concerned about their taxable income. Skelton reported the Centre for Research and Information's finding that among immigrants who had arrived in Canada after 1990, "fully 65 per cent" said that having a gay family member "would make them feel uncomfortable" and attributed this homophobia as a key reason that the newly configured Conservative Party of Canada in 2003 was chipping away at the Liberal domination of the immigrant vote at the turn of the twenty-first century.[1]

Skelton's article was not the only one to make such observations. A special front-page issue of the national *Globe and Mail* newspaper in 2010 featured a report by journalists John Ibbitson and Joe Friesen that opened with a tale told by a Hong Kong migrant in a Toronto suburb. She said that her pastor asked her congregation to support the Conservative Party because they opposed same-sex marriage. Ibbitson and Friesen then noted that Conservatives achieved electoral successes in the 2008 election in six ridings across Canada with "visible minority populations of 20 per cent or higher." They sought to understand what could be making new immigrants espouse a kind of political conservatism that was unexpected because they were supposed to have arrived in Canada due to multicultural policies designed by the Liberal Party. A sociologist at the University of Toronto, Myer Siemiatycki, offered this explanation: "When newcomers come to Canada they bring with them homeland values and traditions, but Canada is not a blank slate. We have a whole bunch of ways—from school to television to the law—that send signals of what the values of this society are."[2]

I want to offer a different interpretation. As transpacific as Cantonese Protestant revivalist theologies might have been in their origins, they were not, I claim, importing their homeland politics. If anything, they were trying to fit into the secular civil societies in which they lived, whether those were places to which they had moved (like the Bay Area and Vancouver) or where they had stayed (like Hong Kong). This kind of legibility required a balancing act. On the one hand, the Cantonese Protestants I spoke to had to maintain their theological convictions, which could be for the most part traced back to the revivalism that regarded their churches as spaces that were supposed to be disentangled from secular politics. But by the 1990s, they also realized that the building spaces in which they gathered and worshipped, as well as the sites where they established parachurch organizations and engaged with the public sphere, were regulated by governments, at least at the local level. Legibility to those governing bodies, as well as to the civil societies from which those states derived their legitimacy, was not optional if they wanted to be able to meet in the buildings of their own choice and be taken seriously as participants in society.

What I want to show in turn is that each civil society to which Cantonese Protestants attempted to be legible also instantiated the secular dream of the Pacific Rim in ever so different ways. Often in transpacific studies, the Pacific Rim is described as a product of American empire, or a reassertion of an abandoned notion of British empire with the foregrounding of Commonwealth nation-states like Canada, Australia, and New Zealand as desirable sites of migration, or even an ongoing contest that extends the United States' Cold War project to contain Chinese communism and nationalisms in various guises and permutations in the region. In such global imaginations, it is as if the Pacific Rim is conceived of as a single sheet, one that holds the scattered sands together. But in each specific place, Cantonese Protestants engaged the structures of specific civil societies—arenas of democratic participation that are also ultimately entangled with states and markets—that were in the thrall of the dream. They may all share similar dreams—multicultural societies, political stability, preparedness for ecological and economic disaster even while pursuing shared transpacific prosperity—but because there is no one institution that unites them, such dreaming works out differently in different civil societies.

Because of the differences among Pacific Rim civil societies, it is also difficult to describe Cantonese Protestants as maintaining transpacific and cross-society networks. Certainly, Cantonese Protestants may consider Hong Kong as a kind of point of common origin, but Hong Kong as a civil society itself has remained very different from, say, the Bay Area and Vancouver. In this chapter, my task is to demonstrate how, far from importing their "homeland politics," Cantonese Protestants actively sought to be legible to the civil societies they lived in while attempting to keep something of their revivalist theological inclinations. I take the three examples that this story of Cantonese Protestants has traversed so far, but there is of course more to this story than San Francisco, Vancouver, and Hong Kong. Certainly, a fuller story could also sketch out Auckland, Sydney, Melbourne, Singapore, Tokyo, Seoul, Seattle, and Los Angeles, among others. The point, however, is simply to show how different these societies are from each other; more examples would simply make the same point. I will move in order through each society as I have traced them in previous chapters, tracking how Cantonese Protestant churches, organizations, and institutions are networked among themselves and contort their narratives of theology to engage their local civil societies legibly. In the Bay Area, the story is an economistic one. Cantonese Protestants have to prove, I show, that their property purchases to house their own institutions add something to the value of local Bay Area economies. In Vancouver, the contest revolves around the meaning of social work, as Cantonese Protestants only seem to become legible when they offer immigrant social services and reorient their institutions to fit that narrative—and even then are still not taken seriously in some quarters as part of Vancouver's multicultural society. Hong Kong presents an even greater challenge after the 1997 handover, as Cantonese Protestant collaboration with the Hong Kong government can be construed as being entangled with an undemocratic state.

And yet, I suggest, there is still a way in which these societies come together. Indeed, I argue that they all still instantiate some version of the Pacific Rim dream, which can be detected in what Cantonese Protestants call the "secular" with which they must engage to be legible. These struggles for secular legibility are precisely that, I also hope to show: struggles that scatter Cantonese Protestants as sand on sheets that instantiate the dream in differing ways. Yet out of the scattering, I suggest, emerges a new consensus among Cantonese Protestants about what they think would be legible to those societies. Out of these struggles for legibility, new theologies emerge that alter not only the practices of Cantonese Protestantism but also their position among Pacific Rim civil societies. The task of this chapter is ultimately to narrate those fresh theological syntheses, which are particular to each society where Cantonese Protestants live.

REAL ESTATE PASTORS: MARKET LEGIBILITY IN THE BAY AREA

When Crosspoint Church of Silicon Valley attempted to purchase new property in 2008, its skirmish with the Milpitas urban economic plan illustrated in a nutshell how Bay Area cities evaluated the importance of religious communities solely in market-driven terms.

Indeed—and perhaps with some irony—Crosspoint Church began in 1999 with Cantonese Protestants conducting market research. Drawing from the successes of the megachurch Saddleback Church of Silicon Valley, Crosspoint's lead pastor, Abraham Chiu, directed his church plant's core group to conduct a social analysis that would determine the best geographic location to plant a Cantonese-speaking evangelical congregation, preferably (as one of its former pastors recalled to me) "on a big street, especially near a freeway exit where you do not have to turn more than three times to get in."[3] The finding from the report was there had been a boom in Cantonese-speaking information technology workers from Hong Kong in the Silicon Valley in the 1990s, specifically between San Jose and South Fremont, where there were excellent school districts.

Crosspoint Church picked the midpoint between Fremont and San Jose: Milpitas. It so happened that at the same time, the Milpitas City Council gave its support to build the $35 million net-worth Milpitas Square Plaza in 1995 and 1996 at the intersection of Highways 237 and 880, which, as Asian American newspaper *AsianWeek* reported at the time, caused an economic boom in Milpitas, with its over twenty Asian restaurants, Asian shops, acupuncture clinic, and the Asian supermarket Ranch 99 Market.[4] That was where Crosspoint decided to begin its efforts in 1999. It held Christmas booths outside of Ranch 99 as well as preview services at the Crowne Plaza Hotel across the street where successful entrepreneurs who happened to be themselves Cantonese Protestant spoke about "personal success."[5] They eventually purchased an industrial site on a main Milpitas throughway, Calaveras Boulevard. The church grew to about four hundred.

In 2007, the church decided that it needed more space. The pastoral leadership met with Milpitas City Hall officials, where they immediately encountered resistance. One of the pastors who was at that meeting, Andy Ching, recalled to me from that meeting, "The vice mayor had an economic plan—it was very obvious—and so he did not welcome churches to come in." The problem, Ching said, was that the site they wanted was "a heavy industrial site," and though they had informally discussed it as a possibility for their church, the vice mayor "said that that place, we will not zone it for churches anymore." Instead, city officials pointed the church to a former landfill as an alternate possibility.

The real problem, the Crosspoint leadership realized, was that the city wanted to maximize space for economic development. Crosspoint's marketing strategy kicked into high gear. Ching told me that these efforts required a multipronged political strategy. "If we were not building a church," he said, "we would never have guessed that there were so many things that I have to consider!" They learned that they needed to have insiders inside city hall, as well as to go to the Rotary Club because "all the key people are there, and you can give them your business card."[6] Simultaneously, the church launched a petition campaign for the church, generating some 1,700 individual letters from residents, business owners, and community workers (including a letter from the boss of a development agency as well as one from the former mayor) that emphasized in its standard form, "They have been here for 8 years serving the Chinese people and the City of Milpitas at Large. Granting the church the use permit would enhance their ability to serve hard working people in our community."[7] They needed an in with God too. The church organized a prayer walk around the proposed project site where church members confessed personal sin and prayed for "God's will" over the project that would be used to "serve" and "glorify God."[8] Finally, they had to refute an environmental hazard report from 2008 that identified in the area "three facilities that store and use toxic gases and that upon an accidental release could impact the project site."[9] The church's report revealed that there was also a hospital nearby and that if the toxic gases were in fact released, it would have a devastating impact on the entire city of Milpitas, not just the one church.

On June 11, 2008, the city government called a public hearing about the church's application for a conditional use permit for the industrial space. The recommendation, according to a report prepared beforehand, was for the Planning Commission to deny it. But community support won the day. Thirty-two congregation members and local community residents testified in person about the church's emotional care for those suffering psychological distress, outreach to international students, practical advice for how to parent children, and integration into Milpitas's economy because churchgoers supported local businesses.[10] The Planning Commission then stated that "just because staff recommended denial on the project they were not discriminating against the church" and approved the application.[11] It paid off. Three years later, the mayor visited a community gym that Crosspoint opened and said to the local press that the church had been granted a final conditional use permit because it had demonstrated its social and economic contributions to Milpitas's civic and market vitality.[12]

Crosspoint's case, I learned as I asked around in my interviews in the Bay Area, was by no means unusual. In fact, on the first day of my fieldwork in the Bay Area, I attended Cornerstone Community Church in San Francisco with some of my relatives. Its founding pastor, Rev. Chanson Lau, was preaching that day. He joked in his sermon that he was known as the "real estate pastor" and that other Bay Area pastors had criticized him for being "worldly." But he was a man of faith, he insisted. That was what his church's property purchases were about.

I learned more about Chanson Lau's real estate escapades when I interviewed him. The story began when he planted Cornerstone Community Church in 1975. Like many Cantonese Protestant pastors of revivalist tendency at the time, he had in fact been on staff at Cumberland Presbyterian Chinese Church in San Francisco's Chinatown and had struck out on his own with about 120 mostly English-speaking young adult members, after which they also developed a large Cantonese-speaking congregation. The church began by renting on Lawton Street in San Francisco's Sunset District. There, Lau attempted his first purchase. It was a two-lot storefront on the same road that cost $300,000 and required $50,000 in down payment. He was unable to raise the sums, he told me, and his own real estate agent had walked out in a huff. But he worked out a deal with the owner's agent, and he also found registering the property "very easy"; all he had to do was to "register the church as the owner with a board of trustees, and then they gave us the nonprofit status."

That was the 1970s. Everything, Lau suggested, changed in the 1990s. With their new available lots, the church launched a private school, Cornerstone Christian Academy. It was such a success that Lau began to be concerned that the storefront aesthetic felt like he was running a "dodgy school." In the late 1990s, he began to search for new property, and that was when he came face-to-face with San Francisco's planning department, with nearly the same problems that Crosspoint ran into ten years later with Milpitas. Cornerstone, he said, wanted a former Lucky's supermarket. He encountered immediate resistance from the planners:

So that department head said that, "Oh, Mr. Lau, you go up to the wall there, and you look at the map. You tell me where you want to buy, and I tell you whether we can zone you for a nonprofit." So I went up there, and I looked at the map, and I pointed to that Lucky's store, that ten acres. I said, "Right here, right here." And he said, "OK, Mr. Lau, if I give you that ten acres to be a church, you look around. Where are the residents around here, what other areas they can go shopping? OK? Even if you have the money to buy up that ten acres, I cannot zone it for you as a church because it has to be a marketplace." So that is why the reason now in San Francisco, all this city planning department, they have the responsibility which part they can zone it for nonprofit or for business.

Lau said that the church met with similar difficulties when he bought the former premises of Simpson Bible College (incidentally, Lau's alma mater) on Silver Avenue. After the purchase, planners ordered Cornerstone's new building to be retrofitted for an earthquake, citing the 1989 earthquake in San Francisco that had caused the Bay Bridge and other buildings to collapse. The church spent another $10 million over the next three years, retrofitting the wings of the buildings for classrooms and building a new cafeteria, while Lau also purchased a closing Catholic high school on nearby Cambridge Avenue, which they obtained with relative ease because the planning department wished for it to remain within the confines of nonprofit organization zoning.[13] In each of these cases, Cornerstone discovered that private property purchases could not be conducted between private hands as they used to be in the 1970s. The municipal planning department also had a say, often an economic one.

Across the Bay in Oakland, there were similar developments. The Bay Area Chinese Bible Church (BACBC) and its Chinese Christian Schools (CCS) had also been renting since the 1970s—apartment buildings, in their case, until in the 1980s the San Leandro Unified School District rented out school buildings to them. In 2002, they decided to buy property in Alameda from property tycoon Ron Cowan. Senior pastor Steve Quen told me in an interview that although negotiations with Cowan were going well, local neighborhood activists challenged the project at Alameda City Hall on April 20, 2002. Although they had a number of private gripes about the church—the church was unsupportive of gay rights, it was also three times larger than the largest church in the city, some raised the problem of the school having "hygiene" issues—the formal complaint was that the school's presence would cause traffic and noise disruptions to the neighborhood and thus disrupt Alameda's community plans.

The school's superintendent, former attorney Robin Hom, offered a detailed response as to how traffic, noise, and size would be limited, and the city approved their application.[14] But BACBC also wanted to do more. After consulting with the socially engaged pastor Rev. Sherman Williams of Fremont Community Church, BACBC organized a Love Alameda Day, where they cleaned up public properties in the city while also framing CCS's vision, Quen said, as a "community outreach" as an educational institution in the "top few percentiles in academics" to "go into the community where the church can't go."[15] There was a business dimension too. Hom told me that the school was conceived as a "ministry of the church," but "we have some business aspects because we have paying customers, and because of our size, what we do has an impact on the church, but from a regular organizational structure, that's where we fall in."[16] In the eyes of the church and the school, it was not enough to meet the city's minimal standards of why they had to be there. They had to show what their contribution was, framed in the deliverable metrics of tangible community service, academic excellence, and business structure.

There is yet another parallel to note. The Bay Area headquarters a Chinese health products company, Prince of Peace Enterprises. Its chief executive officer, Kenneth Yeung, was also once on staff in San Francisco's Cumberland Presbyterian Chinese Church. As I recounted in chapter 2, he had begun his career as a social worker, then worked for the church, and then was encouraged by his senior pastor at Cumberland to venture out into secular business territory.

When I went to visit Yeung at his offices, his receptionist handed me a cup of ginseng tea and an informational folder. Flipping through the materials, I learned of Prince of Peace Enterprises' very impressive story of business success. The company started by selling Chinese diet tea in the early 1980s. It was also a distributor of international products to Californian drugstores and supermarkets, such as the pain-relieving Tiger Balm from Singapore, the Swiss Ricola cough drops, Ferrero Rocher chocolates from Italy, Delacre cookies from France, St. Honore mooncakes from Hong Kong, and Almond Rocha from the United States. I found myself reflecting at that point in my reading that Yeung may well have been responsible for many of my own delightful childhood memories eating these snacks, often acquired through church networks.

With their business empire in place, they joined the Ginseng Board of Wisconsin in the 1990s, growing American-sourced ginseng and extracting its essences in China to create various teas and health food products, including ginseng root, ginseng candies, premium biscuits, and health supplements. ("So that's how Mom got into ginseng," I said to myself.) With an annual turnover of some $40 million (according to the booklet), Prince of Peace Enterprises' 72,000 square-foot headquarters is located in Hayward, with branches in Los Angeles, New York, Hong Kong, Macau, various sites in China, and Kuala Lumpur, with subsidiary companies like Global Marketing Associates and New Jamaican Gold supplying the processed products for the company's sales.

When I asked Yeung about Prince of Peace Enterprises' relevance to civil society—he did, after all, have a social work and ministry background—he told me, "I don't believe in big government." He talked about how some inspection workers had been hired at the United States Department of Agriculture who had little experience of his imported Chinese mooncakes that had preserved eggs enclosed in the baked goods. Yeung said that these workers argued without precedent that these products should have been refrigerated, leading to a costly legal battle and a scientific study that delayed the product's sale before the Chinese Mid-Autumn Festival and resulted in a major loss of profits. Yeung contended that "smaller business just cannot survive." "It's because government has become an extra burden to the business," he said, "too many regulations."

Yeung's focus on business became a model of best practice for a number of Cantonese Protestant churches and institutions in the Bay Area. His small government politics enabled, he imagined, the ability for organizations to operate efficiently. But they also needed to live "ethically" in the "marketplace" synthesis of "business, education, and government," he insisted. "If I'm in business," he continued, "if I don't have good morals, especially Chinese going so often to China, I could have a girlfriend there or something. Then I end up hurting my business because I'm distracted or a lot of things that people would suspect, *Are you a legitimate*

Christian? You may cheat your wife; you may cheat me!"[17] Although Yeung did not explicitly reference local Bay Area Cantonese Protestant scandals, several other interviewees noted that the 1990s and 2000s was a time of tremendous institutional restructuring. Some staff members at one organization described what they called a "great earthquake" they experienced in 1995, when two staff members attempted to make everything "subservient to foreign missions" by shutting down the organization's various local missions and publication departments. These actions resulted in the resignation of the entire board and the dismissal of the entire staff, as well as an institutional split in which the staff members who were more radical about "foreign missions" broke off to start another organization while the original organization underwent a painful restructuring process.[18] This crisis was not an isolated incident: another high-profile organization had originally worked with staff split between two institutional headquarters locations, only to experience what a staff member called "chaos" when staff from these two sites disagreed.[19]

And then there were the sex scandals.[20] The most prominent and publicly discussed one concerned CCS, BACBC's school. In 1994 and 1995, the school's founder, Pastor Louis Lightfoot, was credibly accused of inappropriately touching the students and fled to Kentucky to escape investigation. Quen had to clean up the mess. He told me that the real problem was that the church had been overly structured around Lightfoot's magnetic personality.[21] Under Quen, BACBC restructured the balance of power in the church and the school. In so doing, what emerged was a leadership model that operated on the principles of shared responsibility and business accountability. In 2011 and 2012, this model was touted as best practice at leadership summits organized by none other than Proposition 8's Hak-Shing William Tam. Tam said that the main problem he saw in the "Chinese church" was that organizational leadership was often concentrated in a single leader. As he said in our interview of the church that he attended, "I want Christian leaders now to think big and have a higher capacity of accepting challenges, new leaders, new ideas, so that we can advance. The reason why this church is that big is because we have team leadership. We don't have one leader and call all the shots, everybody admiring you. It's not the way to go."[22] Tam's summits, which were released as a set of twelve DVDs, also included speeches from family psychologist Dr. Melvin Wong, financial adviser Lam Sau Wing, writer Cecilia Yau, and Prince of Peace's Kenneth Yeung, with the main message advocating the decentralization of Cantonese Protestant leadership within their organizations.

Part of this vision also involved churches that could be economically self-sustaining. Yeung's business vision influenced one pastor in San Jose, Rev. Abraham Poon, to transform his congregational structure. Poon told me that he met Yeung on an airplane in the 1970s from Hong Kong to Calgary, when they both first moved to North America. By the 1990s, Poon had himself become a prominent Cantonese Protestant pastor through his work at the San Jose Christian Alliance Church (SJCAC); he was also well spoken in English and Mandarin.[23] He said that he felt Yeung's influence especially in his convictions that good business practices should shape every organization. In 2005, this vision led SJCAC to take on the project of Living Stones Village (LSV) in which they attempted to transform an orphanage in Guangxi Province in the People's Republic of China into a "self-sustaining" operation. Buying up eighty acres of land, LSV's orphanage turned into a plan for an entire village composed of a business strip of twenty stores, a local bilingual school with community arts courses, and a church, the proceeds of which would feed back into the orphanage's operations. This philosophy of self-sustenance in turn fed back into the church itself. Poon called together a symposium called Vision 2020 to "bring the church into the community," inviting business leaders to teach his church and others in attendance how to become "Christian businesses." Poon explained, "I think the days for full-time ministers is over; it should be believers, and I think everybody should have a full-time job." Poon then saw his vision through. He remodeled his own church's structure after LSV to incorporate a "for-profit" preschool and Chinese school. In turn, Poon then changed his day job scope from the work of pastoral ministry to fundraising for LSV.[24]

Yeung's business model also inspired Chinese Christian Herald Crusades (CCHC) to turn itself into an economically self-sustaining organization. The story goes right back to the home congregation that has been in the background of this Bay Area revivalist narrative in chapter 2, Cumberland Presbyterian Chinese Church. In 1989, Cumberland's mission pastor, Susanna Lau, began making concerted efforts in San Francisco's Chinatown to formulate a local evangelical "holistic" mission based on her doctoral studies at Fuller Theological Seminary.[25]

Her efforts attracted CCHC, a Cantonese Protestant social services organization that was based solely at the time in New York City, to open a San Francisco branch on Cumberland premises. With that also came a local version of their free newspaper, *Herald Monthly*, for which Lau organized a distribution circuit through various Cantonese Protestant churches and a local board, including radio host David Pang and family values activist Hak-Shing William Tam, that would tailor its contents to Bay Area issues.

As CCHC's operations expanded, the organization sought to engage in Cantonese radio too. That effort came into play in 1998 when the chief executive officer of the United Commercial Bank, Lam Sau Wing, took early retirement at the age of forty-five and joined CCHC's planning committee.[26] Lam tapped Pang and Tam to run the radio ministry. Pang told me that this show was different from his secular one. "At first, we thought there were some things on my radio show that we thought that we could not say," he said, "because at the end of the day, I was a working staff there." Unlike Pang's secular show, CCHC's show, titled *Conversations at Eight O'Clock Sharp*, ran with an explicitly Christian program that tackled various topics every day: health on Mondays, family on Tuesdays, finances on Wednesdays, and social issues on Thursdays. Interestingly, these themes were exactly the same ones covered on the "everyday life" issues on Pang's secular show, but the difference was that they could speak explicitly on the CCHC venue about faith.[27]

Just before I came to the Bay Area to do research, CCHC also went the self-sustaining route, again under Lam's executive directorship. Closing its San Francisco office, CCHC established a more permanent place in 2010 on a new property in Oakland's Chinatown on Eighth Avenue. Speaking in a spring 2011 promotional video, Lam attributed these property purchases—in words not unlike Chanson Lau, Steve Quen, Robin Hom, Kenneth Yeung, and Abraham Poon—to divine guidance:

> Even though CCHC has been in the Bay Area for the last almost twenty years, it has always been renting properties, not purchasing property. I had this very deep feeling in my heart that God will gift a place for us. Last March when we signed the contract, we could never have imagined this because we did not even have $500,000 to buy it. But we knew that this was the place that God had gifted to us,

so we knew that God would take care of it, so with faith, we signed the contract and then we began to fundraise.

By November 19, 2010, the doors of CCHC opened. In a promotional video, Lam said, "Seven months ago, we did not imagine it would go so smoothly that we could use cash to buy this place." These permanent facilities have afforded CCHC a site from which to build their Herald Music ministry, their radio show, their tutorial programs, their local evangelism training courses, and a cancer care outreach in which lay ministers are trained to visit cancer patients throughout the Bay Area. All of these ministries require only about a $700,000 annual budget due to the heavy flow of volunteers.[28] It is sustained in turn by the business elements of this ministry: a Hong Kong–style Chinese bakery adjacent to the new CCHC premises called Bread of Life Bakery, with Hong Kong pastry chef Chu Chun Wing at the helm making Hong Kong–style buns and "world class" egg tarts. By the time I was doing my research, this bakery had expanded into venues in San Francisco Chinatown's Portsmouth Square and in the heavily Chinese American–populated Richmond District, though recent reports reveal that it has unfortunately pulled back severely from its operations.[29] The egg tarts really were delicious.

The vision of Bay Area civil society that emerges from these stories is economistic on two levels. It appears that two dynamics were at play both within and surrounding Cantonese Protestant churches and institutions in the 1990s. Within the church, there was already a drive for institutional restructuring due to the advent of scandal. Influential Cantonese Protestants, such as Kenneth Yeung, Lam Sau Wing, David Pang, and Hak-Shing William Tam, laid the groundwork for a business transformation of these institutions, with their emphases on leadership teamwork and economic self-sustainability. These transformations were well timed for a second dynamic, which seemed to be a shift in urban planning philosophy in the Bay Area. Those shifts had something to do with the dream of the Pacific Rim. Milpitas Square, for example, was an explicit attempt to use Asian businesses to ratchet up the city's economy. But in so doing, churches and organizations were well poised to become legible to those city governments—and indeed, in some cases, at larger scales too—emphasizing their economic contribution in private sector revitalization, academic excellence, and volunteer services. Theologically, Cantonese

Protestant institutions in the Bay Area might be said to have undergone a market translation in the 1990s and 2000s. God was still in the picture—very prominently, in fact. But the church was no longer simply a revivalist space, quite unlike the first transformation in the 1970s. It was also a site of best market practice sustained by the divine and legitimized by their moral integrity, situated in a Pacific Rim society where that was the only way they were legible enough to secure property purchases anyway.

"A DIFFERENT KIND OF CHURCH": SOCIAL WORK IN METRO VANCOUVER

In Vancouver, a question that kept coming up in my interviews was whether the historically revivalist organization Chinese Christian Mission (CCM) Canada had more or less replicated the United Chinese Community Enrichment Services Society (SUCCESS) in a "Christian" way.

It was a good question, largely because most of the founders of SUCCESS in 1973 were also Christian, of the Cantonese Protestant variety. In 1977, SUCCESS hired Angela Kan, a Hong Kong social worker who was also Cantonese Protestant, who was very successful in obtaining public and private funding for migrant settlement programs at the time, especially Vietnamese refugees. In 1987, Lilian To—another Cantonese Protestant—succeeded Kan. *Chinatown News* praised the move as one that would expand SUCCESS's services to include "preventive and counseling programs to help immigrants make adjustments in Canadian society," including "marital and peer counseling, family education, citizenship awareness and seniors visiting seniors," as well as a "street youth centre" and anti-racist programming.[30]

SUCCESS was not a faith-based organization. Still, it had its miracle stories. David Lam, a Christian real estate businessman and lieutenant-governor of British Columbia, was one of SUCCESS's earliest donors.[31] He recalled in one of SUCCESS's commemorative booklets that the organization was once approaching dire financial straits. Its founder, Lilian To, also a Cantonese Protestant, "started to cry," he wrote, "for all those new immigrants who needed the helping hand of SUCCESS." Lam then gathered a sum that "was in fact larger than all my savings," she testified. "Miraculously, I made enough money to donate to SUCCESS and the Chinese Cultural Centre in the end. And what I earned after that far exceeded what I could imagine. I knew it was all for God's bounty."[32]

But the point was that as personally religious as Lilian To, David Lam, and Angela Kan might have been, SUCCESS itself was not faith based. When I was doing my research in 2011 and 2012, the chief executive officer of SUCCESS was Thomas Tam. He was also a Cantonese Protestant. He emphasized to me, "SUCCESS is not a partisan or religious organization. It's a social service organization. So we are very careful not to give the public the impression that we are affiliated with any certain religion or any political party." He stressed to me that they had to preserve their "neutrality" because SUCCESS's staff and clientele represented a diversity of religions, ethnicities, and partisan loyalties. What was Christian—and specifically Cantonese Protestant—about it was incidental, he explained. It was more that there was an outsized representation of Christians among social workers in Hong Kong, he said, and in the 1970s and 1980s, they were in "high demand" in Canada. "And we got ten points in the immigration process," he said, referring to the "point scale" that Canadian immigration authorities used to score its applicants. "So social worker among the professions gets a higher score. So it's very easy to come here."[33]

The question was whether there could be a version of SUCCESS that could be explicitly faith based. That was what the board members of CCM Canada began to imagine for themselves in the 1990s. CCM Canada was the Canadian branch of its parent revivalist mission agency founded by Rev. Thomas Wang—the same one who had later spearheaded the American Return to God Prayer Movement in the mid-2000s—and headquartered in California. But the Canada outfit, it turns out, had quite a bit of autonomy.

In the late 1990s, one of CCM Canada's board members was Rev. Edwin Kong, the senior pastor at Vancouver's Christ Church of Canada. He told me that he was frustrated that his pastoral duties did not include community engagement. During a sabbatical, he reflected on "how the church should go into the community and how SUCCESS has inspired me."[34] Then, in 1999, Kong learned there was space to try some of his new ideas out. The City of Burnaby had just approved the plans to build Crystal Mall, an Asian shopping center, on a site that had been previously zoned for an unsuccessful community center.[35] In October

1999, Kong, his church's architect, Kingsley Lo, and CCM Canada's lawyer, William Lim, proposed to the city that the community center, which was subsequently incorporated in the plans for the mall, be rezoned as a "House of Worship."[36] They met with immediate resistance. The neighbors alleged that a church would be a dead spot in the mall because it would be vacant during the weekdays. Kong was ready with a reply. At a public hearing in November, he said that CCM was a "non-traditional church" that "will hold worship services during the week instead of the usual Sundays" and would "also run many programs that will seek to meet the spiritual and social needs of the general population in the Lower Mainland," including a "seniors center, a youth center, women center, counseling service, etc." that would be "readily accessible to the public by transits, by vehicle, or walking distance." He went further. Most planning models, he said, "push churches to the edge of cities to expand." By contrast, CCM's proposal to build its facilities in a mall represented innovative "21st Century city planning" that "will set a precedent model for other N.A. [North American] cities."[37] He then produced 47 individual letters in support of the application (and 3 opposed), a supportive petition with a total of 578 individual signatures (and one opposed with 10 signatures). Fifteen Burnaby residents, Crystal Mall shopkeepers, and CCM representatives also spoke in person in favor of the project.

And so it was that the City of Burnaby approved CCM Canada's application to be a "church" in Crystal Mall.[38] CCM Canada then made a few bold changes. A new mission statement came into play: "Bringing the church into the world, and bringing the world into the church." They hired the former head of SUCCESS, Angela Kan, as their new executive director. They invited the Hong Kong grassroots ministry pioneer Rev. Lo Lung Kwong (see chapter 2) to speak on how the church could practice "social concern" in the secular public sphere more effectively. These activities shifted CCM Canada from a model of evangelism that was based, in Kong's words, on "proselytizing, turning the world off." Now CCM Canada would "do what the community needs" as a form of "local mission." They enacted an emergency social services program that distributed earthquake kits. They started a youth ministry to train young leaders. They launched a women's group, a dance club, a children's day camp, activities for the elderly, art clubs, a cancer care and brain injury support group, a counseling center, and various other "interest groups."[39]

It was a supermarket model, Kong told me. "You go to the Bay," he said, referencing the Hudson's Bay Company department store, "they have everything. You go to Superstore, they have everything. We should be sensitive to the need of the society and tap the resources from the Christian community, according to the needs. . . . Whatever resources we can tap, then we offer, and we do our best."[40] Kan agreed. For her, the difference between her old and new places of employment lay in whether someone needed a service or a community: "SUCCESS: oh, you know, finding employment? Find SUCCESS la. Don't know English? Find SUCCESS. If CCM can say, 'Oh, you have needs, if you are lonely, you're sick, find CCM, someone will help you, someone will care for you'—that's what we want to do, so we interact with this society, and another service is counseling." A faith-based organization, she elaborated, could evangelize as a form of care, whereas a secular one could not. "Because of professional ethics," she said, "I cannot say, 'I'm a Christian. Do you want me to pray for you?'" or that "Christian teaching's biggest message is forgiveness," even though "each of us have many baggage, maybe you hurt other people or other people hurt you" in the context of "parents-children relationships, broken for many decades that they have a cold war at that time, or husband and wife, all those, like infidelity and things."[41]

A new narrative emerged at the time among Cantonese Protestants in Vancouver that their own faith-based organizations, and even churches, could sometimes deliver better services than SUCCESS. There was some of the revivalist story about how public funding limits what an institution can do. One CCM Canada staff member told me that SUCCESS was too reliant on government money. As a result—at least according to this respondent—its department for home "visitation" had been cut as well as its "cancer care department."[42] Those departments, she said, moved over to CCM Canada. At Ambassadors for Christ (AFC), a staff member said, "We do academic consultation"—a student tutoring service—"because SUCCESS does not have a department like that." In fact, AFC was the go-to, he said, for anything involving students, even for SUCCESS, he claimed. If there was a settlement case and students were involved, AFC would get a call from SUCCESS. "If I remember rightly," he said, "we are the only nonprofit organization that does this."[43]

Some actual church congregations—the traditional kind, as opposed to CCM Canada's "nontraditional" format—also tried to get involved in social services. Kong cited the North Shore Pacific Grace Church's community center as a direct inspiration for the work of CCM. Its founder, Rev. Abraham Lau, said to me, "I began a center to hope to serve this society. Our ultimate goal was still evangelism; that was what we wanted to do. Some people there didn't know what was going on, but the leaders, we want to build up the church."[44] At another church, Vancouver Chinese Evangelical Free Church, Rev. Edward Lee told me that because of where they were—a former gas station on the eastern fringe of Vancouver—the Cantonese-dominant church had to minister to the neighborhood, which he said was mostly Mandarin speaking. "Maybe it's God who planted us there," he said. "We don't know."[45] So too, Angela Kan's own home congregation, Lord's Grace Church, experienced a similar shift. In 2000, they hired Rev. Paul Chan, who was trained as an urban missiologist at Eastern Baptist Seminary. He had also served as a former associate pastor in a downtown church in Vancouver, First Baptist Church, where (as he told me) he had been the first chair of their urban mission consultation in 1999.[46] When he got to Lord's Grace Church, he issued a "Senior Pastor's Dream" to be "committed geographically" to its local Vancouver neighborhood, Kitsilano, even though, as his deacon board chair Walter Wong noted at the time, the demographics there were not predominantly Chinese.[47] Chan and Wong began a "community witnessing department" in the Chinese congregation that hosted neighborhood dinners and movie nights for their non-Chinese neighbors, setting up a large screen in the church in 2010 for neighborhood broadcasts of Vancouver's Winter Olympics.[48]

Even the Vancouver Chinese Evangelical Ministerial Fellowship (VCEMF)—the very same pastors' association that some Cantonese Protestants claimed was apolitical and apathetic—eventually changed. Under the leadership of Rev. James Ip and Rev. Wayne Lo, VCEMF took on distinctively social engagement initiatives from 2010 to 2012. Ip told me that VCEMF historically followed the conventions of the "old pastors" by caring for fellow Chinese clergy's "spiritual health." He then cited Jesus's command to be "salt and light" and a "city on a hill" (Matthew 5:13–16) and said that VCEMF needed to extend that care toward "social concern," though he clarified that he did not mean to politicize the pastors or tell them how to vote.[49]

Instead, one area of focus for VCEMF was mobilizing young people. There was, some of my interviewees told me, a Cantonese-speaking ministry at the University of British Columbia and Simon Fraser University called the Church Revival Youth (CRY) Network. Their mission, one of their pastoral leaders told me, was to pray for the breakdown of "spiritual strongholds" of emotional, moral, psychological, and spiritual "bondage," which means "we're not just praying for local churches, but we're praying for the larger society, for universities, the campuses, for the city's welfare, because our vision is much larger than one or two churches; it's about Greater Vancouver, and we want to see God's kingdom on earth as it is in heaven."[50] One of these "strongholds," which VCEMF and the CRY Network identified, was the expansion of Edgewater Casino in downtown Vancouver. Ip was also a member of the Vancouver Not Vegas coalition, which opposed this building project. He told me that he was the only pastoral representative of the Chinese Christian community at the city's public hearing. He was also a former urban planner in Hong Kong. Shoring up his professional and community credentials, he said that he told the city that the expansion of the casino would spread crime and corrupt the morals of young people. After the meeting, he got the CRY Network involved. He knew that one activity that the CRY Network did was to go on "prayer walks" to bless university campuses in Vancouver. And so it was that the CRY Network came out to city hall the next time Ip was there for yet another hearing.[51] Due to exam season, the numbers were low, CRY Network representatives told me, but the important thing for them was that they were there.[52]

It is with this context that VCEMF found themselves offended, astonished even, that they and the Cantonese Protestants they claimed to represent were still seen as illegible in some quarters of Vancouver civil society. Around the time my research started in 2011, the religion and diversity beat reporter for the *Vancouver Sun*, Douglas Todd, wrote a piece on "Chinese Christians" and Chinese New Year. He was curious about how they had picked up the "common habits of Western society" while integrating Buddhist traditions whenever they celebrated Chinese New Year. He spoke with Langara College instructor Li Yu, who had argued in a book chapter on Chinese Christians in *Asian Religions in British Columbia* that Christianity deserved to be considered a

"Chinese religion." Li told him, "The Chinese churches strengthen people's original identity, not their Canadian identity. Whether that is good or not depends on how you see it."[53]

VCEMF wrote a scathing response that was printed on Todd's blog *The Search*. They retorted that many members of Chinese churches "participate actively in conferences and seminars together with their counterparts of mainstream churches." They also serve as "dedicated volunteers" in Canadian civil society and state institutions, they wrote, and they "watch and follow NHL hockey games on a regular basis," cheered for the Canadian teams during the 2010 Winter Olympics, celebrate Christmas "like mainstream citizens celebrate that season, buying gifts, decorating their homes, donating to charity organizations and sharing with the less fortunate," and have transcended their English-language barriers by developing "personal friendships with Canadians of other ethnic groups through sports, cooking, gardening, parenting, charity, and political activities." VCEMF was aghast that they had been portrayed, as they said, as "mono-cultural." Chinese Christians in Vancouver, they further pressed the point, "accept the fact that Canada is already a multicultural society and that they will do their part for the well-being of the society in their different capacities in it."[54]

VCEMF had taken Todd's article as a betrayal. Cantonese Protestants were already integrated into Vancouver's civil society, they were saying, since the 1970s when SUCCESS started. It was how they were originally legible in Canadian civil society, and in the 1990s and 2000s, Cantonese Protestant churches, missions agencies, and interchurch networks also reoriented themselves for social services after the model laid out by SUCCESS, with some degree of success themselves. But still, Todd's article portrayed them, with Li's help, as an ethnic ghetto.

That, I suggest, said something about the problems of the Pacific Rim dream in Vancouver. Certainly, communities like those of Cantonese Protestants contributed to the mosaic of multiculturalism that made up the city and its suburbs. But at the end of the day, what being multicultural also meant was that each community was seen as taking care of their own, even if SUCCESS offered a range of services, churches reached out to their neighborhoods, VCEMF helped stop casino expansion, and CCM Canada called itself a "nontraditional" church. That they were not portrayed as legible contributors to Vancouver's civil society probably says more about Vancouver and the narratives of the Pacific Rim that shape the city than them. They were themselves so far beyond the question of whether to integrate and to serve the community that they were in fact fighting about how to do it, with or without public funding.

BREAKTHROUGH OR THE NARROW ROAD? CRITIQUING THE POST-HANDOVER HONG KONG STATE

If Cantonese Protestant legibility required—at least from the perspective of how Cantonese Protestants read the civil societies they lived in—market integration in the Bay Area and social service delivery in Vancouver, then in Hong Kong after the 1997 handover, the issue at hand was whether Protestant churches and organizations should collaborate with the city's government. This question was, I learned during my 2012 fieldwork, an existential one. The Hong Kong government was technically the administration of the city as a Special Administrative Region (SAR) of the PRC, constitutionally existing in a "one country, two systems" framework with the mainland. It put the city in an interesting position vis-à-vis the dream of the Pacific Rim, as it was at once part of the transpacific integration in its place as a cosmopolitan city, but questions could now be raised about whether working with its government meant in some way having to collaborate with a Chinese party-state that had its own designs for the city's international reputation. Could Cantonese Protestants work with such a system that was in fact becoming increasing aligned with the PRC and still uphold democratic principles?

Perhaps no institution illustrates how dramatic this question has become than the saga of Breakthrough Youth Ministries and its Youth Village near the top of the Sha Tin hills in Hong Kong. Breakthrough had come to prominence in 1970s Hong Kong civil society under the leadership of the late Josephine So Yan Pui, with events like the Golden Jubilee incident galvanizing Protestant clergy activism at the time. When So died in 1981, Breakthrough's new leader was Dr. Philemon Choi Yuen-wan.

Choi made his mark on the organization by deciding, well before the 1997 handover, to stay in Hong Kong. In fact, shortly after the United Kingdom and the PRC signed the 1984 Joint Declaration returning Hong Kong to Chinese sovereignty in 1997, Breakthrough, under

Choi's direction, purchased property, their outlet on Kowloon's Jordan Street that has served as a counseling center. In the early 1990s, they bought property again, this time for the Youth Village. "The reason why the Youth Village was even undertaken was as a symbol, as a sign, at a time of growing unease and fear in Hong Kong about 1997," Breakthrough's architect Freeman Chan said to me in an interview. Choi's task was, in Chan's words, "to put a line in the sand that we will not cross. That line is, we will not leave Hong Kong."

Trying to get land in Hong Kong put Breakthrough in touch with the state. That formal process began in the 1991, when Hong Kong was still under British rule. At that time, Breakthrough applied to purchase land in Sha Tin in the New Territories. The application reached the desk of the chief secretary, Sir David Ford. Chan remembers that Ford was impressed by the youth work done by Breakthrough. He "put his informal stamp of approval on it," Chan recalled, writing a private letter to commend Philemon Choi for his good work. Ford also carbon copied this note to all of the government departments to expedite his application.[55] "That's how things work in government," Chan said. "It was a learning curve for me."

Getting the site for the Youth Village meant that Breakthrough could expand its services. Prior to the Youth Village, Breakthrough had operated as an organization independent of the government. Its focus had been on its counseling services, youth programs, and a monthly magazine. With a larger parcel of land, Chan designed a "youth village" that could serve as a campground in which pilot projects for disadvantaged youth in Hong Kong could be developed to help the government make policy around youth and poverty. Chan completed the project in 1996, together with a chapel without pews in which a church for disabled persons called the Ark Community met.[56]

In 1997, Hong Kong became an SAR of the PRC. Breakthrough was still in touch with the state, but it was a new government. Their main contact became the new chief executive (CE), businessman Tung Chee Hwa. Like Ford, Tung was also impressed with Breakthrough's youth work when he visited the Youth Village in 1998. In fact, the *South China Morning Post* reported that Tung "was impressed by the participants' awareness of topical issues." He also "watched youngsters practicing rock climbing, an activity aimed at nurturing self-confidence and team spirit among participants," and "toured the Xyber Café in the village and saw young people learning to communicate on the Internet."[57]

That is the story of how Philemon Choi found himself working with the SAR government. In 1998, Tung appointed Choi to be commissioner for youth. He told me that from there he became a member of the Central Policy Unit, a group representing economic and social sectors of Hong Kong society to examine and propose government policies. Choi also joined some nine committees concerning poverty, youth, and childhood. All of this activity made Choi susceptible to accusations that he had actually become a member of the state. In an interview, Choi made sure I understood which side he was actually on, that he was taking a "prophetic stance" as an unpaid volunteer working with the government:

> I am not in the government structure. I am someone who's inside making a statement, and they know where I come from. People say, "Even Tung Chee Hwa you will help!" My response is, of course, I believe God has appointed these government officials and put them in charge, and if he's willing to listen to someone who works with young people, then so be it. But I will never take his pay, I will never get his pay. If I get paid from government, I become one of them.[58]

And indeed, some of Choi's policies led to progressive reform on education and employment among youth. In 2001, Choi conducted studies on unemployed and "nonengaged" youth ("NEY," as he called them). Working with research teams from the Chinese University of Hong Kong and Hong Kong Polytechnic University, the project, titled "Spread Your Wings," concluded that the causes of NEY unemployment usually came down to mental health and family dysfunction and that these factors could be ameliorated by building up trade skills. In response, Choi started six Youth Colleges to train NEY in creative design, hip-hop dancing, hairdressing, and cooking. He also became chair of politician Henry Tang's Commission on Poverty's subcommittee on adolescence and children, where he proposed a Child Development Fund in 2004. The scheme worked through a "targeted savings" clause in which every family would be obligated to save HK$200 monthly for their child. Those savings would be matched by the government. Youth who successfully saved for two years would be rewarded with a $3,000 bonus. The money would incentivize new business start-ups. Each young person would also receive one-to-one mentoring over two years to discern a career path. Those mentors were usually Protestant Christians.[59]

Breakthrough Youth Village became the site of many a pilot project. They researched youth civic engagement, gambling, pornography usage, romantic lives, literacy, video and online gaming, social media usage, occult practices, friendship networks, family relationships, interpersonal skills, and preferred college majors.[60] They also relaunched *Breakazine*, a periodical that attempted to tap into what its editor Pakkin Leung called the "individual and ego-centric narrative" of its readers.[61]

For project implementation, Choi organized the Hong Kong Church Network for the Poor (HKCNP). With business consultant Susanna Hui at the helm, HKCNP gathered the three interchurch bodies—the Hong Kong Christian Union, the Hong Kong Church Renewal Movement, and the Hong Kong Christian Council (HKCC)—along with some nineteen directors from a variety of faith-based organizations to implement Breakthrough's ideas. The Child Development Fund, for example, used the HKCNP to source its mentorship program. HKCNP's hallmark was the Love Food Bank. Government welfare, Hui told me, lasted only six weeks. The Love Food Bank extended it to three months. It allowed for churches to "care for the individual," Hui added, using "food as a means to get a person into the church doors" to receive this care.[62]

Breakthrough also influenced other organizations that were not under its umbrella. Shirley Loo, the longtime chief editor for *Breakthrough Magazine* in the 1990s, told me that Breakthrough was her "Shaolin forest." In 2001, she launched Family Heartware, a publication outlet for her books on family, parenting, and marriage with the central theological focus that "women are good, whole, and beautiful," capable of "dreaming for God" without needing to despise their self-image or to find their wholeness solely in motherhood. Connecting with two other pastors' wives, Loo developed the Family Development Foundation in 2005, a small organization from which Loo speaks at schools on youth issues and holds courses on mental illness and women's dignity.

What was interesting was the way Loo, like Choi, had been drawn into government work. She told me that she was asked in the late 1990s to "do a small favor" to promote the Independent Commission Against Corruption. She said that from that point, she was drawn into several government committees, including the Action Committee Against Narcotics (ACAN), the Education Resource Committee, the Social Welfare Department Family Life Education Resource Development Centre, the Quality Education Fund, and the School Site Allocation Committee. She also became part of Henry Tang's Family Council, an umbrella gathering of the Commissions on Youth, Women, and the Elderly. Like Choi, her involvement in these committees, she clarified, did not make her part of the system. She told me that she instead presents a "family voice" that stems from her spiritual practice, which is drawn from a devotional called *Time with Abba* that she says gives her a "clear mind." She was living her "calling," she said, to the "secular world," which meant that she often sought to link social ills with systemic family problems. The result was that she sometimes felt marginalized in these meetings, but she saw herself as an effective advocate too. She recalled that after a long debate, ACAN changed the Cantonese description of illicit drugs from "endangering substances" to "toxic substances," highlighting the "poison" of illicit drugs in their damage to bodies and families.[63]

The Breakthrough model positioned Protestant organization leaders as internal critics to Hong Kong's government system. It was also not the only game in town, though even its critics had to admit that Breakthrough had paved the way for their critique too. The opponents to Breakthrough's state-centric model tended to coalesce around an organization called the Hong Kong Christian Institute (HKCI), which was founded in 1988 by the trans-denominational HKCC then-chair Rev. Kwok Nai Wang. HKCI's board also featured Protestants in the revivalist camp, such as the China Graduate School of Theology's Dr. Carver Yu, on its board. In its early days, it even collaborated with Breakthrough. As a staff member at Breakthrough told me, HKCI was much more focused on "social concern" issues than Breakthrough, which was good because "your whole organization has an engine of its own."[64] Similarly, one staff member at an organization with revivalist roots told me that the difference of theologies did not place either him or his organization in diametrical opposition to HKCI or any ecumenical organization, for that matter. "I actually know HKCI very well," he said, "and I know where their predicament is; they can't be too vague on their position [about policy issues], but there needs to be balance, but they need to participate in civic action, and they have, and I think that's a good thing."[65] There was also the example of the Hong Kong Church Renewal Movement, which Kwok himself founded in 1985. In 2000, its head became Rev. Wu Chi Wai, and its focus turned from the original practice of neighborhood social engagement toward developing pastoral leaders within the church, a "not very obvious" social engagement, as Wu put it.[66] But that was also the point. Its purview now also included developing relationships with those in the Breakthrough model, especially through the HKCNP.

The trick was to bring Protestants of the Breakthrough model and the HKCI practice together. In September 1987, some in the revivalist tradition founded the *Christian Times*. They pulled the Hong Kong newspaper *Sing Tao Daily*'s managing editor Lee Kam Hung in as their volunteer editor and flanked him with Carver Yu as the managing editor. In the 1990s, the *Christian Times* provided a space for pastors and the church to discuss how to help the church during what they called the "immigration trend," the large-scale immigration of church pastors and leaders to metropolises in the Pacific Rim leading up to 1997.

In an interview, Lee Kam Hung described the *Christian Times* as a unique publication, founded by revivalists but not "evangelistic" in its aims. Instead, the paper walked a "narrow road," he said. It was a forum for discussing issues like "social justice," "the problems that the church must handle," "politics," and "a lot of ethical and moral issues." The approach of the newspaper was to allow for what he called a "plurality of voices." As he put it,

> We have elevated a platform: in the Chinese church, we are the one and only place that truly has different voices, including those that the church likes to hear and those that the church does not like to hear, those that the church can accept, and those that the church probably can't accept—must force itself to accept—those voices, they all appear here. So you will seldom see all of those people talking with each other, and yet all of them can write here in the *Christian Times*. This is the unique thing. Usually, as far as the positions are from each other, they will never meet.[67]

In the 2000s, those contrasts became magnified with the sexuality debates. Those in the Breakthrough model may have advocated for the family in the government. But organizations like HKCI moved into coordinating roles to advocate for social justice for marginalized grassroots populations, including sex workers, sexual minorities, and migrant workers, and to organize demonstrations for democracy in Hong Kong. The *Christian Times* brought them into conversation.

When Kwok Nai Wang retired in 2000, his successor was a feminist theologian from Chung Chi Divinity School, Rose Wu Lo Sai. Wu had been a prominent figure in Hong Kong's feminist liberation movement. In the 1990s, she founded the Hong Kong Women's Christian Council and the Christian queer movement. As HKCI's general secretary at the time of research in 2012, Fan Lap Hin, explained to me, Wu's time at HKCI shifted the organization toward grassroots social movements. "She is a feminist," he said, "so in sexual minority rights and human rights, it got stronger. HKCI at that time became a site for identity politics. . . . We got more involved in civil society. We started to run together with the weakest in society and also got involved with civic issues." Because of this work with sexual minorities, Wu and HKCI were often criticized by STL and HKSCS. As Fan noted, they were often the first two names on their "pro-gay" PowerPoint slides.[68] Wu herself was careful not to frame her critics as enemies. She simply highlighted her ideological differences with them. "Their democracy is very different," she said to me. "I think we have to be careful about this. They talk about the good of the family. They add some things about economics, to decrease tax. In fact, the tax is the problem. They want it so that some people don't want to pay tax. So you see, it's very middle class. This is a middle-class agenda." She too described her long-standing work as "democracy as a way of life," which necessarily challenged undemocratically structured systems.[69] HKCI in turn promoted this theology by holding classes, publishing books and a monthly journal, and giving talks at churches on social justice, human rights, and feminist solidarities.

One model for what HKCI did followed the theologian Raymond Fung Wai Man's argument that the Christian doctrine of sin is that the marginalized are "sinned against" by the political economic system.[70] HKCI attacked Hong Kong's policy structure that favored, at least in HKCI's analysis, property owners over against renters, temporary migrant workers, and sexual minorities. Siding with the economically marginalized created a coalition between HKCI's progressive Protestants and the Catholic Church's activism for the "right of abode," which referred to the constitutionally guaranteed right under Article 24 of the Basic Law to reside in and receive benefits from Hong Kong after working for seven years. Indeed, the retired Catholic bishop of Hong Kong, Joseph Cardinal Zen Ze-kiun, told me that the foremost social issue in Hong Kong was the right of abode. He said that the Hong Kong public had been misled by political propaganda about the depletion of resources in Hong Kong that would come about if the right of abode were to extend to migrant workers and persons in the PRC seeking family reunification with relatives in Hong Kong.[71]

Zen and his diocesan Justice and Peace Commission, led by human rights activist Jackie Hung Ling-Yu, worked with HKCI on right of abode. For Wu, HKCI's educational efforts in this regard formed a "minority dissenting voice" among Protestants in Hong Kong, who remained politically apathetic on this issue. "On domestic migrant workers," she said, "Hong Kong people think of them as 'others,' but in fact, they are two hundred thousand people serving some two hundred thousand families. At home, my mother also relies on an Indonesian domestic worker; that's why I can be at this interview!" Wu argued that because "we are becoming more globalized, a global village," migrant workers as "visitors" had the same rights as Hong Kong people when they were visitors in other places.[72] Her statements about Protestant political apathy were not unfounded. When I spoke to one high-level Protestant denominational leader, he said that these matters of secular legality did not require the church to take an absolute position, as these matters fell under the state's governance, not the church's.[73] Focus group members in Sha Tin also emphasized that unlike same-sex marriage, which "clearly" opposed Scriptural teaching, the right of abode was not a matter for Christian reflection.[74] While a focus group member in Tuen Mun observed that equal treatment under the law mandated that all who work in Hong Kong for seven years should be entitled to the right of abode, another respondent in the same group argued that this model could prove to be economically unsustainable.[75] As one focus group member in Kwun Tong expressed, this point about health benefits became abundantly clear to her when she was pregnant. She reasoned that domestic workers and mothers from China might take up more hospital beds, so it was not in her interest to support them.⁷⁶ Finally, most agreed that the right of abode was not an item for theological reflection. It was something for them to talk about solely as private citizens.

HKCI's willingness to take a minority stance within Hong Kong Protestantism, it must be emphasized, did not signal a separate political development from something like Breakthrough. It was more of a disagreement about what to do about the post-handover state. Directly contrasting the Breakthrough model, these groups argued that Christian independence from state power was necessary if the church were to speak directly about human dignity in a civil society whose policy structure constantly threatened to erode human rights. The word that they used to encapsulate this forceful speech was "truthfulness." It came up in an informal group conversation with one theology student who was writing a doctoral dissertation on the work of the German theologian Dietrich Bonhoeffer, who thought a great deal about what he called "telling the truth."⁷⁷ Some "friendships" really do affect "truthfulness," this member said to the group, in the sense that how one tells truth is altered based on one's subjective relationships. "Truthfulness" subsequently became the calling card for interviews and further group conversations with this group of people.⁷⁸

One church congregation that arguably embodied this kind of "truthful" theology was Senlok Christian Church in Shaukeiwan. Its pastor, Rev. Timothy Lam Kwok Cheung, told me that he was cognizant that various journalists have painted him as a "political" pastor with a "political church." He had "no interest in politics," he said, despite evidence that seemed to point otherwise. He showed me a window marquee outside his church that made an impassioned statement for pro-democratic Sinophone movements with large Chinese characters, making reference to democratic figures who were part of Sinophone popular consciousness in 2012. He also acknowledged that a variety of pro-democracy activists and political leaders attended his church, notably Kowloon West's Legislative Council member Raymond Wong Yuk Man, who had made a name for himself for his fiery political speeches, one time in 2008 even throwing bananas at CE Donald Tsang for reducing elderly pensions. Lam told me, "My church has political people. Yuk Man is very good, sitting in the back with his grandson. He doesn't do naughty things here. He is an ordinary brother."

Lam then clarified that he was not interested in politics, but he certainly was interested in policies. In 2012, he launched My Brother's Keeper. It was a forty-day campaign of solidarity with what he called "street sleepers" (Cantonese, *lousukze*). He said that he refused to call them "homeless" (Cantonese, *mougaaze*) because they still considered the places they were living with their fellow "street sleepers" their home. During this campaign, Lam slept nightly on the street with fellow street sleepers and ate congee with them. He also witnessed how the police searched the street sleepers three times in a given night and confiscated their belongings, ostensibly to clear the streets for cleaning. Lam wrote a letter of complaint to the police commissioner. He said that it led to an immediate change in police behavior when Lam was sleeping there.

Lam also discovered that Hong Kong's social work department had neglected street-sleeping individuals. He had developed a hospital visitation routine with an elderly, disabled street sleeper and was dismayed to learn that the hospital discharged him prior to the social work department assigning him a place to live. Lam's elderly friend found himself sleeping under a bridge without access to food for two days. Lam called the social work department, he said. He learned that the social worker required this paralyzed man to visit him twice a week in his office, and because the man did not have the access or ability to do so, he had been discharged. Lam told me, "These forty days have uncovered the injustices of policy. These professional social workers do nothing, and this is my example."[79]

Lam may have denied that he was interested in politics, but a group that called themselves Narrow Church were outspoken about their political interests. I met one of their members in an overpriced American-style coffee shop in a mall. He explained that he was a pastor, but his church was not a typical one. It was called Narrow Church, he said, after Jesus's dictum that the way is straight, the gate narrow.

Narrow Church's origins, my respondent told me, lay in a group of the Chinese University of Hong Kong's Chung Chi Divinity School graduates.[80] In 2009, they decided to protest an event called the Global Day of Prayer. The Global Day of Prayer was organized by Linda Ma, who is married to the evangelist Fredrick Ma Si Hung. They had attended another event also called the Global Day of Prayer in South Africa, that one led by a Bay Area revivalist they discovered to be their long-lost relative Jaeson Ma.[81] In 2005, the Hong Kong version was launched. The event featured the CE and regime officials leading large prayer gatherings of some three hundred churches and forty thousand Christians in two stadiums in Hong Kong.[82] The divinity students decided that the Global Day of Prayer was an act of church collusion with government officials and compromised the church's ability to act truthfully. They organized a Facebook event titled the Alliance for the Return to the Christian Spirit to protest the gatherings in 2009 and 2010.

My Narrow Church respondent then asked me if I had heard of the band called Hallelujah Get Out. I had not. It was a protest worship troupe, he explained, that had formed while they were protesting the demolition of a village called Tsoi Yuen Tsuen in the New Territories in 2011 to prepare for a high-speed light rail from Hong Kong to Shenzhen. Narrow Church formed their own worship band called Hallelujah Get Out and went to Tsoi Yuen Tsuen "every other day" in January 2010, my respondent said. "*Haaaa-leeee-luuu-jah GET OUT!*" the band would sing to the authorities as they moved from corner to corner within the town.[83] These acts proved controversial within Protestant circles at large and were widely discussed during my fieldwork. At a public lecture on "social concern" that I attended at a revivalist organization, I learned that one Tsoi Yuen Tsuen protester was denied baptism at a megachurch.[84]

As my respondent was describing these Narrow Church escapades, his church friends arrived. They held in their hands a *Ming Pao* newspaper, opened to a full-page statement that had been taken out by a number of pastors and theologians and signed with over eight hundred names. The context was the CE elections in March 2012. The situation surrounding the election was said to be "dangerous," as I heard it described in a church on my first Sunday of fieldwork, for two reasons. First, the candidacy of the politician generally thought to be favored to win, Henry Tang, had become mired in scandal. A few days before Tang filed his intention to run for CE, the news media had discovered that there was an "illegal structure" under his home, in the sense that he did not have a building permit for it. After a series of cagey responses from Tang as to how this basement could have gotten there without his knowing, his wife, Lisa Kuo Yu-chin, stepped forward at a press conference to say that it was she who had wanted to have that segment of their home built. He then said that he had not paid attention to the plans his wife had laid out because they were having "marital problems" at the time, which was further embarrassing because he was a publicly professing Protestant Christian who had worked on family issues in the Hong Kong government and had let his wife take the heat for him.[85] The public frenzy that these events created eventually lost Tang the favor of the Election Committee, which transferred its approval to the openly pro-Beijing candidate Leung Chun-ying, known more popularly as C. Y. Leung.

Second, the CE who was still in office before the March election, Donald Tsang, found himself embroiled in a corruption scandal. There were already troubling reports circulating in the news that he had been entangled in conflicts of interest with his close personal contacts with the very property tycoons whose power in Hong Kong he had enabled with his stated agenda to turn the city into an international financial center. He had been traveling in their private jets and yachts, the news stories said. Then, after all of that, was the grand revelation. He had been spotted sitting with organized crime members in a casino in Macau, another sign of conflict of interest but this time with the underworld.[86]

The statement spoke of the "anger and disappointment" about the conduct of the candidates in the CE elections. It then issued a cautionary warning for its readers not to act out of a feeling of "anger and helplessness" because "wrong choices at this moment will cause irreparable disasters in the future." Instead, it called on electors to be responsible to "public opinion," on candidates to return to the path of "honesty," and on Hong Kong society to remove the barriers to universal suffrage. Quoting the biblical words of the prophet Micah (6:8), the authors accused Hong Kong people at large of caving in to "greed" and "fragmentation" and demanded that they "do justice, love mercy, and walk humbly with your God."[87]

Thrusting the newspaper in our faces, my new friends, as they began describing themselves after a short time, decried what they felt was the statement's toothless prescriptions, as it failed in their view to analyze why Hong Kong politics had remained undemocratic since the 1997 handover. They explained that they were going to go home to plan a protest that would be a lot more "radical" than what they considered the tepid response of the eight hundred signatories in *Ming Pao*. I was invited, so we got on the train together. There was a television encased in the wall broadcasting the news. A cardinal in a red hat, the diocesan Hong Kong Bishop John Tong Hon, came on the screen. As he appeared on the news, I said to my new friends that that was "Tong Hon" on the screen. They looked, and so it was; they were impressed that even I knew who he was. We could not quite make out what he was saying, but I heard in Cantonese something to the effect of, "Let he who is without sin cast the first stone."[88] My friends told me to repeat what they thought I said. I did. They were upset.

As we arrived at one of the church members' home, I learned we were in charge of writing a prayer text that Christians could chant during the protest. A banner had already been prepared for the purpose; we were going to march the next day under the words, "我們憤怒了" (*ngo mun fan nou liu*, "We are pissed off!"). The news about Tong, though, led to some debate about how to write the prayer text and not only among the Narrow Church members in the room, who were eating takeout food and serving plum wine. It turns out that I had heard correctly, that Tong really had said, "Let he who is without sin cast the first stone," about Tsang, whom Tong described in the same press conference as a committed Roman Catholic. They decided to take after the imprecatory psalms in the Bible and use an expletive to "mouth curse" Tong.

After writing the text, they forwarded it to their ecumenical partners who were supposed to colead the pre-protest prayer rally. The phone began to ring nonstop. There were Catholics, they explained to me as the various calls came in (they were helping me with my research, they said), who objected to a description of their bishop with such rude language and threatened to pull out of the rally. There were also "evangelicals," they said, whose allegedly middle-class sensibilities were offended by Cantonese cuss words in a prayerful text. Heated words began to rise from the table, with some claiming that these objections arose from being tied to a church establishment that had too much institutional baggage. Then the whole group told me that I should interview all these other people to get a fuller picture of Christian political engagement in Hong Kong, especially those who took exception to Narrow Church. A number of the research connections I made in my time in Hong Kong can be traced to this dinner meeting. They seemed especially excited to connect me to those who objected to their antics. They also introduced me to the pleasures of plum wine, which caused me to hiccup. As they drove me back to the train station, one of them exclaimed from the back of the car, "Justin, you are drunk!"

It is the ire with which Narrow Church has critiqued those it deems "pro-government" collaborators with the state that has drawn the most controversy. One HKCC representative lamented the way in which he had been "demonized" by Narrow Church for his reluctance to critique the Hong Kong government.[89] Chung Chi Divinity School's dean, Rev. Lo Lung Kwong, exclaimed that Narrow Church's members were in fact his own divinity students, but they had taped a vulgar sign of protest on a toilet in his church's restroom. He observed that this "lack of respect" meant that even though he saw common points of dialogue with them, he was personally reluctant to engage them in conversation.[90] Breakthrough's Philemon Choi also became a target of these protests because of his relationships with high-ranking officials like former CE Tung Chee Hwa and the Family Council's Henry Tang. Choi said that they were "hypocrites" who did not pay attention to the policy action research that he was doing within the state to subvert its unjust policies from within.[91]

And yet, in this division between Breakthrough and Narrow Church, there was remarkable agreement. Even Choi had to admit that the post-handover state in Hong Kong—a contest in and of itself over the content of the dream of the Pacific Rim—was flawed at best and had to shore up its legitimacy by attending to the material needs of the city's population. The question was whether working within the structures of the state from within or opposing it from outside was the better approach. From both approaches, theologies also emerged, with the Breakthrough model adopting a posture of spiritual purity from within the system, while HKCI and Narrow Church took on the mantle of "truthfulness." But both theological approaches also revealed the real place of the church in Hong Kong society. They were all critics of the post-handover state, in one way or another, as it navigated Hong Kong's new place in the Pacific Rim, both in the international order and as a city under the undemocratic rule of Chinese sovereignty. The question was where they chose to launch their democratic critiques.

CONCLUSION: THE PACIFIC RIM AS PACIFIC WORLD

As I was in the later stages of working on this book manuscript, one venue at which I workshopped this work was the American Studies

Association. Outsiders to American studies may be forgiven for thinking that the field is dedicated to promoting the interests of the United States. For the most part, it is not. Instead, it is invested in a critique of what has come to be known, perhaps problematically, as American empire, which, broadly speaking, describes the emergence of the United States as a world power after World War II and the expansion of its power in reconstructing Europe, containing communism in Asia, and exerting a great deal of geopolitical influence in Latin America.[92]

The panel I was on focused on the Pacific dimensions of American empire. It brought together two speakers, Yale historian Alvita Akiboh and me. There seemed to be an ideological division between the two of us, at least on the surface. Akiboh spoke at length about her project on what she and others have called Pacific worlds, the emergence of Indigenous and local realities in the Pacific region that contest colonial and postcolonial structures.[93] She said that in her first-year course on the history of Pacific worlds, she has to tell students that they will not be studying the integration of Asians into the Americas, as the "Pacific Rim" is but one world in this region and often the most hegemonic one. I, on the other hand, talked precisely about the "Pacific Rim," as I told the story of the formation that has enabled people like the Cantonese Protestants I discuss in this book to move between Hong Kong and metropolitan areas like Vancouver and the Bay Area across the Pacific Ocean. For this, our moderator Judy Tzu-Chun Wu gently challenged me. The Pacific Rim, she pointed out, is often taken as one that silences Pacific worlds; why was I so invested in the concept? I replied that the Pacific Rim indeed does do that, but it also is the vehicle for the narratives I unfold about the Asians who move into American, Canadian, and Oceanic worlds as part of a very powerful dream about an integrated region between the Asia-Pacific and the Americas.

And yet, what I have shown in this chapter is that the Pacific Rim is also not one world. It is better described as an association of several worlds, each rooted in the various civil societies that are shot through with different imaginaries of what the Pacific Rim could be, what it means to integrate Asia and the Americas, and what material transformations would be entailed by such imaginations beginning especially in the 1990s and then carried forward into the 2000s. In these societies, Cantonese Protestants arguably had to change the way they do the theological work of articulating the place of God and the church in a secular society. Their orientation may have been shaped by revivalist practice, but ideological shifts in Pacific Rim societies required them, especially when purchasing property, to become newly legible. What this means is that there was also no overarching transpacific Cantonese Protestant bloc that I could detect. Cantonese Protestant communities and networks were far too busy vying for legibility in the societies where they lived to form something like that.

The question, then, is whether there is *any* cohesion to the Pacific Rim dream across the various secular societies that it encompasses. It is to that larger scope that I finally turn as we consider what Cantonese Protestants might show us as to how their own civil societies shape their theologies as they participate in secular democratic processes.

CHAPTER FIVE

The Fading Shadow of Tiananmen

Chinese Christians and Electoral Democracy

From whom do the kings of the earth collect duty and taxes—from their own sons or from others?
—Matthew 17:25

INTRODUCTION: THE WOUND OF HISTORY

As I was returning to the place I was staying in the Bay Area from a day of interviews in 2011, I received an urgent phone call from one of my respondents. I had spoken with this person about how some Christians in San Francisco and San Jose had liaised with student movement leaders from the Tiananmen Beijing Spring when they came to the United States in 1989. From April 15 to June 4 of that year, the democracy movement in Beijing had culminated in a series of demonstrations, occupations, hunger strikes, civil society education teach-ins, and even a rock concert tour on the central square named for the Gate of Heavenly Peace: Tiananmen. There was a violent crackdown on the protests in early June, ordered by hard-liners in the Chinese Communist Party (CCP). They were remembered with the name of the last day before the demonstrations were fully stamped out, 6/4.[1]

The Cantonese Protestants who spoke with me were not the only ones who remembered watching the vivid images of the protests and then the military crackdown on television. Scholars from the time as ideologically and disciplinarily diverse as Francis Fukuyama, Giorgio Agamben, and Richard Madsen (and for that matter, different even on the question of whether they even cared about China in any politically meaningful way) commented on how Tiananmen had interrupted the common story about liberal progress in the world—precisely the stuff that composes the dream of the Pacific Rim—by ending on the completely wrong note: in the tragedy of tanks, as opposed to an opening to a future of democratic coexistence.[2] It was also my first childhood memory. I was living in the Bay Area and just about to turn three. After the crackdowns, a song came out from Taiwan titled "The Wound of History," which commemorates the events on the square as a wound that, unhealed, is ready to explode in remembrance. It is still often sung at Tiananmen commemorations and calls for redress. I sang that song so much at home and at church that an uncle made me a cassette tape with it on loop, as if to say that my history began just as the Pacific Rim's was wounded.[3]

On the phone, my respondent apologized for not telling me the entire context of how to go about talking to people about Tiananmen, even though it was indeed very important to the Pacific Rim context in which they moved. I had written to a contact mentioned in the research interview with this person—on the advice of the interviewee, no less—and the message had sent him into a frenzy. He had apparently gone into business in the People's Republic of China, where mention of the incident is officially censored. From my email request for an interview, he had begun telling others in the Cantonese Protestant networks I was moving through that I was putting people into danger. My respondent clarified that she did not think I was endangering anyone, especially not her, and my conscience was clear too. My research, after all, was not about Tiananmen—it was about Cantonese Protestants and their engagements with Pacific Rim civil societies—and it only ever seemed to come up whenever I asked my interviewees how they became involved in politics. But this encounter made clear to me that Tiananmen was a sensitive topic, whether on this side of the Pacific or the other.

As I continued my research, I gained an unexpected insight. It struck me how many other pastors, church leaders, parachurch organizations, and businesspeople also found themselves attempting to break into the PRC market in the 1990s and 2000s. These activities sat awkwardly with all the buzz about Tiananmen just a few years before. They made me wonder whether this email recipient really had that much to worry about.

Relatedly, it also did not have to be the case that one had to have switched sides on the PRC to move away from the 6/4 moment, even if one might personally claim to have been catalyzed by the movement. One pastor I spoke to in Vancouver traced his origin story to Tiananmen. "The one single event that influenced me to care more about the society or maybe nation, the society," he said, "it's because in 1989, June 4, Tiananmen incident." He explained that he had already moved to Canada and was in fact on vacation when he saw it happening on the news. When he returned to Vancouver, he saw that "Canada also had many Christians who were very upset this whole massacre, and in the meantime, I was always impacted by this event, and I thought, *Lord, what thing can you use me in?*"[4] But most of the interview then proceeded to be about educating Cantonese Protestants about what he saw as the dangers of same-sex marriage. In so doing, he also spoke about how he shifted his partisan allegiances to the Conservative Party of Canada, even though one of the more vocal Liberal Party candidates at the time, Raymond Chan (who went on to be elected as member of parliament [MP] of Richmond), had openly condemned the crackdowns. This pastor's political changes, in turn, could be said to reflect broader shifts in Canadian politics. By the 2000s, it was the Conservative Party that became popularly perceived as the one that stood up to the PRC, while the Liberals sought to liberalize Canada-China trade, although what seemed to matter more to my interviewee was the Conservatives' views on sexual morality.

The events of Tiananmen also had a shattering impact on Hong Kong at that time. On June 4 itself, about one million people took to the streets in a kind of solidarity of grief, both with those in Beijing and among themselves. Popular sentiment had it that it was as if their worst fears about their city's upcoming transfer of sovereignty to the PRC in

1997 were coming true. In the wake of Tiananmen, an estimated 1 percent of the city's population of five million at the time left Hong Kong in 1990, mostly for cities around the Pacific Rim to escape potential political instability.[5] Almost immediately after the handover, the democracy movement that had sprung up in the 1970s with the collaboration of both Protestant and Catholic leaders found itself having to advocate for the practice of autonomy promised in the "one country, two systems" framework worked out in the 1984 Joint Declaration between the United Kingdom and the PRC and enshrined in Hong Kong's mini-constitution, the Basic Law. But that, too, led to ideological contradiction. "One country, two systems," after all, was a PRC framework, invented by Deng Xiaoping himself, as a not-so-subtle test drive in Hong Kong before they would try to implement it with Taiwan reunification. Those who sought to work with that system, however democratically minded they felt themselves to be—and indeed, however much some of them called for 6/4 redress—often found themselves called out as part of an undemocratic establishment.

What struck me, in other words, was how the initial wound of Tiananmen seemed to have faded in significance in all three places—not that it had healed but that it also seemed that Cantonese Protestants had moved on, regardless, at least in their public activities, which seemed to revolve around practices of democracy that centered on electing political representatives they felt best represented their interests. There was a realism that appeared to take over from the romance of 1989. It seemed that in the Bay Area, the discourse among Cantonese Protestants had almost entirely shifted from remembering the events of 6/4 toward focusing on what those events enabled in a Sinophone world: doing business with PRC partners in ways that strengthened the political networks of Chinese Americans in their local civil societies and voting in politicians they thought could represent them in strategic positions, such as in the case of the 2011 mayoral elections in San Francisco. In Vancouver, Tiananmen was described as a kind of political awakening but only initially for a liberal democratic politics. More often, Cantonese Protestants would invoke Tiananmen as that which sparked the need for political discernment among Cantonese Protestants and would then go on to talk about how they had switched allegiances to the Conservative Party, mostly due to its perceived conservatism on sexual morality. Hong Kong was even more different. For Cantonese Protestants and their allies in the Catholic Diocese, Tiananmen made them aware that the shifting political structures of the city in the wake of the 1997 handover were points for theological reflection. But "one country, two systems," they would find, was a system invented by the very establishment that perpetrated the crackdowns, which meant that the optics of secular engagement with that framework cast those who participated in it as undemocratic colluders, regardless of any participant's privately held democratic convictions.

What I attempt to do here is to demonstrate that there is a kind of thematic unity—a sheet, if you will—that ties the dream of the Pacific Rim together for Cantonese Protestants in their theological considerations. That unifying sensibility, I claim in this chapter, is a vague sense of electoral democracy among Sinophone communities, one that is often secular and somewhat motivated by Tiananmen as an origin story but often departing from it in surprising and sometimes unpredictable ways. The common threads of departure tended to come together around some kind of democratic sensibility they understood as "Chineseness" in the sense that people, especially those who have to live with the word "Chinese," should be free to choose their own representatives to work among the structures of Pacific Rim civil societies and even to change them according to their visions of how a society ought to be structured.[6] But what that process required was for Cantonese Protestants to build coalitions outside of their communities for society-wide political legitimacy. It was often in that process that theological compromises had to be made.

"A CAPITAL FOR THE ASIAN AMERICAN COMMUNITY": CHINESE CHRISTIANS AND SAN FRANCISCO CITY POLITICS

As I conducted research in the Bay Area in 2011, a major event that came up in my interviews was the mayoral race that culminated in a municipal election in the city of San Francisco on November 8, 2011. What made the competition interesting was the field of candidates. Four out of the six finalists were Asian American, competing, in the words of one of these aspirational characters, to govern "a capital for the Asian American community" in an election that "could be a watershed moment for the community."[7] In the end, the incumbent, a Chinese American named Ed Lee, won with nearly 60 percent of the votes. But the other three Asian

Americans were experienced political hands too. Jeff Adachi was the city's public defender. David Chiu was a San Francisco city supervisor. Leland Yee was a California state senator.

What was interesting to me was that there did not seem to be any overt Chinese Christian, much less Cantonese Protestant, campaigning in these elections. A friend in San Francisco did mention that I should perhaps look into whether Christians were helping David Chiu, but the only reference I could find to David Chiu being at a church in 2011 was to him receiving an award from the Buddhist Women's Association of the Southern Alameda County Buddhist Church in Union City, California.[8] When I asked one of my respondents point-blank whether he knew of any Chinese Christians helping anyone, he joked that the most he knew about was that Leland Yee "tells me that he married in Grace Cathedral and he don't go to church every week."[9]

It would have been easy for me to think of the 2011 mayoral races in San Francisco as unimportant to my project. And yet, when I was interviewing Cantonese Protestants involved in the Bay Area's Cantonese-speaking secular media in the late 1980s through the 1990s, they, to my surprise, told me about their involvement in San Francisco politics, which included these mayoral races but were not limited to them. In particular, two Cantonese Protestant characters I spoke with stood out: the political operative James Yu and a self-proclaimed "political woman" I pseudonymize as Lavender Leung. Both were practicing Protestant Christians. They also had very different views of how politics should be conducted and spoke of their involvement in city politics, including the election, in vastly divergent terms. The story that I tell traces their political involvement in San Francisco's civil society and culminates in the mayoral races.

Different as these characters were, the one thing the two of them, and the mayoral candidates too, seemed to have in common was that they did not seem to have had much to do at all with the events of Tiananmen in 1989. At the same time, it should *also* be said that, as I gathered from other respondents, Tiananmen activism paved the way for the emergence of Chinese American business-friendly politics in the Bay Area.

In fact, there had been a network of Cantonese Protestants, or perhaps several, involved in Tiananmen in 1989. However, those networks had been composed of a very different cast of characters, who at the time also had very different political orientations from their current practices. It was widely known, one respondent said, that San Jose Chinese Baptist Church's former senior pastor, Rev. Daniel Ng Chung-man (who is now senior pastor of the Hong Kong evangelical megachurch Kong Fook Evangelical Free Church in Admiralty—and a vocal critic of the post-2014 Hong Kong protests, to boot), coordinated a coalition of Chinese churches in San Jose, San Francisco, and the East Bay.[10] He called this network Chinese Christians in Action (CCIA), with its Chinese name being the Christians Love China Association (Cantonese, *geiduktou oiwaawui*, 基督徒愛華會). As another interviewee put it, CCIA's work was to "reach out to those who came out," referring to the dissidents who were leaving China.[11] One minister in the Silicon Valley, where some of the prayer meetings were held, said "a lot of churches band together and some offer help to get the dissidents outside of China. We more or less provided spiritual counseling, like Chai Ling's husband—before their divorce—they came to Christ, and a lot of other things, cared for some of their needs. That's all we did. We did not get involved in any protests."[12] Other respondents remember intercongregational prayer meetings at local churches they described as an "awakening."[13]

What is interesting is what happened to these interchurch networks. One parachurch leader in the Bay Area told me that he and others joined an organization that vehemently has nothing to do at all with Tiananmen, Thomas Leung Insing's Cultural Regeneration Research Society (CRRS). CRRS sought to broker contacts between intellectuals in the PRC and their counterparts in Sinophone communities around the world, as well as to organize poverty alleviation and anti-corruption efforts in the PRC itself.[14] Leung himself told me that his departure from Vancouver's Regent College in 1993 to found CRRS coincided with two Bay Area parachurch leaders contacting him. What was fascinating in my interview with Leung was his insistence that he had taken no position at all on Tiananmen at the time. Indeed, given his proximity to the PRC's central government, it is clear to me, at any rate, that he really did not have anything to do with it. But the people who contacted him said that they themselves did.[15] One respondent in the Bay Area directly linked his work with CRRS with his personal political awakening during Tiananmen. "By the grace of God," he said, "we've been quite active in China, and I use that as a so-called platform. . . . So I think that's the 6/4 movement, I guess the sequel and consequence of that." This respondent was on CRRS's board at the time that I did this research. He clarified to me that the Bay Area office for CRRS was in fact quite small compared to the ones in Vancouver and in Los Angeles. "We have no staff," he said, "only volunteers. We only have staff in Southern California"—accentuating the point that maybe his story was just a local quirk in the Bay Area.[16]

Neither Lavender Leung nor James Yu seemed to have much to do with CRRS. But I met Lavender because of a secular event that someone who was involved with CRRS, the radio host David Pang (whom I discussed in chapters 3 and 4), was hosting at the Chinese Cultural Center in San Francisco's Chinatown during my fieldwork in 2011. Pang was the master of ceremonies, Lavender among the organizers. It was there that I met Lavender, who soon had me meet her at her restaurant for an interview. There, Lavender told me how she had begun her entry into politics. She said that she held press conferences to complain about how city policy affected her private property.[17] She complained that a pothole outside her new Chinese restaurant in 1998 prevented her from being able to erect a handicapped access walkway to her restaurant and that the planning department had taken too long to fix it due to bureaucratic red tape. Realizing that she was being racially marginalized, she held a press conference with several city politicians. Her antics garnered her the moniker of "that political woman" in San Francisco's city hall. Lavender said that she herself was a Protestant Christian, though her networks did not seem to be.

James Yu had also been involved in political activities, both broadcasting his mostly pro-business views on Cantonese radio and television as well as working behind the scenes, since the 1990s. It was in speaking to him that I learned that the mayoral races in San Francisco were more important than I thought they would be to my project. Indeed, it was another respondent who told me that interviewing Yu was a must. "We stay up very late talking about politics," she said, "and he is very involved, much more than me."[18] Yu also recounted the rumors about himself. "Sometimes I get involved," he said to me, "and people say slanderous things about me too: 'Waa, Dr. Yu does politics. Don't get near him!'"

In 2011, Yu was also a vice chair on the San Francisco board of the Asian Pacific American Political Action (APAPA) group, an organization that tried to turn out the Asian American vote in California. In fact, I first learned of APAPA from Yu. After I interviewed him, he asked me to run an errand for him. Since I had borrowed a car to get around the Bay Area for my fieldwork, he asked me to pick up posters for a Gospel cruise he was organizing and then distribute them throughout San Francisco's Chinatown with one of his friends from APAPA, a man named Richard Ow.

The funny thing was that Ow was not a Christian, APAPA was a thoroughly secular organization, and yet they were the people tasked with promoting the Gospel cruise. When I interviewed Ow, he told me that the agenda of APAPA's founder revolved purely around turning out the Chinese American vote from his base in Fresno in California's Central Valley almost two hundred miles south of the Bay Area. Yu, he told me, headed the newly formed Bay Area chapter of APAPA in 2011, and his objective was to mobilize awareness among Chinese Americans about the San Francisco mayoral races. For example, there was a meet-the-candidates dinner event at the Imperial Garden Seafood Restaurant on San Bruno Avenue, down the street from where Ow and I had our interview. Yu would be the master of ceremonies, I was told.

In fact, Yu's efforts garnered APAPA a wide range of political ideologies, often in ways that were asymmetrical with his own. In stark contrast to Yu's affinity for a pro-business, free-market ideology, Ow described himself as a "Democrat" who was "progressive," by which he meant that he was out to help "poor people, you know, the underpaid workers, you know, the tenants, you know. Yes, I'm a progressive!"[19] That was not all. It turns out that Ow was a marriage commissioner and was one of the officials officiating same-sex marriages in 2004.[20] In fact, that was a sore spot in his relationship with Christians, he suggested. "See, lots of Christians think that a supporter of gay is a terrible person, it's no good, no good," he said. "But you cannot tell me I'm a terrible person. I know that, but I just tell you what I am, and these are open record, lots of people knows it." He had, he then told me, developed his political relationship with the Chinese Christian Union (CCU) when they worked against gambling in Chinatown in 1995.[21] They had opposed the introduction of the first site in San Francisco that would enable horse-race gamblers to place their bets in a facility not located on a racetrack. Joining the Coalition Against Off-Track Betting Parlor in Chinatown, the CCU teamed up with the Chinatown Merchants Association to block this experimental gambling site at the Grand Palace on 950 Grant Avenue in San Francisco, a site owned by the well-connected Fang family.[22] The CCU opposed the offtrack betting site with a rationale that combined family values with an Asian American image. Ow, one of then-mayoral candidate Willie Brown's political operatives, worked directly with the CCU at the time, in particular with the progressive activist Alan Wong. As Ow explained it, the CCU opposed the site because it tore apart Chinese Christian families, as "the man will skip town and then left the wife to get wealthy, and many of these situations happened in the congregations, so they're against it."[23] His long track record, in other words, meant that he also saw himself as having credibility with Chinese Christians, even if most of it was established by working with progressives in the community.

The local chapter of APAPA, I then learned, was not only ideologically diverse but also geographically so. They came from all over the Bay Area, if not also from different parts of California more generally. This geographic diffusion upset Lavender Leung. She criticized APAPA for bringing people who could not vote in the city for political events. "These people always come from Fremont," she said. "They use one car and drive them to come here to listen. They just listen. They don't know what the real situation is here. And sometimes people come from the Bay Area, or people come from Fresno." Lavender was also upset about how Yu organized a meeting between mayoral incumbent Ed Lee and Chinese Christian pastors. It turned out that most of those ministers did not live in the city. She said that Yu had not been clear about the meeting place, so the CCU pastors who did reside in San Francisco had not been able to find the room until halfway through the meeting, and the ones who could not vote in the city had all the good spots. "James has no right," Lavender exclaimed. "He is not a pastor and he is a Republican. He has no power, and his church is in Fremont! With San Francisco, he has no involvement there! What relation does he have to this city? So he makes an appointment, people think he is a pastor—he's a dentist, do you think that's good?"[24]

Lavender suggested that these appeals to churches were politically futile. At one level, churches were reluctant to get involved with their campaigns because it might compromise their churches' political neutrality. One San Francisco pastor corroborated this claim. He told me that during election season, some candidates for mayor, city supervisor, and the school board tried to solicit attention from his church, to which he was very "selective." "There were times that some other candidates will come to worship in our church," he said, "expecting a chance to speak and well, sometimes I do not allow them to speak."[25] At Cornerstone Evangelical Baptist Church, I also learned that Rev. Chanson Lau had written into his church's constitution a ban on all "political activities" since 1975, which meant that when certain candidates came to pass out literature at Cornerstone, they were turned away because of the church's policy.[26]

Cognizant of this dynamic, Lavender told me that she pursued a different strategy. Instead of tapping the churches, she became directly involved in San Francisco mayoral incumbent's Ed Lee's reelection campaign in 2011. Having previously worked for now-disgraced former city supervisor Ed Jew in his municipal campaigns, Lavender was well positioned to be tapped by city hall insiders for her political insight.[27] Although a younger Chinese American formally managed Lee's campaign, Lavender told me that she became the de facto spokeswoman for the campaign toward Chinese American communities, urging them to vote for a candidate who was Chinese. Knowing that the ballot was structured so that voters would write their top three choices in the city's "ranked-choice vote" system, Lavender encouraged those she spoke with to put Ed Lee first, followed by their choice of David Chiu, Leland Yee, or Jeff Adachi. Moreover, because she was conversant in Cantonese and Mandarin, she was able to help the Ed Lee campaign obtain advertising in the Chinese daily newspaper *Sing Tao Daily*. She also broadcast videos that she made that featured the "Run Ed Run" campaign slogan that had been made popular by Lee's political supporters. "This time," she said, curiously, "Ed will listen to the Christians," though it was unclear what she meant by this except that she herself was a Christian and perhaps more politically effective than other Cantonese Protestants.[28] And yet, the results speak for themselves, if Leung is to be believed. Lee soared to the top of the 2011 mayoral races, initially gaining 30.75 percent of the ranked-choice vote. He was elected with 59.64 percent of the final vote.

Democratic organizing, in other words, turned out to be hard work, with disconnects among how Cantonese Protestants imagined how civil society worked, how they formed their political networks, and how they mobilized and engaged. In the Bay Area, what seems to have happened was that Cantonese Protestants, initially galvanized by the emotion of Tiananmen, quickly found themselves in pro-business networks that sought to forge connections with the People's Republic of China while leveraging their communities for family values and business-friendly policies. These voices were amplified on the radio as some Cantonese Protestants, like James Yu, found their way to the secular airwaves. But the amplification of their networks did not mean that the actual work of organizing was so simple. It turned out that addressing a crowd and mobilizing communities were two different things, and it was here that operatives like Richard Ow and Lavender Leung shone. Political work meant much more than trying to get churches, which tended to have an apolitical strain anyway, on side. It literally required campaign work and participation in city politics, and whether one was Cantonese Protestant (like Lavender) or not (like Ow) did not matter much.

On reflection, I was right, to some extent, to think that Chinese Christians did not matter much to the 2011 mayoral races in San Francisco despite its high concentration of Asian American candidates. Churches were not involved, the Cantonese Protestants who were did so almost for secular reasons, and the candidates themselves did not claim to represent any sort of Chinese Christianity. But what was intriguing was the way that these municipal elections divided Cantonese Protestants across the Bay Area all the same, though again not for theological reasons. The divisions had to do with methodology, with what it meant to engage in secular politics, what communities to mobilize, and what levers of power to pull. These distinct coalitional geographies in turn suggest that what drove Cantonese Protestant engagements with the mayoral races was not some kind of coherent political theology. Instead, it was the secular realities of electoral politics in the City by the Bay that divided them as they formulated their strategies for engagement, sometimes blurring the lines between the secular and the religious.

VOTING FOR "CHINESE CULTURE"? CHINESE CHRISTIANS AND THE CONSERVATIVE PARTY OF CANADA

A few days after I defended my doctoral prospectus in 2011, the Canadian Broadcasting Corporation (CBC) featured a story about the emergence of "Chinese Christians," broadly construed, in Canadian politics. A committee member asked me if I had seen it. It was relevant to my project, he said, especially because it focused on Chinese Christian activities in Vancouver. I thanked him for the lead.

Of course, the timing of the story had nothing to do with my research starting, though it was fortuitous. It was about a month before the 2011 Canadian federal elections. The Conservative Party of Canada was seeking a broader mandate, a majority in Parliament after having governed as a minority government since 2006. In doing so, they found themselves embroiled in a minor scandal. A memorandum authored by the multiculturalism secretary Jason Kenney leaked on March 20. It was titled "Breaking Through: Building the Conservative Brand in Cultural Communities." It was a set of PowerPoint slides that outlined the Conservative Party campaign strategy, but it was also topped by a cover sheet with the official letterhead of the federal multiculturalism office.

In the slides, Kenney described a strategy to win over immigrant communities that made up 54 percent of the Greater Toronto Area (GTA) and 41 percent of Metro Vancouver. "If GTA South Asians were to form a city," he highlighted and boldfaced, "it would be the third largest city in the country." So too, the "Chinese market," where the overwhelming majority of Cantonese and Mandarin speakers in the provinces of Ontario and British Columbia reportedly lived in the cities, needed to be tapped, especially with advertisements on radio and television. Kenney identified ten federal ridings across Canada where it would be important to run candidates who appealed to those people, four of which were in Metro Vancouver.[29] In two of them, the party placed Chinese Christian candidates, Wai Young in Vancouver-South and Ronald Leung in Burnaby-Douglas. They also ran the incumbent Alice Wong, who had in 2008 finally defeated Raymond Chan, the Liberal Party's longtime MP in the majority-Chinese suburb of Richmond. All three—or four, if one were to include the unseated Chan—emerged from Cantonese-speaking Protestant Christian networks.

The CBC picked up on the Chinese Christian dimension of this strategy. Adrienne Arsenault, one of the mainstay correspondents for CBC's nightly news *The National*, gathered a large group of mostly Mandarin speakers. She asked them if it was their first time voting. As the hands went up in assent, she asked them what their political principles tended to be. One woman earnestly picked up a Bible and declared it the basis of her vote. The segment then cut to an interview with a Cantonese-speaking pastor who was supposed to be representing Metro Vancouver's Chinese Christian communities, Rev. Wayne Lo from the Christian Social Concern Fellowship (CSCF). He explained to Arsenault that those biblical values tended to align with "Chinese culture," especially on "traditional family values" and toughness on crime.[30]

But as I seek to show here, the larger story of Metro Vancouver's Cantonese Protestants in the Canadian 2011 federal elections demonstrates that they were not trying to impose either their sense of "Chineseness" or their faith onto the world. They were working to transcend their own community politics and enter into the partisan machines that powered federal elections.

Those electoral endeavors also had their roots, to some extent, in Tiananmen, though like their counterparts in the Bay Area, it was certainly not a direct line from the events of 1989 to the Conservative Party. Once again, the cast of characters was very different in the late 1980s. The story begins with Rev. Lo Sek Wai, who in 1989 was the senior pastor at New Life Chinese Lutheran Church. Though he was from Hong Kong, Lo started a Bible study in Mandarin as an outreach to overseas PRC students. "Strangely," he recalled, "I became the leader."[31] When the events of June 4 unfolded, Lo organized a group of Cantonese Protestants in his church basement to organize a series of protest events. The first event that this basement group planned was a candlelight vigil at St. John's Shaughnessy Anglican Church on June 6. Some five thousand people attended (according to the *Vancouver Sun*'s religion reporter Douglas Todd, "roughly 400 Caucasians" were in that number), filling up the already-sizable church sanctuary and overflowing onto Granville Street.[32] The vigil's marshal, Bill Chu, one of the members of the basement group, recalled, "So the whole block was filled with people, and what was most amazing is as a Christian, that was the first time we see so many teary-eyed, not a single happy face."[33] The next development happened on June 18. The basement group renamed itself the Vancouver Society in Support of the Democratic Movement in China and organized a large-scale demonstration with "all the Chinese communities, not just Christian, and all concerned, Caucasians, other ethnic groups" in Vancouver's downtown.[34]

It was at this second meeting that Lo met the emerging human rights activist Raymond Chan. At the June 18 protest, Chan called for a further demonstration after Lo's. It was then that Raymond Chan became known as a Tiananmen redress organizer. Chan issued a complaint via video "to the government of the People's Republic of China for their massacre in Peking, Tiananmen, on June the Fourth." He continued, "The killing of thousands of people has aroused the anger of the world, particularly the overseas Chinese." Calling immediately for redress and accountability, Chan stressed that he was simply calling on the Chinese government to enforce its own citizens' constitutional rights. "We are not asking to overthrow the government," he said. "All we are asking to do is for the government to enforce their own constitution, and to have the People's Congress be elected and have democracy realized in China." For Chan, political ideology mattered less than the general fact of the rule of law. "Whatever," he concluded, "whether it's a Communist country, whether it's a Communist country that dominates, whatever. We don't care. All we want is a government that would have democracy and guarantees liberties and human rights."[35]

Chan's emergence as a Tiananmen activist effected a parting of ways between Tiananmen redress activism and Christian engagement with civil society. Chan formed an organization that took the original name of Lo's basement group, the Vancouver Society in Support of the Democratic Movement (VSSDM) in China, and organized the annual memorial vigil in Vancouver. On the encouragement of then–San Jose pastor Rev. Daniel Ng Chung-man, Lo's basement group renamed themselves the Christians in Support of the Democratic Movement in China—or Chinese Christians in Action (CCIA), for short—in order to differentiate themselves from Chan's work, the same name as Ng's Bay Area counterpart at the time.[36] Sometimes VSSDM and CCIA collaborated. Chan himself became a Christian around this time, though he threw himself into politics and by 1993 was running as the Liberal Party candidate for the mostly Chinese suburb of Richmond.

CCIA, by contrast, attempted to intervene into "Chinese culture" in Vancouver by shifting it from what CCIA considered a self-interested consciousness to a democratic one. In the early 1990s, they organized Chinese New Year booths at a mall in Vancouver. "We were welcomed by Oakridge Mall," Lo told me, "because we create traffic to the mall during Chinese New Year and our event is not commercial—we only sell Chinese crafts, paintings, and posters—so the management welcomed us."[37] CCIA set up a show stage for song and dance performing groups, a lion dance, and craft booths, and they were supported by public appearances by British Columbia's lieutenant governor David Lam and acclaimed social worker Angela Kan. The objective of their exhibit was to change the Chinese New Year seasonal greeting from *gung hei fat choi* (Cantonese, "congratulations, make lots of money") to *peng on hei lok* (Cantonese, "peace and happiness"). CCIA's leader, Bill Chu, told the *Vancouver Sun* that "the old greeting grew out of millennia of political oppression in China . . . [when] the Chinese channeled their energy into making money" because they could not effect political change.[38] From there, CCIA also became involved in Indigenous politics, as Chu discovered a similar experience of oppression with the Tiananmen crackdown among the Lil'wat people on Mount Currie as they faced down government and corporate incursions on their territory. But as Chu told me, by the 1990s, he was also operating with a very small crew. Most of his followers had gone over to CRRS, where their leader, Thomas Leung Insing, continued the line on "Chineseness" in hopes of influencing PRC politics.[39]

By the early 1990s, the stage was set for Cantonese Protestants to enter the fray of Canadian electoral politics, somewhat on the legacy of Tiananmen. It was poetic that Raymond Chan ran for Parliament in 1993 on the basis of his Tiananmen credibility, and it was because of it that some Cantonese Protestant clergy, even the ones who later became embedded in the Conservative Party, openly supported him. One minister, for example, recalls that Raymond Chan emerged on the scene claiming to be a Christian. "At first," Lo said, "he claimed, *I am a Christian*, you help me to be elected as a Christian politician, that kind of saying. And I think he drew a lot of votes from the Christian voters in Richmond at that time."[40] Another pastor in Vancouver's Chinatown corroborated this statement: "I think at that time, in the early '90s, even the pastors, they wrote in the newspaper, they said, I vote him just because he is Chinese . . . in, I think it's *Truth Monthly*."[41] Stephen Cheung, a financial adviser who later became a Conservative Party operative, also remembers that the Chinese community favored Raymond Chan simply because he was Chinese. "When we first came in 1992," he said, "because in the Chinese community, different activities, Chinese schools, those connections, my wife . . . and her friends, they did some volunteering, not me. That was when Raymond Chan was coming out to be elected, and he was a Chinese."[42] Rev. Lo Sek Wai added that he supported Chan's candidacy "personally," adding, "I encouraged them to participate in the election but not to mention any names in favor of any person."[43]

Having successfully elected Chan, many of my respondents said that disillusionment set in fairly quickly. One story, litigated mostly in the pages of *Truth Monthly*, focused on how his claims to Christian faith were suspect because he had offered joss stick incense at a Buddhist temple on Chinese New Year in 1997. In that very newspaper, Chan explained that as the secretary of state for the Asia-Pacific region, it was his duty to perform the ceremony because "we must know that our country, Canada, is composed of different religions, different races, different backgrounds of people" and thus must be inclusive of all citizens. To that end, he accepted the invitation to perform the ceremony because "as elected Members of Parliament and ministers, I cannot [decline] because they are not Christians, as that would deprive people who believe in other religions access to government opportunities; in addition, the commemorative ancestral rituals are not religious, but commemorate Canada's Chinese ancestral contributions." Because he believed that God ultimately guided the actions of Parliament, he did not feel that his actions were un-Christian.[44] Chan's statement garnered a rebuke from *Truth Monthly*'s founder and editor, Peace Evangelical Church's revivalist legend David Ng Chu-kwong. "You've tried very hard to avoid being misunderstood," Ng wrote, "but the result is that you are unsuccessful because there are still very many people who think you are mistaken, because the Christian expression for 'reverence for one's ancestors' is not 'incense,' but 'fresh cut flowers' and 'silent' commemoration." Ng concluded that all of these actions must have occurred because Chan "had not believed in the Lord for too long."[45]

Ng's narrative about Chan came to dominate Cantonese Protestant discourse about him, and the Liberal Party more generally. One pastor told me that he realized "everyone figured out that he is Chinese, you vote him, he may be for the party, not for the community. Now I think the Chinese is more understanding on how to vote."[46] In the Richmond focus group, the participants agreed that the party was often more important than the candidate. Mrs. Chin mentioned that this axiom held true if only the candidate were not Raymond Chan, for, as they put it, "he had credibility issues." Mr. and Mrs. Yang then clarified that "it's not what he says on the platform," for "he says one thing and does another," telling his constituents one thing while voting differently in Parliament. "He just wanted to secure his vote, and many people saw that, so he lost the election," Mrs. Yang said. When I asked them to clarify what upset them so much, Mrs. Yang brought up the joss stick incident again: "Raymond Chan's problem was that he burned incense and worshipped ancestors. That's the problem. Because he said that he was Christian, people said, 'No, that's not Christian,' and then they began to pay attention to what he did—is it really for us? That's how they discovered that he said one thing and did another."[47]

And so it was that by the late 1990s and early 2000s, the electoral loyalties of Cantonese Protestants began to switch from the Liberal Party to the Canadian Alliance Party, which became the newly formed Conservative Party of Canada. As some Conservative Party operatives who were Cantonese evangelicals told me, their first taste of right-of-center politics came from their support for Stockwell Day, a former pastor and socially conservative politician from British Columbia's Okanagan Valley who was campaigning in the 2000 federal elections to become leader of the Canadian Alliance Party (formerly the Reform Party).[48] The local Reform candidate in Richmond was Joe Peschisolido, a Roman Catholic businessman from Ontario who had recently moved to Richmond. As the political operative Kenny Chiu put it, they made the radical move of "not supporting a Chinese candidate"—that is, the Liberal Party's Raymond Chan—in the 2000 election but to support Peschisolido instead.[49] Peschisolido engaged local business and church networks, successfully coasting to a victory over Raymond Chan, while Day nominally won the Canadian Alliance leadership, though he lost it to Stephen Harper in 2002 after an internal party referendum.[50] At that point, Peschisolido shocked voters by walking across the floor to join Prime Minister Jean Chrétien's Liberal Party. Chiu's press release on behalf of the Canadian Alliance Party's Richmond Constituency Association expressed "an enormous sense of betrayal" on the part of Peschisolido's supporters. "The action is also considered dishonorable to those friends who fought shoulder to shoulder with him against the Liberals 2000 campaign," the statement added. "It is a serious letdown especially to those who made personal sacrifices in going door knocking with him, and to those who donated money to his campaign."[51] Peschisolido paid for his actions. In the run-up to the 2004 election, Raymond Chan defeated

Peschisolido for the Liberal Party's nomination, ousting Peschisolido from Parliament.

Chan's foibles and Peschisolido's betrayal paved the way for the emergence of Alice Wong as a candidate for the newly formed Conservative Party of Canada in the Richmond riding in 2004. Originally in 1999, she had been a Canadian Alliance candidate in the Vancouver-Kingsway riding, where she lived and went to church at Vancouver Chinese Evangelical Free Church (VCEFC).[52] When she was defeated in that riding, Rev. Wayne Lo advised her to try her chances in Richmond, upon which she contacted Kenny Chiu (as Chiu told me) in 2002.[53] With that, she was connected with all of Peschisolido's former Chinese supporters. As Mr. Ping also told me, curious individuals at VCEFC's sister church, the Richmond Chinese Evangelical Free Church, vetted her understanding of Richmond's local politics, the role of a volunteer in her campaign, and the degree to which she shared their values.[54]

Still, Alice Wong's 2004 campaign was considered a disaster. Mr. Ping said that one of the key problems was that Raymond Chan was still touting his identity as a "Christian," which meant that Christians were still voting for him as the safe option. He also remembered the campaign as "full of high passion" but "lacking in manpower and support," resulting in a loss that left them "discouraged and discontent with their own efforts."[55] Stephen Cheung, who functioned in 2004 as the Conservative Party's riding director, told me that Peschisolido's betrayal continued to bite them, in addition to the problem that their volunteers had "no experience."[56] Kenny Chiu said the problem was that the concentration of Cantonese Protestants in the campaign led to "a very narrow imagination" that was unable to build a grassroots coalition that could include a diverse group of potential Conservative voters, such as "disillusioned [New] Democrats, social conservatives, non–social conservatives, fiscal conservatives, libertarians, Hong Kong, Taiwan, PRC, churches, and temples." Raymond Chan handily defeated Wong in the 2004 elections by 4,747 votes.

After Wong's defeat in 2004, Kenny Chiu worked to reconsolidate the Conservative Party's stronghold in Richmond. Chiu told Wong (as he related to me), "I told her that I wouldn't support her because she had to learn her lesson, so we both knew that the next candidate would not be Alice." Instead, the director of Focus on the Family Canada, Darrel

Reid, became the federal candidate in Richmond. Chiu, who had assured Reid that he need not be Chinese to run in Richmond, said that the "maturing Alice Wong machinery with its factions united went behind Darrel, and Alice Wong volunteered for him." In contrast to Wong's 2004 campaign, Reid's was fully secular and focused on his contributions to the Chinese Canadian community through historical head tax redress. Chiu instructed Reid to attend a visit from Prime Minister Paul Martin to Vancouver's Chinatown where he would address head tax redress activists.[57] From this meeting, Reid understood that the Conservative Party needed a position on head tax redress, from which he assembled a quick bullet-point list in twenty-four hours that declared that there would be a "formal apology," followed by a "reconciliation" dialogue as well as a material "redress," after which a "fund" would be set aside to make sure that such legislation "doesn't happen again."[58] Although Reid did not win the election, his bullet points had been forwarded to Stephen Harper's secretary, Jason Kenney. The story went that Harper subsequently apologized to head tax payers in 2006 when he was made prime minister of Canada.[59]

The year 2006 also saw the emergence of English-speaking Chinese Canadian Protestants from Cantonese Protestant churches in Canadian politics, mostly in the Vancouver-South riding and associated to some degree with the activities of the Pentecostal activist Faytene Kryskow's 4MyCanada, which held an annual rally outside of Parliament to pray for government leaders and touted a socially conservative agenda on sexuality issues.[60] Esther Leung-Kong, an activist associated with this movement (and incidentally, Thomas Leung's daughter), recalled that she participated in Kryskow's activities because "the Liberals were saying that this is what the young people wanted," referring to same-sex marriage, "but these were not our voices, so we wanted to be heard."

Leung-Kong told me that her political awakening led her to organize a series of dialogues with local politicians in Vancouver, regardless of whether she agreed with their positions. She said that she visited Vancouver-Centre Liberal MP Hedy Fry to understand why she was advocating for the legalization of prostitution. Leung-Kong described the meeting with Fry as cordial, with them even reportedly coming to an agreement that "we need to educate women early on, especially those with lower incomes." Leung-Kong subsequently met with politicians who ranged the ideological spectrum, including Vancouver-South Liberal MP Ujjal Dosanjh (whom Leung-Kong described as "resistant to our views"), Burnaby-Douglas NDP MP Bill Siksay ("We didn't know he was a gay activist; we just knew he was a Christian and he and his partner attended the United Church of Christ; it was a good meeting"), New Westminster NDP MP Dawn Black, Surrey North NDP MP Penny Priddy, and Vancouver mayor Sam Sullivan ("We blessed him, and prayed with three people, and when we were done praying, he also prayed, and that shocked us").

Leung-Kong's irenic activities paved the way for the campaign of second-generation Cantonese evangelical Wai Young in the Vancouver-South riding in 2008. Leung-Kong helped Wai Young fight a tough campaign against the Liberal MP incumbent, Ujjal Dosanjh, whom she had visited. He was a formidable opponent, she pointed out, because he himself had been formerly premier of British Columbia before becoming Vancouver-South's federal MP. Leung-Kong emphasized to me that the campaign itself was secular. There were of course prayer meetings that supported Young privately, she said, but the public face of Young's campaign matched the prevailing Conservative Party strategy, which was to appeal to a broad Chinese Canadian electorate. That was challenging, Leung-Kong told me, because Young was an English speaker with limited Cantonese-language skills.[61] Young's campaign was defeated by an extremely narrow margin of twenty votes (16,090 for Young, 16,110 for Dosanjh).

These very strategies from Vancouver-South brought victory to the Alice Wong campaign in Richmond in that same 2008 election cycle. As one of the new campaign managers Sacha Peter said to me, they welcomed Chinese Christians, though they did not tie the campaign to any particular church congregation. "This is a core group of supporters of Alice Wong," he emphasized, "and in no way would I ever try to change our own strategy to reflect different beliefs of this core support. I mean, they're a great group of people, and they're highly motivated, and they highly believe in the Conservative principles, and if I tried to, they'd probably kick me off the campaign."[62]

Indeed, the campaign was better described as a mixing space for various religious groups. As one interviewee admitted, the campaign "did not distinguish between [its volunteers] as Christian or Buddhist; it's the characters that matter because even Caucasians do things differently from the Chinese."[63] In turn, the pastor at the Richmond Chinese Evangelical Free Church at the time of my research, Rev. Anthony Yeung, told me that the church actively "avoided this association" of Alice Wong with their congregation "because it is unfair and negative to Alice Wong." Indeed, he advised his church's fellowship leaders to forgo opportunities to bring Wong in as a fellowship speaker or else "this church will be labeled as an Alice Wong church."[64] So too, when I asked the Richmond focus group if they would vote for Wong if she attended their congregation, they said that they would not. "Yes, we vote for Alice Wong," Mrs. Au said, "but she is only one person, so we must vote for the party, because we are talking about the big picture here, not just one small member, unless she can influence the country as much as Stephen Harper."[65]

Sacha Peter told me that the new 2008 campaign focused instead on being "tighter on message control, carefully preparing and rehearsing what was said, including on the gay marriage issue and the support for traditional marriage." Indeed, this message control strategy was also replicated in the Burnaby-Douglas riding with the Conservative candidacy of a popular Cantonese radio host, Ronald Leung, who adopted a policy that avoided media interviews and public debates as he ran a close race with the NDP incumbent Bill Siksay. In Richmond, Alice Wong attended debates and gave interviews but only on particular messages that the campaign wanted to send: lower taxes and toughness on crime. They also focused their platform through a local "pet issue," the Garden City lands, a contested lot in Richmond's city center that had claims by the federal government, the City of Richmond, the Agricultural Land Commission, and the Musqueam First Nation. Whereas Raymond Chan's platform was to put the land in the hands of the city to build a convention center, Peter strategically maneuvered the Wong campaign to argue that the land should remain "fallow as is," citing the possibility of traffic congestion if the lands were to be developed.[66]

With this tighter form of message control, the socially conservative moral issues for which Alice Wong was originally known became seen as campaign distractions. A high point came in the 2008 campaign's confrontation with a Liberal political smear that attempted to pin Wong to the Canadian Alliance for Social Justice and Family Values Association (CASJAFVA) as a "right-wing organization" that propagated hate speech and that was unduly tied to churches. Chan's campaign press release generated over forty pages of material quoting and translating Alice Wong's Chinese statements into English.[67] It focused on controversial statements from CASJAFVA's convener, lawyer K-John Cheung, asserting that "sexual orientation" had not been adequately defined and that if legislation against sexual orientation discrimination were to be on the books, it "could include heterosexuality, homosexuality, lesbianism, transexuality, pedophilia, polygamy, polyandry, bestiality, sadistic-sexuality, masochistic-sexuality and incestuous sexuality."[68] It then linked Wong to CASJAFVA via several pictures of them at various fundraisers and rallies together, calling her the "go between with CASJAFVA and senior Conservative MPs," especially during an October 2005 fundraiser attended by current prime minister Stephen Harper. The press release then presented the quotes in the context of CASJAFVA newsletters and reproduced emails from Stephen Cheung, linking Wong's team with CASJAFVA. Based on this evidence, Chan called on Stephen Harper to remove Wong as his Richmond candidate because of her "extreme views."[69]

The Alice Wong campaign handily replied to the statement by focusing on an economic message and argued that Chan was posing a distraction from the local Richmond concerns.[70] Turning Chan's allegations that the Wong campaign was mixing politics and religion against him became the prevailing 2008 strategy. Alice Wong was asked at an all-candidates' debate what her position on same-sex marriage was. She said, "My position is, I respect the position of the Parliament which has already dealt with this issue." Chan then retorted that it was the "biggest shame in this campaign" that "Ms. Wong has a different position in front of the Chinese media, and a different position in front of the English media." Wong thundered back,

> You are the person who does the double-talking. My position has always stayed the same, whether it's Chinese or English, but my position right now is that it's the law of the land. The government has already dealt with it, so legally, it's there, but my personal belief has not changed, but it does not matter. What matters is that you told the Chinese media that before you were voted in, you said that you vote against same-sex marriage, but when you got the Minister position,

you don't want to lose that position, you voted against it, you were not telling the same thing to the Chinese media. That is a great lie.[71]

Chan was beaten at his own game. As Chiu put it, it first reminded voters of all the reasons that they had "hated" Raymond Chan in the past for breaking his campaign promises.[72] Second, it demonstrated that Wong's campaign was no longer about social conservatism in Richmond but that her political scope could build broader coalitions than the Cantonese evangelicals with which she had begun. In 2008, Alice Wong received 21,329 (49.77 percent) votes, defeating Raymond Chan by 8,108 votes (18.92 percent).

There was already a basis for a mature Cantonese Protestant approach to coalition building by 2011 when the CBC covered Jason Kenney's leaked immigrant "market" strategy for Conservative Party wins in Vancouver and Toronto. There were, once again, three campaigns in Metro Vancouver that could be seen as having Chinese Christian ties: Wong's in Richmond, Young's in Vancouver-South, and Leung's in Burnaby-Douglas. Wong's was seen as the most experienced, having propelled Wong to victory in 2008 and given her three years of work through which her campaign developed their new "pet issue"—"infrastructure funding."[73] Appealing to Wong's record in Parliament, the campaign argued that Wong had secured funding for the successful construction of the rapid transit Canada Line, joining Richmond with downtown Vancouver. Basing itself on Wong's political capital in Parliament, Wong's campaign contrasted itself with the record of her Liberal opponent, Peschisolido, the MP who had crossed party lines in 2002.

As part of my research, I joined Wong for a day of door-knocking and hung out at her campaign headquarters, which is how I met so many of her operatives, including Peter. From these encounters and the interviews that subsequently followed, I learned that the major strategy in 2011 was to leverage campaign signage to attack Peschisolido's political character. Peter told me that the campaign predicted correctly that Peschisolido would put up signs in "illegal locations" on public sites such as the school board building, city hall, the Garden City Lands, and road medians. When the six thousand "illegal" signs went up, Peter called the City of Richmond to force Peschisolido to play by the rules while issuing a press release that was put in the papers, contrasting how Wong played by the rules while Peschisolido did not.[74] In turn, high school volunteers conducted door-knocking expeditions. On one route on which I accompanied them, the strategy was to bring Alice Wong herself along, having the students knock on the door to ask for permission to put up signs for Wong while Wong herself would rush in to personally greet her constituents, some of whom said to her, "Don't worry, Alice, we like Harper," while another man who passed on the street remarked snidely, "Oh, you are Conservative, and you do not change."

Confident that Wong was assured victory in Richmond because of Peschisolido's poor record, Wong's campaign volunteer staff also attempted to help Wai Young and Ronald Leung. Peter told me that his campaign volunteers "assisted Young's campaign with the electronic structure." Moreover, to compensate for Young's Chinese-language limitations, Kenny Chiu from the Richmond campaign worked as Young's translator. Young also received support from CSCF's Wayne Lo, assuring her of first-generation Cantonese Protestant support despite her second-generation identity. Leung's campaign was more problematic. The problem, as Peter put it, was that Leung had a no-interview policy.[75] In my Coquitlam focus group, my respondents lamented what they saw as his political missteps, especially when he refused to attend the all-candidates' debate. "It turned me off when he refused to debate," Mr. Yee said. "It was more door-knocking. We told him that refusing to debate is losing. How can you buy people in the mainstream if you only stay within the Asian community? What about the majority? He needed to publicize more. I was so ticked off. If he wanted to win, he should have gone to three or four debates, but he only showed up one time at Crystal Mall." As he spoke, loud sighs could be heard around the table.[76]

In the end, Alice Wong defeated Joe Peschisolido in Richmond by 17,802 votes. Wai Young unseated Ujjal Dosanjh by 3,900 votes. Ronald Leung lost by 1,011 votes to the NDP candidate, Kennedy Stewart. These successes (and near successes) were only possible, it turns out, to the extent that Cantonese Protestants were able to build coalitions and establish credibility beyond their communities' immediate concerns. What that involved was participating in partisan machinery, first in the 1990s with the Liberals and then in the 2000s with the Conservatives. Tiananmen may have served as an inspiring origin story to some of this political story, though the tale traces much more the political mishaps of the activist who started it all, Raymond Chan. But in the end, the CBC was more correct than they knew. To the extent that Chinese Christians were successful in voting in their own candidates, they had in fact emerged as a force within Canadian politics because they—at least the ones who were going to engage in electoral activities—had made the journey to secular civil society coalition building in Canada, addressing issues they initially did not care about and engaging unexpected allies outside of their communities.

THE PROBLEM OF "PUBLIC THEOLOGY": CONTESTING HONG KONG'S ELECTION COMMITTEE

I began my fieldwork in Hong Kong in February 2012, in the midst of its fourth chief executive (CE) "elections." I was told over and over by my respondents that as a Special Administrative Region (SAR), Hong Kong does not allow for free elections, even though it made provisions to elect eighteen legislators to the Legislative Council in 1991 and stipulates in Article 45 of the Basic Law that "the method for selecting the Chief Executive shall be specified in the light of the actual situation in the Hong Kong SAR and in accordance with the principal of gradual and orderly progress," with the "ultimate aim" as "the selection of the Chief Executive by universal suffrage upon nomination by a broadly representative nominating committee in accordance with democratic procedures."[77] With referenda in the Legislative Council failing to set the date for universal suffrage for 2005, 2007, and 2012, the Beijing regime had at the time of my research tentatively indicated its preference for 2017 to be the year when Hong Kong citizens would directly elect the CE.

Meanwhile, what it meant to have an election for the CE of Hong Kong was actually that there was always an Election Committee that would vote on behalf of the people. Originally called the Selection Committee in 1996 with 400 voting seats, this voting body was renamed the Election Committee in 1998, comprising 800 seats, and has been expanded to 1,200 seats after electoral reforms in 2010. The Election Committee gathered individuals from various professional and political sectors of society, who would then vote for the CE. This voting body also included the six officially recognized religious bodies in Hong Kong:

the Catholic Diocese of Hong Kong, the Chinese Muslim Cultural and Fraternal Association, the Hong Kong Christian Council (HKCC), the Hong Kong Taoist Association, the Confucian Academy, and the Hong Kong Buddhist Association. It was often said that the Election Committee looked to the Beijing central government to see whom it would favor. But when a journalist asked the People's Republic of China leader Jiang Zemin in 2000 whether this was actually the case, he lashed out at what he cast as the low quality of the question and said in English, "Too simple! Sometimes naïve!"[78]

For Protestants and Catholics, ecumenical and evangelical, the events of this fourth CE election in 2012 afforded them an opportunity for continued reflection on the unique political situation of Hong Kong SAR. They often called their reflections "public theology" (Cantonese, *gunggong sanhok*), as these conversations often occurred among academic theologians in Hong Kong as they contested each other over the role of the Christian church in relating to the workings of a secular public sphere, whether that was conceptualized as the state apparatus or the civil society of people who debated governmental actions.

These reflections often came apropos of a democracy movement that was initially galvanized by Tiananmen. The Pro-Chinese Democracy Movement in Hong Kong, headed by the democracy activist Szeto Wah, has existed since 1976, mostly as working alliances between university student groups and radical socialist activists, but the 1989 student movement elicited supportive commentary from Protestant organizations in Hong Kong in May 1989.[79] The sociologist Tinming Ko relates in his sociological study of Protestant ministers in Hong Kong politics that there were numerous "million-people demonstration walks in May 1989" as well as a "China and Hong Kong Young People in One Heart" rally co-organized by Breakthrough Youth Ministries and the Fellowship of Evangelical Students that drew over two hundred thousand students to participate. On May 22, three hundred ministers attended a Pastor Prayer Meeting to pray in solidarity with the Chinese students, after which on May 25, three hundred pastors walked from Wan Chai Methodist Church to deliver a letter in support of the students to the New China News Agency.[80]

Although many of my respondents participated in the Million Man March in Hong Kong against the state brutality of the Beijing regime, few knew that this large-scale demonstration was the result of Protestant conversations with pro-democracy activists in the immediate wake of the military suppression in Tiananmen Square. One of the major mainline Protestant members of the clergy during my research told me about it in an interview. He said that in 1989, he was the pastor at Wan Chai Methodist Church. He recounted how, late one night in early June, he was speaking with several leaders of the democratic student movement in Hong Kong who had camped outside of his church when he heard on the radio that the People's Liberation Army was entering Tiananmen Square. "At that moment, I called Szeto Wah," he said, "and he was unavailable, like *I'm so tired. I have to sleep.* And I woke him up." It was from there, he continued, that they launched the Hong Kong Alliance in Support of Patriotic Democratic Movements in China. "The Alliance phone call," he exclaimed, "I made it! So we started it, and I brought the Christians in, and we decided to start the Alliance."[81]

He told the Christians at the meeting that they would start a Christian alliance as well, known as the Hong Kong Christian Patriotic Democratic Movement (CPDM). Breakthrough's Philemon Choi became its chair. Ko relates Choi's words in his account. CPDM's mission, Choi wrote, was "our response to the love of God" while promoting democracy is "a way to express our faith in loving people," which meant that CPDM "is not a political body" but one that "can help facilitate the democratic movement in Hong Kong and China, and that the righteousness and peace of God be seen in the city we love."[82] Statements of protest issued by a range of Christian organizations then appeared in newspapers following the June 4 event, calling out the Beijing regime on its "bloodshed" and the "massacre" that happened. There was a Million Man March organized by Szeto Wah at Victoria Park before parading through Hong Kong Island in protest. My mainline clergy contact also told me of a demonstration from a mainline church in Kowloon's Yau Ma Tei in which one thousand people came. Another congregation on Hong Kong island also hosted a twenty-four-hour prayer event as Szeto's demonstration started.[83]

One could say that this kind of interinstitutional coalitional organization repeated itself in the formation of the Civil Human Rights Front (CHRF) in 2002. At that time, CE Tung Chee Hwa's Legislative Council began drafting a National Security Ordinance at the request of Beijing's

State Council. Seeking to replace the laws on treason from the British colonial era, this new legislation was based on the Basic Law's Article 23, which stipulated that the city "shall enact laws on its own to prohibit any act of treason, sedition, subversion against the Central People's Government, or theft of state secrets." It would also "prohibit foreign political organizations or bodies from conducting political activities in the Region" and "establishing ties with foreign political organizations or bodies."[84] Alleging that this bill would stifle dissent while eroding the rights of citizens, the National Security Ordinance, known commonly as Article 23 (廿三條例, *jaasaam tiulai*), had already sparked a sixty-five-thousand-person protest on December 15, 2002, and a petition campaign on December 24, 2002, before culminating in the five-hundred-thousand-strong "7/1" demonstration on July 1, 2003, a mass protest that was timed to coincide with the anniversary celebration of the return of Hong Kong to PRC sovereignty. It has since developed into an annual tradition, until the National Security Law, the fulfillment of Article 23's promises, came into place in 2020.

What was interesting about CHRF was how open it was about the religious groups that powered it, though it was really a secular coalition. The Catholic Diocese's Justice and Peace Commission (HKJP) was a major part of its public persona, for example. HKJP's Jackie Hung said that HKJP was a core part of CHRF because few of the other groups took leadership. "If you look at so many groups that are here, there are really only a few bodies who actually do anything," she said, "and those are the Christian groups and the gay and lesbian groups are the most vigorous."[85] The Catholic Diocese, as it happened, was also one of the original critics of Article 23 from the very beginning. The retired Catholic bishop of Hong Kong, Joseph Cardinal Zen Ze-kiun, told me that he had objected to the law's ban on "proscribed societies" that were blacklisted by the central government and forbidden to operate in the SAR.[86] For Zen, one religious example of a "proscribed society" in the PRC was the Falun Gong. "If a sect like the Falun Gong is banned on the mainland and then also should be banned in Hong Kong," he said, "putting it into the anti-subversion law, maybe it will be used tomorrow with the Catholic Church." Zen's most visible contribution to CHRF was that immediately before the march on July 1, 2003, he started the tradition of having a prayer meeting for all participants regardless of religious affiliation that gathered at Victoria Park prior to the larger demonstration. As the five-hundred-thousand-person march proceeded from the park to the Central District, Zen told me that he had withdrawn from the march to pray in solidarity with elderly people and nuns who could not march because it was "a very hot afternoon," starting first at a nearby Catholic parish and then concluding with a mass at St. Joseph's Hospital.[87]

In turn, it was arguable that CHRF itself had Christian origins. When I interviewed HKCI's Fan Lap Hin, he showed me a pro-democracy pamphlet that had the names of key Protestant and Catholic organizations involved in a coalition for universal suffrage and human rights activism. He said, "These are the post-2003 people; that's the network." HKCI had played a critical role in the formation of CHRF because the feminist theologian Rose Wu Lo Sai was HKCI's head at the time and was named the "convener" of the coalition. She had returned in 2000 after receiving her doctorate, with a specialization in feminist and queer theologies, from Episcopal Divinity School in Boston in 1998.[88] She became the director of HKCI after its founder, Rev. Kwok Nai Wang, retired. In September 2002, Wu called together a meeting of thirty-three civil society groups for a discussion of the impending "rumors" that Article 23 legislation might be passed. The group set up two task forces, one focusing on Article 23 and the other on human rights. "Hong Kong only has a human rights legislation, not a committee," Wu told me in an interview, "so we thought that Hong Kong needed a mechanism for that." She also was elated at the group's success turning out the protest on July 1, 2003. "The journalists, the lawyers, the students, the women, the sexual minorities, the church, Christians, the grassroots groups, the laborers, so many groups participated," she related to me, "and I really thought this platform was formed at the right time, and we had a good time to have the CHRF voice, to have that big demonstration."[89]

And yet, core as these Catholic and Protestant institutions may have been to CHRF, the participants in my focus groups in 2012 were both divided and sometimes half-hearted about Article 23 and universal suffrage. One focus group that I conducted in North Point answered vehemently that any protests led by CHRF were nothing close to the panic that they had felt when the Tiananmen incident happened in 1989.[90] At the Tuen Mun focus group, Mrs. Ng expressed that she felt that the activities of some pro-democratic Christian groups were too "violent." "Democracy is necessary," she said, "but if someone uses this to divide this society, for example, the Bible says not to cause dissension. If they are causing chaos, it's no good to attack leaders and to divide the society." Instead, as Mr. Lee said in the same focus group, Hong Kong citizens should use "rational means" to persuade the government to become more democratic.[91]

If anything, much more social attention became focused on the existence of the Election Committee itself, which for my respondents stood for all that was obstructing universal suffrage in Hong Kong. In Sha Tin, Mrs. Cheng recalled that the church underwent some confusion on the Protestant elections because it was not part of HKCC and yet "openly allows individual members to be chosen—we have that, but some churches don't announce it. I know because I talk with other churches' friends." While she understood that one had to be part of HKCC to become an Election Committee member, she noted that her church was not part of HKCC, to which another church member said to her quizzically that she had not in fact heard any announcement from the church that there was an election happening.[92] In a separate group that took place in the same area, Mr. Chu said that he was hesitant to denounce the "small circle elections" because he did not understand what level of electoral consensus constitutes majority rule: "Is it 10 percent? 50 percent? 99 percent? 100 percent?"[93]

In fact, much of what became known as public theology in 2012 concerned the approaches of Catholic and Protestant groups to the Election Committee. Because the Election Committee reserved seats for members of the Catholic Diocese and HKCC, their methods of choosing delegates became sources of theological controversy. Kung Lap Yan, a Protestant liberation theologian at the Chinese University of Hong Kong's Chung Chi Divinity School, instructed me to examine the Roman Catholic approach to the Election Committee as a point of comparison to the one taken by HKCC.[94] And so it was that I found myself, while working on research about Protestants in Hong Kong, interviewing the retired bishop of Hong Kong, Cardinal Zen, about his approach to the Election Committee.

Zen's vehement opposition to Article 23 had garnered him a reputation as an uncompromising and principled spiritual leader in the democracy movement, so much that in 2022, he was arrested as a trustee of the pro-democracy 612 Humanitarian Relief Fund for allegedly violating the National Security Law. But in talking to him, I learned that he could work with the system too. He told me that he had developed an approach to the Election Committee called "passive compliance." At the time, he was a coadjutor bishop—not the main hierarch in the diocese—and there was, in his words, "some quarrel within the Church between the curia and the Justice and Peace Commission" (HKJP) when it came to their involvement in the Election Committee.[95] HKJP, he said, wanted to boycott the elections because they were not democratic. The curia wanted to get involved. The "solution," as Zen put it, was what he called "passive compliance." He acknowledged the merits of HKJP's protest that "this is a small circle, not democratic, we don't want to have such a system. And the Church as such, we don't have to have a part in that." But he also recognized the diocesan curia's wisdom in allowing the Catholic faithful to participate, for "if we boycott, they may accuse us of depriving their rights." Zen's passive compliance thus took the position that "if any Catholic want to join, let him join by himself; we only prove and testify that he is a Catholic" by checking the baptismal and membership records. Zen said that this approach sent the message that the Church was not supportive of the elections, even though there were Roman Catholics in the Election Committee. "No, no, no, the Catholics, they go by themselves," he exclaimed. "They do not represent the Church; they go by their own personal capacity!"[96]

Kung turned out to be right. The Catholic Diocese's posture of passive compliance really was a contrast with HKCC's approach, which was to host free elections for HKCC seats among members of Protestant churches.[97] "I was the one who proposed this more than ten years ago," Lo Lung Kwong told me, in a bid to make the elections somewhat politically legitimate. He said that after he proposed this, he was attacked in the pages of the daily newspaper *Ming Pao* for joining an "unjust election," insinuating that there was a "conspiracy behind you and Beijing's power." Lo retorted that if that were the case, HKCC should have rejected the government's offer for it to take the Election Committee seats in the first place. Having accepted them, it had become a question for Lo of "how to run it as proper as possible so as to involve as many Christians as possible."[98]

Whereas this model remained intact for the first two CE elections in 2002 and 2005, HKCC opened its elections to all Protestant churches in 2007, regardless of whether they were registered with HKCC. That led to megachurches that were not part of the conventional denominational apparatuses in Hong Kong participating. As one official in HKCC put it to me, the Protestant voting process was subjected to "a lot of manipulation of churches because some newer churches really wanted to get into these positions." He said that several of these charismatic groups "really wanted to get into these positions, and their churches are very big, so they only vote for a member within the churches, and all the votes go to that member, and they come out."[99] An Evangelical Free Church pastor, the Rev. Peter Ho, remembered this scenario well. His church, Tung Fook Evangelical Free Church in Causeway Bay, was also a two-thousand-person charismatic megachurch. But he told me that they had not participated in this third election precisely because he saw what other large churches were doing "because our way of voting is not fair." He then described a situation where a large church might put forward ten names from its own congregation and then put a ballot box within their own premises. Some churches, he added, might not have a box. That created a possibility that "the members of that church definitely will vote our own pastor because they don't have to make any effort to go to vote. If you put it outside in a neutral place, so you have to make effort to go there to vote. So I say it's not a fair way to vote."[100]

These disagreements among and around HKCC's approach to the Election Committee led to widespread discussion about the public theology that went behind approaches to the 1,200-person Election Committee of 2012. The term came from revivalist theologians associated with a group called the Hong Kong Christian Union, which represented churches with roots in revivalism and found their intellectual headquarters at institutions like the China Graduate School of Theology (CGST).[101] Attempting to demonstrate their relevance to the Election Committee debates, evangelical theologians like Carver Yu and Kang Phee Sang at CGST argued for public theology as an approach to public affairs that explicitly used Christian theological language for public discourse. Yu laid the groundwork for this kind of public theology in his address to the Lausanne Conference, an international network of contemporary missionaries, in Cape Town in October 2010. The situation facing Hong Kong and the PRC, Yu said, was that "without moral truth, might is right," which would eradicate the "ground of foundational democracy," as "without moral truth, the person only becomes a tool or commodity of the market."[102] Kang, who was new to CGST in 2011, told me that "many things that are in the public are epistemological issues." The key was to find the "metanarrative there" and to challenge the assumption that "religion is private" on the basis of secular societies already having "a kind of what is acceptable and what is not acceptable, what is good and what is evil."[103] The implication, Kang then wrote in the *CGST Bulletin*, was that "in a free and democratic society, it is every citizen's right to public space," which meant that if certain citizens were religious, they should be allowed to speak with a distinctively theological voice, claiming against the metanarrative of the public square that "the God we believe in is Lord of the public space."[104] Yu and Kang were saying, in other words, that it was not so much the Election Committee that mattered but whether the Protestants elected to it could speak within it using explicitly Christian language to challenge it on its democratic problems.

Public theology in turn immediately came under contest for providing a theological justification for cooperating with the Election Committee. Kung told me that he had argued that, in fact, the "good witness" of the church would have been to "not vote" and thus expose "how ridiculous such an election is."[105] Some of Kung's students at Chung Chi Divinity School followed through with their mentor's critique by registering themselves as a voting constituent with the HKCC internal elections for the committee seats as Narrow Church in 2011 for the explicit purpose of making a mockery of the elections from within the system. One of its members, Takchi "Fastbeat" Tam, revealed to me that as soon as they were registered, Narrow Church submitted an advertisement to several pro-democracy newspapers, including *Ming Pao*, that "welcomed the entire Hong Kong's seven million people to be a Christian for one day" so that they could oppose the "small circles election" on October 30, 2011.[106] They printed a Narrow Church Christian membership card that readers could detach, wrote out the Apostles' Creed, and told their readers to recite it. On recitation, the reader was now a Christian, at least temporarily so, and could participate in the Protestant elections as a member of Narrow Church.[107] They then instructed them to cast blank votes with statements like, "This is evil" and "This is a small circle election." Fastbeat said that he calculated that approximately one thousand people became Narrow Church members for that day, as about 10 percent of the ballots turned out blank.[108] The HKCC officials I spoke with, including Lo Lung Kwong, expressed annoyance at these tactics.[109] It also means that they worked.

The long-standing scandal of the Election Committee was in turn, by March 2012 when I was in full swing in my fieldwork, compounded by the scandals that happened among both the outgoing CE Donald Tsang and the two viable CE candidates, Henry Tang and Leung Chun-ying (better known as C. Y. Leung), that I related in the previous chapter. As I noted in chapter 4, several Protestant clergy in Hong Kong issued a statement in *Ming Pao* on March 2, 2002, that was signed by some eight hundred Protestant leaders from across the ideological spectrum. The statement excoriated the various scandals that they alleged were undermining the political legitimacy of the elections. It "deplored the Chief Executive Election that used various misdemeanor shocks as a point of attack and struggle" (referring to the exposés about one of the candidates, Henry Tang, having erected an illegal structure in his home) while "exposing how the political circle is connected with the interests of the business community" (referencing the revelations that CE Donald Tsang had taken personal favors from property tycoons and organized crime groups). It then made three appeals. First, it called on the 1,200 members of the Election Committee to "vote based on their conscience," listening to the "voice of the seven million Hong Kong people" without attempting to flatter the elites. Second, it called on whoever would win the CE elections to "repair public confidence" by being politically transparent. Third, it demanded that Hong Kong society "remove obstacles to the implementation of universal suffrage," for the current electoral system was now revealed to "create more conflicts of interest and social differences."[110]

The statement took on a life of its own over the course of my fieldwork as it went through the rigamarole of the Protestant public theology debate. Both those who were close to the existing regime and progressive activists who demonized it found fault with the statement. As both of these sets of respondents told me, it had been subjected to revisions that had undermined its legitimacy by removing direct accusations against Tang and Tsang so that it would read in general terms about voting "based on conscience" and the need to rebuild public trust.[111] For some revivalists I spoke with, even these revisions were not compassionate enough. Breakthrough's Philemon Choi told me that he did not sign the statement because it was, in his words, "too self-righteous because it condemns Henry Tang: you have justice, but where is the mercy? When Nathan confronted David, he did so humbly and gently, so he responded with repentance."[112] Choi then said that he had personally confronted Tang, and "he wept, because I treated him as a real person and did not label him as evil."[113] Megachurch pastor Rev. Peter Ho also refused to sign the statement, again because "we ourselves, we are not doing the proper way." Ho observed that "maybe their [the Christian leaders'] home also has some kind of illegal structure" and that the public should be more forgiving of these politicians' private lives.[114] Ho had a point. After the elections, it turned out that C. Y. Leung also had built some structures at his houses on the Peak without the proper permits.[115]

On the other hand, there were accusations that the revisions of the statement indicated that Protestant leaders supported the "small circle election" as an undemocratic exercise. As the architect of the HKCC elections, Lo Lung Kwong told me in our interview that "these criticisms are schizophrenic because they themselves rely on public opinion." Still, he accepted that those like him in the public sphere always received criticism, even to the point of heightening their public persona.[116] At Narrow Church, Fastbeat elaborated on his criticisms in our interview. He said that he had spoken to a number of Protestant clergy and that they were more or less fatalistic about the Election Committee. "This is our reality," he summarized his interpretation of their sentiments, "to be either for Tang or for Leung. There is no way out." He then said that they chose Tang as the lesser of the two evils. Tang, Fastbeat told me, had once given an interview on celebrity pastor Enoch Lam's television show in which he had told Christians that he would "use love to govern Hong Kong." That he had been interviewed on this popular show was suggestive of the way the wind among some Protestants was blowing, Fastbeat suggested. Then Fastbeat recounted the *Ming Pao* statement's revision process and suggested that those who were in on it knew that Tang's personal scandals would propel Leung Chun-ying to become the new CE. He speculated that this statement veiled their pragmatic support for Leung so that Lo would be able to tell

Leung that "you are the voice of the people" while telling the signatories that Leung had been elected "based on their conscience."[117]

Whether Fastbeat's speculations were in fact true is beside the point. But HKCI's Fan Lap Hin drove home the problem to me. The statement, he said, attempted to "use politics to make an impact, for example, like making a statement," but those politics seldom produced structural changes since the "method of protest" reinforced the system and did nothing in fact to change the mechanisms of power.[118] In 2012, those structures in Hong Kong crystallized around the problem of the Election Committee, the symbol that stood in for democratic longings in a city that was run in fundamentally undemocratic ways. But what that meant was that the Election Committee—indeed, the nature of the Hong Kong elections in 2012—was the secular force that shaped what was being called public theology. Gone again were the concerns of Tiananmen, much less the conception of the church as separate from the government. By 2012, it was a system that was external to churches that became the theological shaping force, forcing it to reckon with an internally contradictory electoral apparatus and begging the question of what democracy could possibly mean, even if everyone for or against it generally agreed that it was to be desired.

CONCLUSION:
THE CALCULATIONS OF DEMOCRATIC ENGAGEMENT

In each of these Pacific Rim civil societies, the problem that Cantonese Protestants faced when it came to political engagement with electoral politics was a proverbial "damned if you do, damned if you don't" dilemma. At face value, the revivalist theology that came to dominate Cantonese Protestantism across the Pacific Rim in the 1970s had an easy answer to the problems of secular politics. The purity of the church's space, this theological narrative went, should be guarded at all costs, even at the expense of engagement with the important social and political issues of the day.

The problem is that Cantonese Protestants, as I have been showing, do not live simply in the vacuum of the church. Some of their politics may, on the face of it, be motivated by the socially conservative issues of sexuality and private security. But more important, even what is private—like personal prosperity and business success—requires some level of engagement with the system that may enable or inhibit it (or sometimes both).

The case might be made that the events in 1989 on Tiananmen Square provoked a kind of theological reflection among Cantonese Protestants across these Pacific Rim civil societies about the importance of the systems that they have lived within and those in which they currently reside. But as I hope to have shown, Tiananmen was but a moment of provocation; the story then leaves it behind, in most cases, mostly due to the subsequent urgency for democratic participation in the 1990s and 2000s. Because their communities did not exist in theological vacuums, they found themselves getting involved, at the time of my research, in the San Francisco mayoral races in 2011, the Canadian federal elections also in 2011, and the debates about the Election Committee in Hong Kong in 2012.

This dynamic of having a system to work within is suggestive for an interpretation of the structures of Pacific Rim civil societies themselves. The systems are secular; Cantonese Protestants cannot participate in them by tooting their own revivalist theological horns. There is, as the anthropologist Talal Asad puts it, a process of translation whereby their motivations need to be legible in terms of a calculative politics.[119] What is interesting about these secular translations that enable political participation is that they are also not optional. Cantonese Protestants have become integrated into the democratic worlds of Pacific Rim civil societies through the narratives of "Asian America" in San Francisco, "Chinese Christians" in federal electoral ridings in Metro Vancouver, and public theology in Hong Kong's political system. This integration, I have suggested in this chapter, is ironically that which seems to scatter Cantonese Protestant communities and networks internally as they disagree about their modalities of engagement with worlds outside the church. But there is general agreement that it is necessary, regardless of whether one might frame it theologically as evil. In such sheets of scattered sand, such agreement about democracy, however vague it might be, is remarkable. The sheet of the Pacific Rim, in other words, may well be a vaguely democratic one, but the various versions of democracy that Cantonese Protestants might advocate are the sands scattered on it.

Epilogue

Ten Years

You, my brothers, were called to be free.
—Galatians 5:13

On October 21, 2016, the group the Ten Years Workshop hosted a screening of the award-winning set of film shorts known as *Ten Years* at the evangelical Tenth Church Vancouver. It would have been a bit *leung*, as Cantonese slang has it for something that is really on the nose, to call the event "Ten Years at Tenth." They opted for "Ten Years: A Community Conversation."[1]

Ten Years is a compilation of five films that together depict a dystopian future of a Hong Kong without democracy and the freedoms guaranteed in the Basic Law. The first short imagines a plot by the authorities to pass a National Security Bill on the basis of a concocted emergency, with the police and organized crime collaborating to stage a political assassination. The second follows the activities of a couple who use taxidermy to preserve objects from bulldozed buildings, the last being one of the couple's own body. In the third, viewers follow the travails of a taxi driver who cannot speak Mandarin in a city that is mandating language change from Cantonese. The fourth is a fictional documentary that speculates about a self-immolation of radical activists in front of the Liaison Office of the People's Republic of China (PRC) in Hong Kong. The fifth tells the story of a grocer who gets in trouble for putting the label "local egg" on the eggs he is selling, as words like "local" have been banned from Hong Kong for being suggestive of the ideology that the city should be autonomous from the mainland.[2]

The films were made in 2015, shortly after the formal eviction of the 2014 Umbrella Movement street occupations. Those protests had begun after the extended lead-up of the Occupy Central with Love and Peace (OCLP) movement since January 16, 2013. After police fired tear gas on a protesting crowd attempting to occupy the government areas of Admiralty on September 28, tens of thousands of Hong Kong residents descended on the streets. Their slogans evolved into a demand, for OCLP had called for "genuine universal suffrage" for candidates not pre-vetted by Beijing. For seventy-nine days, they held the government district of Admiralty, the commercial center of Causeway Bay, and the local neighborhoods of Mong Kok. *Ten Years* was made after these protests were cleared without their demands being met. The prediction in the films was that if protections could not be secured for Hong Kong's civil society freedoms, then in ten years, the city would be completely subsumed under the legal structures of the mainland.

The joke is that it only took five years. In 2019, the Hong Kong government put forward a bill that, if passed, would amend the criminal code to allow for the extradition of anyone in Hong Kong to any requesting jurisdiction that claimed that that person had committed a crime. Fearing that the amended law would be used against dissidents (the claim was that the PRC could claim that any of its critics had committed a crime against the state), millions of the city's residents came out for a series of protests that lasted from mid-June through the beginning of the COVID-19 pandemic in 2020. On June 30, 2020, Beijing imposed the National Security Law on the city, effectively quelling the visibility of the protests and driving talk of them underground. Although the government initially gave assurances that the law would not be used retroactively, it did spell out broad infractions related to secession, subversion, terrorism, and collusion with foreign forces. In October 2021, court rulings opened the door for the retroactive use. By March 28, 2022, 183 persons had been arrested on allegations that they violated the law. On May 10 and 11, the trustees of the 612 Humanitarian Relief Fund, a group that paid the legal defense fees of protesters who could not pay for their own lawyers, were all arrested on charges of foreign collusion. Among those detained was Cardinal Zen, now ninety years old.

It had, I realized, been ten years since I had spoken to Zen during my fieldwork in Hong Kong. He was eighty then. By the time this book is published, it will have also been ten years since I wrote the doctoral dissertation on which it is based. As I shifted gears from the radical revisions to that text to the mental space where I had the capacity to write this epilogue, I thought about what I had been doing in the intervening decade between that exercise and this manuscript. I felt like I had gotten caught up in this drama of democracy that befell Hong Kong, so much that it shifted my research agenda. And yet, it felt like a recapitulation of the sheets of scattered sand that have undergirded this book, only with the specter of post-2012 Chinese nationalism vying for power as yet another sheet on the Pacific Rim.

The group calling itself the Ten Years Workshop was actually a loose coalition of mostly Cantonese-speaking Protestants who had found ourselves thrown together by the Umbrella Movement in 2014. During the 2019 Anti-Extradition Law Amendment Bill protests, it called itself Vancouver Christians for Love, Peace, and Justice (VCLPJ). I was not part of the organizing committee for the 2016 event—by the time it happened, I was living in Chicago and teaching Asian American studies at Northwestern University—but they insisted that I give the opening remarks by prerecorded video, mostly because I had led the editing on a book titled *Theological Reflections on the Hong Kong Umbrella Movement*, which had just come out that year.

But what interested me was how the event recapitulated many of the threads of my research. The film itself had the same kind of Christian influence as Hong Kong's politics and protests. One of its producers was a Protestant Christian, Andrew Choi, the son of Breakthrough's longtime general secretary Philemon Choi. He too delivered remarks by video at the event, which was in turn promoted as a church event.

On its Eventbrite page, Ten Years Vancouver called the proceedings a "community screening" that "asks Christians in Vancouver to collectively reflect on God's heart when it comes to Hong Kong's relationship with China. We invite you to watch the award-winning film *Ten Years* to learn about the fears of Hongkongers and to prayerfully consider how God might be inviting you to respond."[3] There was, of course, no way to tell if it was only Christians who attended (probably not; it was a free movie screening and a popular one at that). The six hundred free tickets on Eventbrite were all gone within a matter of weeks, and a plan had to be instated to arrange for those without tickets to line up at the front door, be counted to see if letting them in would violate the fire code, and then be ushered inside. This ticketing policy was a possibility because the group had acquired the rights to screen the film from the distributor Golden Scene for free. Because it was not for commercial purposes—it was a community event for theological reflection at a church—the film company had just let them have it for the night.

The specific church at which this event was held, Tenth Church Vancouver, was also significant and not only because it bore the name "Tenth." It had a reputation among Cantonese Protestants as the congregation that their second-generation English speakers tended to run off to when they got tired of their parents' churches.[4] There was some irony to this cycle. The flagship Cantonese Protestant church in Vancouver, the Chinese Alliance Church, had in fact started in the basement of what was originally called Tenth Avenue Alliance Church. But because the all-white congregation would not let Chinese people join their church, they had searched for other pastures, beginning in Chinatown, purchasing property on Knight Street in the 1970s and expanding in the 1990s to Marine Drive with their Fraserlands congregation, now an independent entity in and of itself. The new pastor in the 1990s, Ken Shigematsu, came in from Irvine, California, with a multicultural mission born out of what was being called the "silent exodus" in Asian American evangelical circles—he had been a co-pastor to the Korean American evangelical visionary Dave Gibbons as they planted Newsong Church as a model for this kind of thing—and to his church flocked young people from Chinese and Korean congregations all over Metro Vancouver.[5]

Part of the Ten Years Workshop organizing team also remembered Tenth's reputation for social justice, a memory in which Cantonese

Protestants played a significant part. In 2007, the municipal government had imposed on the church the requirement of a social services permit for a homeless shelter and food program that, incidentally, the city's own advocate for the homeless, Judy Graves, had had a hand in starting. With some interreligious encouragement, the church decided to fight the imposition, which they did and won. The coalition that grew up around the church was called Faith Communities Committed to Solidarity for the Poor (FCCSP). Helming FCCSP was none other than Bill Chu, the Tiananmen activist who worked for First Nations land rights and Chinese Canadian reconciliation with them (see chapter 5).

There was some speculation in 2016 that there might be trouble at Tenth Church Vancouver for hosting the screening of *Ten Years*, but there were no security problems and everything went smoothly. The same could not be said of a prayer meeting that VCLPJ planned at Tenth Church on August 18, 2019. According to a Facebook post by the group that was later included on the *Church for Vancouver* blog's roundup on the event, one hundred demonstrators followed the "Pray for Hong Kong" event to the church and loudly protested it from outside, waving PRC flags, chanting pro-China slogans, and taking pictures of participants in the prayer meeting.[6] Those in the church felt so unsafe that they had the police create exit pathways so that they could escape the premises. The event was postponed to September 8.

The counterprotest to VCLPJ generated a variety of reactions. An Eastern Catholic priest, Fr. Richard Soo, SJ—and incidentally, my pastor currently—was a member of the VCLPJ. He penned an editorial for the local Catholic newspaper that was then reprinted in the *Vancouver Sun* insisting that he would not stay quiet despite intimidation because the Bible called for such acts of justice.[7] In an interview with Douglas Todd for the *Vancouver Sun*, another VCLPJ figure, Rev. Samuel Chiu, said that he understood the protests to be divisive among Chinese Christians—and in his case, Cantonese Protestants—in Metro Vancouver. "I'm being pressed by some local Chinese people to not be so vocal," he said. "Some church elders are coming up to me and saying, 'Stop talking about the protests.' It shocked me."[8]

But perhaps one of the most interesting questions that came to me about the VCLPJ derived from an Asian American journalist going by "D. Cheng" who interviewed me for the evangelical magazine

Christianity Today. Cheng had heard about the Tenth prayer meeting, but they wanted to take the conversation out of Canada and make a connection to Chinese *American* churches. When they spoke with me, they said that they had already spoken with sociologist Fenggang Yang, who told them that he did not think that Chinese American churches would throw their weight behind the Hong Kong protests. There had been an influx of Mandarin-speaking PRC-based migration, he said, and churches that had both "very nationalistic Chinese Christians and more democratic Chinese Christians" would find it "hard . . . to have any meaningful conversation."[9]

Yang was right, of course, but I still had to have a think about Cheng's question. There had indeed been some very visible Chinese American protests, often associated with the right, in the time after my research had ended in 2012. I had heard, for example, of not only Chinese Americans (mostly from my Protestant students at Northwestern whose parents were Trump supporters) but also Chinese *Canadians* openly supporting the election of Donald Trump to the presidency in 2016.[10] A lawsuit in 2014 bent on striking down affirmative action at Harvard University resulted in the United States Supreme Court deciding to do just that in 2023. Although it was formally filed by conservative activist Edward Blum, the media positioning of the case relied heavily on the support of Chinese Americans who feel that race quotas disadvantage them for admission, even though they are technically a racial minority in the United States.[11] So too, on February 20, 2016, a widely publicized Chinese American protest moved through Brooklyn calling for justice to be served for a police officer, Peter Liang. Liang had fired his gun into what he thought was an empty stairwell and accidentally killed a Black man, Akai Gurley. In what seemed the complete opposite of what a movement like Black Lives Matter might have called for, what the protesters meant by "justice" was that they wanted him to be acquitted, as they felt that he, as an Asian American, was being scapegoated for white supremacist police violence against Black people. In one video, a protester explained that Asian Americans were not "aligning ourselves with white privilege"—in fact, she said that "Chinese people, Asian people, need to understand that we do not have white privilege," which she took to mean "wanting to be put above the law"—and that she was protesting because "Peter Liang took the fall for the sins of a country."[12] The slippage between "Chinese people" and "Asian people" was telling. In the aftermath of the protests, some journalists also followed the repercussions of the case to the PRC, where they found that both online conversation and state media were covering it with some attention.[13]

The trouble with all of these examples, with the fascinating links between events and issues that used to be covered under the banner of Asian American and Asian Canadian identity to the rising specter of Chinese nationalism across the Pacific, was that it was difficult to find a church angle for any of them. I also did a quick search to see if anyone I had interviewed in the Bay Area had been involved in these movements or had said anything about Hong Kong. I found nothing. But the silence was also pregnant. "Just as Hong Kong Christians mostly want peace," I said, "those in the diaspora also want peace in their churches and in Hong Kong." I then gave myself permission to give voice to some of my frustrations with the silence. "One of my long-standing concerns about the Chinese church is that when stuff happens that is upsetting to people in general, they don't want to talk about it," I continued. "Because they don't want to talk about it, they don't want to learn about it. But in not talking about it, they are talking about it."[14]

When the article came out, I couldn't believe I had actually brought myself to say what I really thought. It was my sheet of scattered sand explanation, still me saying that the ideological disunity in Chinese Christianity, and especially in Cantonese Protestantism, belied unexpected unities but not among the ideologies, not even, say, opposition to same-sex marriage and transgender rights or motivations based on private property interests. The unity could be found instead in the sheet, the field of disagreement, and if one looked closely, it was usually a secular structure to which Cantonese Protestants were responding. Here, those structures were on the surface related to the Hong Kong protests. But as Yang was suggesting, a new hegemon had also arisen to contest ideological power on the Pacific Rim. It was the specter of Chinese nationalism—the very anxiety raised by *Ten Years*—as a possibly new dominating secular force that engendered both protest and passivity all over the Pacific Rim. That was, I came to realize, what was different about the post-2012 era, and I came to that realization by admitting that I too was but a grain of sand on this sheet.

The concept I have returned to time and again to make sense of this research is what the literary scholar Shu-mei Shih calls the Sinophone Pacific. Some of my colleagues in the emerging field of Chinese Christianities, especially those in theology and religious studies, have told me in passing conversation that they are skeptical about this term "Sinophone" because it sounded like the "Sino-centrism" of what they called Sino-theology, which is heavily focused on the inculturation of Christian theology in Chinese national contexts. Initially, I shared their skepticism. To me, the prefix "Sino-" signaled a fixation on "China" as well. The field of China studies, for example, was the domain of "sinologists" who seemed to me notoriously fixated on the nation. There was a darker element too.[15] Since 2015, the Chinese Communist Party, under the leadership of Xi Jinping, has been trying to implement policies of Sinicization for religious groups throughout the PRC. The idea is that the various religions in China would become avenues for the patriotic propagation of "Chinese" values. In this way, Tibet's Buddhist institutions have been hollowed out, Uyghur Muslims in Xinjiang have been sent to reeducation camps, a secret deal has been struck with the Vatican through which party officials would appoint Catholic bishops, crosses in Christian churches have been taken down, and icons of the government leadership have been put up, all in the name of Sinicization.

I first heard about the Sinophone from Ting Guo, who was writing her manuscript on the political usage of "love" in China at the time and was one of the main cohosts of the Mandarin-language *Shicha Podcast*, an attempt to discuss critical theory and contemporary issues with young audiences throughout the Mandarin-speaking world. I learned quickly that what Shih means by the Sinophone is precisely the opposite of Sinicization. Indeed, for Shih, it refers to any community that has the burden of speaking a "Sinitic language" that brings it, often unwillingly, into contact with the hegemony of Chinese nationalism.[16] Guo later became one of my coauthors for projects related to the Hong Kong protests, and she invited me as one of her collaborators to her class on modern Sinophone worlds to talk about how I came to learn about the term. "From you," I said, adding that I had to "unlearn" my "toxic masculinity" to engage with feminist scholarship to understand the term more fully. "Be like Justin," she tweeted after that session.[17]

In what is becoming a bipolar world where the dimension of the transpacific has become even more exacerbated, Shih's concept of the Sinophone, developed in what must seem now as the halcyon days of the mid-2000s when she could still write of films in post-handover Hong Kong as caught between "nostalgia" and the "neurosis" of finding itself newly attached to a "nation," remains a way forward for communities that now have to live between these two competing nationalisms.[18] One piece that I learned about from *Shicha Podcast* was the journalist E. Tammy Kim's article in the *Columbia Journalism Review* titled "Transnationally Asian." What Kim stresses are the informal messaging networks among transpacific families, as well as community journalist collectives that have reported extensively on protests and democratization throughout Asia, that in fact bind Asian communities together across borders much more strongly than any nationalist ideology can. Moving off the fixation in many Asian American circles around aspirations for representation in politics and popular culture, Kim argues that what is much more commonly in vogue, albeit sometimes hidden by its informalities, are the practices of care that she identifies within these kinship and translocal networks that operate in their own languages and vocabularies instead of the stories of the dominant nationalist structures that seem to be in power.[19]

Cantonese Protestants, I suggest, remain important as actors in these informal networks as they negotiate these shifts in Pacific Rim secularities. Ten years between the dissertation and the book manuscript has afforded me a clarity in what those transformations might be. In that time, Chinese nationalism seems to have itself developed into a powerful set of dreams about the greatness of the Chinese nation. The Pacific Rim, once developed by Anglo-American hegemonic powers as an attempt to control the Pacific region and to contain China's growth, has become much more of a fusion of these two nationalist ideations and is probably open to more. Yet what is common between both fantasies is that they can only be used to power institutions operating at local levels, and when they work powerfully, they project a kind of secular hegemony into which communities like Cantonese Protestants need to find some level of legibility. Such a dynamic may continue to lead to ideological fragmentation as theological transformation is seldom a matter of consensus. But it also does provide a sheet, one that after the time I have studied in this book, may seem new with the expansion of Chinese nationalism and yet remains a continuation of the same story. The secular dreams of the Pacific Rim are evolving, and so the story of Cantonese Protestants and communities like theirs in their struggles for freedom on the one hand and legibility on the other will most likely continue, even well beyond these last ten years.

NOTES

PREFACE

1. See Justin K.H. Tse, *Religious Politics in Pacific Space: Grounding Cantonese Protestant Theologies in Secular Civil Societies* (PhD diss., University of British Columbia, 2013).

2. Ian Young, "School Transgender Policy Row," *South China Morning Post*, May 22, 2014, https://www.scmp.com/news/world/article/1517362/school-transgender-policy-angers-vancouvers-chinese-christians.

3. Douglas Todd, "Metro Vancouver's Chinese Christians Wrestle with Morality of Homosexuality," *Vancouver Sun*, June 28, 2013, D5. See also Justin K.H. Tse, "'Fraught' Chineseness: 'Chinese Christians' in the *Vancouver Sun*," in *Ecclesial Diversity in Chinese Christianity*, ed. Alexander Chow and Easten Law (New York: Palgrave, 2021), 183–207.

4. Statistics Canada, "Religion (95) and Visible Minority Groups (15) for Population, for Canada, Provinces, Territories, Census Metropolitan Areas and Census Agglomerations, 2001 Census—20% Sample Data. 2001 Census. Statistics Canada Catalogue Number 97F0022XCB2001005," May 13, 2003, https://www150.statcan.gc.ca/n1/en/catalogue/97F0022X2001005.

5. See Justin K.H. Tse, "Making a Cantonese-Christian Family: Quotidian Habits of Language and Background in a Transnational Hongkonger Church," *Population, Space, and Place* 17, no. 6 (2011): 759.

6. Timothy Tseng and James Chuck, eds., *2008 Report: Bay Area Chinese Churches Research Project Phase II: A Program Initiative of the Institute for the Study of Asian American Christianity (ISAAC)* (Castro Valley, CA: Institute for the Study of Asian American Christianity, 2008), 4–10.

7. Hong Kong Christian Council, *Survey Report on Public Perception of Protestantism in Hong Kong, 2021* (Hong Kong: Hong Kong Christian Council, 2021). I am thankful to Francis Yip for supplying me with this report.

8. Ting Guo, "Politics of Love: Love as a Religious and Political Discourse in Modern China through the Lens of Political Leaders," *Critical Research on Religion* 8, no. 1 (2020): 39–52.

9. Gary Okihiro, *Third World Studies: Theorizing Liberation* (Durham, NC: Duke University Press, 2016).

10. This list is far from exhaustive, but the range of theoretical work that remarkably is in agreement on a revisionist account of secularization that revolves around the transformations of theology, while debating how such theological shifts should be interpreted and assessed, includes Alasdair McIntyre, *After Virtue: A Study in Moral Theory* (Notre Dame, IN: University of Notre Dame Press, 1981); Talal Asad, *Formations of the Secular: Christianity, Islam, Modernity* (Stanford: Stanford University Press, 2003) and *Secular Translations: Nation-State, Modern Self, and Calculative Reason* (New York: Columbia University Press, 2018); John Milbank, *Theology and Social Theory: Beyond Secular Reason*, rev. ed. (Oxford: Blackwell, 2006); Charles Taylor, *A Secular Age* (Cambridge, MA: Belknap, 2007); Saba Mahmood, *Politics of Piety: The Islamic Revival and the Feminist Subject* (Princeton: Princeton University Press, 2004); Winnifred Favers Sullivan, *The Impossibility of Religious Freedom* (Princeton: Princeton University Press, 2005); Judith Butler, *Parting Ways: Jewishness and the Critique of Zionism* (New York: Columbia University Press, 2012); Gil Anidjar, *Blood: A Critique of Christianity* (New York: Columbia University Press, 2014); Elizabeth Shakman Hurd, *Beyond Religious Freedom: The Global Politics of Religion* (Princeton: Princeton University Press, 2015); Joan Wallach Scott, *Sex and Secularism* (Princeton: Princeton University Press, 2017); Jeffrey Redding, *A Secular Need: Islamic Law and Secular Governance in Contemporary India* (Seattle: University of Washington Press, 2020); Darryl Li, *The Universal Enemy: Jihad, Empire, and the Challenge of Solidarity* (Stanford: Stanford University Press, 2020). For a text on secularization in Asia, see Peter van der Veer, *The Modern Spirit of Asia: The Spiritual and the Secular in China and India* (Princeton: Princeton University Press, 2014).

11. See Ki Joo Choi, *Disciplined by Race: Theological Ethics and the Problem of Asian American Identity* (Eugene, OR: Pickwick, 2019); Jonathan Tran, *Asian Americans and the Spirit of Racial Capitalism* (New York: Oxford University Press, 2022). My sympathies lie with their willingness to engage the category of "Asian American" as a theological problematic as it is lived out in community life. I am also aware of Joel Robbins, *Theology and the Anthropology of Christian Life* (New York: Oxford University Press, 2020). However, I am wary of using theological categories in ways that overdetermine what my respondents are actually saying and doing. Even if they use the terms of theology, they may be using them in creative and unpredictable ways that may even be unmoored from historical Christian traditions but speak to a secular age. Examples of this kind of work include Hussein Ali Agrama, *Questioning Secularism: Islam, Sovereignty, and the Rule of Law in Modern Egypt* (Chicago: University of Chicago Press, 2012); Mayanthi L. Fernando, *The Republic*

Unsettled: Muslim French and the Contradictions of Secularism (Durham, NC: Duke University Press, 2014); Saba Mahmood, *Religious Difference in a Secular Age: A Minority Report* (Princeton: Princeton University Press, 2016); Angie Heo, *The Political Lives of Saints: Christian-Muslim Mediation in Egypt* (Berkeley: University of California Press, 2018).

12. Robbie Goh, "Noah's Ark: Evangelical Christianity and the Creation of a Value Environment in Hong Kong," *Material Religion* 10, no. 2 (2014): 208–32. I invited Goh to be a keynote speaker at a graduate conference on migration that I co-organized at the University of British Columbia (where I was based) and the National University of Singapore (where Goh was a dean at the time). Because he was in town for the conference, he attended my first-year spring review as a doctoral student and heard my initial musings on the ark. His argument that the ark somehow promotes an environmentalist ethic, based on his own visits to the ark before the operation shut down in 2011, is of course entirely his own.

13. Jaeson Ma, "Pray for Edison Chen, Me, and the World," JaesonMa.com, April 29, 2008, http://web.archive.org/web/20081028181303.

14. Stephen Kurczy, "Chinese Explorers Stand by Claim of Noah's Ark Find in Turkey," *Christian Science Monitor*, April 30, 2010, https://www.csmonitor.com/World/Global-Issues/2010/0430/Chinese-explorers-stand-by-claim-of-Noah-s-Ark-find-in-Turkey.

15. ArkWhy.org, "呼籲 [Call]," January 29, 2011, http://web.archive.org/web/20111203201637. A group calling itself ArkWhy challenged TME's findings on Mount Ararat on the basis of biblical archaeology, even marshalling the written testimony of creation scientists in the United States to call attention to problems in carbon dating.

16. Doug Ward, "Chan Accuses Rival of Using Churches," *Vancouver Sun*, January 17, 2006, A4.

CHAPTER ONE

1. Aihwa Ong, *Flexible Citizenship: The Cultural Logics of Transnationality* (Durham, NC: Duke University Press, 1999), 19.

2. Ackbar Abbas, *Hong Kong: Culture and the Politics of Disappearance* (Minneapolis: University of Minnesota Press, 1997), 7.

3. Christine Mok and Aimee Bahng, "Transpacific Overtures: An Introduction," *Journal of Asian American Studies* 20, no. 1 (2017): 1–9.

4. Aihwa Ong and Donald Nonini, eds., *Ungrounded Empires: The Cultural Politics of Modern Chinese Transnationalism* (New York: Routledge, 1997).

5. Ong, *Flexible Citizenship*, 3. Ong's counterstudy to this story of capital accumulation is a study of Cambodian refugee migrants to the San Francisco Bay Area; in this way, the Bay Area becomes a site of contestation among multiple

transpacific class narratives. Aihwa Ong, *Buddha Is Hiding: Refugees, Citizenship, the New America* (Berkeley: University of California Press, 2003).

6. Kris Olds, *Globalization and Urban Change: Capital, Culture, and Pacific Rim Mega-projects* (New York: Oxford University Press, 2001); Katharyne Mitchell, *Crossing the Neoliberal Line: Pacific Rim Migration and the Metropolis* (Philadelphia: Temple University Press, 2004).

7. Sin Yih Teo, "Dreaming inside a Walled City: Imagination, Gender, and the Roots of Immigration," *Asian and Pacific Migration Journal* 12, no. 4 (2003): 411–38; Johanna L. Waters, *Education, Migration, and Cultural Capital in the Chinese Diaspora* (Amherst, NY: Cambria, 2008); David Ley, *Millionaire Migrants: Trans-Pacific Life Lines* (Oxford: Wiley-Blackwell, 2010).

8. Ley, *Millionaire Migrants*, 255.

9. David Ley and Audrey Kobayashi, "Back to Hong Kong: Return Migration or Transnational Sojourn?," *Global Networks* 5 (2005): 111–28.

10. Johanna L. Waters, "Geographies of Cultural Capital: Education, International Migration and Family Strategies between Hong Kong and Canada," *Transactions of the Institute of British Geographers* 31, no. 2 (2006): 172–92.

11. Jini Kim Watson, *The New Asian City: Three-Dimensional Fictions of Space* (Minneapolis: University of Minnesota Press, 2011).

12. Bruce Cumings, "Rimspeak; or, the Discourse of the 'Pacific Rim,'" in *What's in a Rim? Critical Perspectives on the Pacific Region Idea*, ed. Arif Dirlik (Boulder: Westview, 1993), 30.

13. Arif Dirlik, "The Asia-Pacific Idea: Reality and Representation in the Invention of a Regional Structure," *Journal of World History* 3, no. 1 (1992): 61.

14. Arif Dirlik, "Introducing the Pacific," in *What's in a Rim? Critical Perspectives on the Pacific Region Idea*, ed. Arif Dirlik (Boulder: Westview, 1993), 4.

15. On American imperialism, see Daniel Immerwahr, *How to Hide an Empire: A History of the Greater United States* (New York: Farrar, Straus and Giroux, 2019). Although some might find the term "American empire" controversial, the theologian Reinhold Niebuhr did not seem to mind gesturing toward America as an imperial power when he wrote about it as such in *The Irony of American History* in 1953. In the wake of the United States leading the effort to contain communism in Korea, he remarked that the "final height of irony is reached by the fact that the most powerful nation in the alliance of free peoples is the United States," a society that claims to be innocent of global domination. See Reinhold Niebuhr, *The Irony of American History*, in *Reinhold Niebuhr: Major Works on Religion and Politics*, ed. Elisabeth Sifton (Washington, DC: Library of America, 2015), 467.

16. One of the pioneering studies of Pacific decolonization, American imperialism and militarism, and Asian nationalisms and struggles for self-determination is Bruce Cumings, *The Origins of the Korean War*, vol. 1: *Liberation and the Emergence of Separate Regimes, 1945–1947* (Princeton: Princeton University Press,

1981); *The Origins of the Korean War*, vol. 2: *The Roaring of the Cataract, 1947–1950* (Princeton: Princeton University Press, 1981). More recent studies include Ji-Yeon Yuh, *Beyond the Shadow of Camptown: Korean Military Brides in America* (New York: New York University Press, 2002); Jodi Kim, *Ends of Empire: Asian American Critique and the Cold War* (Minneapolis: University of Minnesota Press, 2010); Simeon Man, *Soldiering through Empire: Race and the Making of the Decolonizing Pacific* (Berkeley: University of California Press, 2018); Wen-Qing Ngoei, *Arc of Containment: Britain, the United States, and Anticommunism in Southeast Asia* (Ithaca: Cornell University Press, 2019); Christine Hong, *A Violent Peace: Race, U.S. Militarism, and Cultures of Democratization in Cold War Asia and the Pacific* (Stanford: Stanford University Press, 2020); Aimee Bahng, "The Pacific Proving Grounds and the Proliferation of Settler Environmentalism," *Journal of Transnational American Studies* 11, no. 2 (2020): 45–73.

17. Recent histories of the model minority myth and its creation of a problematic transpacific narrative for Asian Americans include Ellen D. Wu, *The Color of Success: Asian Americans and the Origins of the Model Minority* (Princeton: Princeton University Press, 2014); Madeline Hsu, *The Good Immigrants: How the Yellow Peril Became the Model Minority* (Princeton: Princeton University Press, 2015); Jane H. Hong, *Opening the Gates to Asia: A Transpacific History of How America Repealed Asian Exclusion* (Chapel Hill: University of North Carolina Press, 2019).

18. "Settler colonialism" refers to the act of clearing space of Indigenous peoples to enable their replacement by laborers engaged in resource extraction. See Patrick Wolfe, *Settler Colonialism and the Transformation of Anthropology: The Politics and Poetics of an Ethnographic Event* (New York: Cassell, 1999). One of the most systematic transpacific studies of settler colonialism is Gary Okihiro's "spacetime" trilogy: *Island World: A History of Hawai'i and the United States* (Berkeley: University of California Press, 2008); *Pineapple Culture: A History of the Tropical and Temperate Zones* (Berkeley: University of California Press, 2009); *The Boundless Sea: Self and History* (Berkeley: University of California Press, 2019). For studies of settler colonialism and ecological devastation in the Pacific, see Rob Wilson, *Reimagining the American Pacific: From* South Pacific *to Bamboo Ridge and Beyond* (Durham, NC: Duke University Press, 2000); Candace Fujikane and Jonathan Y. Okamura, eds., *Asian Settler Colonialism: From Local Governance to the Habits of Everyday Life in Hawai'i* (Honolulu: University of Hawai'i Press, 2008); J. Kēhaulani Kauanui, *Colonialism and the Politics of Sovereignty and Indigeneity* (Durham, NC: Duke University Press, 2008); Michelle Nancy Huang, "Ecologies of Entanglement in the Great Pacific Garbage Patch," *Journal of Asian American Studies* 20, no. 1 (2017): 95–117; Camille Fojas, Rudy P. Guevarra Jr., and Nitasha Tamar Sharma, *Beyond Ethnicity: New Politics of Race in Hawai'i* (Honolulu: University of Hawai'i Press, 2018); Maile Arvin, *Possessing Polynesians: The Science of Settler*

Colonial Whiteness in Hawai'i and Oceania (Durham, NC: Duke University Press, 2019); Nitasha Tamar Sharma, *Hawai'i Is My Haven: Race and Indigeneity in the Black Pacific* (Durham, NC: Duke University Press, 2021).

19. Viet Thanh Nguyen and Janet Hoskins, "Introduction: Transpacific Studies: Critical Perspectives on an Emerging Field," in *Transpacific Studies: Framing an Emerging Field*, ed. Janet Hoskins and Viet Thanh Nguyen (Honolulu: University of Hawai'i Press, 2014), 1–38.

20. On racial melancholia, especially in Asian American studies, and its psychoanalytic engagements, see Anne Anlin Cheng, *The Melancholy of Race: Psychoanalysis, Assimilation, and Hidden Grief* (New York: Oxford University Press, 2001); David Eng, *Racial Castration: Managing Masculinity in Asian America* (Durham, NC: Duke University Press); David Kyuman Kim, *Melancholic Freedom: Agency and the Spirit of Politics* (New York: Oxford University Press, 2007); Jinah Kim, *Postcolonial Grief: The Afterlives of the Pacific Wars in the Americas* (Durham, NC: Duke University Press, 2019).

21. See Kandace Chuh, *Imagine Otherwise: On Asian Americanist Critique* (Durham, NC: Duke University Press, 2003). Chuh argues that the field of Asian American studies is "subjectless," that the "Asian American" in the discipline is not so much an idealized personal figure but rather the transpacific social field and its structures.

22. Shu-mei Shih, "The Concept of the Sinophone," *PMLA* 126, no. 3 (2010): 709–18.

23. See Rey Chow, "On Chineseness as a Theoretical Problem," *boundary 2* 25, no. 3 (Autumn 1998): 1–24; Ien Ang, *On Not Speaking Chinese: Living between Asia and the West* (New York: Routledge, 2001); Allen Chun, "Fuck Chineseness: On the Ambiguities of Ethnicity as Culture as Identity," *boundary 2* 23, no. 2 (1996): 111–38; Lawrence J. C. Ma, "Space, Place, and Transnationalism in the Chinese Diaspora," in *The Chinese Diaspora: Space, Place, Mobility, and Identity*, ed. Lawrence J. C. Ma and Carolyn Cartier (Lanham, MD: Rowman & Littlefield, 2003), 1–50; Wang Gungwu, "Chineseness: The Dilemmas of Place and Practice," in *Cosmopolitan Capitalists: Hong Kong and the Chinese Diaspora at the End of the Twentieth Century*, ed. Gary G. Hamilton (Seattle: University of Washington Press, 1999), 118–34. Rey Chow's theoretical work in her classic *Protestant Ethnic and the Spirit of Capitalism* also alludes to the problems of "Chineseness" as an "ethnicity" but offers a broader theorization of ethnic categories in a purportedly multicultural world. See Rey Chow, *The Protestant Ethnic and the Spirit of Capitalism* (New York: Columbia University Press, 2002). Chun's colorful article has been expanded into the much more respectable Allen Chun, *Forget Chineseness: On the Geopolitics of Cultural Identification* (Albany: State University of New York Press, 2017).

24. Some prefer the term "banana" to describe a positionality like mine, as it plays on being "yellow" on the outside and "white" on the inside. I follow the

sociologist and novelist Louis Chu's preference for *jook sing* in his novel *Eat a Bowl of Tea* where "jook sing" implicitly describes a kind of existential emptiness and unreliable narration as it somatically manifests in the Cantonese protagonist's experience of erectile dysfunction. Sometimes this inner vacuousness can, as in the novel, generate a hysterical search for a substantive identity. See Louis Chu, *Eat a Bowl of Tea: A Novel* (New York: Lyle Stuart, 1961).

25. Henry Yu, "The Intermittent Rhythms of the Cantonese Pacific," in *Connecting Seas and Connected Oceans: Indian, Atlantic and Pacific Oceans and China Seas Migrations from the 1830s to the 1930s*, ed. Donna R. Garbaccia and Dirk Hoerder (Leiden: Brill, 2011), 393–414.

26. For more on the Asian American movement, see Daryl J. Maeda, *Chains of Babylon: The Rise of Asian America* (Minneapolis: University of Minnesota Press, 2009); Karen Ishizuka, *Serve the People: Making Asian America in the Long Sixties* (London: Verso, 2016).

27. I was interviewed about this phenomenon in 朱楠 [Chu Lam], "新移民改變宗教團體文化 [New immigrants are changing the culture of religious communities]," *Sing Tao Daily*, February 3, 2011.

28. Interestingly enough and in contrast to this sentiment against the War on Terror, one Cantonese Protestant radio personality, Raymond Kwong, wrote a post on the politically conservative blog *Free Republic* in 2003 lambasting "the liberals" for opposing the Iraq War while allegedly covering former American president Bill Clinton's tracks during his impeachment trial in 1998. See Raymond Kwong, "What Hypocrisy and Double Standard about Bush Landing on Carrier!," *Free Republic*, May 9, 2003, http://www.freerepublic.com/focus/f-news/903430/posts.

29. Focus group, Fremont, California (I), October 11, 2011.

30. Board of Education, Burnaby School District 41, "Policy #5.45.00: Sexual Orientation/Gender Identity."

31. Jennifer Moreau, "Mayor Says Hatred Tends to Spread," *Burnaby Now*, November 17, 2011, https://www.burnabynow.com/local-news/mayor-says-hatred-tends-to-spread-2931718; Jennifer Moreau, "Voice Pledges to Be 'a Thorn in Their Side,'" *Burnaby Now*, November 23, 2011, https://www.burnabynow.com/local-news/voice-pledges-to-be-a-thorn-in-their-side-2934809.

32. CTV, "'Disturbing' Video Linked to Burnaby Trustee Candidate," CTV News, November 17, 2011, https://bc.ctvnews.ca/disturbing-video-linked-to-burnaby-trustee-candidate-1.727197.

33. Focus group, Burnaby, British Columbia, January 16, 2012.

34. For a comprehensive study of Fr. Franco Mella's liberation theology that emphasizes his nonviolent principles, see Lai Tsz-him, "A Nonviolent Model of Liberation Theology: A Dialogue with Maoism," *Ching Feng* 17, no. 1–2 (2018): 43–66.

35. For more on Protestant and Catholic involvement in "right to abode" activism in Hong Kong, see Justin K.H. Tse, "One Family, Many Systems? Ecumenical

Alliances and the Defense of the Domestic in Post-handover Hong Kong," in *Gathered in My Name: Ecumenism in the World Church*, ed. William T. Cavanaugh (Eugene, OR: Cascade, 2020), 105–24.

36. Focus group, Sha Tin, Hong Kong (II), April 1, 2012.

37. "爭居權火燒入境處 50 傷 7 危全港震 [50 injured, 7 killed in arson fire during protest for Hong Kong's right of abode]," *Hong Kong Daily News*, August 3, 2000. I am grateful to the Hong Kong theologian Lai Tsz-him for helping me figure out what event to which these respondents were referring.

38. ATV World Newsline with Michael Chugani, "Benny Tai and Priscilla Leung," *ATV World Newsline*, June 2, 2013. See Ben2015Ben, "ATV World Newsline (Michael Chugani) with Priscilla Leung, Benny Tai," YouTube, June 3, 2013, https://youtu.be/hm7beyGxYvI.

39. Fion Li and David Tweed, "Support for Occupy Hong Kong over Vote Waning, Group Says," *Bloomberg*, September 2, 2014, http://www.bloomberg.com/news/2014-09-02/support-for-occupy-hong-kong-over-vote-waning-group-says.html.

40. This comment came in response to a conference paper I presented at the American Academy of Religion in 2016 in a session titled "Local Knowledge of 'Chinese Religions.'" See Justin K.H. Tse, "Canto-theologies in the Umbrella Movement: Christians and Cantonese Heroes in Protest," paper presented at the Annual Meeting of the American Academy of Religion, San Antonio, November 19–22, 2016. I am grateful to Ting Guo for organizing this session.

41. "The sheet of scattered sand" is my own translation of the colloquial Cantonese phrase I encountered in my fieldwork, translated from 一盤散沙 (Cantonese, *yut pun san saa*). The official translation of Sun Yat-sen's original formulation, 一片散沙, uses the word "loose" where I use "scattered." "Loose," however, does not really capture the meaning of *san* (散), which includes a sense of not only that something appears to be disunited and fragmented but that it is that way because it has been made to be that way. "Scattered" is therefore my preferred translation. The 盤 (*pun*) is perhaps the more real contention because as the epigraph of this book also has it, Sun's formulation was indeed 一片散沙. A *pin* (片) can refer to a "sheet" but also a "piece" or a "slice" of something, which suggests that in the text of the *Three Principles*, it can almost be said to function as a kind of contradictory phrase, as how can one have a "piece" of scattered sand, or even a slice of it, unless one is referring to the scattered sand itself as a sheet, which in any case is not the popular understanding of the term? As Sun says in one of the passages he uses it in, those who use it—who at the time were critics of his nation-building idea—are "holding their spear to the shield," which is a Chinese wisdom phrase that denotes self-contradiction. The translation choice here, then, is my way of dealing with how this term has moved from its official place in Sun's writings to a popular Cantonese colloquialism that I encountered in my ethnography. In the Cantonese (*pun*)—and not the *Three Principles* (*pin*)—there is a container for the sand to be scattered onto or even into. A container, as I say in the manuscript also, is not what constitutes the sands but is

external to them. A container, however, does not need to be specific about its depth; one can scatter sands onto a plate or a pan, or as I have long conceived of it in my mind, a baking sheet. In each case, the container is still plausibly a *pun*. My sense is that the translation here does matter as a contribution to transpacific and Sinophone studies more generally, where there are attempts to capture the fragmentation and disunity of what has in the past been called the "Chinese diaspora," which is a term I do not use in the manuscript as the overwhelming consensus in the literature is that "diaspora," much as it also has to do with scattering, implies a homeland, which in the case of Sinophone subjects is deeply problematic because it is not always clear that there is a "China" that they belong to. See L. Ma, "Space, Place, and Transnationalism in the Chinese Diaspora"; Chun, "Fuck Chineseness."

42. Sun Yatsen, "The Principle of Nationalism: Lecture 1, Delivered on January 27, 1924," in *San Min Chu I: The Three Principles of the People*, trans. Frank W. Price (Taipei: Government Information Office, 1990), 4.

CHAPTER TWO

1. Lian Xi, *Redeemed by Fire: The Rise of Popular Christianity in Modern China* (New Haven: Yale University Press, 2010); Christie Chow, *Schism: Seventh-Day Adventism in Post-denominational China* (Notre Dame: University of Notre Dame Press, 2021).

2. Timothy Tseng, "Trans-Pacific Transpositions: Continuities and Discontinuities in Chinese North American Protestantism since 1965," in *Revealing the Sacred in Asian and Pacific America*, ed. Jane Naomi Iwamura and Paul Spickard (New York: Routledge, 2003), 241–71.

3. Philemon Choi, research interview, March 14, 2012.

4. Research interview, April 13, 2012.

5. Research interview, April 13, 2012.

6. Research interview, April 25, 2011.

7. Choi, research interview; see also Philip Teng, *Who Am I?* [in Chinese] (Hong Kong: Dao Sing Publishers, 1980); Ronald Y. K. Fung and Carver T. Yu, eds., *A Life of Ministry: Essays Presented to Philip Teng on His 60th Birthday by Members of the Faculty of the China Graduate School of Theology* (Hong Kong: China Alliance Press, 1982).

8. See Lian, *Redeemed by Fire*. Lian tells the intricate story of how Chinese revivalists sometimes, problematically, aligned themselves with the Kuomintang.

9. Stephen Yuanlian Chiu and Sun Lingli, *One Hong Kong Dollar Trip, Seven Thousand American Dollar Miracle* [in Chinese] (Hong Kong: China Bible Seminary Publishing Department, 1978).

10. Thomas Wang, "The God of John Sung Can Revive Us Too," in *Diary of John Sung: Extracts from His Journals and Notes*, ed. Levi Sung, trans. Thng Peng Soon (Singapore: Genesis, 2012), 420–22.

11. Hsu, *The Good Immigrants*.

12. Fenggang Yang, "Chinese Conversions to Evangelical Christianity: The Importance of Social and Cultural Contexts," *Sociology of Religion* 59 (1998): 237–57. See also Carolyn Chen, *Getting Saved in America: Taiwanese Immigration and Religious Experience* (Princeton: Princeton University Press, 2006). Chen argues that religious experience intensifies as part of the transpacific immigrant process of assimilation.

13. Amy Tan, *The Joy Luck Club* (New York: Ivy, 1989), 6. See also Amy Tan, *The Kitchen God's Wife* (New York: Ivy, 1991), 7. In the latter, the protagonist's father is a former pastor at FCBC.

14. Tseng and Chuck, *The 2008 Report*, 61.

15. Research interview, June 9, 2011.

16. James Chuck, "Where Are the Chinese Churches Heading in the 1970's?," paper presented at the Chinese Christian Union, San Francisco, February 28, 1970; quoted in Tseng, "Trans-Pacific Transpositions," 263–64.

17. I am very grateful to Timothy Tseng for graciously providing documents on the Tahoe conference and CONFAB that he had accessed from the Edwar Lee papers at the Ethnic Studies Department at the University of California, Berkeley. I also thank Rev. James Chuck for giving me the CONFAB conference proceedings. I have also used these documents to write Justin K.H. Tse, "Liberal Protestant Chinatown: Social Gospel Geographies in Chinese San Francisco," *Chinese America: History and Perspectives* (2015): 29–46. I am grateful to the Chinese Historical Society of America for granting me permission to reprint these portions in this book.

18. Tahoe Rethinking Commission, *Tahoe Rethinking Commission Report* (San Francisco: Lake Tahoe Chinese American Youth Conference, 1949). I work here from Timothy Tseng's notes on the document, which I am grateful to him for sharing.

19. Horace Cayton and Anne Lively, *The Chinese in the United States and the Chinese Christian Churches* (New York: National Council of Churches, 1955). I am grateful to Rev. James Chuck for donating his copy of the report to me.

20. CONFAB, *Chinese Churches Today and Tomorrow* (San Francisco: National Conference of Chinese Churches in America, 1955).

21. Alan Wong, research interview, July 17, 2011.

22. James Chuck, research interview, June 11, 2011.

23. Helen Jin Kim, "Niseis of the Faith: Theologizing Liberation in the Asian American Movement" (unpublished BA thesis, Stanford University, 2006). Other accounts of Protestant churches being involved in the Asian American movement can be found in William Wei, *The Asian American Movement* (Philadelphia: Temple University Press, 1993); Russell Jeung, *Faithful Generations: Race and New Asian American Churches* (New Brunswick, NJ: Rutgers University Press, 2005). San Francisco State College was renamed San Francisco State University in 1972 after the strikes.

24. Perhaps the most detailed account of the strikes themselves can be found in Karen Umemoto, "'On Strike!' San Francisco State College Strike, 1968–69: The Role of Asian American Students," *Amerasia Journal* 15, no. 1 (1989): 3–41. See also Ishizuka, *Serve the People*, and Okihiro, *Third World Studies*.

25. Alan Wong, research interview. See Umemoto, "On Strike," 11, for a more detailed story that happened to "A. W."

26. "Presbyterian Church in Chinatown PCC—Faith in Action: Mei Lun Yuen (2012)," 2012, http://www.pccsf.org/faithinaction/meiLunYuen.html.

27. "Mei Lun Yuen Use Permit Application Unanimously Approved by Commission," *East-West: The Chinese American Journal*, January 26, 1977, 1. See also Kim, *Niseis of the Faith*, 60–62, for a detailed account of this story. See also Harry Chuck and Josh Chuck, dirs., *Chinatown Rising* (San Francisco: Center for Asian American Media, 2019).

28. Frank Mar, *I Remember* (Oakland: KTVU, 1984), 12.

29. See Mar, *I Remember*. Additional information here was provided in Katie Choy-Wong, research interview, June 17, 2011; Russell Yee, research interview, July 6, 2012.

30. Jeung, *Faithful Generations*, 26. Jeung acquired this estimate from Frederick Bird, *A Study of Chinese Churches in the San Francisco Bay* Area (N.p.: Bureau of Community Research, 1968). See also Timothy Tseng, "Protestantism in Twentieth-Century Chinese America: The Impact of Transnationalism on the Chinese Diaspora," *Journal of American East-West Relations* 13 (2004–2006): 129–30, n24.

31. James Chuck, "The National Conference of Chinese Christian Churches, Inc.: A Brief Chronology," in CONFAB, *Growing Deep, Reaching Out: Discerning God's Direction for His People* (San Francisco: National Conference of Chinese Christian Churches, Inc., 1998).

32. Tseng and Chuck, *The 2008 Report*, 117.

33. Tseng and Chuck, *The 2008 Report*, 114.

34. Tseng and Chuck, *The 2008 Report*, 113. Lord's Grace Christian Church has since moved in 2000 to Mountain View. I am grateful to Rev. Andy Ching, a former pastor there, for confirming this information in Andy Ching, research interview, December 13, 2012.

35. Tseng and Chuck, *The 2008 Report*, 98.

36. Tseng and Chuck, *The 2008 Report*, 119.

37. Frank Mar, "A New Wind Is Blowing," in *The Theologies of Asian Americans and Pacific Peoples*, ed. Roy I. Sano (Berkeley: Asian Center for Theology and Strategies, Pacific School of Religion, 1973), 434. See also Tseng, "Protestantism in Twentieth-Century Chinese America," 31. Tseng cites the original working paper in a collection edited by Wesley Woo that was later published in the Pacific Asian Center for Theologies and Strategies Reader but makes the same observation about Mar's inclination to include "separatist evangelical organizations."

38. Chinese Christian Mission, *50th Anniversary Booklet* (Petaluma: Chinese Christian Mission, 2011), 9.

39. Wally Yew, research interview, June 7, 2011. When I interviewed Yew, he was at CCM in the capacity of ministry ambassador.

40. Cumberland Presbyterian Chinese Church, *Celebrating 100 Years of Ministry, 1894–1994: A Call to Mission . . . the Mission Continues* (San Francisco: Cumberland Presbyterian Chinese Church. 1994), 5. See also Alan Wong, research interview. Wong was also an elder at Cumberland Presbyterian Chinese Church and opposed this move. He told me that he was outvoted. Ernest Chan's actions were thus "controversial" as they engendered some contestation.

41. Tseng and Chuck, *The 2008 Report*, 42.

42. James Chuck, *An Exploratory Study of the Growth of Protestant Chinese Churches in San Francisco, 1950–1982* (Berkeley: Bay Area Chinese Churches Research Project, 1996), 48; Tseng and Chuck, *The 2008 Report*, 63.

43. Tseng and Chuck, *The 2008 Report*, 52.

44. Kenneth Yeung, research interview, December 8, 2011.

45. Chinese Independent Baptist Church, *Centennial Celebration* (Oakland, CA: Chinese Independent Baptist Church, 2009), 11–13.

46. Russell Yee, research interview.

47. Steve Quen, research interview, December 20, 2011.

48. Alvin Louie, "Should an ABC Pastor Study Chinese?," in *A Winning Combination: ABC/OBC*, ed. Cecilia Yau (Petaluma: Chinese Christian Mission, 1986), 131–41.

49. *Chong v. Lee* (1981), 29 B.C.L.R. 13, para. 1. *Chong v. Lee* was itself a significant case in Canadian jurisprudence relating to religion. This case especially set precedent for the relation between the theology of churches and the jurisdiction of the courts in future cases that seemed to always involve Asian Canadian Protestant churches.

50. *Chong v. Lee*, para. 3.

51. See Stephen Lee, "A Brief Survey on the History of Christ Church of China, Vancouver," in *75th Anniversary Thanksgiving Report*, ed. Victor Lee, Allen Liu, Pat Fung, and Stephen Lee (Vancouver: Christ Church of China, 1986), 21. In Lee's account in the church's seventy-fifth anniversary booklet, this allegation can be refuted from the church's meeting minutes on January 11, 1972, and October 22, 1978, where it states that persons applying for membership who have already been baptized may be those initiated by either sprinkling or immersion.

52. *Chong v. Lee*, para. 4.

53. *Chong v. Lee*, para. 8.

54. Jiwu Wang, *"His Dominion" and the "Yellow Peril": Protestant Missions to Chinese Immigrants in Canada, 1859–1967* (Ottawa: Wilfred Laurier University Press, 2006), 67. See also Paul Yee, *Saltwater City: An Illustrated History of the Chinese in Vancouver* (Maderia Park, BC: Douglas and McIntyre, 2006), 19.

55. Lee, "A Brief Survey on the History of Christ Church of China, Vancouver," 19.

56. Halya Kuchmij, dir., *Generations: The Chan Legacy* [DVD] (Toronto: CBC Learning, 2007). Rev. Chan Sing Kai later became the pastor of the Chinese Methodist Church in Oakland's Chinatown and thus one of Rev. Edwar Lee's predecessors. I am also grateful to Todd Wong, whom I met at the Asian Canadian Writers' Workshop, for insisting that I include information from this documentary in my work.

57. Wang, *"His Dominion" and the "Yellow Peril*," 61, 64.

58. David Chuenyuen Lai, *Chinatowns: Towns within Cities in Canada* (Vancouver: University of British Columbia Press, 1988), 129; Kay Anderson, *Vancouver's Chinatown: Racial Discourse in Canada, 1875–1980* (Montreal: McGill-Queen's University Press, 1991), 196, 199.

59. This was reported in the city council proceedings on November 14, 1967, citing the solicitor general's letter from September 19, 1967, and can be found in the City of Vancouver Archives MCR 1-102, vol. 97, p. 309. I am grateful to the City of Vancouver Archives for directing me to this source.

60. See Robert Chan and Ruth Chan, eds., *The Red River Years: The Winnipeggers in the Potter's Hand* (Hong Kong: MI Design, 2014).

61. Augustus Chao and Sylvia Yu, *Serving God with Heart and Soul: The Life of Pastor Augustus Chao* (Vancouver: Canadians for Historical Justice and Racial Reconciliation, 2002), 79.

62. Chao and Yu, *Serving God with Heart and Soul*, 81.

63. Lee, "A Brief Survey on the History of Christ Church of China, Vancouver," 20.

64. David Leung, "David Poon," in *Leaders Who Shaped Us: Canadian Mennonite Brethren*, ed. Harold Jantz (Toronto: Kindred Productions, 2010), 276.

65. Lee, "A Brief Survey on the History of Christ Church of China, Vancouver," 20.

66. Leung, "David Poon," 277–78.

67. Lee, "A Brief Survey on the History of Christ Church of China, Vancouver," 21.

68. Gentle Lee, *His Name Is Wonderful—the Autobiography of Gentle Lee* [in Chinese] (Hong Kong: Chinese Alliance Press, 2006), 57–58.

69. Research interview, November 11, 2011. When I was a child, my father also used to tell me stories about these picketers. I never imagined that this story would take on significance for my research.

70. Lee, *His Name Is Wonderful*, 59.

71. Lee, *His Name Is Wonderful*, 59–60.

72. Lee, "A Brief Survey on the History of Christ Church of China, Vancouver," 22.

73. Research interview, May 10, 2011.

74. Edwin Kong is quoting directly here from Acts 6:4.

75. Edwin Kong, research interview, May 3, 2011.

76. See A. E. Sweeting and P. Morris, "Educational Reform in Post-war Hong Kong: Planning and Crisis Intervention," *International Journal of Educational Development* 13, no. 3 (1993): 201–16.

77. Beatrice Leung has since become professor in the Department of Politics and Sociology at Lingnan University in Hong Kong and writes on Sino-Vatican relations and church-state interactions in Hong Kong. See Beatrice Leung, *Sino-Vatican Relations: Problems in Conflicting Authority, 1976–1986* (Cambridge: Cambridge University Press, 2009); Beatrice Leung and Shun-Hing Chan, *Changing Church and State Relations in Hong Kong, 1950–2000* (Hong Kong: Hong Kong University Press, 2003). While Leung and Chan's history of church-state relations covers the educational services provided by her own order, the Precious Blood sisters, it omits the Golden Jubilee incident; Leung and Chan, *Changing Church and State Relations in Hong Kong*, 30–40.

78. John-Baptist Wu, *Thanks Precious Blood Golden Jubilee School*, pastoral letter, June 2, 1978, http://www.catholic.org.hk/v2/en/message_jw/y1978_7_gj.html.

79. Franco Mella, research interview, March 15, 2012; Jackie Hung, research interview, March 26, 2012. Both Franco Mella and the Justice and Peace Commission's director Jackie Hung Ling-Yu expressed that this was a devastating blow. When the Justice and Peace Commission reopened, it only issued statements and did research until 1997, when the new political situation brought about by the handover to Chinese sovereignty pushed it to become more vocal and participatory in Hong Kong's political contestations.

80. These two research interviews took place on March 16, 2012, and March 21, 2012, respectively.

81. Lo Lung Kwong, "Begging to Have a Double Portion of Your Spirit," in *Death Be Not Proud Conference* (Hong Kong: China Alliance Press, 2002), 141.

82. Sweeting and Morris, "Educational Reform in Post-war Hong Kong," 209–11.

83. For two sympathetic and critical accounts of CCCOWE's usage of the term "Chineseness," see Judith Nagata, "Christianity among Transnational Chinese: Religious versus (Sub)Ethnic Affiliation," *International Migration* 43, no. 3 (2005): 99–130; Jonathan Tam, "Renegotiating Religious Transnationalism: Fractures in Transnational Chinese Evangelicalism," *Global Networks* 19, no. 1 (2019): 66–85.

84. Harold J. Ockenga, "Challenge to the Christian Culture of the West," in *Fuller Voices: Then and Now*, ed. Russell P. Spittler (Pasadena: Fuller Theological Seminary, 2004), 17. Ockenga's speech at Fuller Theological Seminary's first convocation is widely taken to be one of the foundational moments in evangelicalism as an attempt to showcase itself as an intellectual movement. See Molly Worthen, *Apostles of Reason: The Crisis of Authority in American Evangelicalism* (New York: Oxford University Press, 2013).

85. Research interview, April 13, 2012.

86. Josephine So Yan Pui, *Death, Be Not Proud*, trans. Ho Hing Kay (Hong Kong: Breakthrough, 1989), 96–98.

87. Yam Chi Keung, "Engagement in Television by Protestant Christians in Hong Kong," *Studies in World Christianity* 11 (2005): 87–105.

88. Research interview, March 16, 2012.

89. Ruth Chan, research interview, January 5, 2013. Chan is not using "mainline" in a technical sense here but in a much looser way to talk about the "church establishment." Because Breakthrough Youth Ministries was not part of any church, its existence and status as "evangelical" were questioned.

90. Christian Organizations Joint Statement, "Addressing the Golden Jubilee Incident's Situation" [in Chinese], *Breakthrough Magazine*, June 1978, 19. I am grateful to Sookit Li for scanning a copy of this page for me.

91. Josephine So Yan Pui, "A Statement on Our Statement" [in Chinese], *Breakthrough Magazine*, June 1978, 20. I am grateful to Sookit Li, once again, for scanning a copy of this page for me.

92. Tinming Ko, *The Sacred Citizens and the Secular City: Political Participation of Protestant Ministers in Hong Kong during a Time of Change* (Farnham: Ashgate, 2000), 31.

93. Chu Yiu Ming, research interview, April 3, 2012.

94. Lo Lung Kwong, research interview, March 29, 2012.

95. Chu Yiu Ming, research interview.

96. Lo Lung Kwong, research interview.

97. Alexander Chow, *Chinese Public Theology: Generational Shifts and Confucian Imagination in Chinese Christianity* (New York: Oxford University Press, 2018). Of particular importance in Chow's analysis is how he distinguishes among various models of contemporary Chinese intellectual currents that position Christian theology in relation to the party-state, civil society, and market socialism.

CHAPTER THREE

1. For a theoretical account of why geographers insist on grounding transnational networks in the stubbornly limiting physicality of everyday lives, see David Ley, "Transnational Spaces and Everyday Lives," *Transactions of the British Institute of Geographers* 29, no. 2 (2004): 151–64. See also Olds, *Globalization and Urban Change*; Teo, "Dreaming inside a Walled City"; Mitchell, *Crossing the Neoliberal Line*; Ley and Kobayashi, "Back to Hong Kong"; Waters, "Geographies of Cultural Capital"; Waters, *Education, Migration, and Cultural Capital in the Chinese Diaspora*; Ley, *Millionaire Migrants*; David Ley, "A Regional Growth Ecology, a Great Wall of Capital and a Metropolitan Housing Market," *Urban Studies* 58, no. 2 (2000): 297–315.

2. Thomas Wang, research interview, July 6, 2011. Wang emphasized to me that it was the first time that he had seen "Chinese Christians" do anything of the sort. See also Deborah Lee and Lina Hoshino, dirs., *In God's House: Asian American Lesbian and Gay Families in the Church* [DVD] (Berkeley: Progressive Films, 2007). The 2004 rallies were described as a surprise and shock from Chinese Christian communities typically seen as apolitical.

3. John Ibbitson and Joe Friesen, "The Growing Ties of Immigrants and Conservatives," *Globe and Mail*, October 4, 2010, A1.

4. One of the most detailed accounts of this liberal imaginary around sexuality is Jo Becker, *Forcing the Spring: Inside the Fight for Marriage Equality* (New York: Penguin, 2014).

5. Focus group, Richmond, British Columbia, October 11, 2011.

6. Research interview, June 14, 2012.

7. California Ballot Proposition 8, "Eliminates the Right of Same-Sex Couples to Marry. Initiative Constitutional Amendment," California State Elections (November 4, 2008).

8. For the behind-the-scenes story, see Becker, *Forcing the Spring*.

9. See *Perry et al. v. Schwarzenegger*, 704 F.Supp.2d 921 (N.D. Cal., 2010), Decision, 5–7. Judge Vaughn Walker recounts how the plaintiffs advanced a case based on the Fourteenth Amendment of the United States Constitution that had not been engaged in previous litigation on same-sex marriage. The Fourteenth Amendment guarantees equal protection under the law, with discrimination only permitted in cases that pass "strict scrutiny" for the public interest of state security. I also write about this in "The Privacy of Hak-Shing William Tam: Imagining Asian Families in Proposition 8 in California," *Journal of Asian American Studies* 26, no. 1 (2023): 63–85, and am grateful to the journal for allowing me to reuse parts of this article for this book.

10. *Perry et al. v. Schwarzenegger*, 704 F.Supp.2d 921 (N.D. Cal., 2010), Trial Transcript, 1928. The smoking gun they are referring to is Hak-Shing William Tam, "What If We Lose?," Presence Ministry, September 4, 2009 (available in *Perry v. Schwarzenegger*, 704 F.Sup.2d 921 [N.D. Cal, 2010], Deposition of Hak-Shing William Tam, December 1, 2009, "What If We Lose" Letter).

11. *Perry*, Trial Transcript, 1922. This is a quote from Tam's website, 1man 1woman.net, "Homosexuality Linked to Pedophilia?," n.d., https://web.archive.org /web/20100222094656.

12. *Perry*, Trial Transcript, 1957.

13. *Perry*, Trial Transcript, 1914.

14. *Perry*, Trial Transcript, 1963.

15. *Perry*, Trial Transcript, 2003.

16. Hak-Shing William Tam, research interview, June 28, 2011.

17. *Perry*, Decision, 22. What the decision does not seem to take into account, however, is Tam's testimony that he had actually broken the Statement of

Unity twice when he spoke with the *San Jose Mercury News* on one of the Asian American Yes on 8 rallies and when he had spoken to a Chinese newspaper reporter about "sibling marriage." The defensive strategy seems to have been to render Tam's participation in the Statement of Unity as an indicator that he tended to act autonomously from ProtectMarriage.com and that his actions could not always be pinned on the umbrella organization. See *Perry*, Trial Transcript, 1970–71.

18. *Perry*, Trial Transcript, 1916, 1920.

19. *Perry*, Trial Transcript, 1907.

20. Hak-Shing William Tam, *Church, Stand Up as Salt and Light! Biblical Responses to Social Challenges Today* (Sunnyvale, CA: Traditional Family Coalition, 2006), ii.

21. As an effort to stall gay and lesbian high school dropout rates in the 1980s by child psychologist Virginia Uribe in Los Angeles, Project 10 was successfully implemented in Southern California in 1989 despite the vehement opposition of Rev. Louis Sheldon's Traditional Values Coalition. See Virginia Uribe, "Project 10: A School-Based Outreach to Gay and Lesbian Youth," *High School Journal* 77, no. 1–2 (1994): 108–12; Virginia Uribe, "The Silent Minority: Rethinking Our Commitment to Gay and Lesbian Youth," *Theory into Practice* 33, no. 3 (1994): 167–72. When Project 10 became an initiative in San Francisco's public schools, a conservative grassroots coalition that included Chinese Americans opposed it on the grounds that, as the National Association for Research and Therapy on Homosexuality's Dr. Joseph Nicolosi had it, counseling centers would channel teens with same-sex desires into a politically "gay" identity by activist counselors. See Joseph Nicolosi, "The Six Fallacies behind 'Project 10,'" Queer Resources Directory: Family Research Council, 1993, http://www.qrd.org/qrd/religion/anti/FRC/project.10-family.research.council.letter.

22. Hak-Shing William Tam, "Why I Helped Start Prop 8," *TFC Newsletter* 3, no. 3 (2008): 1.

23. Janet Jakobsen, *Working Alliances and the Politics of Difference: Diversity and Feminist Ethics* (Bloomington: Indiana University Press, 1998), 133. Jakobsen writes about the CFA as she shows that socially conservative movements tend to work on the strategy of "working alliances," including across racial lines, and advocates for feminist movements to be reconceptualized in similar terms.

24. Hak-Shing William Tam, research interview.

25. *Perry*, Trial Transcript, 1963.

26. Hak-Shing William Tam, research interview.

27. On Asian American presence among the marriage commissioners in 2004, see Mabel Teng, "The Right Place at the Right Time: Cultural and Political Controversy of San Francisco's Gay Marriage," *Amerasia Journal* 32, no. 1 (2006): 63–66.

28. Katherine T. Phan, "Q&A with Rev. Raymond Kwong," *Christian Post*, May 22, 2004, http://www.christianpost.com/news/q-a-with-rev-raymond-kwong-2690/.

29. Hak-Shing William Tam, research interview.

30. David Pang, research interview, December 13, 2011.

31. Chinese Family Alliance, "Traditional Family Day," April 25, 2004, http://web.archive.org/web/20060218220843.

32. Ulysses Torassa, "Thousands Protest Legalizing Same-Sex Marriage; Asian Americans, Christians Rally in Sunset District," *San Francisco Chronicle*, April 26, 2004, B1.

33. In addition to photographs uploaded to the Chinese Family Alliance's Homestead website at the time, this event was also recorded by the photographic and videographic recording services of a pastor who ran a small organization in the suburbs that broadcast biblical teaching to the PRC. See research interview, July 8, 2011.

34. *Perry*, Trial Transcript, 1907.

35. Thomas Wang, "Epilogue," in *America, Return to God*, ed. Thomas Wang (Sunnyvale, CA: Great Commission Center International, 2006), 126.

36. Thomas Wang, "'My People Have Changed God!,'" in *America, Return to God*, ed. Thomas Wang (Sunnyvale, CA: Great Commission Center International, 2006), 38.

37. Thomas Wang, introduction to *America, Return to God*, ed. Thomas Wang (Sunnyvale, CA: Great Commission Center International, 2006), 4.

38. As a point of clarification, former Louisiana Republican state representative Tony Perkins is the current president of the Family Research Council. The Family Research Council was itself originally founded in 1981 by socially conservative family psychologist and political commentator Dr. James Dobson as the political arm of his nonprofit organization Focus on the Family. The organizations have been administratively separate since 1992.

39. Hak-Shing William Tam, research interview.

40. *Perry*, Trial Transcript, 1899–1910, 1977.

41. *Perry et al. v. Schwarzenegger*, 704 F.Supp.2d 921 (N.D. Cal., 2010), Deposition of Hak-Shing William Tam, December 1, 2009. The video evidence is listed as Exhibit PX2542. I collated this list of Tam's media appearances in 2008 from the deposition.

42. Hak-Shing William Tam, "TFC Helped Pass Prop 8," *TFC Newsletter* 3, no. 3 (2008): 3. Tam differentiates here between the October 12 "prayer rally," which was co-organized by American Return to God Prayer Movement and TFC, and the rally in Cupertino on October 19. The only numerical estimate he gives is for the Cupertino rally. Videos of the October 12 rally show Portsmouth Square in Chinatown as crowded during the speeches, with a counterprotest to the side. See Outlook Video, "Proposition 8 Rally and Counter Rally—Pt. 2 Raw Video," October 31, 2008, https://www.youtube.com/watch?v=DTyjy4go4Gg.

43. CounterCounterCulture, "After-Action Report: Cupertino Open Air Rally in Support of Marriage and California's Proposition 8," *Free Republic*, October 20,

2008, http://www.freerepublic.com/focus/f-news/2109993/posts; 1man1woman.net, "Protect Traditional Marriage Cupertino Rally," n.d., http://1man1woman.net/cupertino_pic.html; Traditional Family Coalition, "List of Activities of Traditional Family Coalition" [in Chinese], http://tfcus.homestead.com/Events.html. Curiously, this list omits the October 12 rally and says that Tam was in Los Angeles for a conference on "Sexual Brokenness."

44. See CounterCounterCulture, "After-Action Report"; Traditional Family Coalition, "List of Activities of Traditional Family Coalition."

45. Ken McLaughlin, "Survey: Asian-Americans Overwhelmingly against Outlawing Gay Marriage," *San Jose Mercury News*, October 15, 2008, B1. Indeed, as the National Asian American Survey led by Karthick Ramakrishnan, Janelle Wong, Taeku Lee, and Jane Junn at the University of Southern California noted in the same article, a marked 57 percent of Asian Americans opposed Proposition 8 in October 2008, a surprise to many who would have assumed that this community would be more conservative on sexuality issues. See Janelle Wong, S. Karthick Ramakrishnan, Taeku Lee, and Jane Junn, *Asian American Political Participation: Emerging Constituents and Their Political Identities* (New York: Russell Sage Foundation, 2011).

46. Network on Religion and Justice, "No to Prop 8 Counter-Rally (to the Yes on Prop 8 Rally)," Past Events, October 12, 2008, http://www.netrj.org/?p=pastevents&id=18.

47. Research interview, July 10, 2011.

48. Franco Kwan, research interview, July 8, 2011.

49. Gerry Shih, "Chinese Christians Are the Focus of Same-Sex Marriage Case," *New York Times*, January 22, 2010, 19A.

50. Liu Tong, research interview, June 27, 2011.

51. Hak-Shing William Tam, research interview.

52. Research interview, December 13, 2012.

53. Research interview, July 18, 2011.

54. Focus group, San Jose, California, December 5, 2011.

55. Lam Sau Wing, "5 November 2008," *MoneyRadio* [audio], November 5, 2008, http://www.moneyradio.org.

56. David Pang, research interview.

57. Hak-Shing William Tam, research interview.

58. Focus group, Fremont, California (I).

59. Focus group, Fremont, California (II), December 3, 2011.

60. David Pang, research interview.

61. "哪一政黨最值得贏到你神聖的一票 [Which of the parties deserves your most sacred vote]" [Email], April 25, 2011; "With vigilance, please cast your ballot on May 2 / and a few issues here / - pls invite 10 friends to do the same" [Email], April 28, 2011. I am grateful to one of my interviewees for forwarding both the Chinese and English versions of the email to me. They are formatted almost exactly

alike, without much substantial difference in translation. I am quoting from the English one.

62. Focus group, Richmond, British Columbia, October 10, 2011.
63. Research interview, May 31, 2011.
64. Research interview, March 21, 2012.
65. Raymond Chan, "Raymond Chan on Criminal Code," House of Commons Hansard #218 of the 35th Parliament, 1st session, June 14, 1995, http://openparliament.ca/debates/1995/6/14/raymond-chan-2/only/.
66. Research interview, May 10, 2011. *Truth Monthly* became a politically conservative forum of sorts following the passage of the C-41 and C-33 sexual orientation bills, as its contributors paid attention to the left-leaning BCTF in 1996 and 1997. The events also coincided with a lawsuit that Langley's Trinity Western University filed against BCTF's guild, the BCCT, when they were denied accreditation because a "covenant" that all faculty, students, and staff signed prohibited homosexual practices. See *Trinity Western University v. British Columbia College of Teachers*, [2001] 1 S.C.R. 772, 2001 SCC 31.
67. Jeremy Torobin, "Investigation to Examine Police Action at Rally Clash," *Vancouver Sun*, August 9, 1997, A15.
68. Bill Chu, research interview, May 20, 2011.
69. K-John Cheung, research interview, June 3, 2011.
70. Canadian Alliance for Social Justice and Family Values Association, "Some of the More Important Works Done by CASJAFVA in the Past Ten Years for Your Information," 2012, http://www.canadianalliance.org/english/index.php.
71. K-John Cheung, research interview.
72. Research interview, May 5, 2011.
73. Research interview, July 17, 2012.
74. Focus group, Coquitlam, British Columbia, July 6, 2012.
75. Wayne Lo, research interview, May 14, 2011.
76. Research interview, April 28, 2011.
77. Research interview, May 3, 2011.
78. Wayne Lo, email correspondence, June 22, 2012.
79. Research interview, May 27, 2011.
80. Research interview, April 29, 2011.
81. Research interview, April 28, 2011.
82. Research interview, April 26, 2011.
83. Research interview, October 20, 2011.
84. Focus group, Richmond, British Columbia.
85. Focus group, Coquitlam, British Columbia.
86. Research interview, May 10, 2011.
87. Research interview, May 11, 2011.
88. Focus group, Richmond, British Columbia.
89. Focus group, Burnaby, British Columbia.

90. Focus group, Richmond, British Columbia.
91. Research interview, May 5, 2011.
92. Research interview, May 13, 2011.
93. There was also a school trustee, Chak Kwong Au, who successfully ran for city council at the time. He was widely known to be a Cantonese Protestant as well as a practicing psychotherapist. However, his political platform emphasized his commitments to multiculturalism, anti-racism, and democratic consultation in civil society. See City of Richmond, "Councillor Chak Kwong Au," https://www.richmond.ca/cityhall/council/about/members/ChakKwongAu.htm.
94. Moreau, "Mayor Says Hatred Tends to Spread"; Moreau, "Voice Pledges to Be 'a Thorn in Their Side.'"
95. Research interview, May 17, 2011.
96. Research interview, May 5, 2011.
97. Focus group, Burnaby, British Columbia.
98. Daniel Cheung, *Too Bright: An Insider's Discourse of the Society for Truth and Light* [in Chinese] (Hong Kong: Dirty Press, 2009).
99. Kung Lap Yan, ed., *Religious Right* [in Chinese] (Hong Kong: Dirty Press, 2010).
100. Kwan Kai Man, research interview (II), April 2, 2012.
101. Choi Chi Sum, research interview, March 26, 2012.
102. Kung Lap Yan, research interview, March 22, 2012.
103. Kwan Kai Man, research interview (I), March 23, 2012.
104. Choi Chi Sum, research interview.
105. Kwan Kai Man, research interview (I).
106. Choi Chi Sum, research interview.
107. Kwan Kai Man, research interview (II). I am deeply thankful for this generous conversation Kwan had with me.
108. Kwan Kai Man, research interview (II).
109. Kwan Kai Man, *Reflections on Human Rights and Homosexuality* [in Chinese] (Hong Kong: China Alliance Press, 2000).
110. The Hong Kong Catholic Diocese took a different approach. They first issued a statement that the diocese "vehemently object[s] to such cruel action infringing the rights of our followers." See "Hong Kong's Catholics Condemn Gay Activists for Disrupting Mass," *China Daily*, August 18, 2003, https://www.chinadaily.com.cn/en/doc/2003-08/18/content_255971.htm. Jackie Hung at the diocese's Justice and Peace Commission told me that her office's active role in advocating for the human rights of sex workers and sexual minorities convinced Bishop Joseph Zen Ze-kiun he should dialogue with these *tongzhi* activists. Jackie Hung, research interview, March 26, 2012. At a meeting arranged between the diocese and the *tongzhi* movement, Zen explained to the activists, "We have our doctrine, but whatever we could do to help you, we did," such as supporting the colonial government's decriminalization of homosexuality in 1991 and supporting an equal opportunity law against

discrimination for employment and property ownership. Joseph Zen, research interview, March 30, 2012.

111. Research interview, March 23, 2012.

112. Tim Cribb, "Justice for All: Gay Lobby Groups and Religious Bodies Appear Set for a Showdown as the Government Moves a Step Closer to Formulating Anti-discrimination Laws,' *South China Morning Post*, January 27, 2005, A16. I am thankful to Kwan Kai Man for providing this article.

113. Kwan Kai Man, research interview (I).

114. Research interview, March 23, 2012.

115. Choi Chi Sum, research interview.

116. Research interview, March 23, 2012.

117. Kwan Kai Man, research interview (I); research interview, March 23, 2012.

118. Research interview, March 23, 2012.

119. Kwan Kai Man, research interview (II).

120. See Ip King-Tat, ed., *The Ends of the Rainbow: 200 Days of Dispute over the SODO Legislation* [in Chinese] (Hong Kong: Key Road Press, 2005).

121. According to Hong Kong Catholic Diocese's Justice and Peace Commission's Jackie Hung, Bishop Zen himself had endorsed the Justice and Peace Commission's decision to have the *tongzhi* group lead the protest, despite the complaints of conservative Catholics who were presumably more in line with the diocese's Marriage Advisory Council, whose official position opposed SODO. Arguing that she had decided to put the gay rights group in the front because "my base is that we are all equal, that we are all the same," she recalled that STL "boycotted" them on the one hand, while conservative Catholics complained to Bishop Zen. Zen listened to Jackie Hung's explanation that "the demonstration's main theme is still universal suffrage, and that we are talking about electing the chief executive, electing the Legislative Council, we're not talking about homosexuality, but we feel that in this movement, they have their contribution." According to Hung, Zen then endorsed her decision. Jackie Hung, research interview.

122. Choi Chi Sum, research interview; see also Jackie Hung, research interview; Rose Wu, research interview, March 22, 2012.

123. Most of my information on the *Gay Lovers* documentary and the ensuing case *Cho Man Kit v. Broadcasting Authority*, HCAL69/2007 (2008), comes from Kwan Kai Man, research interview (II).

124. Kwan Kai Man, research interview (II).

125. Christian Times, "Who Is the Moral Taliban?," *Christian Times*, June 10, 2007, http://christiantimes.org.hk/Common/Reader/News/ShowNews.jsp?Nid=42002&Pid=5&Version=0&Cid=220&Charset=big5_hkscs.

126. Labour and Welfare Bureau, "Administration's Paper on the Proposed Amendment to the Domestic Violence Ordinance (Cap. 189)," Panel on Welfare Services, Hong Kong, CB(2)341/08-09(03) (2008).

127. Research interview, March 23, 2012. It is important to note here that the Catholics themselves were divided. Whereas the Marriage Advisory Committee likely attended the meeting to express socially conservative voices, the Justice and Peace Commission supported the amendments. As Jackie Hung told me, the Catholic Diocese's Justice and Peace Commission argued to Joseph Cardinal Zen that "if only because of the wording, someone was badly injured and the law does not protect them, then the Catholic Diocese has a huge sin on its hands." Jackie Hung, research interview.

128. Dony Wong, "'Domestic Violence Ordinance' Yan Fook Church's Rev. Patrick So《家庭暴力條例》恩福堂蘇穎智牧師," YouTube, January 10, 2009, https://web.archive.org/web/20170331072807/https://www.youtube.com/watch?v=gNkoY6xuNO8&feature=related.

129. Research interview, March 23, 2012.

130. Pak Yiu Yick, "蘇穎智收皮! 明光社食蕉! 蔡志森無恥! [Patrick So, shut up! STL, eat bananas! Choi Chi Sum, no shame!]," YouTube, February 14, 2009, https://www.youtube.com/watch?v=UjLU1_zOKak.

131. Research interview, April 16, 2012.

132. Kwan Kai Man, research interview (II).

133. Focus group, Tuen Mun, Hong Kong, March 18, 2012.

134. Because homosexuality was decriminalized in 1991, Mr. Lam was likely referring to the SODO, the *Gay Lovers*, or the DVO episodes in STL's activism.

135. Focus group, Sha Tin, Hong Kong (II), April 1, 2012.

136. Choi Chi Sum, research interview.

137. Choi Chi Sum, research interview.

138. Research interview, March 21, 2012.

139. Kwan Kai Man, research interview (II).

CHAPTER FOUR

1. Chad Skelton, "The Shifting Immigrant Vote," *Vancouver Sun*, June 19, 2004, C1.

2. Ibbitson and Friesen, "The Growing Ties of Immigrants and Conservatives." This particular article is simply about immigrant shifts from the Liberal Party of Canada to the Conservative Party mostly due to same-sex marriage, but the earlier entry in the series references nervousness about the Canadian multicultural project in the face of new religious nationalisms at the time. See Ingrid Peritz and Joe Friesen, "Multiculturalism's Magic Number," *Globe and Mail*, October 1, 2010, A16.

3. Andy Ching, research interview.

4. Nina Wu and Bert Eljera, "The Malls of Asian America," *AsianWeek*, April 1, 1998, http://web.archive.org/web/20110603230741.

5. Crosspoint Church of Silicon Valley, "Crosspoint Community Survey and Lucky Draw," 1999, http://www.crosspointchurchsv.org/events/events_spe_122599.html; Crosspoint Church of Silicon Valley, "March 19 (Sunday) Special Preview Service III," 2000, http://www.crosspointchurchsv.org/events/events_spe_031900.html.

6. Andy Ching, research interview.

7. Petition to Milpitas City Planning Commission, May 19, 2008, in Milpitas Planning Commission, Public Hearing: Conditional Use Permit No. UP07-0001, Crosspoint Church of Silicon Valley. The letter from the former mayor, dated May 17, 2008, argues that "churches like Crosspoint play a vital roll [sic] in the welfare of our community" and that "the City of Milpitas has a history of support for churches and has profited from the ministry of these churches toward making Milpitas the ideal community it is."

8. Crosspoint Church of Silicon Valley, "Crosspoint Prayer Walking" (Milpitas, CA: Crosspoint Church of Silicon Valley, July 22, 29, 2007). This was a handout that Rev. Andy Ching supplied to me, for which I am grateful.

9. Milpitas Planning Commission, Agenda Report, Item 6: Conditional Use Permit No. UP07-0001, Crosspoint Church of Silicon Valley, City of Milpitas, June 11, 2008, 4.

10. Milpitas Planning Commission, Agenda Report, Item 6: Conditional Use Permit No. UP07-0001, Crosspoint Church of Silicon Valley, City of Milpitas, June 11, 2008, 6–10.

11. Milpitas Planning Commission, Planning Commission Subcommittee Minutes, City of Milpitas, June 11, 2008, 10.

12. Avni Nijwahan, "Crosspoint Church Opens Rec Center: Church Opens an 11,000 Square-Foot Gym Which They Plan to Eventually Share with the Public," *Milpitas Patch*, September 19, 2011, http://milpitas.patch.com/groups/volunteering/p/crosspoint-church-opens-recreation-center.

13. Chanson Lau, research interview, June 24, 2011. Lau's remarks on the Silver Avenue property can be corroborated by San Francisco City Planning Commission, Motion No. 14051: Adopting Findings Related to the Authorization of a Conditional Use Pursuant to Application No. 94.555C by the City Planning Commission to Allow the Expansion of an Existing Private Religious School and a Planned Unit Development to Allow Modification of the Front Setback and Rear Yard Open Area Requirements, as well as Review for Consistency with Section 101.1 of the City Planning Code of the Seismic Retrofit, Partial Demolition and Construction of an Addition to an Architecturally Significant Building in an RH-1 (Residential House, One-Family) District and a 40-X Height and Bulk District," San Francisco City Planning Commission, Case No. 94.555C, 801-831 Silver Avenue.

14. Robin Hom, "Re: Bay Area Chinese Bible Church/Chinese Christian Schools. Final Development Plan (FDP01-05) and Major Design Review (DR-OI-108) for 1801 North Loop Road," Letter to Planning & Building Services Department, Alameda, California, April 11, 2002, in James M. Flint, "City Council

Review of Appeal of Planning Board Approval of Final Development. Plan FDP01-05 and Major Design Review DR01-108 to Allow a Private School in Harbor Bay Business Park. Applicant: Chinese Bible Church. Appellants: Andrea Scarnecchia, Nick Correia, Michelle Stempien, Richard Davis," Interdepartment Memorandum, Alameda, California, April 16, 2002.

15. Steve Quen, research interview, December 20, 2011.

16. Robin Hom, research interview, December 8, 2011.

17. Kenneth Yeung, research interview, December 8, 2011.

18. Research interviews, June 7, 2011, June 8, 2011, June 9, 2011, June 29, 2011, July 17, 2011.

19. Research interview, December 20, 2011.

20. There were other cases of sexual misconduct scandals within Cantonese evangelical congregations and faith-based organizations in the 1990s for which I have received documentation. In fact, my father wrote his doctor of ministry dissertation at Western Seminary on them in 2003. One of these cases happened at the congregation in which I was raised as a child and was handled by my father on behalf of the pastoral staff. My father was in turn helped by another senior leader at another influential church that had experienced the same ordeal in the early 1990s. Separately, one of my research respondents also passed me a confidential report of a woman who was sexually harassed by a prominent evangelist who served as the board member of an influential faith-based organization. My source told me that when he confronted this organization, they referred him to their lawyers, which reinforces the privacy of the case. See Philip Tse, "Effectual Procedures for Dealing with Pastoral Sexual Misconduct in Chinese Churches" (DMin diss., Western Seminary, 2003).

21. Steve Quen, research interview.

22. Hak-Shing William Tam, research interview, June 28, 2011.

23. Abraham Poon, research interview, July 1, 2011. In the 1990s, Poon also became involved with praise-and-worship music, he said. He told me he provided charismatic "spiritual cover"—a prayerful pastoral form of leadership—since 1999 for the Taiwanese American praise-and-worship group Stream of Praise, because its founder, the Rev. Sandy Yu, was married in his church. Stream of Praise is a collective based in Southern California whose worship music has been influential throughout Chinese churches and often comprised the Mandarin Chinese songs of the Cantonese congregations that I visited throughout my fieldwork. In addition, SJCAC was reputed to be the originating church for Pastor Liu Tong's charismatic, Mandarin-speaking megachurch, River of Life Christian Center in Santa Clara in 1998.

24. Abraham Poon, research interview. Poon cited Nigerian pastor Sunday Adelaja and his book *Church Shift* (2008) as the influence for this vocational shift among pastors. See Sunday Adelaja, *Church Shift: Revolutionizing Your Faith, Church, and Life for the 21st Century* (Lake Mary, FL: Charisma House, 2008).

25. Susanna Lau, research interview, July 16, 2011. I am grateful to Lau for supplying me with a ministry development paper she wrote for a course during her studies at Fuller Theological Seminary in 1992. In it, she argues the church should be a space that serves new Chinese migrants through a "holistic" theology. One example she gave was Cumberland Church's English class, which developed into a "friendship club" within the English class that became a Saturday night worship service in its own right in the early 2000s, running in the evenings with about forty to sixty people weekly. It also connected Lau to a network of social services organizations that served the Chinese migrants coming to the friendship club, what Lau called the Chinatown Program Network, conceiving of the church as the "fish-pond" where there "should be a channel for the fish to flow into the pond from the ocean which is the community." A key example was Lau's connection to the Presbyterian Church's Cameron House and its counseling, employment, and drug rehabilitation departments, as well as secular agencies like the Mental Health Services, Self-Help for the Elderly, On Lok Lifeways, the Chinese Newcomers Service Center, and the Chinese Union. See Susanna Lau, "Direction of San Francisco Chinatown Ministry Development for Cumberland Presbyterian Chinese Church of San Francisco," unpublished paper for Fuller Theological Seminary, Pasadena, CA, December 1992, 20.

26. Lam Sau Wing declined to be interviewed for scheduling purposes. As a result, my knowledge of his work is drawn from his MoneyRadio website, public documents, and interviews with his colleagues Susanna Lau, research interview; David Pang, research interview; and Ernest Lam, research interview, June 14, 2011.

27. David Pang, research interview.

28. CCHC SF, "角聲美西北地區分會 - 新辦公大樓 [CCHC West Coast Northern California—new building] Spring 2011," YouTube, May 9, 2011, https://www.youtube.com/watch?v=GfNHC42foKU. The video is no longer accessible online, but I have access to it from my own archives.

29. CCHC SF, "角聲生命麵包工程之發展史 [CCHC Bread of Life Bakery Service]," YouTube, August 14, 2012, https://www.youtube.com/watch?v=5pQ3cnJDL9I. The video is no longer accessible online, but I have access to it from my own archives.

30. SUCCESS, *Lilian To: A Life of Devotion* (Vancouver: SUCCESS, 2005), 61.

31. Reginald H. Roy, *David Lam: A Biography* (Toronto: Douglas and McIntyre, 1996), 174.

32. SUCCESS, *Lilian To*, 10.

33. Thomas Tam, research interview, July 27, 2011.

34. Edwin Kong, research interview, May 3, 2011.

35. See City of Burnaby, "Rezoning Reference #9/96: Crystal Square. Metrotown—Area 14—North Block," May 23, 1996. The land on which Crystal Mall stood was purchased by Crystal Square Development Corporation in 1996 and rezoned by

the City of Burnaby "for a major mixed-use development over a site encompassing 85% of the overall block" of previously public lands. Its facilities included "a two-storey podium which accommodates a market, retail stores, restaurants, a food fair, a three cinema complex, office uses, hotel service facilities, and *an adult community facility*" (emphasis mine).

36. Burnaby City Council, "Item 04—Rezoning Reference #99-44: Manager's Report," City of Burnaby, October 14, 1999. The contention was that the original zoning did not allow for a church.

37. Edwin Kong, "RZ #99-44: Letter from the Rev. Edwin Kong," City of Burnaby Public Hearing, November 16, 1999.

38. Burnaby City Council, "Item 02—'Burnaby Zoning Bylaw 1965, Amendment Bylaw No. 54, 1999'—Bylaw No. 11028," in "Public Hearing Minutes: 1999 November 23," City of Burnaby, November 23, 1999. I am grateful to Therese Nielsen, the administrative assistant at the City of Burnaby's Planning Department, for her assistance in locating the documents referenced here, including Rev. Edwin Kong's letter.

39. Edwin Kong, research interview; see also Angela Kan, research interview, April 28, 2011.

40. Edwin Kong, research interview.

41. Angela Kan, research interview.

42. Research interview, April 28, 2011.

43. Research interview, May 27, 2011.

44. Abraham Lau, research interview, May 5, 2011. When I interviewed Rev. Abraham Lau, he was senior pastor at Vancouver Chinatown's Christ Church of China.

45. Edward Lee, research interview, May 30, 2011.

46. Paul Chan, research interview, June 3, 2011.

47. Paul Chan, *Senior Pastor's Dream: 2001 and Beyond* (Vancouver: Lord's Grace Church, 2000). I am grateful to Rev. Ted Ng, a former pastor at Lord's Grace Church, for supplying me with this document.

48. Walter Wong, research interview, April 29, 2011.

49. James Ip, research interview, June 3, 2011. In 2012, Rev. James Ip's return to Hong Kong marked the end of his service with VCEMF.

50. Research interview, April 26, 2011.

51. James Ip, research interview.

52. Research interview, May 27, 2011.

53. Douglas Todd, "Chinese Celebrate Festival despite Shift in Religious Beliefs; Metro Vancouver's 100,000-Strong Chinese Christian population Continues to Observe Lunar New Year despite Its Roots in Buddhism," *Vancouver Sun*, February 5, 2011, A13; see also Li Yu, "Christianity as a Chinese Belief," in *Asian Religions in British Columbia*, ed. Larry DeVries, Don Baker, and Dan Overmyer (Vancouver: University of British Columbia Press, 2010), 233–48. Li made these comments

based on the chapter he had contributed to *Asian Religions in British Columbia*. I also engage this episode in "'Fraught' Chineseness."

54. Douglas Todd, "Evangelical Chinese Christians Respond to Feb. 5th Piece," *The Search*, February 14, 2011, http://blogs.vancouversun.com/2011/02/14/evangelical-chinese-christians-respond-to-feb-5th-piece.

55. Freeman Chan is also the architect behind a number of schools and public buildings in Hong Kong. His most well-regarded piece is the Man Meets Heaven pool at the Chinese University of Hong Kong.

56. Freeman Chan, research interview, March 16, 2012. I write about this episode also in "Under the Umbrella: Grounded Christian Theologies and Democratic Working Alliances in Hong Kong," *Review of Religion and Chinese Society* 2, no. 1 (2015): 122–25. I am grateful to the *Review of Religion and Chinese Society* for granting me permission to reuse some of this material and what I wrote for them in this book.

57. South China Morning Post Reporter, "Tung Urges Youth to Help Community," *South China Morning Post*, November 18, 2011, http://www.scmp.com/print/article/262680/tung-urges-youth-to-help-community.

58. See Tse, "Under the Umbrella," 124.

59. Philemon Choi, research interview, March 14, 2012.

60. See Breakthrough Youth Ministries, *Breakthrough Youth Research Archives*, http://www.breakthrough.org.hk/ir/researchlog.htm.

61. Pakkin Leung, research interview, April 2, 2012.

62. Susanna Hui, research interview, March 21, 2012.

63. Shirley Loo, research interview, March 22, 2012.

64. Research interview, April 2, 2012.

65. Research interview, March 27, 2012.

66. Wu Chi Wai, research interview, April 10, 2012.

67. Lee Kam Hung, research interview, April 5, 2012.

68. Fan Lap Hin, research interview, March 13, 2012.

69. Rose Wu Lo Sai, research interview, March 22, 2012.

70. See Raymond Fung, "Compassion for the Sinned Against," *Theology Today* 37, no. 2 (1980): 162–69.

71. Joseph Zen, research interview, March 30, 2012.

72. Rose Wu, research interview, March 22, 2012.

73. Research interview, March 19, 2012.

74. Focus group, Sha Tin (II), April 1, 2012.

75. Focus group, Tuen Mun, March 18, 2012.

76. Focus group, Kwun Tong, April 13, 2012.

77. See Dietrich Bonhoeffer, "What Is Meant by Telling the Truth," in *Ethics 1949*, pt. 5, trans. Neville Horton Smith (New York: Simon & Schuster, 1995), 358–68.

78. Research interview, March 13, 2012.
79. Lam Kwok Cheung, research interview, March 9, 2012.
80. Research interview, March 2, 2012. I followed up on this interview on March 22, 2012.
81. Jaeson Ma, *The Blueprint: A Revolutionary Plan to Plant Missional Communities on Campus* (Ventura: Regal Books, 2007), 94–95. In his book, Jaeson Ma tells the story of how he discovered that he was related to Frederick Ma Si Hung and Linda Ma, for both were from Swatow and that his father was Frederick Ma's half brother but had been separated during the Cultural Revolution. Jaeson Ma grew up in San Jose, California, living an early life of crime before becoming a charismatic Christian evangelist attempting to bring revival to university campuses. His friendship with the Ma couple in Hong Kong led to the emergence of the Global Day of Prayer, which in turn generated the protests of the Alliance of the Return to the Christian Spirit.
82. Ma, *The Blueprint*, 96. In a research interview I had with an HKCC representative, I learned that Linda Ma's Global Day of Prayer took place in June and was a charismatic event. It was different from the HKCC's World Day of Prayer, which was a mainline ecumenical effort that took place in March that had been renamed from the Women's World Day of Prayer in 1963. The Global Day of Prayer took place from 2005 to 2010 and was discontinued afterward. The World Day of Prayer began in the 1960s and continues to be an HKCC initiative. See research interview, March 19, 2012.
83. Research interview, March 2, 2012, March 9, 2012, March 22, 2012.
84. I followed up on this ethnographic encounter with research interview, March 19, 2012.
85. See Eddie Luk and Phila Siu, "It's All My Fault!," *Standard*, February 17, 2012, https://www.thestandard.com.hk/sections-news-print/119828/It's-all-my-fault!
86. See "曾蔭權敗走江湖派對 [Donald Tsang goes to the party of the rivers and lakes]," *Oriental Daily*, February 20, 2012, A2, https://orientaldaily.on.cc/cnt/news/20120220/00174_001.html; Enid Tsui, "Hong Kong's Tsang Faces Corruption Probe," *Financial Times*, February 29, 2012, http://www.ft.com/intl/cms/s/0/f5055f20-628b-11e1-872e-00144feabdc0.html. The "rivers and lakes" is a martial euphemism for the underworld.
87. "憂憤填膺、信念不移: 一群基督徒對特首選舉惡聞劣行的回應 [Filled with indignation, faith unwavering: The response of a group of Christians to the disturbing news of the chief executive elections]," *Ming Pao*, March 2, 2012, A17. The full statement can be found online at "超過八百信徒教牧聯署 – 回應特首選戰惡聞劣行 [More than 800 believers and pastors jointly sign—response to chief executive elections disturbing news]," *Christian Times*, March 2, 2012, https://christiantimes.org.hk/Common/Reader/News/ShowNews.jsp?Nid=71328&Pid=5&Version

=0&Cid=220&Charset=big5_hkscs. After beginning fieldwork in late February 2012, I received this statement from a respondent in my email on February 27, 2012, with a deadline to sign by February 28, 2012.

88. See Kahon Chan, "Legco Committee Leaves Tsang's Inquiry to ICAC: Motion to Invoke Powers under P&P Ordinance Closed," *China Daily*, March 3, 2012, https://www.pressreader.com/china/china-daily-hong-kong/20120303/282746288698491.

89. Research interview, March 19, 2012.

90. Lo Lung Kwong, research interview, March 29, 2012.

91. Philemon Choi, research interview.

92. One of the best introductions to American studies as a discipline is George Lipsitz, *American Studies in a Moment of Danger* (Minneapolis: University of Minnesota Press, 2001). An update can be found in Barbara Tomlinson and George Lipsitz, "American Studies as Accompaniment," *American Quarterly* 65, no. 1 (2013): 1–30.

93. See Matt K. Matsuda, *Pacific Worlds: A History of Seas, Peoples, and Cultures* (Cambridge: Cambridge University Press, 2012). I am also influenced by Gary Okihiro's prescription to reframe the "Pacific" as "Oceania" to center Pacific Islanders and the routes of the sea. See Gary Okihiro, *American History Unbound: Asians and Pacific Islanders* (Berkeley: University of California Press, 2015).

CHAPTER FIVE

1. One of the most important scholarly accounts of the Tiananmen Beijing Spring is Craig Calhoun, *Neither Gods nor Emperors: Students and the Struggle for Democracy in China* (Berkeley: University of California Press, 1994). Calhoun's intervention is to characterize the events on Tiananmen Square in 1989 as an experiment in the usage of public space for the development of civil society in market socialism.

2. See Richard Madsen, *China and the American Dream* (Berkeley: University of California Press, 1995); Francis Fukuyama, "The End of History?," *National Interest* 16 (Summer 1989): 3–18; Giorgio Agamben, *The Coming Community*, trans. Michael Hardt (Minneapolis: University of Minnesota Press, 1990).

3. I write more about this formative experience in Justin K.H. Tse, "蒙上眼睛，就以爲看不見 Repress Your Eyes, So You Thought Couldn't See It: My Aunties and Uncles Taught Me to Feel the World When I Was Three," *Inheritance*, June 4, 2020, https://www.inheritancemag.com/stories/meng-shang-yan-jing-jiu-yi-wei-kan-bu-jian-repress-your-eyes-so-you-thought-you-couldnt-see-it.

4. Research interview, May 14, 2011.

5. See Ronald Skeldon, "Emigration and the Future of Hong Kong," *Pacific Affairs* 63 (1990): 502. Skeldon compiled this estimate from the Government

Secretariat in Hong Kong. This figure is also cited in Wong Siu-lun, "Emigration and Stability in Hong Kong," Social Sciences Research Centre Occasional Paper 7, Department of Sociology, University of Hong Kong, 1992, 3.

6. One of the most subtle critiques of the usage of the Tiananmen Beijing Spring to forge a fictional sense of identity around "Chineseness" is Ang, "On Not Speaking Chinese," 21–36.

7. Chris Fan, "David Chiu Wants to Pedal His Way into San Francisco History," *Hyphen: Asian America Unabridged*, August 8, 2011, https://hyphenmagazine.com/blog/2011/08/david-chiu-wants-pedal-his-way-san-francisco-history. Fan clarifies that *Hyphen*'s glowing profile of David Chiu's candidacy requires "full disclosure—in addition to attending early Hyphen meetings, he later helped to secure space for Hyphen at the offices of Chinese for Affirmative Action," though he is "not currently involved with Hyphen."

8. See Mercury News, "Asian American Festival Brings People to Union City Church," *San Jose Mercury News*, May 21, 2011, https://www.mercurynews.com/2011/05/21/asian-american-festival-brings-people-to-union-city-church/.

9. Research interview, July 4, 2011.

10. Lo Sek Wai, research interview, March 21, 2012. I name Lo here because he publicly presents himself in all three of my sites as having his origin story tied to Tiananmen.

11. Research interview, June 8, 2011.

12. Research interview, July 1, 2011. Chai Ling's autobiography places the date of her Christian conversion in 2009 in New York. See Chai Ling, *A Heart for Freedom: The Remarkable Journey of a Young Dissident, Her Daring Escape, and Her Quest to Free China's Daughters* (Carol Stream, IL: Tyndale, 2011).

13. Focus group, Fremont, California (I).

14. Research interview, December 13, 2011.

15. Thomas Leung, research interview, November 1, 2012.

16. Research interview, December 13, 2011.

17. Research interview, November 30, 2011. "Lavender Leung" asked me to neither record nor use her actual name in this study, although she did sign a consent form to be interviewed and joked that she suspected that her actual identity could probably be discerned from her responses, especially if I referred to her as "that political woman." The quotes from her are from my detailed notes of the interview. Because her last name is not actually "Leung," I will refer to her as "Lavender" for reasons of consonance.

18. Research interview, June 30, 2011.

19. Richard Ow, research interview, July 4, 2011.

20. Ow's involvement as a marriage commissioner in the events of 2004 are documented in Steve Rubenstein, "Mad Dash to S.F. City Hall to Say 'I Do'/2 Groups Trying to Halt Same-Sex Unions Must Wait until Tuesday," *San Francisco Chronicle*, February 14, 2004, https://www.sfgate.com/news/article/Mad-dash-to-S-F

-City-Hall-to-say-I-do-2-2822920.php; Jane Ganahl, "Love Stories/Doug and Eric: Zing Went the Strings," *San Francisco Chronicle*, March 14, 2004, https://www.sf gate.com/news/article/Mad-dash-to-S-F-City-Hall-to-say-I-do-2-2822920.php.

21. Richard Ow, research interview.

22. Steven A. Chin, "Off-Track Betting Proposal Draws Protests: Chinatown Churches Fight Parlor at Fang's Grand Palace," *San Francisco Examiner*, October 19, 1995, A1. I also write about this case in "Liberal Protestant Chinatown."

23. Richard Ow, research interview.

24. Research interview, November 30, 2011.

25. Research interview, July 17, 2011.

26. Chanson Lau, email correspondence, November 15, 2012. The exact wording as Lau sent it to me was from Article II-C from the church's Articles of Incorporation: "No substantial part of the activities of this corporation shall consist of carrying on propaganda, or otherwise attempting to influence legislation, and the corporation shall not participate or intervene in any political campaign (including the publishing or distribution of statements) on behalf of any candidate for public office."

27. In 2008, Ed Jew pleaded guilty to charges of perjury, as he had violated the residency requirements of a San Francisco city supervisor, and of extortion toward small-business owners.

28. Research interview, November 30, 2011.

29. Paul Wells, "Jason Kenney's Plan for Breaking through in Ethnic Communities," *MacLean's*, March 3, 2011, https://www.macleans.ca/politics/ottawa/jason-kenneys-plan-for-breaking-through-in-ethnic-communities/. The full leaked document is provided as part of Wells's piece. For *MacLean's* full coverage of Kenney's multicultural strategy for the Conservative Party of Canada, see Alec Castonguay, "The Inside Story of Jason Kenney's Campaign to Win Over Ethnic Votes: The Secret to the Success of Canada's Immigration Minister," *MacLean's*, February 2, 2013, https://www.macleans.ca/news/canada/welcome-to-my-world/.

30. Adrienne Arsenault, "Diversity among Voters," in *Road Stories: Vancouver*, CBC News, April 4, 2011, http://www.cbc.ca/thenational/indepthanalysis/story/2011/04/04/national-roadstoriesvancouver.html. The story has since been taken offline from the CBC's website, but I discuss it in my dissertation research as well as in Justin K.H. Tse, "Asian Religions Aren't That Exotic," *Ricepaper Magazine* 16, no. 4 (2012): 12, 15.

31. Lo Sek Wai, research interview. See Douglas Todd, "Protest Leader Proud: Cleric Also Shy about Role," *Vancouver Sun*, June 8, 1989, B11. I also write about Lo in "'Fraught' Chineseness." I am grateful to Wipf & Stock for granting me permission to reuse parts of what I wrote for them in this book.

32. Todd, "Protest Leader Proud," B11.

33. Bill Chu, research interview.

34. Lo Sek Wai, research interview.

35. These are transcribed parts of Raymond Chan's protest speech, a video of which I acquired from a research respondent.

36. Lo Sek Wai, research interview.

37. Lo Sek Wai, research interview.

38. See Kevin Griffin, "Chinese-Canadians Reaching Out with Year of the Monkey Festivities: Traditions Bent to Bridge Gap," *Vancouver Sun*, January 31, 1992, B2. They also seemed unaware that the Chinatown Merchants' Association had also set up a Chinese New Year parade at the Pacific National Exhibition.

39. See Tse, "'Fraught' Chineseness."

40. Research interview, May 14, 2011

41. Research interview, November 11, 2011.

42. Stephen Cheung, research interview, August 31, 2011.

43. Lo Sek Wai, research interview.

44. Raymond Chan, "My Response: A Deeper Experience of Democracy" [in Chinese], *Truth Monthly*, April 1997, http://www.truth-monthly.com/issue43/04oo.html.

45. David Ng, "Our Advice to Our Christian Brother, Raymond Chan," *Truth Monthly*, April 1997, http://www.truth-monthly.com/issue43/04pp.html.

46. Research interview, November 11, 2011.

47. Focus group, Richmond, British Columbia.

48. Stephen Cheung, research interview; Kenny Chiu, research interview.

49. Kenny Chiu, research interview.

50. Stephen Cheung, research interview.

51. conniew, "Richmond News release re: Joe Peschisolido," *Free Dominion—Principled Conservative—Party and Canadian Politics—Canada Blogs*, 2013, http://freedominion.com.pa/phpBB2/viewtopic.php?p=26253. Peschisolido made a comeback in the 2015 federal elections and defeated Kenny Chiu, who became a Conservative Party candidate, in the Steveston-Richmond East riding. In 2019, Chiu defeated Peschisolido and became the riding's MP. He lost his seat in 2021 to the Liberal Party's Parm Bains.

52. I name both Vancouver Chinese Evangelical Free Church and Richmond Chinese Evangelical Free Church because respondents referred to them on the record.

53. Wayne Lo, research interview; Kenny Chiu, research interview.

54. Research interview, May 11, 2011.

55. Research interview, May 11, 2011.

56. Stephen Cheung, research interview.

57. Kenny Chiu, research interview.

58. Darrel Reid Campaign, "Reid Calls for Apology, Reconciliation on Head Tax Issue," Darrel Reid Campaign Office, Conservative Party of Canada, 2006. I am thankful to Kenny Chiu for providing me with copies of this press release in both English and Chinese in Kenny Chiu, email correspondence, July 4, 2012.

59. There will be some understandable debate about the role of these Conservative Party operatives in the head tax redress, though some of the literature has reflected on the politics of the Conservative Party in making this apology. In private conversation, some head tax activists repudiated the idea that the Conservative Party's inner echelons were instrumental in the head tax redress effort, as there is a long history of wrangling with the various political parties that culminated in the class action suit *Mack v. Attorney General of Canada* (2002), 165 OAC 17 (CA). My conclusion is there might be a "both-and" here: first, there was a coalition of head tax redress groups advocating from without the government for head tax redress, but second, those in the inner echelons of Conservative Party politics, such as Darrel Reid, Jason Kenney, and Stephen Harper, felt the need to do this because of Reid's Richmond campaign. See David Dyzenhaus and Mayo Moran, eds., *Calling Power to Account: Law, Reparations, and the Chinese Canadian Head Tax* (Toronto: University of Toronto Press, 2005); Pauline Wakeham, "The Cunning of Reconciliation: Reinventing White Civility in the 'Age of Apology,'" in *Shifting the Ground of Canadian Literary Studies,* ed. Smaro Kamboureli and Robert Zacharias (Waterloo, ON: Wilfrid Laurier University Press, 2012), 209–33; Matt James, "Neoliberal Heritage Redress," in *Reconciling Canada: Critical Perspectives on the Culture of Redress*, ed. Jennifer Henderson and Pauline Wakeham (Toronto: University of Toronto Press, 2013), 31–46. I coauthored a conference paper on the American and Canadian apologies for Chinese exclusion with Christian ethicist Grace Kao. See Grace Y. Kao and Justin K.H. Tse, "Redress for Chinese North Americans, Racial Justice for All," paper presented at the Second Biennial Conference of the Society of Race, Ethnicity, and Religion, Iliff School of Theology, Denver, April 17–29, 2005.

60. Marci McDonald, *The Armageddon Factor: The Rise of Christian Nationalism in Canada* (Toronto: Vintage Canada, 2011), 13–17.

61. Esther Leung-Kong, research interview, July 17, 2012.

62. Sacha Peter, research interview, October 7, 2011.

63. Research interview, May 16, 2011.

64. Anthony Yeung, research interview, May 10, 2011.

65. Focus group, Richmond, British Columbia.

66. Sacha Peter, research interview.

67. I thank Sacha Peter, Alice Wong's campaign manager, for providing me with the complete text of both Raymond Chan's campaign press release and the Conservative response, as well as for videos of Raymond Chan's 1993 political campaign and the debate between Alice Wong and Raymond Chan on same-sex marriage in 2008. Peter also introduced me to the delights of the all-day breakfast at Cookie's Grill in Chilliwack, British Columbia, which was a highlight of our interview.

68. Chan's campaign was quoting from Canadian Alliance for Social Justice and Family Values Association, *English-Chinese Bi-monthly Magazine* 48 (June 2003); Canadian Alliance for Social Justice and Family Values Association, *English-Chinese Bi-monthly Magazine* 66 (July/August 2006), 2.

69. Raymond Chan, Press Release, September 30, 2008.

70. Alice Wong Campaign, "Response to Raymond Chan's Desperate Attack," September 30, 2008. Humorously, an appendix to this release points out that CASJAFVA had also previously endorsed Liberal Party candidates, such as Ujjal Dosanjh, Joe Peschisolido, and Sam Comuzzi, as well as Vancouver's then-mayor Sam Sullivan. Rhetorically, it concluded, "Are the Liberals saying that **Ujjal Dosanjh**, **Sam Sullivan**, and **Joe Comuzzi** are responsible for all of CASJAFVA's publications or statements?" (emphases original).

71. This exchange in October 2008 took place during the all-candidates' debate in Richmond, British Columbia, during the 2008 Canadian federal elections. I am grateful to Sacha Peter for providing this video in Sacha Peter, email correspondence, November 16, 2012. See also "Election '08," *Richmond News*, October 8, 2008, A09. I am grateful to *Richmond News* for providing me with this document of the candidates' platforms in their own words.

72. Kenny Chiu, research interview.

73. Sacha Peter, research interview.

74. Sacha Peter, research interview; Alice Wong Campaign, "Obeying the Law with Campaign Sign Placement: Respecting Property Rights of Others," March 28, 2011.

75. Sacha Peter, research interview.

76. Focus group, Coquitlam, British Columbia.

77. Article 45, Basic Law of the Hong Kong Special Administrative Region of the People's Republic of China.

78. Jiang's entire tirade can be found—with subtitles accounting for his switches among Mandarin, Cantonese, and English—at Shanghaiist, "Jiang Zemin Berates Hong Kong Journalist," Facebook, October 3, 2014, https://www.facebook.com/watch/?v=10152728897091030.

79. Pik Wan Wong, "The Pro-Chinese Democracy Movement in Hong Kong," in *The Dynamics of Social Movements in Hong Kong*, ed. Stephen Wing Kai Chiu and Tai-lok Lui (Hong Kong: Hong Kong University Press, 2000), 55–90.

80. Ko, *The Sacred Citizens and the Secular City*, 38–39. I am also grateful to one respondent who offered me her entire personal archive of Tiananmen press clippings from Hong Kong that corroborates the story that Ko tells.

81. Research interview, March 29, 2012.

82. Philemon Choi, "Hong Kong Christian Patriotic Democratic Movement" [in Chinese], in *Christian Witnesses in Hong Kong*, ed. Kwok Nai Wang and Agatha Mei Yuk Wong (Hong Kong: Hong Kong Christian Institute, 1991), 101–4, as quoted in Ko, *The Sacred Citizens and the Secular City*, 39.

83. Research interview, March 29, 2012.

84. Article 23, Basic Law of the Hong Kong Special Administrative Region of the People's Republic of China.

85. Jackie Hung, research interview.

86. National Security Bill, "A bill to amend the Crimes Ordinance, the Official Secrets Ordinance and the Societies Ordinance pursuant to the obligation imposed by Article 23 of the Basic Law of the Hong Kong Special Administrative Region of the People's Republic of China and to provide for related, incidental and consequential amendments," Hong Kong Legislative Council, October 7, 2003, DMA#72814v.5, s. 16.6.

87. Joseph Zen, research interview.

88. See Rose Wu, "A Story of Its Own Name: Hong Kong's *Tongzhi* Culture and Movement," in *Off the Menu: Asian and Asian North American Women's Religion and Theology*, ed. Rita Nakashima Brock, Jung Ha Kim, Kwok Pui Lan, and Seung Ai Yang (Louisville: Westminster John Knox Press, 2007), 275–92.

89. Rose Wu, research interview.

90. Focus group, North Point, March 4, 2012.

91. Focus group, Tuen Mun.

92. Focus group, Sha Tin, Hong Kong (I), March 25, 2012.

93. Focus group, Sha Tin, Hong Kong (II).

94. Kung Lap Yan, research interview.

95. By the curia, Cardinal Zen meant the "diocesan curia"—that is, the chief officials of the local diocese who assist the bishop in his governing duties.

96. Joseph Zen, research interview. Hong Kong's Anglican primate, Archbishop Paul Kwong, observes that Zen's "passive compliance" somewhat contradicted the approach of his predecessor, John Baptist Cardinal Wu, whose 1989 pastoral letter *Marching into the Bright Decade* in Kwong's interpretation called the Catholic Church in Hong Kong to perform a ministry of reconciliation in the new social and political structures of post-1997 Hong Kong. See Paul Kwong, *Identity in Community: Toward a Theological Agenda for the Hong Kong SAR* (Zurich: LIT, 2008), 133.

97. For the HKCC's involvement in the construction of Basic Law itself, see also Shun-Hing Chan, "Nationalism and Religious Protest: The Case of the National Day Celebration Service Controversy of the Hong Kong Protestant Churches," *Religion, State and Society* 28, no. 4 (2000): 359–83.

98. Lo Lung Kwong, research interview.

99. Research interview, March 19, 2012.

100. Peter Ho, research interview, March 9, 2012.

101. This use of the term "public theology" is inspired by theologian Max Stackhouse, who writes that a "theology" can be considered "public" because it is "that which we as Christians believe we have to offer the world for its salvation is not esoteric, privileged, irrational, or inaccessible" but is rather "both comprehensible and indispensable for all, something that we can reasonably discuss with Hindus and Buddhists, Jews and Muslims, Humanists and Marxists." Moreover, "such a theology will give guidance to the structures and policies of public life," which "must

imply a viable element of justice." See Max L. Stackhouse, *Public Theology and Political Economy: Christian Stewardship in Modern Society* (Grand Rapids: Eerdmans, 1987), xi.

102. Lausanne Movement, "Pluralism and Truth in Asia—Carver Yu," YouTube, September 27, 2011, http://www.youtube.com/watch?v=X0ydIlVwmeY.

103. Kang Phee Sang, research interview, March 29, 2012.

104. Kang Phee Sang, "Christian Faith and Public Values," *CGST Bulletin*, April–June 2012, 1.

105. Kung Lap Yan, research interview.

106. Takchi Tam, research interview, March 9, 2012.

107. See Narrow Church, "Opposing the State-Market-Church Nexus, the Only Act They Can Make Is 'Greed'!," *Ming Pao*, October 26, 2011, A19. Images can be found on Narrow Church's Facebook page at 基督路小教會(專頁) [Narrow Church (Focused Page)], Facebook, October 28, 2011, https://www.facebook.com/narrowchurch/photos/218414118225914.

108. Takchi Tam, research interview.

109. Research interview, March 19, 2012; Lo Lung Kwong, research interview.

110. "憂憤填膺、信念不移 [Filled with indignation, faith unwavering: The response of a group of Christians to the disturbing news of the chief executive elections," *Ming Pao*, March 2, 2012, A17.

111. Interestingly, I learned this story from two people who would have found themselves ideological opponents in research interview, March 9, 2012; research interview, March 14, 2012.

112. Philemon Choi is referring to the story of King David's adulterous relationship with Bathsheba, the wife of one of his "mighty men," Uriah the Hittite, in 2 Samuel 11–12. After attempting to cover up the affair by having Uriah killed in battle, the prophet Nathan confronted David with a parable of a rich man with a flock of sheep stealing a poor man's lamb. Using the story to provoke David to outrage, Nathan told David, "You are the man!" driving home David's personal guilt. Choi interpreted this story as demonstrating that guilt needed to be personally and tactfully confronted, not publicly protested.

113. Philemon Choi, research interview.

114. Peter Ho, research interview.

115. See Lai Ying-tat, "C. Y. Leung Admits Liability for Illegal Structures," *South China Morning Post*, November 23, 2012, https://www.scmp.com/news/hong-kong/article/1089352/cy-leung-admits-liability-illegal-structures. At the time, the Leung administration posted a thirty-page report on the structural irregularities of his Peak houses on the CE website.

116. Lo Lung Kwong, research interview.

117. Takchi Tam, research interview.

118. Fan Lap Hin, research interview.

119. See Asad, *Secular Translations*.

EPILOGUE

1. Ten Years Workshop, "Ten Years: A Community Conversation 十年: 社區放映會," Eventbrite, October 21, 2016, https://www.eventbrite.ca/e/ten-years-a-community-screening-tickets-27551636687.
2. "Extras," dir. Kwok Zune; "Season of the End," dir. Wong Fei-pang; "Dialect," dir. Jevons Au; "Self-Immolator," dir. Kiwi Chow; and "Local Egg," dir. Ng Ka-leung, in Ng Ka-leung, Mandrew Kwan, Jevons Au, Frankie Chan, and Andrew Choi, prods., *Ten Years* (Hong Kong; Golden Scene, 2015).
3. Ten Years Workshop, "Ten Years."
4. See Esther Yuen, "Mass Exodus: Constrained by the Traditional Views of Their Churches, Many Young Chinese Christians Are Seeking a New Congregation, Leading to Friction within the Community," *Pacific Rim Magazine* 2, no. 13 (2011): 8. The two churches Yuen writes about are Tenth Church Vancouver and Faith Community Christian Church. It was through this article that I came to know both communities with some degree of intimacy over the course of my Vancouver fieldwork.
5. I write about Ken Shigematsu and Tenth Church Vancouver in Justin K.H. Tse, "Hearing a Different Kind of Evangelical: Profile: Pastor Ken Shigematsu," *Ricepaper Magazine* 16, no. 3 (2012): 54–57; Justin K.H. Tse, "Difference and the Establishment: An Asian Canadian Senior Pastor's Evangelical Spatiality at Tenth Avenue Alliance Church in Vancouver, BC," *Relegens Thréskeia* 3, no. 2 (2014): 24–56. The original journalism on Dave Gibbons that gave rise to the term "silent exodus" can be found at Doreen Carvajal, "Column One: Trying to Halt 'Silent Exodus': More Korean American Ministers Are Reaching Out to Keep Younger Immigrants. They Offer More Relevant Sunday Services and a Cultural Bridge to U.S. Life," *Los Angeles Times*, May 9, 1994, https://www.latimes.com/archives/la-xpm-1994-05-09-mn-55636-story.html; Helen Lee, "Silent Exodus: Can the East Asian Church Reverse the Flight of Its Next Generation?," *Christianity Today* 40, no. 9 (1996): 50–53.
6. Flyn Ritchie, "Pro-China Mob Harassed 'Pray for Hong Kong' Group at Tenth Church: Statement," *Church for Vancouver*, August 20, 2019, https://churchforvancouver.ca/pro-china-mob-harassed-pray-for-hong-kong-group-at-tenth-church-statement/. This article reproduces the text of VCLPJ's Facebook post. I am also thankful to Chris Chiu for providing me with his archive of press reports about this incident.
7. Richard Soo, "Keeping Quiet about Hong Kong 'Not an Option': Priest," *B.C. Catholic*, September 4, 2019, https://bccatholic.ca/voices/richard-soo-sj/keeping-quiet-about-hong-kong-not-an-option-priest; Richard Soo, "Father Richard Soo: Is the Church a Sanctuary or a Target?," *Vancouver Sun*, September 6, 2019, https://vancouversun.com/opinion/op-ed/father-richard-soo-is-the-church-in-canada-a-sanctuary-or-target.
8. Douglas Todd, "70s Hymn an Anthem for Protesters," *Vancouver Sun*, September 7, 2019, H3.

9. D. Cheng, "Praying for Hong Kong Can Be Politically Disruptive—Even in America: Why Chinese Diaspora Churches Remain Silent while Christians in Hong Kong Take to the Streets," *Christianity Today*, November 18, 2019, https://www.christianitytoday.com/news/2019/november/hong-kong-chinese-diaspora-churches-north-america-response.html.

10. See Douglas Todd, "Chinese Christians for Trump," *Vancouver Sun*, November 1, 2016, https://vancouversun.com/news/staff-blogs/chinese-christians-for-trump. I wrote this guest post on Douglas Todd's blog on what I learned about Chinese Canadians supporting the Trump campaign from my social media feed.

11. The case is *Students for Fair Admissions Inc. v. President and Fellows of Harvard College*, 600 US 181 (2023).

12. David Chen, "Women Explains Protests for Peter Liang," YouTube, February 22, 2016, https://www.youtube.com/watch?v=h6rPTvI91lY. The affective conflicts in Asian American consciousness when it came to the Peter Liang protests are eloquently articulated by Jay Caspian Kang, "How Should Asian-Americans Feel about the Peter Liang Protests?," *New York Times Magazine*, February 23, 2016, https://www.nytimes.com/2016/02/23/magazine/how-should-asian-americans-feel-about-the-peter-liang-protests.html.

13. For reporting on how the Peter Liang case has been narrated in relation to Chinese nationalism, see Emily Rauhala, "Peter Liang Case Echoes All the Way to China," *Washington Post*, February 25, 2016, https://www.washingtonpost.com/news/worldviews/wp/2016/02/25/peter-liang-case-echoes-all-the-way-to-china/; Brian Hioe, "Peter Liang in China," *New Bloom Magazine*, March 1, 2016, https://newbloommag.net/2016/03/01/peter-liang-in-china/.

14. Cheng, "Praying for Hong Kong."

15. Shu-Mei Shih, "Introduction: What Is Sinophone Studies?," in *Sinophone Studies: A Critical Reader*, ed. Shu-mei Shih, Chien-hsin Tsai, and Brian Bernards (New York: Columbia University Press, 2013), 7. Shih admits that in "the past few years, scholars have used the term *Sinophone* for largely denotative purposes to literally mean 'Chinese-speaking' or 'written in Chinese.'"

16. Shih, "Introduction," 11.

17. Ting Guo, "Me: Would You Like to Share with the Class How You Got into the Notion of #SinophoneStudies? @DrJustinTse: I Heard It from You, Ting. I Let Go of My Toxic Masculinity and Listened. Be like Justin. Class, Stay Tuned for Week 8 'Sinophone' Transnationalities #ChinaFromTheInsideOut," Twitter, September 30, 2021, https://twitter.com/tingguowrites/status/1443517663741812737.

18. See Shu-mei Shih, "After National Allegory," in *Visuality and Identity: Sinophone Articulations across the Pacific* (Berkeley: University of California Press, 2007), 140–64.

19. E. Tammy Kim, "Transnationally Asian: A New Media Neighborhood for an Emerging World," *Columbia Journalism Review*, July 21, 2020, https://www.cjr.org/special_report/transnationally_asian.php. I first learned of this article from

時差 In-betweenness, "#05 两极化时代的异乡人 | In-betweenness in Polarised Times," *Shicha Podcast*, August 21, 2020, https://shicha.buzzsprout.com/1171871/5088386-05-in-betweenness-in-polarised-times.

BIBLIOGRAPHY

*Of making many books there is no end, and much
study wearies the body.*
—Ecclesiastes 12:12

1man1woman.net. "Homosexuality Linked to Pedophilia?" N.d. https://web.archive.org/web/20100222094656.
———. "Protect Traditional Marriage Cupertino Rally." N.d. http://1man1woman.net/cupertino_pic.html. [No longer available.]
爭居權火燒入境處 50 傷 7 危全港震 [50 injured, 7 killed in arson fire during protest for Hong Kong's right of abode]." *Hong Kong Daily News*, August 3, 2000.
Abbas, Ackbar. *Hong Kong: Culture and the Politics of Disappearance*. Minneapolis: University of Minnesota Press, 1997.
Adelaja, Sunday. *Church Shift: Revolutionizing Your Faith, Church, and Life for the 21st Century*. Lake Mary, FL: Charisma House, 2008.
Agamben, Giorgio. *The Coming Community*. Translated by Michael Hardt. Minneapolis: University of Minnesota Press, 1990.
Agrama, Hussein Ali. *Questioning Secularism: Islam, Sovereignty, and the Rule of Law in Modern Egypt*. Chicago: University of Chicago Press, 2012.
Alice Wong Campaign. "Obeying the Law with Campaign Sign Placement: Respecting Property Rights of Others." March 28, 2011.
———. "Response to Raymond Chan's Desperate Attack." September 30, 2008.
Anderson, Kay. *Vancouver's Chinatown: Racial Discourse in Canada, 1875–1980*. Montreal: McGill-Queen's University Press, 1991.
Ang, Ien. *On Not Speaking Chinese: Living between Asia and the West*. New York: Routledge, 2001.
Anidjar, Gil. *Blood: A Critique of Christianity*. New York: Columbia University Press, 2014.

ArkWhy.org. "呼籲 [Call]." January 29, 2011. http://web.archive.org/web/20111203201637/http://arkwhy.org/#.

Arsenault, Adrienne. "Diversity among Voters." *Road Stories: Vancouver, CBC News*, April 4, 2011. http://www.cbc.ca/thenational/indepthanalysis/story/2011/04/04/national-roadstoriesvancouver.html.

Arvin, Maile. *Possessing Polynesians: The Science of Settler Colonial Whiteness in Hawai'i and Oceania*. Durham, NC: Duke University Press, 2019.

Asad, Talal. *Formations of the Secular: Christianity, Islam, Modernity*. Stanford: Stanford University Press, 2003.

———. *Secular Translations: Nation-State, Modern Self, and Calculative Reason*. New York: Columbia University Press, 2018.

ATV World Newsline with Michael Chugani. "Benny Tai and Priscilla Leung." *ATV World Newsline*, June 2, 2013.

Bahng, Aimee. "The Pacific Proving Grounds and the Proliferation of Settler Environmentalism." *Journal of Transnational American Studies* 11, no. 2 (2020): 45–73.

Basic Law of the Hong Kong Special Administrative Region of the People's Republic of China.

BBC. "Embassy Strike a 'Mistake.'" *BBC News*, May 8, 1999. http://news.bbc.co.uk/2/hi/europe/338557.stm.

Becker, Jo. *Forcing the Spring: Inside the Fight for Marriage Equality*. New York: Penguin, 2014.

Board of Education, Burnaby School District 41. "Policy #5.45.00: Sexual Orientation/Gender Identity." Burnaby School District 41.

Bonhoeffer, Dietrich. "What Is Meant by Telling the Truth." In *Ethics 1949*, pt. 5, translated by Neville Horton Smith, 358–68. New York: Simon & Schuster, 1995.

Breakthrough Youth Ministries. *Breakthrough Youth Research Archives*. http://www.breakthrough.org.hk/ir/researchlog.htm.

Burnaby City Council. "Item 02—'Burnaby Zoning Bylaw 1965, Amendment Bylaw No. 54, 1999'—Bylaw No. 11028." In "Public Hearing Minutes: 1999 November 23." City of Burnaby, November 23, 1999.

———. "Item 04—Rezoning Reference #99-44: Manager's Report." City of Burnaby, October 14, 1999.

Butler, Judith. *Parting Ways: Jewishness and the Critique of Zionism*. New York: Columbia University Press, 2012.

Calhoun, Craig. *Neither Gods nor Emperors: Students and the Struggle for Democracy in China*. Berkeley: University of California Press, 1994.

California Ballot Proposition 8. "Eliminates the Right of Same-Sex Couples to Marry. Initiative Constitutional Amendment." California State Elections. November 4, 2008.

Canadian Alliance for Social Justice and Family Values Association. *English-Chinese Bi-monthly Magazine* 48 (June 2003).

———. *English-Chinese Bi-monthly Magazine* 66 (July/August 2006).

———. "Some of the More Important Works Done by CASJAFVA in the Past Ten Years for Your Information." 2012. https://web.archive.org/web/20110725135733.

Carvajal, Doreen. "Column One: Trying to Halt 'Silent Exodus': More Korean American Ministers Are Reaching Out to Keep Younger Immigrants. They Offer More Relevant Sunday Services and a Cultural Bridge to U.S. Life." *Los Angeles Times*, May 9, 1994. https://www.latimes.com/archives/la-xpm-1994-05-09-mn-55636-story.html.

Castonguay, Alec. "The Inside Story of Jason Kenney's Campaign to Win Over Ethnic Votes: The Secret to the Success of Canada's Immigration Minister." *MacLean's*, February 2, 2013. https://www.macleans.ca/news/canada/welcome-to-my-world.

Cayton, Horace, and Anne Lively. *The Chinese in the United States and the Chinese Christian Churches*. New York: National Council of Churches, 1955.

CCHC SF. "角聲生命麵包工程 之 發展史 [CCHC Bread of Life Bakery Service]." YouTube, August 14, 2012. https://www.youtube.com/watch?v=5pQ3cnJDL9I.

———. "角聲美西北地區分會 - 新辦公大樓 [CCHC West Coast Northern California—new building] Spring 2011." YouTube, May 9, 2011. https://www.youtube.com/watch?v=GfNHC42foKU.

Chai Ling. *A Heart for Freedom: The Remarkable Journey of a Young Dissident, Her Daring Escape, and Her Quest to Free China's Daughters*. Carol Stream, IL: Tyndale, 2011.

Chan, Kahon. "Legco Committee Leaves Tsang's Inquiry to ICAC: Motion to Invoke Powers under P&P Ordinance Closed." *China Daily*, March 3, 2012. https://www.pressreader.com/china/china-daily-hong-kong/20120303/282746288698491.

Chan, Paul. S*enior Pastor's Dream: 2001 and Beyond*. Vancouver: Lord's Grace Church, 2000.

Chan, Raymond. "My Response: A Deeper Experience of Democracy." [In Chinese.] *Truth Monthly*, April 1997. http://www.truth-monthly.com/issue43/04oo.html.

———. Press Release. Raymond Chan Campaign. September 30, 2008.

———. "Raymond Chan on Criminal Code." House of Commons Hansard #218 of the 35th Parliament, 1st session, June 14, 1995. http://openparliament.ca/debates/1995/6/14/raymond-chan-2/only/.

Chan, Robert, and Ruth Chan, eds. *The Red River Years: The Winnipeggers in the Potter's Hand*. Hong Kong: MI Design, 2014.

Chan, Shun-Hing. "Nationalism and Religious Protest: The Case of the National Day Celebration Service Controversy of the Hong Kong Protestant Churches." *Religion, State and Society* 28, no. 4 (2000): 359–83.

Chao, Augustus, and Sylvia Yu. *Serving God with Heart and Soul: The Life of Pastor Augustus Chao*. Vancouver: Canadians for Historical Justice and Racial Reconciliation, 2002.

Chen, Carolyn. *Getting Saved in America: Taiwanese Immigration and Religious Experience*. Princeton: Princeton University Press, 2006.

Chen, David. "Women Explains Protests for Peter Liang." YouTube, February 22, 2016. https://www.youtube.com/watch?v=h6rPTvI91lY.

Cheng, Anne Anlin. *The Melancholy of Race: Psychoanalysis, Assimilation, and Hidden Grief*. New York: Oxford University Press, 2001.

Cheng, D. "Praying for Hong Kong Can Be Politically Disruptive—Even in America: Why Chinese Diaspora Churches Remain Silent while Christians in Hong Kong Take to the Streets." *Christianity Today*, November 18, 2019. https://www.christianitytoday.com/news/2019/november/hong-kong-chinese-diaspora-churches-north-america-response.html.

Cheung, Daniel. *Too Bright: An Insider's Discourse of the Society for Truth and Light*. [In Chinese.] Hong Kong: Dirty Press, 2009.

Chin, Steven A. "Off-Track Betting Proposal Draws Protests: Chinatown Churches Fight Parlor at Fang's Grand Palace." *San Francisco Examiner*, October 19, 1995, A1.

Chinese Christian Mission. *50th Anniversary Booklet*. Petaluma: Chinese Christian Mission, 2011.

Chinese Family Alliance. "Traditional Family Day." April 25, 2004. http://web.archive.org/web/20060218220843.

Chinese Independent Baptist Church. *Centennial Celebration*. Oakland, CA: Chinese Independent Baptist Church, 2009.

Chiu, Stephen Yuanlian, and Sun Lingli. *One Hong Kong Dollar Trip, Seven Thousand American Dollar Miracle*. [In Chinese.] Hong Kong: China Bible Seminary Publishing Department, 1978.

Cho Man Kit v. Broadcasting Authority, HCAL69/2007 (2008).

Choi, Ki Joo. *Disciplined by Race: Theological Ethics and the Problem of Asian American Identity*. Eugene, OR: Pickwick, 2019.

Choi, Philemon. "Hong Kong Christian Patriotic Democratic Movement." [In Chinese.] In *Christian Witnesses in Hong Kong*, edited by Kwok Nai Wang and Agatha Mei Yuk Wong, 101–4. Hong Kong: Hong Kong Christian Institute, 1991.

Chong v. Lee (1981), 29 B.C.L.R. 13.

Chow, Alexander. *Chinese Public Theology: Generational Shifts and Confucian Imagination in Chinese Christianity*. New York: Oxford University Press, 2018.

Chow, Christie. Schism: *Seventh-Day Adventism in Post-denominational China*. Notre Dame, IN: University of Notre Dame Press, 2021.

Chow, Rey. "On Chineseness as a Theoretical Problem." *boundary 2* 25, no. 3 (Autumn 1998): 1–24.

———. *The Protestant Ethnic and the Spirit of Capitalism*. New York: Columbia University Press, 2002.

Christian Organizations Joint Statement. "Addressing the Golden Jubilee Incident's Situation." [In Chinese.] *Breakthrough Magazine*, June 1978, 19.

Christian Times. "超過八百信徒教牧聯署 - 回應特首選戰惡聞劣行 [More than 800 believers and pastors jointly sign—response to chief executive elections

disturbing news]." March 2, 2012. https://christiantimes.org.hk/Common
/Reader/News/ShowNews.jsp?Nid=71328&Pid=5&Version=0&Cid=220
&Charset=big5_hkscs.
———. "Who Is the Moral Taliban?" June 10, 2007. http://christiantimes.org.hk
/Common/Reader/News/ShowNews.jsp?Nid=42002&Pid=5&Version=0&Cid
=220&Charset=big5_hkscs.
朱楠 [Chu Lam]. "新移民改變宗教團體文化 [New immigrants are changing the culture of religious communities]." *Sing Tao Daily*, February 3, 2011.
Chu, Louis. *Eat a Bowl of Tea: A Novel*. New York: Lyle Stuart, 1961.
Chuck, Harry, and Josh Chuck, dirs. *Chinatown Rising*. San Francisco: Center for Asian American Media, 2019.
Chuck, James. *An Exploratory Study of the Growth of Protestant Chinese Churches in San Francisco, 1950–1982*. Berkeley: Bay Area Chinese Churches Research Project, 1996.
———. "The National Conference of Chinese Christian Churches, Inc.: A Brief Chronology." In CONFAB, *Growing Deep, Reaching Out: Discerning God's Direction for His People*. San Francisco: National Conference of Chinese Christian Churches, Inc., 1998.
———. "Where Are the Chinese Churches Heading in the 1970's?" Paper presented at the Chinese Christian Union, San Francisco, February 28, 1970.
Chuh, Kandace. *Imagine Otherwise: On Asian Americanist Critique*. Durham, NC: Duke University Press, 2003.
Chun, Allen. *Forget Chineseness: On the Geopolitics of Cultural Identification*. Albany: State University of New York Press, 2017.
———. "Fuck Chineseness: On the Ambiguities of Ethnicity as Culture as Identity." *boundary 2* 23, no. 2 (1996): 111–38.
City of Burnaby. "Rezoning Reference #9/96: Crystal Square. Metrotown—Area 14—North Block." May 23, 1996.
City of Richmond. "Councillor Chak Kwong Au." https://web.archive.org/web/202 20320203546.
CONFAB. *Chinese Churches Today and Tomorrow*. San Francisco: National Conference of Chinese Churches in America, 1955.
conniew. "Richmond News Release Re: Joe Peschisolido." *Free Dominion—Principled Conservative—Party and Canadian Politics—Canada Blogs*, 2013. http://freedominion.com.pa/phpBB2/viewtopic.php?p=26253. [No longer available.]
CounterCounterCulture. "After-Action Report: Cupertino Open Air Rally in Support of Marriage and California's Proposition 8." *Free Republic*, October 20, 2008. http://www.freerepublic.com/focus/f-news/2109993/posts.
Cribb, Tim. "Justice for All: Gay Lobby Groups and Religious Bodies Appear Set for a Showdown as the Government Moves a Step Closer to Formulating Anti-discrimination Laws." *South China Morning Post*, January 27, 2005, A16.

Crosspoint Church of Silicon Valley. "Crosspoint Community Survey and Lucky Draw." 1999. https://web.archive.org/web/20090922030439.

———. "Crosspoint Prayer Walking." Milpitas, CA: Crosspoint Church of Silicon Valley, July 22, 29, 2007.

———. "March 19 (Sunday) Special Preview Service III." 2000. http://www.crosspointchurchsv.org/events/events_spe_031900.html. [No longer available.]

Cruickshank, Ainslie. "Hundreds Gather in Vancouver to Protest Police Violence, as Hong Kong's Government Puts Controversial Extradition Bill on Hold." *Toronto Star*, June 15, 2019. https://www.thestar.com/vancouver/2019/06/15/hundreds-gather-in-vancouver-to-protest-police-violence-in-hong-kong-as-government-puts-controversial-extradition-bill-is-put-on-hold.html.

Cumberland Presbyterian Chinese Church. *Celebrating 100 Years of Ministry, 1894–1994: A Call to Mission . . . the Mission Continues*. San Francisco: Cumberland Presbyterian Chinese Church, 1994.

CTV. "'Disturbing' Video Linked to Burnaby Trustee Candidate." *CTV News*, November 17, 2011. https://bc.ctvnews.ca/disturbing-video-linked-to-burnaby-trustee-candidate-1.727197.

Cumings, Bruce. *The Origins of the Korean War*, vol. 1: *Liberation and the Emergence of Separate Regimes, 1945–1947*. Princeton: Princeton University Press, 1981.

———. *The Origins of the Korean War*, vol. 2: *The Roaring of the Cataract, 1947–1950*. Princeton: Princeton University Press, 1981.

———. "Rimspeak; or, the Discourse of the 'Pacific Rim.'" In *What's in a Rim? Critical Perspectives on the Pacific Region Idea*, edited by Arif Birlik, 29–47. Boulder: Westview, 1993.

Darrel Reid Campaign. "Reid Calls for Apology, Reconciliation on Head Tax Issue." Darrel Reid Campaign Office, Conservative Party of Canada, 2006.

Diana. "Disgrasian of the Weak! Hak-Shing William Tam." *DisgrasianTM*, January 22, 2010. https://web.archive.org/web/20111225185429.

Dirlik, Arif. "The Asia-Pacific Idea: Reality and Representation in the Invention of a Regional Structure." *Journal of World History* 3, no. 1 (1992): 55–79.

———. "Introducing the Pacific." In *What's in a Rim? Critical Perspectives on the Pacific Region Idea*, edited by Arif Dirlik, 3–11. Boulder: Westview, 1993.

Dyzenhaus, David, and Mayo Moran, eds. *Calling Power to Account: Law, Reparations, and the Chinese Canadian Head Tax*. Toronto: University of Toronto Press, 2005.

Eng, David. *Racial Castration: Managing Masculinity in Asian America*. Durham, NC: Duke University Press.

Fan, Chris. "David Chiu Wants to Pedal His Way into San Francisco History." *Hyphen: Asian America Unabridged*, August 8, 2011. https://hyphenmagazine.com/blog/2011/08/david-chiu-wants-pedal-his-way-san-francisco-history.

Fernando, Mayanthi L. *The Republic Unsettled: Muslim French and the Contradictions of Secularism*. Durham, NC: Duke University Press, 2014.

"憂憤填膺、信念不移:一群基督徒對特首選舉惡聞劣行的回應 [Filled with indignation, faith unwavering: The response of a group of Christians to the disturbing news of the chief executive elections]." *Ming Pao*, March 2, 2012, A17.

Fojas, Camille, Rudy P. Guevarra Jr., and Nitasha Tamar Sharma, eds. *Beyond Ethnicity: New Politics of Race in Hawai'i*. Honolulu: University of Hawai'i Press, 2018.

Fujikane, Candace, and Jonathan Y. Okamura, eds. *Asian Settler Colonialism: From Local Governance to the Habits of Everyday Life in Hawai'i*. Honolulu: University of Hawai'i Press, 2008.

Fukuyama, Francis. "The End of History?" *National Interest* 16 (Summer 1989): 3–18.

Fung, Raymond. "Compassion for the Sinned Against." *Theology Today* 37, no. 2 (1980): 162–69.

Fung, Ronald Y. K., and Carver T. Yu, eds. *A Life of Ministry: Essays Presented to Philip Teng on His 60th Birthday by Members of the Faculty of the China Graduate School of Theology*. Hong Kong: China Alliance Press, 1982.

Ganahl, Jane. "Love Stories/Doug and Eric: Zing Went the String." *San Francisco Chronicle*, February 14, 2004. https://www.sfgate.com/news/article/Mad-dash-to-S-F-City-Hall-to-say-I-do-2-2822920.php.

Goh, Robbie. "Noah's Ark: Evangelical Christianity and the Creation of a Value Environment in Hong Kong." *Material Religion* 10, no. 2 (2014): 208–32.

Griffin, Kevin. "Chinese-Canadians Reaching Out with Year of the Monkey Festivities: Traditions Bent to Bridge Gap." *Vancouver Sun*, January 31, 1992, B2.

Guo, Ting. "Beyond Sing Hallelujah to the Lord: Diffused Religion and Religious Co-optation through Hong Kong Protests." *Journal of the American Academy of Religion* 90, no. 4 (2022): 937–53.

———. "Me: Would You Like to Share with the Class How You Got into the Notion of #SinophoneStudies? @DrJustinTse: I Heard It from You, Ting. I Let Go of My Toxic Masculinity and Listened. Be like Justin. Class, Stay Tuned for Week 8 'Sinophone' Transnationalities #ChinaFromTheInsideOut." Twitter, September 30, 2021. https://twitter.com/tingguowrites/status/1443517663741812737.

———. "Politics of Love: Love as a Religious and Political Discourse in Modern China through the Lens of Political Leaders." *Critical Research on Religion* 8, no. 1 (2020): 39–52.

Heo, Angie. *The Political Lives of Saints: Christian-Muslim Mediation in Egypt*. Berkeley: University of California Press, 2018.

Hioe, Brian. "Peter Liang in China." *New Bloom Magazine*, March 1, 2016. https://newbloommag.net/2016/03/01/peter-liang-in-china/.

Hom, Robin. "Re: Bay Area Chinese Bible Church/Chinese Christian Schools. Final Development Plan (FDP01-05) and Major Design Review (DR-OI-108) for 1801 North Loop Road." Letter to Planning and Building Services Department,

Alameda, California, April 11, 2002, in James M. Flint, "City Council Review of Appeal of Planning Board Approval of Final Development. Plan FDP01-05 and Major Design Review DR01-108 to Allow a Private School in Harbor Bay Business Park. Applicant: Chinese Bible Church. Appellants: Andrea Scarnecchia, Nick Correia, Michelle Stempien, Richard Davis." Interdepartment Memorandum, Alameda, California, April 16, 2002.

Hong, Christine. *A Violent Peace: Race, U.S. Militarism, and Cultures of Democratization in Cold War Asia and the Pacific*. Stanford: Stanford University Press, 2020.

Hong, Jane H. *Opening the Gates to Asia: A Transpacific History of How America Repealed Asian Exclusion*. Chapel Hill: University of North Carolina Press, 2019.

Hong Kong Christian Council. *Survey Report on Public Perception of Protestantism in Hong Kong, 2021*. Hong Kong: Hong Kong Christian Council, 2021.

"Hong Kong's Catholics Condemn Gay Activists for Disrupting Mass." *China Daily*, August 18, 2003. https://www.chinadaily.com.cn/en/doc/2003-08/18/content_255971.htm.

Hsu, Madeline. *The Good Immigrants: How the Yellow Peril Became the Model Minority* Princeton: Princeton University Press, 2015.

Huang, Michelle Nancy. "Ecologies of Entanglement in the Great Pacific Garbage Patch." *Journal of Asian American Studies* 20, no. 1 (2017): 95–117.

Hui, Vikki. "Richmond Church Holds Vigil for Tiananmen Square Massacre Victims and Hong Kong." *Richmond News*, June 4, 2022. https://www.richmond-news.com/local-news/richmond-church-holds-vigil-for-tiananmen-square-massacre-victims-and-hong-kong-5444530.

Hume, Stephen. "Groups Make 'Reconciliation' Happen, Quietly and Effectively." *Vancouver Sun*, February 16, 2007, A13.

Hurd, Elizabeth Shakman. *Beyond Religious Freedom: The Global Politics of Religion*. Princeton: Princeton University Press, 2015.

Ibbitson, John, and Joe Friesen. "The Growing Ties of Immigrants and Conservatives." *Globe and Mail*, October 4, 2010, A1.

Immerwahr, Daniel. *How to Hide an Empire: A History of the Greater United States*. New York: Farrar, Straus and Giroux, 2019.

時差 In-betweenness. "#05 两极化时代的异乡人 | In-betweenness in Polarised Times." *Shicha Podcast*, August 21, 2020. https://shicha.buzzsprout.com/1171871/5088386-05-in-betweenness-in-polarised-times.

In re Marriage cases, 43 Cal. 4th 757 (2008).

Ip King-Tat, ed. *The Ends of the Rainbow: 200 Days of Dispute over the SODO Legislation*. [In Chinese.] Hong Kong: Key Road Press, 2005.

Ishizuka, Karen. *Serve the People: Making Asian America in the Long Sixties*. London: Verso, 2016.

Jakobsen, Janet. *Working Alliances and the Politics of Difference: Diversity and Feminist Ethics*. Bloomington: Indiana University Press, 1998.

James, Matt. "Neoliberal Heritage Redress." In *Reconciling Canada: Critical Perspectives on the Culture of Redress*, edited by Jennifer Henderson and Pauline Wakeham, 31–46. Toronto: University of Toronto Press, 2013.

———. "Wrestling with the Past: Apologies, Quasi-apologies, and Non-apologies in Canada." *In The Age of Apology: Facing Up to the Past*, edited by Mark Gibney, Rhoda E. Howard-Hassmann, Jean-Marc Coicaud, and Niklaus Steiner, 137–53. Philadelphia: University of Pennsylvania Press, 2008.

Jeung, Russell. *Faithful Generations: Race and New Asian American Churches*. New Brunswick, NJ: Rutgers University Press, 2005.

Kang, Jay Caspian. "How Should Asian-Americans Feel about the Peter Liang Protests?" *New York Times Magazine*, February 23, 2016. https://www.nytimes.com/2016/02/23/magazine/how-should-asian-americans-feel-about-the-peter-liang-protests.html.

Kang Phee Sang. "Christian Faith and Public Values." *CGST Bulletin*, April–June 2012, 1.

Kao, Grace Y., and Justin K.H. Tse. "Redress for Chinese North Americans, Racial Justice for All." Paper presented at the Second Biennial Conference of the Society of Race, Ethnicity, and Religion, Iliff School of Theology, Denver, April 17–29, 2005.

Kēhaulani Kauanui, J. *Colonialism and the Politics of Sovereignty and Indigeneity*. Durham, NC: Duke University Press, 2008.

Kim, David Kyuman. *Melancholic Freedom: Agency and the Spirit of Politics*. New York: Oxford University Press, 2007.

Kim, E. Tammy. "Transnationally Asian: A New Media Neighborhood for an Emerging World." *Columbia Journalism Review*, July 21, 2020. https://www.cjr.org/special_report/transnationally_asian.php.

Kim, Helen Jin. "Niseis of the Faith: Theologizing Liberation in the Asian American Movement." Unpublished BA thesis, Stanford University, 2006.

———. *Race for Revival: How Cold War South Korea Shaped the American Evangelical Empire*. New York: Oxford University Press, 2022.

Kim, Jinah. *Postcolonial Grief: The Afterlives of the Pacific Wars in the Americas*. Durham, NC: Duke University Press, 2019.

Kim, Jodi. *Ends of Empire: Asian American Critique and the Cold War*. Minneapolis: University of Minnesota Press, 2010.

Ko, Tinming. *The Sacred Citizens and the Secular City: Political Participation of Protestant Ministers in Hong Kong during a Time of Change*. London: Ashgate, 2000.

Kong, Edwin. "RZ #99-44: Letter from the Rev. Edwin Kong." City of Burnaby Public Hearing, November 16, 1999.

Kuchmij, Halya, dir. *Generations: The Chan Legacy*. [DVD.] Toronto: CBC Learning, 2007.

Kung Lap Yan, ed. *Religious Right*. [In Chinese.] Hong Kong: Dirty Press, 2010.

Kurczy, Stephen. "Chinese Explorers Stand by Claim of Noah's Ark Find in Turkey." *Christian Science Monitor*, April 30, 2010. https://www.csmonitor.com/World/Global-Issues/2010/0430/Chinese-explorers-stand-by-claim-of-Noah-s-Ark-find-in-Turkey.

Kwan Kai Man. *Reflections on Human Rights and Homosexuality*. [In Chinese.] Hong Kong: China Alliance Press, 2000.

Kwong, Paul. *Identity in Community: Toward a Theological Agenda for the Hong Kong SAR*. Zurich: LIT, 2008.

Labour and Welfare Bureau. "Administration's Paper on the Proposed Amendment to the Domestic Violence Ordinance (Cap. 189)." Panel on Welfare Services, Hong Kong. CB(2)341/08-09(03), 2008.

Lai, David Chuenyuen. *Chinatowns: Towns within Cities in Canada*. Vancouver: University of British Columbia Press, 1988.

Lai Tsz-him. "A Nonviolent Model of Liberation Theology: A Dialogue with Maoism." *Ching Feng* 17, no. 1–2 (2018): 43–66.

Lai Ying-tat. "C. Y. Leung Admits Liability for Illegal Structures." *South China Morning Post*, November 23, 2012. https://www.scmp.com/news/hong-kong/article/1089352/cy-leung-admits-liability-illegal-structures.

Lam Sau Wing. "5 November 2008." *MoneyRadio* [audio], November 5, 2008. http://www.moneyradio.org.

Lau, Susanna. "Direction of San Francisco Chinatown Ministry Development for Cumberland Presbyterian Chinese Church of San Francisco." Unpublished paper for Fuller Theological Seminary, Pasadena, December 1992.

Lausanne Movement. "Pluralism and Truth in Asia—Carver Yu." YouTube, September 27, 2011. http://www.youtube.com/watch?v=X0ydIlVwmeY.

Law, Violet. "Hong Kong Finds Flickers of Hope in Ukraine's Winter on Fire." *Al Jazeera*, September 6, 2019. https://www.aljazeera.com/news/2019/9/6/hong-kong-finds-flickers-of-hope-in-ukraines-winter-on-fire.

Lee, Deborah, and Lina Hoshino, dirs. *In God's House: Asian American Lesbian and Gay Families in the Church*. [DVD.] Berkeley: Progressive Films, 2007.

Lee, Gentle. *His Name Is Wonderful—the Autobiography of Gentle Lee*. [In Chinese.] Hong Kong: Chinese Alliance Press, 2006.

Lee, Helen. "Silent Exodus: Can the East Asian Church Reverse the Flight of Its Next Generation?" *Christianity Today* 40, no. 9 (1996): 50–53.

Lee, Stephen. "A Brief Survey on the History of Christ Church of China, Vancouver." In *75th Anniversary Thanksgiving Report*, edited by Victor Lee, Allen Liu, Pat Fung, and Stephen Lee, 19–22. Vancouver: Christ Church of China.

Leung, Beatrice. *Sino-Vatican Relations: Problems in Conflicting Authority, 1976–1986*. Cambridge: Cambridge University Press, 2009.

Leung, Beatrice, and Shun-Hing Chan. *Changing Church and State Relations in Hong Kong, 1950–2000*. Hong Kong: Hong Kong University Press, 2003.

Leung, David. "David Poon." In *Leaders Who Shaped Us: Canadian Mennonite Brethren*, edited by Harold Jantz, 274–84. Toronto: Kindred Productions, 2010.

Leung, Hillary. "Hong Kong's Summer of Unrest Has Been Drawing Inspiration from Ukraine's Winter on Fire." *Time*, September 24, 2019. https://time.com/5682003/winter-on-fire-hong-kong-protests-ukraine.

Leung, Thomas. *Exploration of the Historical Relationship of Tibet in China*. Vancouver: Cultural Regeneration Research Society, 2009.

———. *Observation of the Human Right Issues in China: Fourteen Years of Cultural Exchange and Charity Service among the Chinese*. Vancouver: Cultural Regeneration Research Society, 2008.

Ley, David. *Millionaire Migrants: Trans-Pacific Life Lines*. Oxford: Wiley-Blackwell, 2010.

———. "A Regional Growth Ecology, a Great Wall of Capital and a Metropolitan Housing Market." *Urban Studies* 58, no. 2 (2000): 297–315.

———. "Transnational Spaces and Everyday Lives." *Transactions of the British Institute of Geographers* 29, no. 2 (2004): 151–64.

Ley, David, and Audrey Kobayashi. "Back to Hong Kong: Return Migration or Transnational Sojourn?" *Global Networks* 5 (2005): 111–28.

Li, Darryl. *The Universal Enemy: Jihad, Empire, and the Challenge of Solidarity*. Stanford: Stanford University Press, 2020.

Li, Fion, and David Tweed. "Support for Occupy Hong Kong over Vote Waning, Group Says." *Bloomberg*, September 2, 2014. http://www.bloomberg.com/news/2014-09-02/support-for-occupy-hong-kong-over-vote-waning-group-says.html.

Li Yu. "Christianity as a Chinese Belief." In *Asian Religions in British Columbia*, edited by Larry DeVries, Don Baker, and Dan Overmyer, 233–48. Vancouver: University of British Columbia Press, 2010.

Lian Xi. *Redeemed by Fire: The Rise of Popular Christianity in Modern China*. New Haven: Yale University Press, 2010.

Lipsitz, George. *American Studies in a Moment of Danger*. Minneapolis: University of Minnesota Press, 2001.

Lo Lung Kwong. "Begging to Have a Double Portion of Your Spirit." In *Death Be Not Proud* Conference, 141. Hong Kong: China Alliance Press, 2002.

Louie, Alvin. "Should an ABC Pastor Study Chinese?" In *A Winning Combination: ABC/OBC*, edited by Cecilia Yau, 131–41. Petaluma: Chinese Christian Mission, 1986.

Luk, Eddie, and Phila Siu. "It's All My Fault!" *Standard*, February 17, 2012. https://www.thestandard.com.hk/sections-news-print/119828/It's-all-my-fault!

Ma, Jaeson. *The Blueprint: A Revolutionary Plan to Plant Missional Communities on Campus*. Ventura: Regal Books, 2007.

———. "Pray for Edison Chen, Me, and the World." JaesonMa.com, April 29, 2008. http://web.archive.org/web/20081028181303.

Ma, Lawrence J. C. "Space, Place, and Transnationalism in the Chinese Diaspora." In *The Chinese Diaspora: Space, Place, Mobility, and Identity*, edited by Lawrence J. C. Ma and Carolyn Cartier, 1–50. Lanham, MD: Rowman & Littlefield, 2003.

Mack vs. Attorney General of Canada (2002), 165 OAC 17 (CA).
Madsen, Richard. *China and the American Dream*. Berkeley: University of California Press, 1995.
Maeda, Daryl J. *Chains of Babylon: The Rise of Asian America*. Minneapolis: University of Minnesota Press, 2009.
Mahmood, Saba. *Politics of Piety: The Islamic Revival and the Feminist Subject*. Princeton: Princeton University Press, 2004.
———. *Religious Difference in a Secular Age: A Minority Report*. Princeton: Princeton University Press, 2016.
Man, Simeon. *Soldiering through Empire: Race and the Making of the Decolonizing Pacific*. Berkeley: University of California Press, 2018.
Mar, Frank. *I Remember*. Oakland: KTVU, 1984.
———. "A New Wind Is Blowing." In *The Theologies of Asian Americans and Pacific Peoples*, edited by Roy I. Sano, 424–36. Berkeley: Asian Center for Theology and Strategies, Pacific School of Religion, 1973.
Matsuda, Matt K. *Pacific Worlds: A History of Seas, Peoples, and Cultures*. Cambridge: Cambridge University Press, 2012.
McDonald, Marci. *The Armageddon Factor: The Rise of Christian Nationalism in Canada*. Toronto: Vintage Canada, 2011.
McIntyre, Alasdair. *After Virtue: A Study in Moral Theory*. Notre Dame, IN: University of Notre Dame Press, 1981.
McLaughlin, Ken. "Survey: Asian-Americans Overwhelmingly against Outlawing Gay Marriage." *San Jose Mercury News*, October 15, 2008, B1.
"Mei Lun Yuen Use Permit Application Unanimously Approved by Commission." *East-West: The Chinese American Journal*, January 26, 1977, 1.
Mercury News. "Asian American Festival Brings People to Union City Church." *San Jose Mercury News*, May 21, 2011. https://www.mercurynews.com/2011/05/21/asian-american-festival-brings-people-to-union-city-church/.
Milbank, John. *Theology and Social Theory: Beyond Secular Reason*. Rev. ed. Oxford: Blackwell, 2006.
Milpitas Planning Commission. Agenda Report, Item 6: Conditional Use Permit No. UP07-0001, Crosspoint Church of Silicon Valley. City of Milpitas, June 11, 2008.
———. Planning Commission Subcommittee Minutes. City of Milpitas, June 11, 2008.
———. Public Hearing: Conditional Use Permit No. UP07-0001, Crosspoint Church of Silicon Valley. City of Milpitas, May 19, 2008.
Mitchell, Katharyne. *Crossing the Neoliberal Line: Pacific Rim Migration and the Metropolis*. Philadelphia: Temple University Press, 2004.
Mok, Christine, and Aimee Bahng. "Transpacific Overtures: An Introduction." *Journal of Asian American Studies* 20, no. 1 (2017): 1–9.
Moreau, Jennifer. "Mayor Says Hatred Tends to Spread." *Burnaby Now*, November 17, 2011. https://www.burnabynow.com/local-news/mayor-says-hatred-tends-to-spread-2931718.

———. "Voice Pledges to Be 'a Thorn in Their Side.'" *Burnaby Now*, November 23, 2011. https://www.burnabynow.com/local-news/voice-pledges-to-be-a-thorn-in-their-side-2934809.
Nagata, Judith. "Christianity among Transnational Chinese: Religious versus (Sub) Ethnic Affiliation." *International Migration* 43, no. 3 (2005): 99–130.
Narrow Church. "Opposing the State-Market-Church Nexus, the Only Act They Can Make Is 'Greed'!" *Ming Pao*, October 26, 2011, A19.
Network on Religion and Justice. "No to Prop 8 Counter-Rally (to the Yes on Prop 8 Rally)." Past Events, October 12, 2008. http://www.netrj.org/?p=pastevents&id=18.
Ng, David. "Our Advice to Our Christian Brother, Raymond Chan." *Truth Monthly*, April 1997. http://www.truth-monthly.com/issue43/04pp.html.
Ng Ka-leung, Mandrew Kwan, Jevons Au, Frankie Chan, and Andrew Choi, prods. *Ten Years* ("Extras," dir. Kwok Zune; "Season of the End," dir. Wong Fei-pang; "Dialect," dir. Jevons Au; "Self-Immolator," dir. Kiwi Chow; "Local Egg," dir. Ng Ka-leung). Hong Kong: Golden Scene, 2015.
Ngoei, Wen-Qing. *Arc of Containment: Britain, the United States, and Anticommunism in Southeast Asia*. Ithaca: Cornell University Press, 2019.
Nguyen, Viet Thanh, and Janet Hoskins. "Introduction: Transpacific Studies: Critical Perspectives on an Emerging Field." In *Transpacific Studies: Framing an Emerging Field*, edited by Janet Hoskins and Viet Thanh Nguyen, 1–38. Honolulu: University of Hawai'i Press, 2014.
Nicolosi, Joseph. "The Six Fallacies behind 'Project 10.'" *Queer Resources Directory: Family Research Council*, 1993. http://www.qrd.org/qrd/religion/anti/FRC/project.10-family.research.council.letter.
Niebuhr, Reinhold. *The Irony of American History*. In *Reinhold Niebuhr: Major Works on Religion and Politics*, edited by Elisabeth Sifton. Washington, DC: Library of America, 2015.
Nijwahan, Avni. "Crosspoint Church Opens Rec Center: Church Opens an 11,000 Square-Foot Gym Which They Plan to Eventually Share with the Public." *Milpitas Patch*, September 19, 2011. http://milpitas.patch.com/groups/volunteering/p/crosspoint-church-opens-recreation-center.
Ockenga, Harold J. "Challenge to the Christian Culture of the West." In *Fuller Voices: Then and Now*, edited by Russell P. Spittler, 11–19. Pasadena: Fuller Theology Seminary, 2004.
Okihiro, Gary Y. *American History Unbound: Asians and Pacific Islanders*. Berkeley: University of California Press, 2015.
———. *The Boundless Sea: Self and History.* Berkeley: University of California Press, 2019.
———. *Island World: A History of Hawai'i and the United States*. Berkeley: University of California Press, 2008.
———. *Pineapple Culture: A History of the Tropical and Temperate Zones*. Berkeley: University of California Press, 2009.

———. *Third World Studies: Theorizing Liberation*. Durham, NC: Duke University Press, 2016.

Olds, Kris. *Globalization and Urban Change: Capital, Culture, and Pacific Rim Megaprojects*. New York: Oxford University Press, 2001.

Ong, Aihwa. *Buddha Is Hiding: Refugees, Citizenship, the New America*. Berkeley: University of California Press, 2003.

———. *Flexible Citizenship: The Cultural Logics of Transnationality*. Durham, NC: Duke University Press, 1999.

Ong, Aihwa, and Donald Nonini, eds. *Ungrounded Empires: The Cultural Politics of Modern Chinese Transnationalism*. New York: Routledge, 1997.

Oriental Daily. "曾蔭權敗走江湖派對 [Donald Tsang goes to the party of the rivers and lakes]." February 20, 2012, A2. https://orientaldaily.on.cc/cnt/news/20120220/00174_001.html.

Outlook Video. "Proposition 8 Rally and Counter Rally—Pt. 2 Raw Video." October 31, 2008. https://www.youtube.com/watch?v=DTyjy4go4Gg.

Pak Yiu Yick. "蘇穎智收皮！明光社食蕉！蔡志森無恥！ [Patrick So, shut up! STL, eat bananas! Choi Chi Sum, no shame!]." YouTube, February 14, 2009. https://www.youtube.com/watch?v=UjLU1_zOKak.

Peritz, Ingrid, and Joe Friesen. "Multiculturalism's Magic Number." *Globe and Mail*, October 1, 2010, A16.

Perry et al. v. Schwarzenegger, 704 F.Supp.2d 921 (N.D. Cal., 2010), Decision.

Perry et al. v. Schwarzenegger, 704 F.Supp.2d 921 (N.D. Cal., 2010), Deposition of Hak-Shing William Tam, December 1, 2009.

Perry et al. v. Schwarzenegger, 704 F.Supp.2d 921 (N.D. Cal., 2010), Trial Transcript.

Phan, Katherine T. "Q&A with Rev. Raymond Kwong." *Christian Post*, May 22, 2004. http://www.christianpost.com/news/q-a-with-rev-raymond-kwong-2690.

"Presbyterian Church in Chinatown PCC—Faith in Action: Mei Lun Yuen." 2012. http://www.pccsf.org/faithinaction/meiLunYuen.html.

Rauhala, Emily. "Peter Liang Case Echoes All the Way to China." *Washington Post*, February 25, 2016. https://www.washingtonpost.com/news/worldviews/wp/2016/02/25/peter-liang-case-echoes-all-the-way-to-china.

Redding, Jeffrey. *A Secular Need: Islamic Law and Secular Governance in Contemporary India*. Seattle: University of Washington Press, 2020.

Richmond News. "Election '08." October 8, 2008, A09.

Ritchie, Flyn. "Pro-China Mob Harassed 'Pray for Hong Kong' Group at Tenth Church: Statement." *Church for Vancouver*, August 20, 2019. https://churchforvancouver.ca/pro-china-mob-harassed-pray-for-hong-kong-group-at-tenth-church-statement/.

Robbins, Joel. *Theology and the Anthropology of Christian Life*. New York: Oxford University Press, 2020.

Robbins, Joel, and Matthew Engelke. "Introduction." *South Atlantic Quarterly* 109, no. 4 (2010): 623–31.

Rocha, Samuel D. *Folk Phenomenology: Education, Study, and the Human Person.* Eugene, OR: Pickwick, 2015.

Roy, Reginald H. *David Lam: A Biography.* Toronto: Douglas and McIntyre, 1996.

Rubenstein, Steve. "Mad Dash to S.F. City Hall to Say 'I Do'/2 Groups Trying to Halt Same-Sex Unions Must Wait until Tuesday." *San Francisco Chronicle*, February 14, 2004. https://www.sfgate.com/news/article/Mad-dash-to-S-F-City-Hall-to-say-I-do-2-2822920.php.

San Francisco City Planning Commission. "Motion No. 14051: Adopting Findings Related to the Authorization of a Conditional Use Pursuant to Application No. 94.555C by the City Planning Commission to Allow the Expansion of an Existing Private Religious School and a Planned Unit Development to Allow Modification of the Front Setback and Rear Yard Open Area Requirements, as well as Review for Consistency with Section 101.1 of the City Planning Code of the Seismic Retrofit, Partial Demolition and Construction of an Addition to an Architecturally Significant Building in an RH-1 (Residential House, One-Family) District and a 40-X Height and Bulk District. San Francisco City Planning Com-mission, Case No. 94.555C, 801-831 Silver Avenue." City of San Francisco, February 1, 1996.

Scott, Joan Wallach. *Sex and Secularism.* Princeton: Princeton University Press, 2017.

Shanghaiist. "Jiang Zemin Berates Hong Kong Journalist." Facebook, October 3, 2014. https://www.facebook.com/watch/?v=10152728897091030.

Sharma, Nitasha Tamar. *Hawai'i Is My Haven: Race and Indigeneity in the Black Pacific.* Durham, NC: Duke University Press, 2021.

Shih, Gerry. "Chinese Christians Are the Focus of Same-Sex Marriage Case." *New York Times*, January 22, 2010, 19A.

Shih, Shu-mei. "The Concept of the Sinophone." *PMLA* 126, no. 3 (2010): 709–18.

———. "Introduction: What Is Sinophone Studies?" In *Sinophone Studies: A Critical Reader*, edited by Shu-mei Shih, Chien-hsin Tsai, and Brian Bernards, 1–16. New York: Columbia University Press, 2013.

———. *Visuality and Identity: Sinophone Articulations across the Pacific.* Berkeley: University of California Press, 2007.

Skeldon, Ronald. "Emigration and the Future of Hong Kong." *Pacific Affairs* 63 (1990): 500–23.

Skelton, Chad. "The Shifting Immigrant Vote." *Vancouver Sun*, June 19, 2004, C1.

So, Josephine Yan Pui. *Death, Be Not Proud.* Translated by Ho Hing Kay. Hong Kong: Breakthrough, 1989.

———. "A Statement on Our Statement." [In Chinese.] *Breakthrough Magazine*, June 1978, 20.

Soo, Richard. "Father Richard Soo: Is the Church a Sanctuary or a Target?" *Vancouver Sun*, September 6, 2019. https://vancouversun.com/opinion/op-ed/father-richard-soo-is-the-church-in-canada-a-sanctuary-or-target.

———. "Keeping Quiet about Hong Kong 'Not an Option': Priest." *B.C. Catholic*, September 4, 2019. https://bccatholic.ca/voices/richard-soo-sj/keeping-quiet-about-hong-kong-not-an-option-priest.

South China Morning Post Reporter. "Tung Urges Youth to Help Community." *South China Morning Post*, November 18, 2011. https://www.scmp.com/article/262680/tung-urges-youth-help-community.

Stackhouse, Max L. *Public Theology and Political Economy: Christian Stewardship in Modern Society*. Grand Rapids: Eerdmans, 1987.

Statistics Canada. "Religion (95) and Visible Minority Groups (15) for Population, for Canada, Provinces, Territories, Census Metropolitan Areas and Census Agglomerations, 2001 Census—20% Sample Data. 2001 Census. Statistics Canada Catalogue Number 97F0022XCB2001005." May 13, 2003. https://www150.statcan.gc.ca/n1/en/catalogue/97F0022X2001005.

Students for Fair Admissions Inc. v. President and Fellows of Harvard College, 600 US 181 (2023).

SUCCESS. *Lilian To: A Life of Devotion*. Vancouver: SUCCESS, 2005.

Sullivan, Winnifred Favers. *The Impossibility of Religious Freedom*. Princeton: Princeton University Press, 2005.

Sun Yatsen. "The Principle of Nationalism: Lecture 1, Delivered on January 27, 1924." In *San Min Chu I: The Three Principles of the People*, translated by Frank W. Price, 1–6. Taipei: Government Information Office, 1990.

Sweeting, A. E., and P. Morris. "Educational Reform in Post-war Hong Kong: Planning and Crisis Intervention." *International Journal of Educational Development* 13, no. 3 (1993): 201–16.

Tahoe Rethinking Commission. *Tahoe Rethinking Commission Report*. San Francisco: Lake Tahoe Chinese American Youth Conference, 1949.

Tam, Hak-Shing William. *Church, Stand Up as Salt and Light! Biblical Response to Social Challenges Today*. Sunnyvale, CA: Traditional Family Coalition, 2006.

———. "TFC Helped Pass Prop 8." *TFC Newsletter* 3, no. 3 (2008): 3.

———. "Why I Helped Start Prop 8." *TFC Newsletter* 3, no. 3 (2008): 1.

Tam, Jonathan. "Renegotiating Religious Transnationalism: Fractures in Transnational Chinese Evangelicalism." *Global Networks* 19, no. 1 (2019): 66–85.

Tan, Amy. *The Joy Luck Club*. New York: Ivy, 1989.

———. *The Kitchen God's Wife*. New York: Ivy, 1991.

Taylor, Charles. *A Secular Age*. Cambridge, MA: Belknap, 2007.

Teng, Mabel. "The Right Place at the Right Time: Cultural and Political Controversy of San Francisco's Gay Marriage." *Amerasia Journal* 32, no. 1 (2006): 63–66.

Teng, Philip. *Who Am I?* [In Chinese.] Hong Kong: Dao Sing Publishers, 1980.

Ten Years Workshop. "Ten Years: A Community Conversation 十年：社區放映會." Eventbrite, October 21, 2016. https://www.eventbrite.ca/e/ten-years-a-community-screening-tickets-27551636687.

Teo, Sin Yih. "Dreaming inside a Walled City: Imagination, Gender, and the Roots of Immigration." *Asian and Pacific Migration Journal* 12, no. 4 (2003): 411–38.

Thompson, Terry L. "Hak-Shing William Tam's Notice of Motion and Motion to Withdraw, and Memorandum of Points and Authorities in Support of Motion to Withdraw." In *Perry v. Schwarzenegger*, 704 F.Sup.2d 921 (N.D. Cal, 2010).
Todd, Douglas. "70s Hymn an Anthem for Protesters." *Vancouver Sun*, September 7, 2019, H3.
———. "Chinese Celebrate Festival despite Shift in Religious Beliefs; Metro Vancouver's 100,000-Strong Chinese Christian Population Continues to Observe Lunar New Year despite Its Roots in Buddhism." *Vancouver Sun*, February 5, 2011, A13.
———. "Chinese Christians for Trump." *Vancouver Sun*, November 1, 2016. https://vancouversun.com/news/staff-blogs/chinese-christians-for-trump.
———. "'Churchy' Christian Becomes Social Activist: Bill Chu Has Been Leading B.C. Protests against Repression Ever since the Uprising in Tiananmen Square in 1989." *Vancouver Sun*, February 24, 1997, B4.
———. "Evangelical Chinese Christians Respond to Feb. 5th Piece." *The Search*, February 14, 2011. http://blogs.vancouversun.com/2011/02/14/evangelical-chinese-christians-respond-to-feb-5th-piece.
———. "Metro Vancouver's Chinese Christians Wrestle with Morality of Homosexuality." *Vancouver Sun*, June 28, 2013, D5.
———. "Protest Leader Proud: Cleric Also Shy about Role." *Vancouver Sun*, June 8, 1989, B11.
Tomlinson, Barbara, and George Lipsitz. "American Studies as Accompaniment." *American Quarterly* 65, no. 1 (2013): 1–30.
Torassa, Ulysses. "Thousands Protest Legalizing Same-Sex Marriage; Asian Americans, Christians Rally in Sunset District." *San Francisco Chronicle*, April 26, 2004, B1.
Torobin, Jeremy. "Investigation to Examine Police Action at Rally Clash." *Vancouver Sun*, August 9, 1997, A15.
Traditional Family Coalition. "List of Activities of Traditional Family Coalition." [In Chinese.] http://tfcus.homestead.com/Events.html.
Tran, Jonathan. *Asian Americans and the Spirit of Racial Capitalism*. New York: Oxford University Press, 2022.
Tse, Justin K.H. "Asian Religions Aren't That Exotic." *Ricepaper Magazine* 16, no. 4 (2012): 10–15.
———. "Attending to the Movements of My Heart: An Asian American Conversion from 'Uniatism' in the 'Model Minority.'" *Logos: A Journal of Eastern Christian Studies* 59, no. 1–4 (2019): 293–312.
———. "Difference and the Establishment: An Asian Canadian Senior Pastor's Evangelical Spatiality at Tenth Avenue Alliance Church in Vancouver, BC." *Relegens Thréskeia* 3, no. 2 (2014): 24–56.
———. "'Fraught' Chineseness: 'Chinese Christians' in the *Vancouver Sun*." In *Ecclesial Diversity in Chinese Christianity*, edited by Alexander Chow and Easten Law, 183–207. New York: Palgrave, 2021.

———. "Hearing a Different Kind of Evangelical: Profile: Pastor Ken Shigematsu." *Ricepaper Magazine* 16, no. 3 (2012): 54–57.

———. "Liberal Protestant Chinatown: Social Gospel Geographies in Chinese San Francisco." *Chinese America: History and Perspectives* (2015): 29–46.

———. "Making a Cantonese-Christian Family: Quotidian Habits of Language and Background in a Transnational Hongkonger Church." *Population, Space, and Place* 17, no. 6 (2011): 756–68.

———. "One Family, Many Systems? Ecumenical Alliances and the Defense of the Domestic in Post-handover Hong Kong." In *Gathered in My Name: Ecumenism in the World Church*, edited by William T. Cavanaugh, 105–24. Eugene, OR: Cascade, 2020.

———. "Religious Politics in Pacific Space: Grounding Cantonese Protestant Theologies in Secular Civil Societies." PhD diss., University of British Columbia, 2013.

———. "蒙上眼睛，就以爲看不見 Repress Your Eyes, So You Thought Couldn't See It: My Aunties and Uncles Taught Me to Feel the World When I Was Three." *Inheritance*, June 4, 2020. https://www.inheritancemag.com/stories/meng-shang-yan-jing-jiu-yi-wei-kan-bu-jian-repress-your-eyes-so-you-thought-you-couldnt-see-it.

———. "The Privacy of Hak-Shing William Tam: Imagining Asian Families in Proposition 8 in California." *Journal of Asian American Studies* 26, no. 1 (2023): 63–85.

———. "A Tale of Three Bishops: Ideologies of Chineseness and Global Cities in Vancouver's Anglican Realignment." *Ching Feng: A Journal on Christianity and Chinese Religion and Culture* 15, no. 1–2 (2016): 103–30.

———. "The Umbrella Movement and the Political Apparatus: Understanding 'One Country, Two Systems.'" In *Theological Reflections on the Hong Kong Umbrella Movement*, edited by Justin K.H. Tse and Jonathan Y. Tan, 21–66. New York: Palgrave, 2016.

———. "Under the Umbrella: Grounded Christian Theologies and Democratic Working Alliances in Hong Kong." *Review of Religion and Chinese Society* 2, no. 1 (2015): 109–42.

Tse, Philip. "Effectual Procedures for Dealing with Pastoral Sexual Misconduct in Chinese Churches." DMin diss., Western Seminary, 2013.

Tseng, Timothy. "Protestantism in Twentieth-Century Chinese America: The Impact of Transnationalism on the Chinese Diaspora." *Journal of American East-West Relations* 13 (2004–6): 121–48.

———. "Trans-Pacific Transpositions: Continuities and Discontinuities in Chinese North American Protestantism since 1965." In *Revealing the Sacred in Asian and Pacific America*, edited by Jane Naomi Iwamura and Paul Spickard, 241–71. New York: Routledge, 2003.

Tseng, Timothy, and James Chuck, eds. *The 2008 Report: Bay Area Chinese Churches Research Project Phase II: A Program Initiative of the Institute for the Study of*

Asian American Christianity (ISAAC). Castro Valley, CA: Institute for the Study of Asian American Christianity, 2008.

Tsui, Enid. "Hong Kong's Tsang Faces Corruption Probe." *Financial Times*, February 29, 2012. http://www.ft.com/intl/cms/s/0/f5055f20-628b-11e1-872e-00144feabdc0.html.

Umemoto, Karen. "'On Strike!' San Francisco State College Strike, 1968–69: The Role of Asian American Students." *Amerasia Journal* 15, no. 1 (1989): 3–41.

Uribe, Virginia. "Project 10: A School-Based Outreach to Gay and Lesbian Youth." *High School Journal* 77, no. 1–2 (1994): 108–12.

———. "The Silent Minority: Rethinking Our Commitment to Gay and Lesbian Youth." *Theory into Practice* 33, no. 3 (1994): 167–72.

van der Veer, Peter. *The Modern Spirit of Asia: The Spiritual and the Secular in China and India*. Princeton: Princeton University Press, 2014.

Wakeham, Pauline. "The Cunning of Reconciliation: Reinventing White Civility in the 'Age of Apology.'" In *Shifting the Ground of Canadian Literary Studies*, edited by Smaro Kamboureli and Robert Zacharias, 209–33. Waterloo, ON: Wilfrid Laurier University Press, 2012.

Wang Gungwu. "Chineseness: The Dilemmas of Place and Practice." In *Cosmopolitan Capitalists: Hong Kong and the Chinese Diaspora at the End of the Twentieth Century*, edited by Gary G. Hamilton, 188–234. Seattle: University of Washington Press, 1999.

Wang, Jiwu. *"His Dominion" and the "Yellow Peril": Protestant Missions to Chinese Immigrants in Canada, 1859–1967*. Ottawa: Wilfred Laurier University Press, 2006.

Wang, Thomas. "Epilogue." In *America, Return to God*, edited by Thomas Wang, 126. Sunnyvale, CA: Great Commission Center International, 2006.

———. "The God of John Sung Can Revive Us Too." In *Diary of John Sung: Extracts from His Journals and Notes*, edited by Levi Sung, translated by Thng Peng Soon, 420–22. Singapore: Genesis, 2012.

———. Introduction to *America, Return to God*, edited by Thomas Wang, 4. Sunnyvale, CA: Great Commission Center International, 2006.

———. "'My People Have Changed God!'" In *America, Return to God*, edited by Thomas Wang, 37–38. Sunnyvale, CA: Great Commission Center International, 2006.

Ward, Doug. "Chan Accuses Rival of Using Churches." *Vancouver Sun*, January 17, 2006, A4.

Waters, Johanna L. *Education, Migration, and Cultural Capital in the Chinese Diaspora*. Amherst, NY: Cambria, 2008.

———. "Geographies of Cultural Capital: Education, International Migration and Family Strategies between Hong Kong and Canada." *Transactions of the Institute of British Geographers* 31, no. 2 (2006): 172–92.

Watson, Jini Kim. *The New Asian City: Three-Dimensional Fictions of Space.* Minneapolis: University of Minnesota Press, 2011.
Wells, Paul. "Jason Kenney's Plan for Breaking through in Ethnic Communities." *MacLean's*, March 3, 2011. https://www.macleans.ca/politics/ottawa/jason-kenneys-plan-for-breaking-through-in-ethnic-communities/.
Wei, William. *The Asian American Movement.* Philadelphia: Temple University Press, 1993.
"哪一政黨最值得贏到你神聖的一票 [Which of the parties deserves your most sacred vote]." [Email.] April 25, 2011. English version: "With vigilance, please cast your ballot on May 2 / and a few issues here / - pls invite 10 friends to do the same." [Email.] April 28, 2011.
Wilson, Rob. *Reimagining the American Pacific: From South Pacific to Bamboo Ridge and Beyond.* Durham, NC: Duke University Press, 2000.
Witkowski, D'Anne. "Creep of the Week: Hak-Shing William Tam." *PrideSource*, January 22, 2010. https://pridesource.com/article/39651.
Wolfe, Patrick. *Settler Colonialism and the Transformation of Anthropology: The Politics and Poetics of an Ethnographic Event.* New York: Cassell, 1999.
Wong, Dony. "'Domestic Violence Ordinance' Yan Fook Church's Rev. Patrick So 《家庭暴力條例》恩福堂蘇穎智牧師." YouTube, January 10, 2009. https://web.archive.org/web/20170331072807.
Wong, Janelle, S. Karthick Ramakrishnan, Taeku Lee, and Jane Junn. *Asian American Political Participation: Emerging Constituents and Their Political Identities.* New York: Russell Sage Foundation, 2011.
Wong, Pik Wan. "The Pro-Chinese Democracy Movement in Hong Kong." In *The Dynamics of Social Movements in Hong Kong*, edited by Stephen Wing Kai Chiu and Tai-lok Lui, 55–90. Hong Kong: Hong Kong University Press, 2000.
Wong Siu-lun. "Emigration and Stability in Hong Kong." Social Sciences Research Centre Occasional Paper 7, Department of Sociology, University of Hong Kong, 1992.
Worthen, Molly. *Apostles of Reason: The Crisis of Authority in American Evangelicalism.* New York: Oxford University Press, 2013.
Wu, Ellen D. *The Color of Success: Asian Americans and the Origins of the Model Minority.* Princeton: Princeton University Press, 2014.
Wu, John-Baptist. *March into the Bright Decade.* Pastoral Letter, Hong Kong Catholic Diocese, May 14, 1989.
———. *Thanks Precious Blood Golden Jubilee School.* Pastoral Letter, Hong Kong Catholic Diocese, June 2, 1978.
Wu, Nina, and Bert Eljera. "The Malls of Asian America." *Asianweek*, April 1, 1998. http://web.archive.org/web/20110603230741.
Wu, Rose. "A Story of Its Own Name: Hong Kong's Tongzhi Culture and Movement." In *Off the Menu: Asian and Asian North American Women's Religion and Theology*, edited by Rita Nakashima Brock, Jung Ha Kim, Kwok Pui Lan, and Seung Ai Yang, 275–92. Louisville: Westminster John Knox Press, 2007.

Yam Chi Keung. "Engagement in Television by Protestant Christians in Hong Kong." *Studies in World Christianity* 11 (2005): 87–105.
Yang, Fenggang. "Chinese Conversions to Evangelical Christianity: The Importance of Social and Cultural Contexts." *Sociology of Religion* 59 (1998): 237–57.
Yee, Paul. *Saltwater City: An Illustrated History of the Chinese in Vancouver*. Madeira Park, BC: Douglas and McIntyre, 2006.
Young, Ian. "School Transgender Policy Row." *South China Morning Post*, May 22, 2014. https://www.scmp.com/news/world/article/1517362/school-transgender-policy-angers-vancouvers-chinese-christians.
Yu, Henry. "The Intermittent Rhythms of the Cantonese Pacific." In *Connecting Seas and Connected Oceans: Indian, Atlantic and Pacific Oceans and China Seas Migrations from the 1830s to the 1930s*, edited by Donna R. Garbaccia and Dirk Hoerder, 393–414. Leiden: Brill, 2011.
Yuen, Esther. "Mass Exodus: Constrained by the Traditional Views of Their Churches, Many Young Chinese Christians Are Seeking a New Congregation, Leading to Friction within the Community." *Pacific Rim Magazine* 2, no. 13 (2011): 8.
Yuh, Ji-Yeon. *Beyond the Shadow of Camptown: Korean Military Brides in America*. New York: New York University Press, 2002.

INDEX

A

Abbas, Ackbar, 4
abortion, 12, 101
Action Committee Against Narcotics (ACAN), 126
Adachi, Jeff, 144, 149
Adelaja, Sunday, 211n24
Adeney, David, 31
Agamben, Giorgio, 140
Akiboh, Alvita, 136
Ambassadors for Christ (AFC), 38, 118
America, Return to God (Wang), 69
American empire, critique of, 8–9, 136, 190n15
American Return to God Prayer Movement, 116, 204n42
Americans for Equal Rights, 64
America Return to God Prayer Movement (ARTGPM), 65, 69, 71
Anglican Church of the Good Shepherd, 44
Anti-Extradition Law Amendment Bill demonstrations (Anti-ELAB demonstrations), 3, 179
Apple Daily newspaper, 23, 89
Ark Community, 123
ArkWhy group, 189n15
Arsenault, Adrienne, 151–52
Article 23. *See* National Security Ordinance
Asad, Talal, 176

Asian American Movement, 11, 28, 35, 39
  Cameron House's link with, 38
  Chinatown congregations in, 36
  CONFAB's involvement in, 42
  involvement of Protestant churches in, 196n23
  reconfiguration of Chinatown churches, 37
  role of Chinatown churches in, 59
Asian Community Mental Health Services, 36–37
Asian Health Services, 36
Asian Law Caucus, 36
Asian Pacific American Political Action (APAPA), 146–48
Asian Pacific Islander initiative, 70
Asian Religions in British Columbia, 120
AsianWeek newspaper, 105
Asia-Pacific, 2–3, 61, 136
  image of, 7–8

B

Bahng, Aimee, 4
Baptist Convention, 30–31
Barton, David, 69
Basic Law of Hong Kong, 16
  Article 23, 167, 168, 169–70
  Article 24, 129
  Article 45, 164

"Bathroom Bill." *See* Bill C-389
Bay Area Chinese Bible Church (BACBC), 108–9, 111
Becker, Jo, 202n4
Bill C-33, 78, 206n66
Bill C-41, 77–78, 206n66
Bill C-389, 76
Black, Dawn, 159
Black Lives Matter movement, 182
Blum, Edward, 182
Boies, David, 64, 65, 69, 70
Bonhoeffer, Dietrich, 130
Bread of Life Bakery of CCHC, 114
Breakazine periodical, 125
Breakthrough Youth Ministries, 50, 201n89
  alliance with HKCC, 54–55
  Breakthrough Magazine, 52–53
  Breakthrough Youth Movement, 51
  Breakthrough Youth Village, 122–23, 125–28
  courses for Fellowship of Evangelical Studies, 89
  engagement with secular institutions and civil society, 58
  and HKCI, 130
  and revivalist separatism, 54
  separation from Narrow Church, 135
  See also Choi Yuen-wan, Philemon
British Columbia College of Teachers (BCCT), 79, 206n66
British Columbia Teachers' Federation (BCTF), 78, 79, 98, 206n66
Brown, Jerry, 64
Brown, Willie, 148
Burnaby Parents' Voice, 13–14, 85
Bush, George W., 64

C
Calhoun, Craig, 216n1
California Ballot Proposition 8, 62, 70, 73, 205n45
  Choi's statement, 98
  "fourteen words" of, 63–64
  power of pastor in case of, 73–74
  Tam's fight for, 65, 72, 111
  TFC and, 75
California Family Council (CFC), 70
Cambodian refugee migrants study, 189–90n5
Canadian Alliance for Social Justice and Family Values Association (CASJAFVA), 76, 79–80, 98, 160–61
Canadian Broadcasting Company (CBC), 23, 150–51, 162, 164
Catholic Church in Hong Kong, 54, 222n96
  activism for "right of abode," 129
Cayton, Horace, 34
CCCOWE. *See* Chinese Coordination Center for World Evangelization
CCIA. *See* Chinese Christians in Action
CCM. *See* Chinese Christian Mission
CCP. *See* Chinese Communist Party
CCS. *See* Chinese Christian Schools
CCU. *See* Chinese Christian Union
CFA. *See* Chinese Family Alliance
CGST. *See* China Graduate School of Theology
CGST Bulletin, 171
Chai Ling, 145, 217n12
Chak Kwong Au, 207n93
Chan, Ernest, 39
Chan, Freeman, 214nn55–56
Chan, Raymond, 77, 141, 151–152, 162, 164, 219n35, 220n67
  about CASJAFVA, 80
  forming VSSDM in China, 153
  frustration with Chinese media, 83
  Tiananmen credibility, 154–55
  and 2004 elections, 157
  vote for Bill C-41, 78
Chan Hay Him, 51, 52
Chan Kin-man, 18

Chan Kin Hong, 89
Chan Sing Kai, 43, 199n56
Chan Wai Ming, Ruth, 53, 201n89
Chan Yu Tan, 43
Chao, Augustus, 44–45
Chao, Calvin, 31
Cheng, D., 181–82
Cheung, Daniel, 87, 98
Cheung, K-John, 79
Cheung, Leslie, 62
Cheung, Stephen, 154, 157
Cheung Chau revivals, 29–30, 31
Child Development Fund, 124, 125
Chin, Gordon, 36
"China and Hong Kong Young People in One Heart" rally, 165
China Graduate School of Theology (CGST), 171–72
Chinatown churches, San Francisco, 33–34, 59
    Asian American movement reconfiguration of, 37
    Cumberland Chinese Presbyterian Church, 39
    See also Silicon Valley churches
Chinatown churches, Vancouver, 59
    Augustus Chao's role, 44–45
    Chong v. Lee case, 42–43, 46–48, 198n49
    founding of Christ Church of China, 43–44
    slum clearance controversy, 45–46
    threat of expropriation, 44
Chinatown Coalition for Better Housing, 35
Chinatown Merchants Association, 148, 219n38
Chinatown News, 115
Chinatown Program Network, 212n25
Chinese American Health Organization, 36
Chinese Baptist Church of San Jose, 37–38

Chinese Bible Baptist Church in Los Altos, 38
Chinese Bible Church of Detroit, 38, 40–41
Chinese Christian Mission, 38
Chinese Christian Mission (CCM), 38–39, 68, 81, 115, 117–18
Chinese Christian Schools (CCS), 41, 108
Chinese Christians in Action (CCIA), 145, 153–54
Chinese Christians Today. See *Chinese Christian Mission*
Chinese Christian Union (CCU), 33, 72, 147–48
Chinese Communist Party (CCP), 9, 31–32, 140, 184
Chinese Convalescent Hospital Committee, 36
Chinese Coordination Center for World Evangelization (CCCOWE), 51, 68
    "Chinese Lausanne," 51
Chinese Family Alliance (CFA), 67–68
Chinese Independent Baptist Church (CIBC), 40, 41
Chinese Methodist Church in Vancouver, 43
"Chineseness," 6, 9, 143, 152, 154, 220n83
Chinese Protestant revivalism in Hong Kong, 28
Chinese Students' Christian Association, 34
Ching, Andy, 105
Chiu, Abraham, 105
Chiu, David, 144, 149, 217n7
Chiu, Kenny, 156, 157, 163, 219n51, 219n58
Chiu, Samuel, 181
Chiu, Stephen, 31–32
Choi, Andrew, 179

Choi Chi Sum, 87, 88, 93, 95, 96, 98
Choi Yuen-wan, Philemon, 31, 122–24, 135, 174, 179, 223n112. *See also* Breakthrough Youth Ministries
Chong v. Lee case, 23, 42–43, 46–48, 198n49
Chow, Alexander, 59, 201n97
Chow, Christie, 27
CHRF. *See* Civil Human Rights Front
Christ Church of China, 42–48, 59, 91
Christian Patriotic Democratic Movement (CPDM), 166
Christians Love China Association, 145
Christian Social Concern Fellowship (CSCF), 14–15, 76, 80–82, 152
Christian Times, 94, 127
Chu, Bill, 78–79, 154
Chu, Louis, 193n24
Chu Chun Wing, 114
Chuck, Harry, 35–36
Chuck, James, 33, 34–35, 196n17
Chugani, Michael, 18
Chuh, Kandace, 192n21
Church, Stand Up as Salt and Light! (Tam), 66
Church Revival Youth Network (CRY Network), 120
Church Shift (Adelaja), 211n24
Chu Yiu-ming, 18, 55, 57–58
CIBC. *See* Chinese Independent Baptist Church
Civil Human Rights Front (CHRF), 91, 93, 166–68
Columbia Journalism Review, 185
Comuzzi, Sam, 221n70
CONFAB. *See* National Conference of Chinese American Churches
Conscience for a Minute and a Half, 74
Conservative Party of Canada, 84, 102, 141, 220n59

Chinese Christians and, 150–64
Conversations at Eight o'Clock Sharp show, 113
CPDM. *See* Christian Patriotic Democratic Movement
Crosspoint Church of Silicon Valley, 105–6
CRY Network. *See* Church Revival Youth Network
Crystal Mall, 116–17
CSCF. *See* Christian Social Concern Fellowship
Cultural Regeneration Research Society (CRRS), 145–46, 154
Cumberland Chinese Presbyterian Church, 39–40
Cumberland Presbyterian Chinese Church, 109, 112, 198n40
Cumings, Bruce, 6, 190n16

D
Deng Xiaoping, 142
"diocesan curia," 170, 222n95
Dirlik, Arif, 6, 7
Dobson, James, 69, 203n38
Doh On Yuen, 36
Domestic Violence Ordinance (DVO), 95–96
Dosanjh, Ujjal, 159, 163, 221n70

E
East Bay Asians for Community Action, 36
East Bay Chinese Youth Council, 36
Eat a Bowl of Tea (Louis Chu), 193n24
Education Resource Committee, 126
Elderly Nutrition Program, 36
Election Committee of Hong Kong, 222n101
  CGST's role, 171–72
  CHRF's role, 166–69

CPDM's role, 166
Fastbeat's speculations, 174–75
HKCC's role, 169, 170–71
Lo Lung Kwong's role, 166, 170, 173, 174
participation in Million Man March, 165–66
religious bodies for voting, 164–65
scandal of, 173–74
selection of Chief Executive (CE), 164
Ends of the Rainbow, The, 93
Equal Opportunity Commission (EOC), 90

F
Faith Communities Committed to Solidarity for the Poor (FCCSP), 181
Faith Community Christian Church, 224n8
Falun Gong, 167
Family and Cohabitation Violence Ordinance, 95–96
Family Development Foundation, 125
Family Heartware, 125
Fan, Chris, 217n7
Fan, Harry, 44
Fan Lap Hin, 128, 168, 175
Far East Broadcasting, 39
Fellowship of Evangelical Studies (FES), 29
First Chinese Baptist Church (FCBC), 33, 34, 39
Fisher, Stephen, 91–92
Forcing the Spring (Becker), 202n4
Ford, David, 123
4MyCanada, 158
Fourteenth Amendment, 202n9
Fremont focus group, 10–13
Friesen, Joe, 102
Fry, Hedy, 158

Fukuyama, Francis, 140
Fuller Theological Seminary in Southern California, 51
Fung Wai Man, Raymond, 56, 128

G
Gam, Samuel King, 39
Gay Lovers documentary, 93–94
Gibbons, Dave, 180
Global Day of Prayer, 131, 132, 215n82
Goh, Robbie, 189n12
Golden Jubilee incident (1978), 49–51, 53–54, 58
Gore, Al, 64
Gore v. Bush case, 64
Grassroots Evangelist Educational Training program, 56
Graves, Judy, 181
Great Commission Center International (GCCI), 68, 70, 98
Great Pacific Garbage Patch, 8
Gurley, Akai, 182

H
Hallelujah Get Out band, 132
Happy Together (film), 62
Harper, Stephen, 158, 161, 220n59
Harvey, David, 5
Henry, Carl, 69
HKJP. *See* Justice and Peace Commission
Ho, Peter, 171, 174
Hom, Robin, 109, 113
homeland politics, 62
critiquing post-handover Hong Kong state, 122–35
real estate pastor's role, 104–15
social work in Metro Vancouver, 115–22
and varieties of secular legibility, 101–4
homosexuality, 12

homosexuality *(cont.)*
   Fisher's consultation to investigate public opinion about, 91, 92
   See also same-sex marriage
Hong Kong, 1, 2, 20–21
   antidemocratic "religious right," 63
   capitalization of "quality of life," 6
   church congregations of Cantonese Protestants, 24–25
   critiquing post-handover Hong Kong state, 122–35
   culture as "politics of disappearance," 4
   flexible citizenship, 4–10
   Million Man March in, 12, 165–66
   revival movement in, 24, 31, 59
   transpacific migration from, 3–4
   See also San Francisco; Vancouver
Hong Kong Alliance for Family, 92
Hong Kong Catholic Diocese, 207n110
   Justice and Peace Commission, 209n127
Hong Kong Christian Council (HKCC), 54–55, 125, 165
   denominational establishment, 57
   Global Day of Prayer, 215n82
   "Gospel for the Poor" theme, 56
   World Day of Prayer, 215n82
Hong Kong Christian Institute (HKCI), 126–30
   Fan Lap Hin and, 128, 168, 175
   role in CHRF formation, 168
Hong Kong Christian Union, 125, 171
Hong Kong Church Network for the Poor (HKCNP), 125, 127
Hong Kong Church Renewal Movement, 125, 127
Hong Kong Protestantism, 28, 29–32
Hong Kong Sex Culture Society (HKSCS), 86, 91
   adoption of secular strategy on religious right, 95–96
   and anti-SODO campaign, 93
   debate over religious right, 88–89
   against gay rights activism, 94
   institutional autonomy, 87
   opposition to *Gay Lovers* documentary, 93–94
   response to *Religious Right*, 87–88
Hope Evangelical Free Church, 39
Hoskins, Janet, 2
"House of Worship," 117
Hsu, Madeline, 32
Humanitarian Relief Fund, 178
Human Rights and Homosexuality (Kwan Kai Man), 91
Hung, Jackie Ling-yu, 129, 200n79, 207n110, 208n121, 209n127
Hyphen (Fan), 217n7

I
Ibbitson, John, 102
Immigration Building fire incident in Hong Kong, 17
Independent Commission Against Corruption, 49, 125
Intercollegiate Chinese Students Association (ICSA), 35
Inter-School Christian Fellowship (ISCF), 29
Intervarsity Christian Fellowship (IVCF), 30, 31
Ip, James, 119
Irony of American History, The (Niebuhr), 190n15

J
Jakobsen, Janet, 203n23
Jew, Ed, 149, 218n27
Jiang Zemin, 165

Joint Declaration (1984), 122–23, 142
jook sing, 10–11, 19, 193n24
Junn, Jane, 205n45
Justice and Peace Commission (HKJP), 129, 167, 170, 200n79

K
Kam Chai. *See* Mella, Franco
Kan, Angela, 115, 117, 119, 154
Kang Phee Sang, 171
Kempling, Chris, 79, 98
Kenney, Jason, 158, 162, 220n59
Ken Shigematsu, 180
Kim, E. Tammy, 185
Knights, Stephen, 31
Kong, Edwin, 47, 116, 213n38
Kotake, Donna, 67–68
Kryskow, Faytene, 158
Kung Lap Yan, 87, 88, 169
Kwan, Franco, 72
Kwan Kai Man, 87
    claims to institutional autonomy, 97
    definition of "sexual orientation," 91
    and HKSCS, 91, 94, 98
    objections to Sexual Orientation Funding Scheme, 90
    about religious right, 96–97
    secular social debate about "sex-culture," 89–90
    and STL, 88–89, 94
Kwok Nai Wang, 56, 126, 128, 175
Kwong, Paul, 222n96
Kwong, Raymond, 68, 193n28

L
LaHaye, Tim, 69
Lam, David, 115, 116, 154
Lam Kwok Cheung, Timothy, 130
Lam Sau Wing, 74, 75, 112, 114, 212n26

Lau, Abraham, 119, 213n44
Lau, Chanson, 39, 107, 113, 210n13, 218n26
Lau, Charter, 14–16, 86
Lau, Susanna, 112–13, 212n25
Lau Chin Sek, 56
Lausanne Conference, 51, 171
Lausanne Movement, 68
Lau Wing Sang, 87
"Lavender Leung," 144, 146, 148, 150, 217n17
Lee, Edward, 34, 119, 143, 199n56
Lee, Gentle, 42–43, 46–47
Lee, Stephen, 43, 45, 198n51
Lee, Taeku, 205n45
Lee Kam Hung, 127
Leung, Lavender, 144, 146, 148–50
Leung, Pakkin, 125
Leung, Priscilla, 18
Leung, Ronald, 151, 160, 163
Leung, Thomas, 158
Leung, Tony, 62
Leung Chun-ying, 133, 173
Leung Insing, Thomas, 145, 154
Leung Kit Fun, Beatrice, 49, 200n77, 200n79
Leung-Kong, Esther, 158–59
Ley, David, 6–7
Liang, Peter, 182, 225nn12–13
Lian Xi, 27, 195n8
Lim, William, 117
Ling-chi Wang, 9
Liu Tong, 72–73, 211n23
Lively, Anne, 34
Li Yu, 120
Lo, Kingsley, 117
Lo, Wayne, 14, 81, 119, 152
Lo Lung Kwong, 50–51, 117, 173, 174
    about bus fare hike in Hong Kong, 55–56

Lo Lung Kwong *(cont.)*
   in Chai Wan labor rights issue, 57–58
   Grassroots Evangelist Educational Training program, 56
   about Narrow Church's students, 135
   about passive compliance, 170
Loo, Dennis, 37
Loo, Shirley, 125
Lord's Grace Christian Church, 37, 197n34
Lo Sek Wai, 152, 154–55, 217n10, 218n31
Louie, Alvin, 41–42
Love Alameda Day, 109
Love Food Bank, 125
Lutzer, Erwin, 69

M
Ma, Jaeson, 131, 215n81
Ma, Linda, 131, 215nn81–82
Mack vs. Attorney General of Canada case, 220n59
Madsen, Richard, 140
Mar, Frank, 36–37
market legibility in Bay Area
   BACBC's story, 108–9
   CCHC's story, 112–14
   Chanson Lau's real estate story, 107–8
   Crosspoint Church's property purchase, 104–7
   Prince of Peace Enterprises' story, 39, 109–10
Martin, Paul, 158
Ma Si Hung, Frederick, 131, 215n81
Mei Lun Yuen Project at Cameron House, 36
Mella, Franco, 15, 50
Metro Vancouver. *See* Vancouver
Million Man March in Hong Kong, 12, 165–66

Milpitas Square, 114
Ming Pao (newspaper), 77, 92, 132, 170, 172, 173, 174
Mitchell, Katharyne, 6
Mok, Christine, 4
Mui, Anita, 62
Mui, Thomas, 72

N
National Conference of Chinese American Churches (CONFAB), 34–35, 39, 196n17
   Chinatown churches association with, 37
   collaboration with immigrant revivalists, 38
   involvement in Asian American movement, 42
National Security Bill, 177
National Security Law (2020), 3, 167, 178
National Security Ordinance, 167
New Life Church, Nazarene, 37
New York Times, 23, 72, 73
Ng, Ted, 213n47
Ng Chu-kwong, David, 31, 155
Ng Chung-man, Daniel, 145, 153
Ng Ka Ling v. Director of Immigration case, 23
Ng Man-lun, 89–90
Nguyen, Viet Thanh, 2, 8
Ng Yuk Secondary School, 51
Nicolosi, Joseph, 203n21
Niebuhr, Reinhold, 190n15
Nielsen, Therese, 213n38
Nonini, Donald, 5
North Point Alliance Church, 32

O
Oakland Chinese Presbyterian Church, 36
Occupy Central with Love and Peace (OCLP), 18, 178

Ockenga, Harold J., 220n84
Olds, Kris, 6
Olson, Theodore, 64
"one country, two systems" framework, 122, 142, 143
Ong, Aihwa, 3, 5–7, 189n5
Ottom, Joe, 45
Ow, Richard, 68, 150

P
Pacific Asian Center for Theologies and Strategies (PACTS), 38
Pang, David, 68–69, 74, 75, 114, 146
"parental rights," 79, 80, 85
Peace Evangelical Fellowship, 31
Perkins, Tony, 204n38
Perry v. Schwarzenegger case, 23
Peschisolido, Joe, 156–57, 162–63, 219n51, 221n70
Peter, Sacha, 159, 160, 220n67, 221n71
Poon, Abraham, 37, 113, 211n23
Poon, David, 45, 46
Presbyterian Church in Chinatown (PCC), 36
Prince of Peace Enterprises, 39, 109–10
Project 10 in Southern California, 66–67, 203n21
Proposition 8. *See* California Ballot Proposition 8
ProtectMarriage.com, 64, 65, 70, 71, 75, 203n17

Q
Quality Education Fund, 126
Quen, Steve, 41, 108, 109, 111, 113

R
Radio Television Hong Kong (RTHK), 93, 94
Ramakrishnan, Karthick, 205n45
"ranked choice vote" system, 149
Re Christ Church of China, 15 E.T.R. 272 (B.C.S.C.), 47
Regina Chinese Alliance Church, 45
Reid, Darrel, 157–58, 220n59
Reiner, Rob, 64
Religious Right (Cheung), 87–88
revivalists/revivalism
    Chinatown organizer's meeting with, 42–48
    and emergence of Pacific Rim secularities, 59–60
    "immigrant" revivalists confronting social justice movements, 33–42
    "student movement" and Hong Kong Protestantism, 28, 29–32
Richmond Chinese Evangelical Free Church, 157, 160, 219n52
"right-to-abode activism," 16–17
"Rimspeak," 6
River of Life Christian Church (ROLCC), 72
Robbins, Joel, 188n11
Roman Catholic Church, 53
RTHK. *See* Radio Television Hong Kong
"Run Ed Run" campaign slogan, 149

S
Saddleback Church of Silicon Valley, 105
same-sex marriage, 24
    Bill C-33, 78
    Bill C-41, 77–78
    Bill C-389, 76
    Cantonese Protestant activism against, 62–63
    CASJAFVA stance, 76, 79–80, 98
    Chan's political campaign, 220n67
    CSCF stance, 76, 80–82
    human rights expansion in Vancouver, 76–77
    pastoral participation on questions of sexual ethics, 77

same-sex marriage *(cont.)*
  religious right among Protestants, 86–98
  representational problems in Vancouver, 75–76, 82–86
  Traditional Family Coalition, 63–75
San Francisco, 1–2, 20–21
  Asian American Movement in, 28
  autonomy of Cantonese Protestants in, 63
  Cambodian refugee migrants study to, 189–90n5
  church congregations of Cantonese Protestants, 24–25
  city politics, 143–50
  market legibility in Bay Area, 104–15
  marriage equality in, 62–63
  See also Chinatown churches, San Francisco; Hong Kong; Vancouver
San Francisco Evangelical Free Church, 39
San Jose Christian Alliance Church (SJCAC), 112, 211n23
San Jose Mercury News, 23, 71, 203n17
SAR. *See* Special Administrative Region
School Site Allocation Committee, 126
Schwarzenegger, Arnold, 64
secularities, 1–4, 99, 121, 140, 143
  business transformation of Cantonese Protestant institutions, 114
  Cantonese Protestants and, 19–21, 23–25, 61–62, 103–4, 143
  citizenship flexibility in Hong Kong, 4–10
  division between Breakthrough and Narrow Church, 135
  interviews, focus groups, and archives, 21–23

  legibility in homeland politics, 101–4
  "one country, two systems" framework, 122
  representation problem in Cantonese Protestants, 86
Selection Committee. *See* Election Committee of Hong Kong
Self-Help for the Elderly, 35
Sen Wong, 40–41
sexual ethics
  activism among Cantonese Protestants, 78–79
  homosexual movement and, 91
  story about pastoral participation on questions of, 77
  See also same-sex marriage
Sexual Orientation Discrimination Ordinance (SODO), 91–93
Sexual Orientation Funding Scheme, 90
Shicha Podcast, 184, 185
Shih, Gerry, 72–73
Shi Junlong, 16
Shu-mei Shih, 1, 9
Siemiatycki, Myer, 102
Siksay, Bill, 76, 159, 160
"silent exodus," 180, 224n5
Silicon Valley churches, 37
  Cantonese-speaking IT workers, 105
  congregations in, 42
  focus group discussion, 73–74
  ROLCC in, 72
  See also Chinatown churches, San Francisco
Silver Bay Youth Conference, 34
Sing Tao Daily newspaper, 127, 149
"Sinophone Pacific," 1, 9–10
Sin Yih Teo, 6
SJCAC. *See* San Jose Christian Alliance Church

Skeldon, Ronald, 216n5
Skelton, Chad, 101, 102
So, Patrick, 88, 96–97
Social Welfare Department Family Life Education Resource Development Centre, 126
social work in Metro Vancouver
  CCM Canada, 115, 116–19
  CRY Network's role, 120
  SUCCESS's role, 115, 118, 121
  VCEMF's role, 119–22
Society for Truth and Light (STL), 86, 87
  adoption of secular strategy on religious right, 95–96
  boycott of *Apple Daily*, 89
  debate over religious right, 88–89
  against gay rights activism, 94
  institutional autonomy, 87
  issues in media ethics, 89–90
  journalism ethics, 89
  opposition to *Gay Lovers* documentary, 93–94
  response to *Religious Right*, 87–88
SODO. *See* Sexual Orientation Discrimination Ordinance
Soo, Richard, 181
South Bay Chinese Baptist Church in Milpitas, 38
South China Morning Post, 23, 123
So Yan Pui, Josephine, 50, 52–54, 122
Special Administrative Region (SAR), 122, 123, 164, 165
"Spread Your Wings" project, 124
STL. *See* Society for Truth and Light
St. Paul's Seven, 29, 30
Stream of Praise, 211n23
SUCCESS. *See* United Chinese Community Enrichment Services Society
Sullivan, Sam, 221n70
Sung, John, 32

Sun Yat-sen, 19–20, 194–95n41
Szeto Wah, 50, 165, 166

T
Tahoe Christian Conference, 33–34
Tai Yiu-Ting, Benny, 18
Tam, Hak-Shing William (Bill), 63, 71, 98, 111, 114, 202n10
  Asian Pacific Islander initiative, 70
  attempt to unite "Chinese Christians," 72
  and CFA's engagement with same-sex marriage, 67–68
  defense strategy in *Perry* case, 75
  deposition of, 204n41
  initiative to oppose Project 10, 66–67
  Portsmouth Square in Chinatown rally show, 203n42
  about same-sex marriage issues, 63–65
  secular talk with Thomas Wang, 68–69
  Shih's statement of ROLCC about, 72–73
  strategy of obfuscation, 66
  testimony about "sibling marriage," 202n17
Tam, Takchi "Fastbeat," 172–75
Tan, Amy, 33
Tang, Henry, 135, 173
Teng, Mabel, 67
Teng, Philip, 31, 32
Tenth Avenue Alliance Church, 45, 180
Tenth Church Vancouver, 180, 181, 224n8
Ten Years (films), 177–78
Ten Years Workshop, 177, 179, 180–81
TFC. *See* Traditional Family Coalition
Theological Reflections on the Hong Kong Umbrella Movement, 179

theological reinterpretation of Pacific Rim, 1
Theology and the Anthropology of Christian Life (Robbins), 188n11
Third World Liberation Front (TWLF), 35
Three Principles of the People, The, 20
Tiananmen Square protests in Beijing, 13, 139–40, 144, 217n6
   impact on Hong Kong, 141–42
   political engagement of Cantonese Protestants, 141–43
Time with Abba, 126
Tinming Ko, 165
To, Lilian, 115, 116
Todd, Douglas, 120, 152, 181
tongzhi movement, 90–91, 94, 96, 207n110
Too Bright (Cheung), 87, 98
Traditional Family Coalition (TFC), 63
   Asian American "Yes on 8" rallies, 70–71
   Asian Pacific Islander initiative, 70
   CFA's engagement with same-sex marriage, 67–68
   debate over same-sex marriage, 64–66
   "fourteen words" of Proposition 8, 63–64
   and GCCI, 70
   parent initiative to oppose Project 10, 66–67
   promoting traditional marriage, 69
   role of Chinese-language radio, 74–75
   Shih's statement of ROLCC about Tam, 72–73
   statements of Silicon Valley church pastors, 73–74
transgender rights, 24, 76, 183
Truth Monthly newspaper, 78, 155, 206n66

Tsang, Donald, 130, 133, 173
Tse, Justin K.H., 196n17
Tseng, Timothy, 27, 196n17, 197n37
Tsoi Yuen Tsuen, 132
Tung Chee Hwa, 123, 135
Tung Fook Evangelical Free Church in Causeway Bay, 171
TWLF. *See* Third World Liberation Front
Tzu-Chun Wu, Judy, 136

U
Umbrella Movement protests (2014), 3–5, 19, 178, 179
United Chinese Community Enrichment Services Society (SUCCESS), 115–18, 121
Uribe, Virginia, 203n21

V
Vacation Bible School, 41
Vancouver, 2, 20–21, 28
   Augustus Chao's role, 44–45
   Cantonese Protestants civil society in, 121–22, 152, 181
   capitalization of "quality of life," 6
   CCIA's intervention into "Chinese culture" in, 153–54
   Chinese Alliance Church in, 48, 180
   Chinese Methodist Church in, 43
   church congregations of Cantonese Protestants, 24–25
   human rights expansion in, 76–77
   out-migration narrative from Hong Kong, 5
   Pacific Rim dream problems in, 61–62, 121
   Pacific Rim vision, 6
   representational problems in, 75–76, 82–86
   secularity of Cantonese Protestants, 63

social work in, 115–22
Tenth Church Vancouver, 180, 181, 224n8
Tiananmen's description in, 142
See also Hong Kong; San Francisco
Vancouver Chinese Evangelical Free Church (VCEFC), 157, 219n52
Vancouver Chinese Evangelical Ministerial Fellowship (VCEMF), 78, 79, 119–21
Vancouver Chinese Presbyterian Church, 44
Vancouver Christians for Love, Peace, and Justice (VCLPJ), 179, 181
Vancouver Society in Support of the Democratic Movement (VSSDM), 153
Vancouver Sun, 23, 101, 120, 152, 154, 181

W
Wai Young, 151, 159
Walker, Vaughn, 202n9
Wang, Thomas, 32, 45, 68, 74, 98
 ARTGPM foundation, 69
 CCM Canada foundation, 116
 about "Chinese Christians," 202n2
 cross-country mission trips, 38
 role in CCCOWE, 51
 Tam's statement with, 68–69, 75
Wang Mingdao, 32
War on Poverty, 34–35
Washroom Bill. *See* Bill C-389
Waters, Johanna, 6
Watson, Jini Kim, 6

Williams, Sherman, 109
Wing So, 39
Winnipeg Chinese Alliance Church, 45
Wong, Alan, 35, 148, 198n40
Wong, Alice, 157–59, 220n67
Wong, Janelle, 205n45
Wong, Melvin, 111–12
Wong, Walter, 119
Wong Kar Wai, 62
Wong Yuk Man, Raymond, 130
Woo, Wesley, 197n37
"working alliances" strategy, 203n23
World Day of Prayer, 215n82
Wu, John, 50, 222n96
Wu Chi Wai, 127
Wu Hung-yuk, Anna, 90
Wu Lo Sai, Rose, 90, 175

Y
Yau, Cecilia, 112
Yee, Leland, 144, 149, 163
Yeung, Anthony, 160
Yeung, Kenneth, 39–40, 109–14
Yeung Kwong, 74–75
Yew, Wally, 38, 198n39
Yu, Carver, 126, 171
Yu, James, 144, 146–47, 149
Yu, Moses, 31

Z
Zen (Ze-kiun), Joseph, 129, 169–70, 207n110, 208n121, 209n127, 222n96
Zephyr Point, 33–34

JUSTIN K.H. TSE is assistant professor of religion and culture at Singapore Management University's College of Integrative Studies. He is the co-editor of *Theological Reflections on the Hong Kong Umbrella Movement*.

www.ingramcontent.com/pod-product-compliance
Lightning Source LLC
Chambersburg PA
CBHW052147310125
21252CB00003B/26